W9-ACV-180

THE NEW CAMBRIDGE SHAKESPEARE

ANTONY AND CLEOPATRA

In this edition of the play David Bevington shows how the theatrical design and imaginative vision of *Antony and Cleopatra* make it one of Shakespeare's most remarkable tragedies.

A substantial critical introduction synthesises the best criticism of the play and presents a fresh consideration of its erotic and political complexities.

The edition is throughout attentive to the play as theatre: a detailed, illustrated account of the stage history is followed, in the commentary, by discussion of staging options offered by the text. The commentary is especially full and helpful, untangling many obscure words and phrases, illuminating sexual puns, and alerting the reader to Shakespeare's shaping of his source material in Plutarch's *Lives*.

This is a scholarly edition, but its scholarship is not intrusive: it will also satisfy those approaching the play for the first time.

THE NEW CAMBRIDGE SHAKESPEARE

Romeo and Juliet, edited by G. Blakemore Evans
The Taming of the Shrew, edited by Ann Thompson
Othello, edited by Norman Sanders
King Richard II, edited by Andrew Gurr
A Midsummer Night's Dream, edited by R.A. Foakes
Hamlet, edited by Philip Edwards
Twelfth Night, edited by Elizabeth Story Donno
All's Well That Ends Well, edited by Russell Fraser
The Merchant of Venice, edited by M. M. Mahood
Much Ado About Nothing, edited by F. H. Mares
The Comedy of Errors, edited by T. S. Dorsch
Julius Caesar, edited by Marvin Spevack
The Second Part of King Henry IV, edited by Giorgio Melchiori
King John, edited by L. A. Beaurline
King Henry VIII, edited by John Margeson
The First Part of King Henry VI, edited by Michael Hattaway
Antony and Cleopatra, edited by David Bevington

ANTONY AND CLEOPATRA

Edited by
DAVID BEVINGTON
Phyllis Fay Horton Professor in the Humanities, The University of Chicago

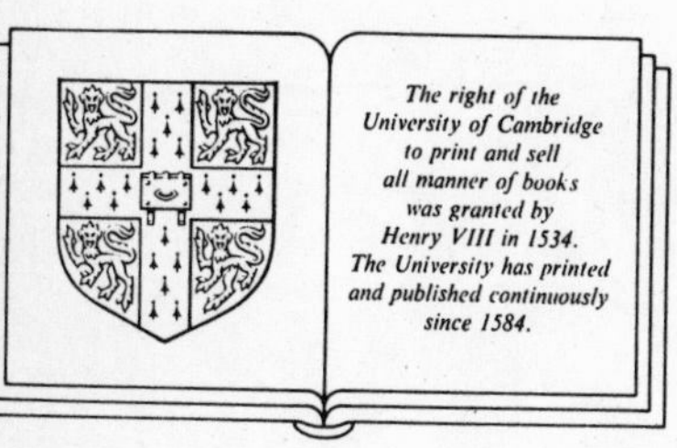

CAMBRIDGE UNIVERSITY PRESS
Cambridge
New York Port Chester
Melbourne Sydney

Published by the Press Syndicate of the University of Cambridge
The Pitt Building, Trumpington Street, Cambridge CB2 1RP
40 West 20th Street, New York, NY 10011, USA
10 Stamford Road, Oakleigh, Melbourne 3166, Australia

First published 1990

Printed in Great Britain at
the University Press, Cambridge

British Library cataloguing in publication data

Shakespeare, William, *1564–1616*
Antony and Cleopatra. – (The New Cambridge
Shakespeare)
I. Title II. Bevington, David
822.3'3

Library of Congress cataloguing in publication data

Shakespeare, William, 1564–1616.
Antony and Cleopatra / edited by David Bevington.
p. cm. – (The New Cambridge Shakespeare)
Bibliography.
ISBN 0-521-25256-3. – ISBN 0-521-27250-5 (pbk.)
1. Antonius, Marcus, 83?–30 B.C. – Drama. 2. Cleopatra, Queen of
Egypt, d. 30 B.C. – Drama. I. Bevington, David M. II. Title.
III. Series: Shakespeare, William, 1564–1616. Works. 1984.
Cambridge University Press.
PR2802.A2B48 1990
822.3'3 – dc20 89–7289 CIP

ISBN 0 521 25256 3 hard covers
ISBN 0 521 27250 5 paperback

BT

THE NEW CAMBRIDGE SHAKESPEARE

The *New Cambridge Shakespeare* succeeds *The New Shakespeare* which began publication in 1921 under the general editorship of Sir Arthur Quiller-Couch and John Dover Wilson, and was completed in the 1960s, with the assistance of G. I. Duthie, Alice Walker, Peter Ure and J. C. Maxwell. *The New Shakespeare* itself followed upon *The Cambridge Shakespeare*, 1863–6, edited by W. G. Clark, J. Glover and W. A. Wright.

The New Shakespeare won high esteem both for its scholarship and for its design, but shifts of critical taste and insight, recent Shakespearean research, and a changing sense of what is important in our understanding of the plays, have made it necessary to re-edit and redesign, not merely to revise, the series.

The *New Cambridge Shakespeare* aims to be of value to a new generation of playgoers and readers who wish to enjoy fuller access to Shakespeare's poetic and dramatic art. While offering ample academic guidance, it reflects current critical interests and is more attentive than some earlier editions have been to the realisation of the plays on the stage, and to their social and cultural settings. The text of each play has been freshly edited, with textual data made available to those users who wish to know why and how one published text differs from another. Although modernised, the edition conserves forms that appear to be expressive and characteristically Shakespearean, and it does not attempt to disguise the fact that the plays were written in a language other than that of our own time.

Illustrations are usually integrated into the critical and historical discussion of the play and include some reconstructions of early performances by C. Walter Hodges. Some editors have also made use of the advice and experience of Maurice Daniels, for many years a member of the Royal Shakespeare Company.

Each volume is addressed to the needs and problems of a particular text, and each therefore differs in style and emphasis from others in the series.

PHILIP BROCKBANK
Founding General Editor

For PHILIP BROCKBANK

CONTENTS

ILLUSTRATIONS

Illustrations 6, 7, 8, 9, 10, 11, and 12 are reproduced by courtesy of the Shakespeare Centre Library, Stratford-upon-Avon.

PREFACE

General editors are an unsung lot. The truth of this dictum has come home to me forcibly through working with Stanley Wells and Gary Taylor on *1 Henry IV* for Oxford, through my own efforts on behalf of the Revels series, and, more recently, through my reliance on the good efforts of Philip Brockbank as Founding General Editor and R. C. Hood as one of the Associate General Editors of the New Cambridge Shakespeare.

I cannot easily say how much I owe these editors. Philip Brockbank, to whom this volume is dedicated and whose recent death we all so much lament, provided a standard and an idea of what this series might be, as much by his life and friendship as by his counselling on matters of interpretation. His quiet insistence on grace of style bespoke the man himself. It has meant a great deal to me that *Antony and Cleopatra* meant so much to Philip.

Robin Hood, as the Associate General Editor assigned to this play, has quietly given a chunk of his life to improving my manuscript. I have acknowledged in the Commentary a number of particular observations made by him, especially on textual matters, but these few citations cannot begin to reflect his contribution. The wording of a considerable number of notes is substantially his, in whole or in part. His cogent arguments on matters of textual choice have won my allegiance and are encoded in the text. He brought to bear a lifetime of studying and teaching this play in the comments he passed on to me, and I have tried to pay him the ultimate flattery not of imitation but of incorporation.

I wish also to thank the Regenstein Library of the University of Chicago, especially its Special Collections division under the curatorship of Robert Rosenthal; the Folger Library, especially Barbara Mowat, editor of *Shakespeare Quarterly*; the Shakespeare Birthplace Trust at Stratford-upon-Avon; Joe Cocks Studio, also in Stratford; and Sarah Stanton, Victoria Cooper, and Paul Chipchase of the Cambridge University Press for invaluable help in the shaping of this volume. It has been an inspiration to correspond with C. Walter Hodges on the fine illustrations he has prepared for this book, and thus to claim as a colleague someone whose visual interpretations of Shakespeare's staging have made a vital difference to me ever since I starting thinking about the subject. I am indebted to Professors David Kastan, James Hammersmith, and Robert Kean Turner for invaluable insights in matters of textual analysis, interpretation, and stage history. I have not shown the manuscript of this book to Janet Adelman or George Walton Williams, but I have gained a great deal from consultations with them in former years and more recently. The notes attempt, inadequately, to record my indebtedness to former editors like Stanley Wells, Emrys Jones, John Dover Wilson, M. R. Ridley, R. H. Case, and many others, and to critics like Janet Adelman, Maynard Mack, and Rosalie Colie. Most of all I have shared the enthusiasms and occasional discouragements of this project with my wife, Peggy.

D.B.

University of Chicago

ABBREVIATIONS AND CONVENTIONS

1. Shakespeare's plays

Shakespeare's plays, when cited in this edition, are abbreviated in a style modified slightly from that used in the *Harvard Concordance to Shakespeare*. Other editions of Shakespeare are abbreviated under the editor's surname (Jones, Kittredge), or, in certain cases, under the series title (Arden, Cam.). When more than one edition by the same editor is cited, later editions are discriminated with a raised figure (Collier²). All quotations from Shakespeare, except those from *Antony and Cleopatra*, use the text and lineation of *The Riverside Shakespeare*, under the general editorship of G. Blakemore Evans.

Ado	*Much Ado About Nothing*
Ant.	*Antony and Cleopatra*
AWW	*All's Well That Ends Well*
AYLI	*As You Like It*
Cor.	*Coriolanus*
Cym.	*Cymbeline*
Err.	*The Comedy of Errors*
Ham.	*Hamlet*
1H4	*The First Part of King Henry the Fourth*
2H4	*The Second Part of King Henry the Fourth*
H5	*King Henry the Fifth*
1H6	*The First Part of King Henry the Sixth*
2H6	*The Second Part of King Henry the Sixth*
3H6	*The Third Part of King Henry the Sixth*
H8	*King Henry the Eighth*
JC	*Julius Caesar*
John	*King John*
LLL	*Love's Labour's Lost*
Lear	*King Lear*
Mac.	*Macbeth*
MM	*Measure for Measure*
MND	*A Midsummer Night's Dream*
MV	*The Merchant of Venice*
Oth.	*Othello*
Per.	*Pericles*
R2	*King Richard the Second*
R3	*King Richard the Third*
Rom.	*Romeo and Juliet*
Shr.	*The Taming of the Shrew*
STM	*Sir Thomas More*
Temp.	*The Tempest*
TGV	*The Two Gentlemen of Verona*
Tim.	*Timon of Athens*

Tit.	*Titus Andronicus*
TN	*Twelfth Night*
TNK	*The Two Noble Kinsmen*
Tro.	*Troilus and Cressida*
Wiv.	*The Merry Wives of Windsor*
WT	*The Winter's Tale*

2. Other works cited and general references

Abbott	E. A. Abbott, *A Shakespearian Grammar*, new edn, 1886 (references are to numbered paragraphs)
Alexander	Peter Alexander (ed.), *William Shakespeare: The Complete Works*, 4 vols., 1951, IV
AR	*Antioch Review*
Arden	*Antony and Cleopatra*, ed. M. R. Ridley, based on the edition of R. H. Case, 9th edn, 1954 (Arden Shakespeare)
Bamborough	J. B. Bamborough, *The Little World of Man*, 1952
Bevington	David Bevington (ed.), *The Complete Works of Shakespeare*, 3rd edn, 1980
Bevington[2]	David Bevington (ed.), *Antony and Cleopatra*, 1988 (Bantam Shakespeare)
Boswell	James Boswell, the younger (ed.), *The Plays and Poems of William Shakespeare* (based on the materials of Edmond Malone), 21 vols., 1821 (Third Variorum)
Bullough	Geoffrey Bullough (ed.), *Narrative and Dramatic Sources of Shakespeare*, 8 vols., 1957–75, V
Cam.	W. G. Clark, J. Glover, and W. A. Wright (eds.), *The Works of William Shakespeare*, 9 vols., 1863–6, VIII (Cambridge Shakespeare)
Capell	Edward Capell (ed.), *Mr William Shakespeare His Comedies, Histories, and Tragedies*, 10 vols., 1767–8, VIII
Capell, *Notes*	Edward Capell, *Notes and Various Readings to Shakespeare*, 3 vols., 1783
Case	*See* Arden
CE	*College English*
Cercignani	Fausto Cercignani, *Shakespeare's Works and Elizabethan Pronunciation*, 1981
Chapman	T. M. Parrott (ed.), *The Comedies of George Chapman*, 1914
Coleridge	Samuel Taylor Coleridge, *Shakespeare Criticism*, ed. Thomas Middleton Raysor, 2nd edn, 2 vols., 1960
Collier	John Payne Collier (ed.), *The Works of William Shakespeare*, 8 vols., 1842–4, VIII
Collier[2]	*The Works of Shakespeare*, 8 vols., 1853, VIII
Collier[3]	*Shakespeare's Comedies, Histories, Tragedies, and Poems*, 6 vols., 1858, VI
Collier[4]	*The Plays and Poems of William Shakespeare*, 8 vols., 1876–8, VII
Collier MS.	Manuscript emendations in John Payne Collier's copy of F2 (the 'Perkins Folio'), probably by Collier himself
Concordance	Marvin Spevack, *The Harvard Concordance to Shakespeare*, 1973
Craig	W. J. Craig (ed.), *The Complete Works of Shakespeare*, 1905

Daniel, *Cleopatra*	Alexander Grosart (ed.), *The Complete Works in Verse and Prose of Samuel Daniel*, 5 vols., 1885, vol. III (references are by act and (where possible) scene; and by through line numbering)
Deighton	Kenneth Deighton, *The Old Dramatists: Conjectural Readings*, 1896, 2nd ser., 1898
Delius	Nicolaus Delius (ed.), *Shakspere's Werke*, 7 vols., 1854–60
Dent	R. W. Dent, *Shakespeare's Proverbial Language: An Index*, 1981
Douce	Francis Douce, *Illustrations of Shakspeare*, 2 vols., 1807
DUJ	*Durham University Journal*
Dyce	Alexander Dyce (ed.), *The Works of William Shakespeare*, 6 vols., 1857, VI
Dyce[2]	*The Works of William Shakespeare*, 9 vols., 1864–7, VII
Dyce[3]	*The Works of William Shakespeare*, 9 vols., 1875–6, VII
EETS	Early English Text Society
ELH	*ELH: A Journal of English Literary History*
ELN	*English Language Notes*
ELR	*English Literary Renaissance*
ES	*English Studies* (Amsterdam)
E&S	*Essays and Studies by Members of the English Association*
ETJ	*Educational Theatre Journal*
F	*Mr William Shakespeares Comedies, Histories, and Tragedies*, 1623 (First Folio)
F2	*Mr William Shakespeares Comedies, Histories, and Tragedies*, 1632 (Second Folio)
F3	*Mr William Shakespeares Comedies, Histories, and Tragedies*, 1663 (Third Folio)
F4	*Mr William Shakespeares Comedies, Histories, and Tragedies*, 1685 (Fourth Folio)
Fitz	L. T. Fitz, 'Egyptian queens and male reviewers: sexist attitudes in *Antony and Cleopatra* criticism', *SQ* 28 (1977), 297–316
Furness	Horace Howard Furness (ed.), *The Tragedie of Anthonie, and Cleopatra*, 1907 (New Variorum)
Globe	W. G. Clark and W. A. Wright (eds.), *Works*, 1864
Goulart	*See* North's Plutarch
Hanmer	Thomas Hanmer (ed.), *The Works of Shakespear*, 6 vols., 1743–4, V
Harrison	Thomas P. Harrison, 'Shakespeare and Marlowe's *Dido, Queen of Carthage*', *UTSE* 35 (1956), 57–63
Heath	Benjamin Heath, *A Revisal of Shakespear's Text*, 1765
Henn	T. R. Henn, *The Living Image*, 1972
HLQ	*Huntington Library Quarterly*
Holinshed	Raphael Holinshed, *The Chronicles of England, Scotland, and Ireland*, 2nd edn, 3 vols., 1587 (references are by volume, book, page, and line)
Hood, R. C.	Information transmitted to the editor by R. C. Hood, Associate General Editor of the New Cambridge Shakespeare
Hudson	Henry N. Hudson (ed.), *The Works of Shakespeare*, 11 vols., 1851–6
Hudson[2]	*The Complete Works of William Shakespeare*, 20 vols., 1880–1, XVI
JAAC	*Journal of Aesthetics and Art Criticism*

Jackson	Zachariah Jackson, *Shakespeare's Genius Justified*, 1819
JEGP	*Journal of English and Germanic Philology*
Johnson	Samuel Johnson (ed.), *The Plays of William Shakespeare*, 8 vols., 1765, VII
Jones	Emrys Jones (ed.), *Antony and Cleopatra*, 1977 (New Penguin)
Jonson	C. H. Herford and P. and E. Simpson (eds.), *Ben Jonson*, 11 vols., 1925–52
Jonson, *Masques*	Stephen Orgel (ed.), *Ben Jonson: The Complete Masques*, 1969
JWCI	*Journal of the Warburg and Courtauld Institutes*
Kittredge	George Lyman Kittredge (ed.), *Sixteen Plays of Shakespeare*, 1946
Knight	Charles Knight (ed.), *The Pictorial Edition of the Works of Shakespeare*, 8 vols., 1838–43, VI
KR	*Kenyon Review*
Kyd	Frederick S. Boas (ed.), *The Works of Thomas Kyd*, 1901
LC	*Library Chronicle* (Univ. of Pennsylvania)
Lettsom	W. N. Lettsom, 'New readings in Shakespeare', *Blackwood's Edinburgh Magazine* 74 (August 1853), 181–202
Linthicum	M. Channing Linthicum, *Costume in the Drama of Shakespeare and His Contemporaries*, 1936
Lyly	R. Warwick Bond (ed.), *The Complete Works of John Lyly*, 3 vols., 1902
MacCallum	M. W. MacCallum, *Shakespeare's Roman Plays and Their Background*, 1910
Madden	D. H. Madden, *The Diary of Master William Silence*, 1897
Malone	Edmond Malone (ed.), *The Plays and Poems of William Shakespeare*, 10 vols., 1790, VII
Marlowe	Fredson Bowers (ed.), *The Complete Works of Christopher Marlowe*, 2 vols., 1973
Mason	John Monck Mason, *Comments on the Last Edition of Shakespeare's Plays* (i.e. the Johnson–Steevens Variorum of 1778), 1785
Milward	Peter Milward, *Shakespeare's Religious Background*, 1973
MLN	*Modern Language Notes*
MLQ	*Modern Language Quarterly*
MLR	*Modern Language Review*
Morris	Helen Morris, 'Shakespeare and Dürer's Apocalypse', *S.St.* 4 (1968), 252–62
Nares	Robert A. Nares, *A Glossary...of Words*, 1822
Nashe	R. B. McKerrow (ed.), *The Works of Thomas Nashe*, 1904–10, with supplementary notes by F. P. Wilson, 5 vols., 1958
Naylor	Edward W. Naylor, *Shakespeare and Music*, 1931
Noble	Richmond Noble, *Shakespeare's Biblical Knowledge and Use of The Book of Common Prayer*, 1935
North's Plutarch	*The Lives of the Noble Grecians and Romans, Compared Together by...Plutarch...Translated out of the Greek into French by James Amyot...and out of French into English by Thomas North*, 1579 (reference numbers are to page and section of the page (e.g. 984B); references to 'The Life of Octavius Caesar Augustus' are to the 1603 and 1612 edns, in which that life, translated by Simon Goulart, appeared)
N&Q	*Notes and Queries*

Odell	George C. D. Odell, *Shakespeare from Betterton to Irving*, 2 vols., 1920
OED	*Oxford English Dictionary*
Onions	C. T. Onions, *A Shakespeare Glossary*, enlarged and revised by Robert D. Eagleson, 1986
Orgel	*See* Jonson, *Masques*
Ovid, *Metamorphoses*	*The Fifteen Books of P. Ovidius Naso, Entitled Metamorphoses*, trans. Arthur Golding, 1567
Oxford	Stanley Wells and Gary Taylor (eds.), *William Shakespeare: The Complete Works*, 1986
Peele	C. T. Prouty (ed.), *The Life and Works of George Peele*, 3 vols., 1952–70 (references are by scene and by through line numbering)
Pembroke, Countess of	The Countess of Pembroke, *Antonie*, 1592, ed. Alice Luce, 1897 (references are by act; and by through line numbers)
Pliny, *Natural History*	*The History of the World, Commonly Called the Natural History of C. Plinius Secundus*, trans. Philemon Holland, 1601
Plutarch, *Moralia*	*The Philosophy, Commonly Called The Morals*, trans. Philemon Holland, 1603
PMLA	*Publications of the Modern Language Association of America*
Pope	Alexander Pope (ed.), *The Works of Shakespear*, 6 vols., 1723–5, V
Pope[2]	*The Works of Shakespear*, 8 vols., 1728
PQ	*Philological Quarterly*
Q	quarto
QQ	*Queen's Quarterly* (Ottawa)
REL	*Review of English Literature* (London)
RES	*Review of English Studies*
Ridley	*See* Arden
RMS	*Renaissance and Modern Studies* (Univ. of Nottingham)
Rowe	Nicholas Rowe (ed.), *The Works of Mr William Shakespear*, 6 vols., 1709, VI
Rowe[2]	*The Works of Mr William Shakespear*, 6 vols., 1709, VI
Rowe[3]	*The Works of Mr William Shakespear*, 8 vols., 1714, VII
SAB	*Shakespeare Association Bulletin*
Schmidt	A. Schmidt (ed.), *Antonius und Cleopatra*, 1870
SD	stage direction
Seager	H. W. Seager, *Natural History in Shakespeare's Time*, 1896, reprinted 1971
Seaton	Ethel Seaton, '*Antony and Cleopatra* and the Book of Revelation', *RES* 22 (1946), 219–24
SEL	*Studies in English Literature, 1500–1900*
SH	speech heading
Shaheen	Naseeb Shaheen, *Biblical References in Shakespeare's Tragedies*, 1987
Sidney, *Apology*	Sir Philip Sidney, *An Apology for Poetry*, in *Elizabethan Critical Essays*, ed. G. Gregory Smith, 2 vols., 1904, I
Singer	S. W. Singer (ed.), *The Dramatic Works of William Shakespeare*, 10 vols., 1856, X
Sisson	C. J. Sisson (ed.), *William Shakespeare: The Complete Works*, 1954

Sisson, *New Readings*	Charles J. Sisson, *New Readings in Shakespeare*, 2 vols., 1956
SJ	*Shakespeare Jahrbuch*
Southern MS.	The Southern MS. notes in F4
SQ	*Shakespeare Quarterly*
S.St.	*Shakespeare Studies* (Univ. of Cincinnati and others)
S.Sur.	*Shakespeare Survey*
Staunton	Howard Staunton (ed.), *The Works of William Shakespeare*, 15 vols., 1881, XIV
Steevens	*The Plays of William Shakespeare*, notes by Samuel Johnson and George Steevens, 10 vols., 1773, VIII (the Johnson–Steevens Variorum)
Steevens^2	*The Plays of William Shakespeare*, 10 vols., 1778, VIII
Steevens^3	*The Plays of William Shakespeare*, 10 vols., 1785, VIII
Steevens^4	*The Plays of William Shakespeare*, 15 vols., 1793, XII
Steevens^5	*The Plays of William Shakespeare*, revised and augmented by Isaac Reed, 21 vols., 1803, XVII
Theobald	Lewis Theobald (ed.), *The Works of Shakespeare*, 7 vols., 1733, VI
Theobald^2	*The Works of Shakespeare*, 8 vols., 1740
Thirlby	Styan Thirlby's conjectures, unpublished, chiefly in the form of manuscript annotations in his copies of eighteenth-century editions
Thistelton	Alfred Edward Thistelton, *Some Textual Notes on The Tragedy of Anthony and Cleopatra*, 1899
TLS	*Times Literary Supplement*
Tyrwhitt	Thomas Tyrwhitt, *Observations and Conjectures upon Some Passages of Shakespeare*, 1766
Upton	John Upton, *Critical Observations on Shakespeare*, 1746
UTSE	*University of Texas Studies in English*
VQR	*Virginia Quarterly Review*
Walker	W. S. Walker, *A Critical Examination of the Text of Shakespeare*, 1860
Warburton	William Warburton (ed.), *The Works of Shakespear*, 8 vols., 1747, VII
Whiter	Walter Whiter, *A Specimen of a Commentary on Shakspeare*, 1794
Wilson	John Dover Wilson (ed.), *Antony and Cleopatra*, 1950 (New Shakespeare)

All quotations from the Bible are taken from the Genevan version (1560) unless otherwise noted.

INTRODUCTION

Date and sources

The latest possible date for *Antony and Cleopatra* is 1608, when, on 20 May, 'A booke Called. Anthony. *and* Cleopatra' was entered in the Stationers' Register by Edward Blount, along with 'A booke called. *The booke of* Pericles *prynce of Tyre*'. Although this same Blount and the younger Jaggard received a licence in November 1623 to include *Antony and Cleopatra* in the Folio among sixteen plays 'not formerly entered to other men' – a licensing that would normally be unnecessary for a play already registered – scholars are generally satisfied that the 1608 entry refers to the play we know.[1] Blount was on friendly terms with Shakespeare's company, the King's Men, and may have undertaken a 'staying entry' in 1608 to prevent piracy by some other publisher. If so, the tactic failed with *Pericles* (which was issued in 1609 by another publisher). *Antony and Cleopatra* at all events remained unpublished until the Folio of 1623.

The earliest possible date for the composition of the play is less easy to determine. Samuel Daniel, who reprinted his *Cleopatra* (1594) for the fourth time in 1607 in a 'newly altered' version, seems to have been influenced by Shakespeare's newly produced play. Daniel alludes to Cydnus as the meeting-place of the lovers and rewrites other passages in which specific word choice seems to echo that of Shakespeare, such as Cleopatra's 'I have both hands and will, and I can die'; compare Shakespeare's 'My resolution and my hands I'll trust' (4.15.51).[2] Such details could have been found in some cases by a consulting of Plutarch or the Countess of Pembroke's *Antonie* (published 1592), but cumulatively they suggest that Daniel found a more immediate and current impetus. And if Daniel did profit from *Antony and Cleopatra* before the end of 1607, the play must have been performed some months earlier; the closing of the theatres on account of the plague in 1607 makes it unlikely that the play could have been performed before Easter of that year.[3]

Shakespeare's new play may also have influenced Barnabe Barnes's *The Devil's Charter*, registered on 16 October 1607 and produced by the King's Men at court on 2 February earlier that same year. Most telling is Barnes's reference to the use of aspics to kill two young princes as they sleep; the aspics are applied to their

[1] See MacCallum, p. 301.

[2] Case, p. xxv. Ernest Schanzer, 'Daniel's revision of his *Cleopatra*', *RES* ns 8 (1957), 375–81, asks sceptically whether most of the changes in Daniel cannot be attributed to his being influenced by the Countess of Pembroke's *Antonie*, but does agree that the verbal closeness of 'None about Caesar trust but Proculeius' (4.15.50) to Daniel argues for direct influence in one direction or the other.

[3] J. Leeds Barroll, 'The chronology of Shakespeare's Jacobean plays and the dating of *Antony and Cleopatra*', in Gordon Ross Smith (ed.), *Essays on Shakespeare*, 1965, pp. 115–62.

breasts and are referred to as 'Cleopatra's birds, / Fed fat and plump with proud Egyptian slime'.[1] To be sure, the printed text claims to offer various corrections and augmentations incorporated in the text in the aftermath of court performance, but the weight of scholarly opinion favours the likelihood that Barnes's indebtedness predates the February performance.[2] If so, the likeliest date for *Antony and Cleopatra* is some time in 1606, probably late in the year.

This dating means that we should be cautious about speaking of *Antony and Cleopatra* as Shakespeare's triumphant emergence from the dark world of *Hamlet*, *Othello*, *Lear*, and *Macbeth*. Even if *Hamlet* and *Othello* substantially predate it, *Lear* is very close though probably slightly earlier, whilst *Macbeth* may be contemporary. If *Pericles* belongs to this period, so too may *Coriolanus* – even *Timon*. There is no clear pattern of development towards a lighter spirit and vision in which to place *Antony and Cleopatra*.[3]

For his chief source Shakespeare turned to 'The Life of Marcus Antonius' in Plutarch's *The Lives of the Noble Grecians and Romans*, as translated by Sir Thomas North from the French of Jacques Amyot and first published in 1579. There Shakespeare found substantially all the narrative content he needed for his play, and extensive portrayals of the major characters (excepting Enobarbus, who is mentioned by Plutarch only briefly).[4] The narrative indebtedness is particularly marked in the second half of the play.

At times the verbal parallels are remarkably close. Shakespeare worked with North's Plutarch in front of him, adapting dialogue and vocabulary closely from what he found in many cases. Compare, for example, the following exchange in 5.2:

> I GUARD What work is here, Charmian? Is this well done?
> CHARMIAN It is well done, and fitting for a princess
> Descended of so many royal kings. (5.2.319–21)

with the original in North:

> One of the soldiers, seeing her, angrily said unto her: 'Is that well done, Charmian?' 'Very well', said she again, 'and meet for a princess descended from the race of so many noble kings.' (1009F–1010A)

There are many such passages,[5] the most famous of which is Enobarbus's narration of the first meeting of Antony and Cleopatra on the river of Cydnus. Here is Shakespeare:

> The barge she sat in, like a burnished throne
> Burned on the water. The poop was beaten gold;

[1] *Ibid.*, p. 149. Barnes may also have been familiar with a similar episode in George Peele's *Edward I*.
[2] E. K. Chambers, *William Shakespeare: A Study of Facts and Problems*, 1930, I, 476–8.
[3] Stanley Wells and Gary Taylor, 'The canon and chronology of Shakespeare's plays', in *William Shakespeare: A Textual Companion*, 1987, pp. 129–30.
[4] Elkin Calhoun Wilson, 'Shakespeare's Enobarbus', in James G. McManaway *et al.* (eds.), *Joseph Quincy Adams Memorial Studies*, 1948, pp. 391–408.
[5] See, for example, 3.6.70 ff., 3.13.150 ff., 2.2.251 ff., and 5.2.199 ff.

Purple the sails, and so perfumèd that
The winds were lovesick with them. The oars were silver,
Which to the tune of flutes kept stroke, and made
The water which they beat to follow faster,
As amorous of their strokes. For her own person,
It beggared all description: she did lie
In her pavilion – cloth of gold, of tissue –
O'erpicturing that Venus where we see
The fancy outwork nature. On each side her
Stood pretty dimpled boys, like smiling Cupids,
With divers-coloured fans, whose wind did seem
To glow the delicate cheeks which they did cool,
And what they undid did. (2.2.201–15)

And here is North:

She disdained to set forward otherwise but to take her barge in the river of Cydnus, the poop whereof was of gold, the sails of purple, and the oars of silver, which kept stroke in rowing after the sound of the music of flutes, hautboys, citterns, viols, and such other instruments as they played upon in the barge. And now for the person of herself: she was laid under a pavilion of cloth of gold of tissue, apparelled and attired like the goddess Venus commonly drawn in picture, and hard by her, on either hand of her, pretty fair boys apparelled as painters do set forth god Cupid, with little fans in their hands with the which they fanned wind upon her. (981)

Many similarly close details follow in the rest of this speech. Yet this remarkable borrowing also illustrates the transforming power of Shakespeare's art, for he repeatedly adds touches of personification, and puts the whole into the mouth of Enobarbus, a wry, humorous Roman soldier whose sardonic perspective adds persuasiveness to the gruff but admiring portrait of the Egyptian queen. Shakespeare also gives Enobarbus an onstage audience for this speech, a pair of dutiful Romans whose curiosity to hear gossip is comically at odds with the normal severity of their lives. Plutarch, by contrast, describes the scene in his own person as narrator, so that the description is accordingly informed by his own outspoken views of the protagonists' behaviour.

On a larger scale, Shakespeare excerpts from his source in a way that gives it dramatic shape. He adapts a historical narrative beginning in 41 BC with the military activities of Lucius and Fulvia through the battle of Actium in 31 BC and down to the lovers' suicides in 30 BC. In contrast to Plutarch's spacious discursive narrative, Shakespeare's play moves with remarkable energy and a sense of the continuous onrush of events, even though it also allows for the passage of time and never loses the expansive sense of ancient history at its most eventful. Shakespeare condenses into Scenes 2 and 3 of Act 1 the news of Fulvia's warring against Lucius, their coming together against Caesar, Labienus's success with the Parthians against Antony in Syria and Lydia, Fulvia's death, and Pompey's threats against Rome, whereas in Plutarch these events are narrated in sequence over a period of years; Fulvia dies in 40 BC, and the meeting with Pompey at Misenum is not until 39 BC.

Another major condensation concerns the breakdown of Antony's marriage to Octavia. Shakespeare shows us a single attempt at mediation by Octavia and a scene of leave-taking between her and Antony at Athens, whereas in Plutarch the matter extends over eight years (from 40 to 32 BC), during which time we hear repeatedly of pregnancies, separations, attempts at reconciliation, and mutual accusations that finally go beyond the reach of compromise. Shakespeare suppresses the distasteful business of the expulsion of Octavia from Antony's house in 33 BC, gives no report of Antony's disastrous campaign in Parthia that reflects such discredit on his soldiership, and leaves the impression that Antony has had no children at all by Octavia ('Have I my pillow left unpressed in Rome, / Forborne the getting of a lawful race', 3.13.108–9). Still further compression of events all but eliminates the interval of time (some months in Plutarch) between the battle of Actium and the death of Antony, and the days between Antony's suicide and that of Cleopatra.

On occasion, Shakespeare also rearranges the order of events. Antony hears the Soothsayer's warning to keep space between himself and Caesar (2.3) before the negotiations with Pompey, not afterwards as in Plutarch. The change makes little difference in the great sweep of events, but it does magnify a quality of rashness in Antony already evident elsewhere in Shakespeare's sources.[1] For the most part, however, Shakespeare is faithful not only to the historical facts but to the spirit of Plutarch's account.

In his presentation of character, Shakespeare goes beyond Plutarch in the direction of a multiplicity of points of view and a paradoxical complexity within the two protagonists. Plutarch views Antony as the victim of a tragic infatuation. Although he plentifully allows Antony to be brave, resourceful, munificent, frank, and charismatic, he makes no attempt to minimise the excesses of Antony's behaviour in Egypt, his financial dishonesty and exploitation of others in order to maintain an entourage of dissipated followers, his indifference to bloodshed, his mistrust of subordinates, his 'mocking and flouting of every man' (981A), his susceptibility to flattery, and his failures of generalship in the Parthian expedition. Similarly, in describing Cleopatra, Plutarch's admiration is real enough for the infinite charm, but the moral conclusion is no less firm and Roman in perspective. Cleopatra's main effect is to 'stir up many vices' as yet hidden in Antony; 'if any spark of goodness or hope of rising were left him, Cleopatra quenched it straight and made it worse than before' (981B). In Egypt, Antony 'spent and lost in childish sports (as a man might say) and idle pastimes the most precious thing a man can spend (as Antiphon saith), and that is, time' (982C–D). Plutarch is plainly distressed to see this great general 'made so subject to a woman's will' (999C). All this is of course in Shakespeare's play as well, but it is expressed by Roman commentators like Demetrius and Philo, or Caesar, or Antony himself when a 'Roman thought' has struck him, and is offset by a contrasting world of pleasure and imagination. Plutarch portrays that Egyptian world in all its exotic splendour, and

[1] MacCallum, p. 334.

makes plain his own fascination as well, but it is the fascination of one who disapproves of a surrender to pleasure of this kind.[1]

The difference is one of emphasis. Shakespeare found in Plutarch a rich complexity in both of his protagonists, one that gave him ample material for his portrayal of their relationship once he set aside the Graeco-Roman perspective of the narrator he found in his original.[2] Plutarch speaks censoriously, and yet he lends support to the idea that Antony and Cleopatra are like demigods. Shakespeare retains much derogatory information not so much in what we see Antony actually do onstage as in what others say about him and what he admits about himself. Yet Shakespeare balances this picture of a tragic fall into enslavement in two ways: by ennobling the vision of love in a fashion that Plutarch could never have sanctioned, and conversely by exploring a darker side of Octavius Caesar's rise to empire than is evident in Plutarch.

Appraisals of Caesar came down to the Renaissance in two contrasting traditions. As a ruler who became the Emperor Augustus after the deaths of Antony and Cleopatra, he offered a positive image of stable rule: he brought to a close a prolonged period of divided authority and ushered in a reign of peace in the Mediterranean world. The empire was thus a potential model for Tudor and Stuart rule in England after the protracted civil wars of the fifteenth century.[3] Ancient historians and poets such as Suetonius, Plutarch, Appian, Livy, Paterculus, Florus, Josephus, Dio Cassius, and Propertius generally concurred in praising Augustus even as they condemned Antony's liaison with Cleopatra.[4] In the medieval period, St Augustine lauded Augustan Rome for its heroism and self-denial, and noted that Augustus had been specially chosen by Providence to reign at the time of Christ's birth, even if Rome was the type of the worldly city as contrasted with the heavenly city of Jerusalem.[5] Dante placed Cleopatra in the second circle of hell among those in whose lives 'Reason by lust is swayed', while

[1] Plutarch himself was a Greek who admired the Roman empire; he was, as T. McAlindon puts it, 'a Platonic transcendentalist with a Ciceronian devotion to morals and the golden mean, an historian who believed in the existence of demi-gods and held that the essentials of Western philosophy are to be found in Greek and Egyptian mythology' (*Shakespeare and Decorum*, 1973, p. 187).

[2] Plutarch writes with a 'rare comprehensiveness of vision', says T. McAlindon, 'in which imagination and reason, sympathy and judicial detachment, often seem at odds' (*Shakespeare and Decorum*, p. 187). See also Barbara Bono, *Literary Transvaluation: From Vergilian Epic to Shakespearean Tragicomedy*, 1984, pp. 153 ff.

[3] James Emerson Phillips, Jr, *The State in Shakespeare's Greek and Roman Plays*, 1940, pp. 188–205.

[4] Suetonius, *The Lives of the Caesars*, Book II, chap. 17, trans. Philemon Holland as *The History of the Twelve Caesars*, 1606; Appian, *The Civil Wars*, Book V, chap. 1, para. 8 ff., trans. W. B. as *An Ancient History and Exquisite Chronicle of the Romans' Wars*, 1578; Livy, in a later epitome of his lost chapters (*periocha*), Books CXXX–CXXXIII; C. Velleius Paterculus, *The Roman History*, Book II, chaps. 82–7; Lucius Annaeus Florus, *Epitome of Roman History*, Book II, chap. 21; Josephus, *The Jewish History*, Book I, chap. 12, para. 5, trans. Thomas Lodge, 1602; Dio Cassius, *Roman History*, Book XLIX, chap. 32; Propertius, *Elegies*, Book III, Elegy 9. See J. Leeds Barroll, 'Shakespeare and Roman history', *MLR* 53 (1958), 327–43, and Marilyn L. Williamson, *Infinite Variety: Antony and Cleopatra in Renaissance Drama and Earlier Tradition*, 1974, pp. 19–43. Janet Adelman, *The Common Liar: An Essay on 'Antony and Cleopatra'*, 1973, pp. 54 ff., stresses more the ambivalence of these sources.

[5] St Augustine, *The City of God*, Book V, chaps. 12–21.

Antony became an example of enslavement to lust in Boccaccio and in subsequent stories of 'the Fall of Princes' written by John Lydgate and others.[1]

This tradition of praise for Augustus and blame for Antony was sustained and amplified in late medieval times and in the Renaissance by Ranulf Higden, Thomas Lanquet, Johannes Sleidanus, William Fulbeck, Jacques Amyot, Thomas North, Philemon Holland, Simon Goulart, Ben Jonson, and others.[2] Castiglione, Montaigne, and Robert Burton refer to Antony and Cleopatra as examples of *Ate*, those whom the gods first make passionate before destroying them.[3] Shakespeare was doubtless aware of this historical judgement, and may even have seen an analogy between Augustus's *pax Romana* and the aspirations of King James I to be an influential peacemaker in Europe[4] – although whether Shakespeare endorsed this pro-Augustan viewpoint is an entirely different matter.

At any rate, the pro-Augustan view was not the only interpretation available to Shakespeare. Even if Octavius Caesar was admired for his statesmanship once he had become emperor, he was frequently criticised (sometimes by the same historians who praised him) as a machiavel for his behaviour during the period of civil strife. Appian, Suetonius, Tacitus, Pedro Mexia, Peter Heylyn, and William Fulbeck all portray him as capable of treachery, callousness, narrow self-interest, and cruelty during his years as triumvir; for some writers, his succession to the imperial title spells the demise of Roman liberty.[5] Shakespeare found elements of this more critical evaluation in Robert Garnier's *Marc Antoine* (1578) and in Samuel Daniel's *Tragedy of Cleopatra* (1594), where Caesar is portrayed as ambitious and bloody even though capable at times of compassion.[6] The Augustus Caesar

[1] Dante, *Inferno*, Canto V, line 63; Boccaccio, *De casibus virorum illustrium*, Book VI, and *De claris mulieribus*, chap. 86. See Franklin Dickey, *Not Wisely But Too Well: Shakespeare's Love Tragedies*, 1957, pp. 144–202.

[2] Ranulf Higden, *Polychronicon*, 1527 (written in the fourteenth century); Thomas Lanquet, *Epitome of Chronicles*, 1549; Johannes Sleidanus (John Sleidan), *Brief Chronicle of the Four Principal Empires ...Babylon, Persia, Grecia, and Rome*, trans. Stephan Wythers, 1563; William Fulbeck, *An Historical Collection of the Continual Factions, Tumults, and Massacres of the Romans and Italians*, 1601; 'Amyot to the Readers', in North's Plutarch, sig. v; Plutarch, *Moralia*, sig. Ggg 2; Simon Goulart, *Life of Octavius Caesar Augustus*, in the 1603 edition of North's Plutarch, pp. 1159–83; Ben Jonson, *The Poetaster*, 1601. See Barroll, 'Shakespeare and Roman history', pp. 338–9, and Howard Erskine-Hill, 'Antony and Octavius: the theme of temperance in Shakespeare's *Antony and Cleopatra*', *RMS* 14 (1970), 26–47.

[3] *The Courtier of Count Baldesar Castilio, Divided into Four Books*, trans. Sir Thomas Hoby, 1588, Book III, sig. Bb6v; Montaigne, *Essays*, II, 33, trans. Donald Frame, 1957, p. 554; Robert Burton, *Anatomy of Melancholy*, Part I, section 2, member 3, subsection 6, and elsewhere. See Dickey, *Not Wisely But Too Well*, pp. 158–9.

[4] H. Neville Davies, 'Jacobean *Antony and Cleopatra*', *S.St.* 17 (1985), 123–58, pushes this purported connection with King James to an extreme.

[5] Appian, *The Civil Wars*, Books III–V; Suetonius, *The Lives of the Caesars*, Book II, chaps. 13 ff.; Tacitus, *Annals*, Book I, chap. 2; Pedro Mexia, *The History of All the Roman Emperors*, trans. W. T., 1604, pp. 29–46; Peter Heylyn (H. Seile), *Augustus: or, an Essay of Those Means and Counsels whereby the Commonwealth of Rome was Altered and Reduced into a Monarchy*, 1632; Fulbeck, *An Historical Collection*, p. 17. See Robert P. Kalmey, 'Shakespeare's Octavius and Elizabethan Roman history', *SEL* 18 (1978), 275–87, and Adelman, *The Common Liar*, p. 55.

[6] Adelman, *The Common Liar*, p. 56.

Shakespeare found in his sources was a complex figure, one that gave him ample evidence of a Rome in which kingdoms are clay.

The ennobling vision of love, generally lacking in Plutarch, came to Shakespeare not only through his imagination and experience but by way of a number of possible sources. Virgil's *Aeneid* exerts a palpable influence, whether directly or as embodied in Renaissance drama and poetry. Like Aeneas, Antony is pulled from erotic entanglement in Africa by the call of Roman destiny and the heroic code of the masculine world. The *pax Romana* established at the end of Shakespeare's play is the subject of Virgil's eulogy. Yet the achievement of the Roman ideal exacts its cost in both works; a drama of love is played out against the epic sweep of history. Like Dido, Cleopatra is a regal figure capable of jealousy and rage, and possesses a nobility equalling that of her lover. Both women bring an abiding interest in fame to their noble suicides.[1] Dido is a sympathetic model for Cleopatra also in Ovid's *Heroides*, where she is the deserted victim; in Chaucer's *The Legend of Good Women* (based on Ovid) and in *The House of Fame*, where Aeneas is condemned by Venus as a traitor in love; and in Marlowe and Nashe's *Dido, Queen of Carthage* (*c.* 1587–93), with its unique blend of the Ovidian and the Virgilian.[2]

Antony and Cleopatra themselves sometimes appear in a partly favourable light in ancient and medieval texts. Although Horace condemns Cleopatra for her wantonness, he does admire her queenly suicide and her proud resolve not to grace Caesar's triumph.[3] In Boccaccio and John Lydgate as well, denunciation is mixed with admiration for the constancy of her devotion. John Gower includes Antony and Cleopatra among a procession of faithful lovers in his *Confessio Amantis*.[4]

Sympathetic interpretations of the famous lovers were available to Shakespeare in the dramatic literature of his own generation. The Countess of Pembroke's *The Tragedy of Antonie* (translated from the French (1578) of Robert Garnier, finished in 1590, published 1592) and Samuel Daniel's *The Tragedy of Cleopatra* (1594) portray the lovers as heroic victims of their own passionate excesses and remorseless destiny, regretfully aware of their failures but ready to face death with resolution and the expectation of an afterlife together in the world of the dead. Even if these severely Senecan closet dramas offered Shakespeare little that he

[1] Reuben A. Brower, *Hero and Saint: Shakespeare and the Graeco-Roman Heroic Tradition*, 1971, pp. 317–53, esp. 319 and 351; Bono, *Literary Transvaluation*, p. 2.

[2] Brower, *Hero and Saint*, p. 352; Ernest Schanzer, *The Problem Plays of Shakespeare*, 1963, p. 160; Harrison, pp. 57–63; J. B. Steane, *Marlowe: A Critical Study*, 1965, p. 30; Robert Miola, *Shakespeare's Rome*, 1983, p. 122; and Adelman, *The Common Liar*, pp. 177–83. Michael Shapiro, 'Boying her greatness: Shakespeare's use of coterie drama in *Antony and Cleopatra*', *MLR* 77 (1982), 1–15, also sees an indebtedness to other pathetic-heroine plays of the coterie drama like *Sophonisba*.

[3] Horace, *Odes*, Book I, Ode 37, and Epode 9. See, for contrasting views of Horace's complex interpretation of Cleopatra, Dickey, *Not Wisely But Too Well*, pp. 146–7; Adelman, *The Common Liar*, p. 56; Williamson, *Infinite Variety*, pp. 19–25; and Perry D. Westbrook, 'Horace's influence on Shakespeare's *Antony and Cleopatra*', *PMLA* 62 (1947), 392–8.

[4] Admiration for Cleopatra is expressed in Boccaccio's *Fiametta* (1343) and in Gower's *Confessio Amantis*, Book VIII, 2751 ff. See Donna Hamilton, '*Antony and Cleopatra* and the tradition of noble lovers', *SQ* 24 (1973), 235–51, and Williamson, *Infinite Variety*, pp. 51–2.

wished to use in the way of dramatic construction and sententious rhetoric, they helped redress the prevalence of condemnation found in some ancient writers, and Daniel's poetic sensitivity to language gave Shakespeare some hints for dialogue and characterisation.[1]

Shakespeare's complex and ennobling vision of love may have come to him ultimately in part from mythology. The stories of Venus and Mars, to which Mardian refers (1.5.19), or Venus and Bacchus (as in North's Plutarch, 981F–982A), were available to Shakespeare in Book VIII of Homer's *Odyssey*, in Ovid's *Metamorphoses*, and, closer to his own theatre, in John Lyly's *Sappho and Phao* (1584), wherein Venus is presented as cunning, erotic, and richly deserving her overthrow by the virtuous Sappho. Yet Venus herself could paradoxically represent chaste love. In the Renaissance allegorical traditions of the *Aphrodite Pandemos* of fruitful nature, or the *Venus armata*, the goddess's conquest of Mars was variously emblematised by Vincentio Cartari and other mythographers as the victory of chaste affection in love or the moral and cosmic triumph of the generative principle over rivalry between the sexes. Renaissance paintings of Mars and Venus exchanging clothing or of Venus and cupids playing with Mars's armour, so suggestive of key scenes in Shakespeare's play, were interpreted as signs of harmonious union.[2] These images were derived ultimately from Lucretius's great invocation to Venus as the goddess of love conquering strife, and from medieval and Renaissance writers like Bernard Silvestris, Alanus de Insulis, Lorenzo Valla, and Erasmus, who coupled Epicurean doctrines of contemplative indifference towards mundane human affairs, scorn for the vicissitudes of fate, and joy in a mortal felicity thus achieved through detachment, with a Christian neo-Platonic emphasis on happiness in this world as an anticipation of heavenly bliss.[3] When Enobarbus says of Cleopatra that 'vilest things / Become themselves in her, that the holy priests / Bless her when she is riggish' (2.2.248–50), he invokes the paradox of the 'Lucretian Venus'. The paradox is eloquently expressed also in the mythographic writings of Natale Conti, in Edmund Spenser's *The Faerie Queene*, and in Elizabethan love lyrics and poems – including Shakespeare's own early *Venus and Adonis* (1593), to which *Antony and Cleopatra* bears more than a passing resemblance.[4]

[1] Other dramatisations of Antony and Cleopatra in this severely Senecan and 'classical' school of writing include Giambattista Giraldi Cinthio's *Cleopatra*, written *c.* 1543, Cesare di' Cesari's *Cleopatra*, 1552, Étienne Jodelle's *Cléopâtre captive*, 1552, a lost version by Fulke Greville (mentioned in Greville's *Life of Sidney*), and *The Virtuous Octavia* by Samuel Brandon, 1598. See Willard Farnham, *Shakespeare's Tragic Frontier*, 1950, pp. 149–50; A. P. Riemer, *A Reading of Shakespeare's 'Antony and Cleopatra'*, 1968, pp. 12–14; and Williamson, *Infinite Variety*, pp. 169–80.

[2] Edgar Wind, *Pagan Mysteries in the Renaissance*, 1968, pp. 75 ff. See also Rudolf Wittkower, 'Transformations of Minerva in Renaissance imagery', *JWCI* 2 (1938–9), 194–205, esp. pp. 202–3, on iconographical reconciliations between Minerva and Venus (*Castitas* and *Voluptas*), signifying the bringing into harmonious control of the lower instincts. Discussed in Adelman, *The Common Liar*, pp. 92–6.

[3] Lucretius, *De rerum natura*, Bernardus Sylvestris, *De mundi universitate*, Alain de Lille (Alanus de Insulis), *De planctu natura*. See Bono, *Literary Transvaluation*, pp. 168 ff., and Adelman, *The Common Liar*, pp. 84–5.

[4] Natale Conti, *Natalis Comitis Mythologiae*, 1581, Book II, chap. 7, pp. 107–8. In Spenser, *The Faerie*

The story of Omphale and Hercules, in which the Amazonian queen subdues the hero and puts him to work spinning among her maids, was widely used in the Renaissance as a cautionary tale of male rationality overthrown by female will. We find it in Philemon Holland's translation (1603) of Plutarch's *Moralia*, in Spenser's *The Faerie Queene*, and in Sir Philip Sidney's *Apology for Poetry*.[1] Shakespeare may well have the story in mind on those occasions when Cleopatra manages the war or drinks Antony to bed dressed in her 'tires and mantles' (2.5.22–3). Yet for all the customary emphasis on the horrors of emasculation by a controlling female, iconographical tradition also offered a more positive image. Hercules was after all a demigod, one of those who, as Plutarch puts it, were 'far stronger than men, and that in puissance they much surmounted our nature, but that divinity which they had was not pure and simple, but they were compounded of a nature corporal and spiritual'.[2] As such, Hercules could be viewed as a creature of paradox, struggling to assert humanity's noble nature over its baser impulses.[3] A particularly revealing iconographical tradition, known as the choice of Hercules between Virtue and Vice, depicts an encounter between the hero and two women, one modest and one brazen. Even though the women appear to represent irreconcilably divergent paths, the point in some interpretations (in Cartari and Conti, for example) is not one of simple moral choice but of perceiving that human completeness requires both pleasure and virtue. Hercules' best choice, as in the parallel myth of the garden of the Hesperides, is to learn to harmonise the *vita activa* and the *vita voluptuosa*.[4] Antony's choice in Shakespeare's play may owe something to this tradition of complex moral evaluation.

Shakespeare makes a repeated point, as does Plutarch, of the identification of

Queene, IV, x, 44 ff., 'Great *Venus*, Queene of beautie and of grace' receives the tribute of 'aboundant flowres' out of the 'fruitfull lap' of the earth and inspires wild creatures to 'seeke to quench their inward fire' in 'generation'. See Adelman, *The Common Liar*, pp. 86–7, and Adrien Bonjour, 'From Shakespeare's Venus to Cleopatra's cupids', *S.Sur.* 15 (1962), 73–80, who observes that Cleopatra accomplishes what Venus of *Venus and Adonis* merely promises; both works employ the paradox of wind that cools even while it kindles, of art and myth that outdo nature, of amorous desire that tames military conquest, and the like. For the argument of this entire paragraph, see Bono, *Literary Transvaluation*, pp. 173–8.

[1] Plutarch, *Moralia*, 'Whether an Aged Man Ought to Manage Public Affairs', p. 386, lines 29–31; *The Faerie Queene*, V, v, 24 ff.; and Sidney, *Apology*, p. 200, where the story is cited as an example of an archetypal comic situation. See J. Leeds Barroll, 'Enobarbus' description of Cleopatra', *UTSE* 37 (1958), 61–78, esp. p. 71; Gordon P. Jones, 'The "strumpet's fool" in *Antony and Cleopatra*', *SQ* 34 (1983), 62–8, p. 65; Schanzer, *The Problem Plays of Shakespeare*, p. 158; and Adelman, *The Common Liar*, p. 81.

[2] Plutarch, *Moralia*, 'Of Isis and Osiris', p. 1297 (lines 2–4).

[3] Eugene Waith, *The Herculean Hero in Marlowe, Chapman, Shakespeare, and Dryden*, 1962, p. 18.

[4] John Coates, '"The choice of Hercules" in *Antony and Cleopatra*', *S.Sur.* 31 (1978), 45–52, citing Erwin Panofsky, *Herkules am Scheidewege*, 1930, and Xenophon, *Memorabilia of Socrates*, Book II, chap. 1, para. 21 ff. See also Schanzer, *The Problem Plays of Shakespeare*, pp. 155–7; Wind, *Pagan Mysteries*, pp. 205–6; Douglas Bush, *Mythology and the Renaissance Tradition in English Poetry*, 1932, rev. edn, 1963, pp. 137–55; and Harry Levin, *The Myth of the Golden Age in the Renaissance*, 1969, p. 134. Ben Jonson's *Pleasure Reconciled to Virtue* (1619) is too late for *Antony and Cleopatra*, but it represents a tradition of harmonising opposites as found earlier in Cartari's *Imagines deorum* (1581) and Conti's *Mythologiae* (1581). Shakespeare shows in *LLL* 4.3.337–8 that he is familiar with popular mythological traditions about Hercules in love.

Vis Amoris.

ALCIDES heere, hath throwne his Clubbe away,
And weares a Mantle, for his Lions skinne,
Thus better liking for to paſſe the day,
With *Omphale*, and with her maides to ſpinne,
To card, to reele, and doe ſuch daily taske,
What ere it pleaſed, *Omphale* to aske.

Si temperata acceſſerit Venus nó alia Dea eſt adeo gratioſa. *Euripides in Medea.*

That all his conqueſts wonne him not ſuch Fame,
For which as God, the world did him adore,
As Loues affection, did diſgrace and ſhame
His virtues partes. How many are there more,
Who hauing Honor, and a worthy name,
By actions baſe, and lewdnes looſe the ſame.

Propert.

Quicquid amor iuſſit, non eſt contemnere tutum,
Regnat et in ſuperos ius habet ille Deos.

1 *Vis Amoris* (Love's Power): Hercules spinning at Omphale's behest. From Henry Peacham's *Minerva Britanna, or a Garden of Heroical Devices* (1612), p. 95

Cleopatra with the goddess Isis of Egyptian mythology. Caesar complains, for example, of reports that Cleopatra has appeared in the market-place at Alexandria and has given audience 'In th'habiliments of the goddess Isis' (3.6.17). According to the myth, Isis, the consort of her brother Osiris, reassembled the parts of Osiris's body when he had been torn apart by his brother Typhon (or Set) and in doing so fashioned a new genital member to replace the one missing piece, thus enabling Osiris to gain immortality and reign as monarch of the underworld. Shakespeare may well have known the invocation at the end of Apuleius's *Golden Ass* in which Isis is identified with the 'celestial' Lucretian Venus, 'who in the beginning of the world didst couple together male and female with an engendered love', and is further identified with 'Dame Ceres, which art the original and motherly nurse of all fruitful things in the earth', as well as with Juno, Bellona, Proserpine, and Hecate.[1]

Isis is further to be identified with Io, whom Jove turned into a heifer in an unsuccessful attempt to evade the wrath of Juno (see 3.10.10–15 of Shakespeare's play).[2] Whether named Io or Isis, the powerful deity thus invoked is the goddess of agriculture, of the moon, of fertility, and of the Nile in its nurturing relation to Osiris, the ocean. Plutarch in his *Moralia* speaks of Isis as the goddess 'of intelligence and motion together', and affirms that her name means 'a motion animate and wise'. Isis is, moreover, of a double nature, both male and female. She is 'the nurse that suckleth and feedeth the whole world'.[3] Osiris in turn is often equated with Bacchus or Dionysus. These images serve collectively to enhance the mythic potency of Antony and Cleopatra, even if the images do not gainsay the worldly failure that is also an integral part of such legends.

Cleopatra's mythic heritage is well summed up by Northrop Frye. Cleopatra, the serpent of the Nile, is a Venus rising from the sea, an Isis, a *stella maris*, a goddess of the moon and the sea. 'She has affinities with a kind of goddess figure that both Hebraic and Classical religions kept trying to subdue by abuse: she is a whore and her children are all bastards; she is a snare to men and destroys their masculinity, making them degenerate slaves like Circe; she is an Omphale dressing her Hercules in women's clothes; she has many characteristics of her sister whore of Babylon.' Yet she is not to be identified with vice, any more than Rome is to be identified with virtue. Her Egypt is instead 'the night side of nature, passionate, cruel, superstitious, barbaric, dissolute, what you will'. She is the 'white goddess' whom it is death to serve, and accordingly *Antony and Cleopatra* is a tragedy of passion and fatal love. Her Egypt is able 'to bring a superhuman vitality out of Antony that Rome cannot equal, not in spite of the fact that it destroys him, but

[1] Apuleius, *Golden Ass*, trans. W. Adlington, 1566, Book II. See Michael Lloyd, 'Cleopatra as Isis', *S.Sur.* 12 (1959), 88–94. Shakespeare may also have consulted Philemon Holland's translation (1603) of Plutarch's *Of Isis and Osiris* (in the *Moralia*); see Harold Fisch, '*Antony and Cleopatra*: the limits of mythology', *S.Sur.* 23 (1970), 59–67.

[2] Robert G. Hunter, 'Cleopatra and the "oestre junonicque"', *S.St.* 5 (1969), 236–8; see also 3.10.14 n. in the Commentary.

[3] *Of Isis and Osiris*, in Plutarch, *Moralia*, p. 1311 (lines 22–7), p. 1304 (line 55), and p. 1301 (lines 6–7). See Lloyd, 'Cleopatra as Isis', pp. 91–2.

because it destroys him'. Cleopatra's mythic ancestry helps illuminate her dangerous fascination and her greatness as a 'counter-historical figure'.[1]

Other possible sources include Book II of Spenser's *The Faerie Queene* and its portrayal of Guyon's temperate resistance to enchantment as contrasted with the enervated surrender of Cymochles to Acrasia. Spenser's own models, Ariosto and Tasso, explicitly compare their protagonists' morally ambiguous amours with the famous love affair of Antony and Cleopatra.[2] English drama and fiction of the 1570s, 80s, and 90s could have provided Shakespeare with a model for Enobarbus in the convention of the protesting soldier, one who, like Hephaestion in John Lyly's *Campaspe* (1584), Sateros in Robert Wilson's *The Cobbler's Prophecy* (*c.* 1589–93), or Antony himself in the anonymous *The Tragedy of Caesar and Pompey, or Caesar's Revenge* (*c.* 1592–6), fulminates briskly against erotic entanglement as inappropriate to a great soldier. Barnabe Rich's *A Right Excellent and Pleasant Dialogue between Mercury and an English Soldier* (1574) offers a similar plea through the voice of an English soldier in debate with the goddess Venus herself.[3] Renaissance manuals of war offered guidelines in military leadership and tactics that Antony so egregiously violates at Actium.[4]

One source or tradition that is particularly hard to gauge is the Christian and moral perspective of Shakespeare's own age. To what extent does Shakespeare consciously or unconsciously impose upon the late pagan world of *Antony and Cleopatra* the sensibilities of post-classical and Renaissance England? In one sense, the play is remarkably free from the moral constraints found in most of Shakespeare's other great tragedies, even in the nominally pagan *Lear*. *Antony and Cleopatra* celebrates an adulterous relationship and ends in noble suicide. Even when the lovers' behaviour is criticised, the terms are Roman: the failures are described as intemperance, inattentiveness to duty, lack of devotion to the best interests of the state, and so on.

[1] Northrop Frye, *Fools of Time*, 1967, pp. 42–74, esp. pp. 49, 59, and 71–3.

[2] *Jerusalem Delivered*, trans. as *Godfrey of Bulloigne* by Edward Fairfax, 1600, Book XVI, stanza 6, where Tasso anticipates his story of Armida's allurement of Rinaldo with a picture of the battle of Actium engraved on the doors of Armida's palace. Cleopatra is referred to in *Orlando Furioso*, trans. John Harington (1591; 2nd edn 1607), Book VII, stanza 19, apropos of Rogero and Alcyna. Ideas of temperance as a mean between the extremes of pleasure and abstemiousness are ultimately indebted to Aristotle's *Nicomachaean Ethics*, Book III, chap. 10, and to Plato's figure of the mind as a chariot drawn by two horses, one temperately honourable and the other ignobly obsessed with glory (*Phaedrus*, in *Works*, ed. H. Stephanus, Paris, 1578, III, 246; referred to in Plutarch, 986D), but Shakespeare need not have had direct knowledge of these sources. See Schanzer, *The Problem Plays of Shakespeare*, p. 158, and Erskine-Hill, 'Antony and Octavius', pp. 28–9.

[3] Paul Jorgensen, 'Antony and the protesting soldiers: a Renaissance tradition for the structure of *Antony and Cleopatra*', in Gordon Ross Smith (ed.), *Essays on Shakespeare*, 1965, p. 163–81; Emrys Jones, *Scenic Form in Shakespeare*, 1971, p. 239.

[4] Paul Jorgensen, *Shakespeare's Military World*, 1956, p. 91. For unconvincing arguments that Shakespeare partly based his portrait of Cleopatra on Queen Elizabeth, and especially on an incident in 1564 when the queen received a delegation from Mary, Queen of Scots, and vividly revealed to the ambassador, Sir James Melville, her sense of feminine rivalry, asking about the colour of Mary's hair, her ability in dancing, etc., see Helen Morris, 'Queen Elizabeth I "shadowed" in Cleopatra', *HLQ* 32 (1969), 271–9, and Keith Rinehart, 'Shakespeare's Cleopatra and England's Elizabeth', *SQ* 23 (1972), 81–6.

Yet the play repeatedly echoes the Book of Revelation in its apocalyptic view of last things,[1] and anticipates a 'time of universal peace' under the Emperor Augustus (4.6.5–6) that, however ironically, reminds us that the birth of Christ is at hand. Other biblical echoes have been adduced, some more persuasive than others.[2] Cumulatively, although they provide little basis for a Christian reading of repentance and preparation for death, they do remind us that *Antony and Cleopatra* could not have been written as it stands in Roman times. The vision of a tragic and ennobling love is indebted to Ovid and Virgil, but it also owes much to the kind of exalted vision of love we find in later Western culture in the *liebestod* of Tristan and Isolde. As J. L. Simmons shows, the Renaissance concept of human love to which Shakespeare is attuned derives its idealism from a kind of syncretic neo-Platonism, justifying romantic love as a human response to manifestations of heavenly beauty even while acknowledging that sexual passion can draw the rational soul away from God. The paradoxical result, qualifying neo-Platonic severity with Aristotelian humanism, is the *via media* of Donne and Spenser, a 'reverend human love' that (as in Sidney's *Astrophil and Stella*) can be seen as ennobling even when adulterous and even when the love object is of dubious worth.[3] Shakespeare wrote about the ancient Roman world pretty much as he found it in Plutarch and his other classical sources, but he also wrote for his own generation.

The contrarieties of critical response

We should hardly be surprised, in view of the opposing or ambivalent interpretations available to Shakespeare of Antony, Cleopatra, and Octavius Caesar, to learn that the play and its characters have evoked widely contrasting responses. 'The woman's a whore, and there's an end on't!', said Dr Johnson of a lady damaged by scandal, and George Bernard Shaw liked to pretend that Johnson had said it of Cleopatra. It agreed with Shaw's own view: 'You can't feel any sympathy with Antony after he runs away disgracefully from the battle of Actium because Cleopatra did', Shaw added. 'If you knew anyone who did that you'd spit in his face. All Shakespear's rhetoric and pathos cannot reinstate Antony after that, or leave us with a single good word for his woman.' The play has 'no moral value whatever'. Its portrayal of love is intolerable because, 'after giving a faithful picture of the soldier broken down by debauchery, and the typical wanton in whose arms such men perish, Shakespear finally strains all his huge command of rhetoric and stage pathos to give a theatrical sublimity to the wretched end of the business, and

[1] Seaton, pp. 219–24; Shaheen, pp. 175–86.

[2] Andrew Fichter, '*Antony and Cleopatra*: "the time of universal peace"', *S.Sur.* 33 (1980), 99–111; John Middleton Murry, *Shakespeare*, 1936, pp. 294–318, esp. p. 303. For a balanced discussion, see J. A. Bryant, Jr, *Hippolyta's View*, 1961, pp. 182–3. Dolora G. Cunningham's assertion of a pattern of Christian repentance and preparation for death in Cleopatra's end, 'The characterization of Shakespeare's Cleopatra', *SQ* 6 (1955), 9–17, has been convincingly refuted by Elizabeth Story Donno, 'Cleopatra again', *SQ* 7 (1956), 227–33.

[3] J. L. Simmons, *Shakespeare's Pagan World: The Roman Tragedies*, 1973, pp. 114–18.

to persuade foolish spectators that the world was well lost by the twain'.[1]

Shaw's opinion, however characteristically overstated, is shared by many who stress the unlawfulness of the famous lovers' conduct and the moral appropriateness of their 'unfortunate end'.[2] For such critics the lovers stand condemned, despite their attractive qualities, as the embodiment of gluttony, lechery, and sloth.[3] The 'base, sensual, and adulterous' nature of their passion expresses itself in the phallic and diabolical symbolism of serpents, witchcraft, and poison, thereby betraying Shakespeare's own immense 'horror of sexuality'.[4] Despite their pretensions to mythic grandeur, Antony and Cleopatra are mere stage figures. 'We are *told* I don't know how many times that [Antony] was a supreme specimen of humanity', complains H. A. Mason, but in fact 'the Antony who is presented dramatically never makes us believe in these reports'.[5] Disillusionment is a common experience for those who read or see the play in these terms: its story of love, which we usually associate with 'a heightened sense of life and fulfilment', leads to nothing.[6] Because Shakespeare is chiefly interested in having us understand the conflicting demands upon Antony, we are not asked to become emotionally involved with the protagonists.[7] The consequence, for A. C. Bradley among others, is that *Antony and Cleopatra* cannot stand in the same rank with *Hamlet*, *Othello*, *Lear*, and *Macbeth*. There is something 'half-hearted', even 'ironical', in Shakespeare's portrayal of the conflict; the play does not stir the tragic emotions fully or attain the 'terrifying and overwhelming power' necessary to the greatest tragedy.[8] In terms of construction as well, some critics find 'a decided falling off' in the handling of the plot.[9]

1 George Bernard Shaw, 'Mr Shaw on heroes', signed 'A.D.', *Liverpool Post*, 19 October 1927, and Preface to *Three Plays for Puritans*, 1906, p. xxviii. Gordon W. Couchman, '*Antony and Cleopatra* and the subjective convention', *PMLA* 76 (1961), 420–5, quotes the following from *Three Plays for Puritans*: 'The very name of Cleopatra suggests at once a tragedy of Circe, with the horrible difference that whereas the ancient myth rightly represents Circe as turning heroes into hogs, the modern romantic convention would represent her as turning hogs into heroes.' For Johnson's remark about Lady Diana Beauclerk, see Boswell, *The Life of Samuel Johnson*, under 7 May 1773.

2 John Dryden, Preface to *All for Love*, 1678.

3 J. Leeds Barroll, 'Antony and pleasure', *JEGP* 57 (1958), 708–20; Barroll, 'Enobarbus' description of Cleopatra', *UTSE* 37 (1958), 61–78; and Dickey, *Not Wisely But Too Well*, pp. 144–60. Irving Ribner, *Patterns in Shakespearian Tragedy*, 1960, p. 172, similarly argues that whatever triumph Antony and Cleopatra may achieve 'is in defiance of the Christian moral order', and 'is rooted in sin'. See also Roy Battenhouse, *Shakespearean Tragedy: Its Art and Its Christian Premises*, 1969, pp. 161–83. For Dr Johnson's opinion, see Walter Raleigh, *Johnson on Shakespeare*, 1908, p. 180.

4 Daniel Stempel, 'The transmigration of the crocodile', *SQ* 7 (1956), 59–72, and David Frost, '*Antony and Cleopatra* – All for Love; or the World Ill-Lost?', *Topic* 7 4 (1964), 33–44, esp. p. 35. See J. P. Brockbank, 'Shakespeare and the fashion of these times', *S.Sur.* 16 (1963), 30–5, on the failure of much criticism and staging of Shakespeare, especially in the nineteenth century, to allow 'too close a contact with Nilus slime'.

5 H. A. Mason, *Shakespeare's Tragedies of Love*, 1970, p. 269. See also E. E. Stoll, *Art and Artifice in Shakespeare*, 1933, pp. 146–7, and Stoll, 'Cleopatra', *MLR* 23 (1928), 145–63.

6 L. C. Knights, 'On the tragedy of Antony and Cleopatra', *Scrutiny* 16 (1949), 318–23; reprinted in *Some Shakespearean Themes*, 1959.

7 William Rosen, *Shakespeare and the Craft of Tragedy*, 1960, pp. 104–60, esp. pp. 133–4.

8 A. C. Bradley, 'Shakespeare's *Antony and Cleopatra*', in *Oxford Lectures on Poetry*, 1909, pp. 285, 290, and 305.

9 Levin L. Schücking, *Character Problems in Shakespeare's Plays*, 1922, p. 135.

Conversely, the vision of ennobling love has had eloquent defenders. Samuel Taylor Coleridge applies the motto *Feliciter audax* to a play he regards as 'perhaps of Shakespeare's plays the most wonderful' because of its 'happy valiancy of style' and its 'insight' into the 'depth and energy' of the lovers' passions.[1] William Hazlitt regards the character of Cleopatra as a 'masterpiece', a 'triumph of the voluptuous, of the love of pleasure and the power of giving it, over every other consideration'.[2] G. Wilson Knight traces a movement in the play's imagery along an ascending scale from 'the material and sensuous, through the grand and magnificent, to the more purely spiritual', by means of which ascent Antony and Cleopatra discover a mutual and transcendental union that amply compensates for the sacrifices of power, warrior-honour, and material magnificence they must make.[3] J. Dover Wilson sees in Antony's majesty, affability, benevolence, liberality, amity, justice, fortitude, and patience in sustaining wrong a 'portrait of true greatness'; Cleopatra too 'must find her true greatness and be touched to finest issues', and does so in Act 5.[4] Even if many of Cleopatra's ardent admirers betray sexist attitudes in praising her for being childlike, passionate, irrational, the guileful 'serpent of old Nile', a 'Lilith who ensnared Adam before the making of Eve', 'the mystery of woman', Blake's 'Eternal Female', 'quintessentiated Eve', and so on,[5] they are at least drawn to the wholeness and complexity of an emotional experience that is at once erotic and sublime.

The sharply divided opinion of critical history has some important consequences for the play itself. Manifestly *Antony and Cleopatra* is, as Ernest Schanzer says, a problem play of sorts, in that it makes us 'unsure of our moral bearings'. The ambiguity perceived by opposing critical traditions, in other words, ought to reside in all of us as audience; we all should experience 'uncertain and divided responses'.[6] Those responses seem structured into the play itself in its many antitheses: Egypt and Rome, the contrary attractions of pleasure and of political or military ambition, and the like. Such polarities are inherent in the life of every individual to a greater or lesser extent. As Stephen Shapiro puts it, the love relationship in *Antony and Cleopatra* is 'structured necessarily by ambivalence and paradox because no simple harmony can resolve the antitheses – ego–objective world, pleasure–pain,

1 Thomas Middleton Raysor (ed.), *Samuel Taylor Coleridge: Shakespeare Criticism*, 2nd edn, 1960, I, 76–9. See also August Wilhelm Schlegel, *Lectures on Dramatic Literature*, trans. John Black, 2nd edn, 1844, pp. 416–17.

2 William Hazlitt, *Characters of Shakespear's Plays*, 1817, new edn, 1906, pp. 74–5. Anna Brownell Jameson, *Characteristics of Women, Moral, Poetical, and Historical*, 3rd edn, 1836, II, 121–4, praises the 'consistent inconsistency' of an antithetical construction that 'dazzles our faculties, perplexes our judgment, bewilders and bewitches our fancy', and produces in us 'a kind of fascination', even if our moral sense rebels against it.

3 G. Wilson Knight, 'The transcendental humanism of Antony and Cleopatra', in *The Imperial Theme*, 1931, rev. edn 1951, pp. 199–262, esp. pp. 204–5.

4 Wilson, pp. xxiv–xxxii.

5 Edward Dowden, *Shakespeare: A Critical Study of His Mind and Art*, 3rd edn, 1881, p. 273; S. L. Bethell, *Shakespeare and the Popular Dramatic Tradition*, 1944, p. 128; A. C. Swinburne, *A Study of Shakespeare*, 1880, p. 189; and Georg Brandes, *William Shakespeare: A Critical Study*, trans. William Archer, Diana White, and others, 1899, p. 462. Cited in Fitz, pp. 297–316.

6 Schanzer, *The Problem Plays of Shakespeare*, pp. 1–2, 6, 146.

activity–passivity – that govern our lives'.[1] The quest for a synthesis thus becomes intensely relevant: are the oppositions dramatised in this play assimilable into a whole view of the human personality? Is the love portrayed an attempt at wholeness or is it polarised into the extremes of lust and chaste marital responsibility? The fact of Antony's tragic fall seems to argue that the task of reconciliation is impossible because the goals are too inherently contradictory, but the dreams of Antony and Cleopatra persuade us that life cannot be sustained without the hope at least of transcendent wholeness. The history of critical reaction suggests that the play is a kind of Rorschach test for us and for those who have written about the play, most of them males. Where Shakespeare stands, and what he makes of Cleopatra, are intriguing questions but difficult to answer, and the very difficulty makes us wonder if the unknowability of authorial judgement is not in fact deliberate,[2] a way of throwing on us as audience the job of sorting out our own responses to the ambivalent pulls of eros and the reality principle that we all have somehow to accommodate.

The ironic gap between word and deed

One thing on which most critics agree, sympathetic or not, is that word and action seldom coalesce in this play; the vows, the dreams, the ideals, the evocation through speech of human greatness in the characters are at odds with what we are allowed to see in their behaviour. Janet Adelman speaks for many when she observes that 'the stage action necessarily presents us with one version of the facts, the poetry with another'.[3] Cleopatra evokes an image of Antony as an emperor, one whose legs 'bestrid the ocean' and whose reared arm 'Crested the world', whose voice was 'rattling thunder' to his enemies and in whose livery 'Walked crowns and crownets' (5.2.81–90). The dying Antony speaks of himself as 'a Roman by a Roman / Valiantly vanquished' (4.15.59–60), that is, one whom no one can conquer but himself (though the phrase allows ironically for a more unflattering reading). In reality, as we see him, Antony is a mixture of greatness and bounty with a disabling self-hatred, erratic judgement in times of crisis, and obsession with a sexual attraction that he himself fitfully condemns as 'idleness' and enslavement to an 'enchanting queen' (1.2.125–7). Similarly, the magic of

1 Stephen A. Shapiro, 'The varying shore of the world: ambivalence in *Antony and Cleopatra*', *MLQ* 27 (1966), 18–32. See also Roberta M. Hooks, 'Shakespeare's *Antony and Cleopatra*: power and submission', *American Imago* 44 (1987), 37–49, for a 'view of the mother–child boundary dilemma as the model for the complications and unresolved tensions of adult sexuality in the play' (p. 37).

2 Norman Rabkin, *Shakespeare and the Common Understanding*, 1967, pp. 185–6; Maynard Mack, '*Antony and Cleopatra*: the stillness and the dance', in Milton Crane (ed.), *Shakespeare's Art: Seven Essays*, 1973, pp. 79–113; Mack (ed.), *Ant.*, 1960, p. 23; Adelman, *The Common Liar*, pp. 15 ff.; Ronald R. Macdonald, 'Playing till Doomsday: interpreting *Antony and Cleopatra*', *ELR* 15 (1985), 78–99; Maurice Charney, *Shakespeare's Roman Plays: The Function of Imagery in the Drama*, 1961; R. A. Foakes, 'Vision and reality in *Antony and Cleopatra*', *DUJ* ns 25 (1964), 66–76; and Robin Lee, *Shakespeare: 'Antony and Cleopatra'*, 1971.

3 Adelman, *The Common Liar*, p. 103. See also Virgil K. Whitaker, *The Mirror Up to Nature: The Technique of Shakespeare's Tragedies*, 1965, p. 280.

language conjures up for us (in Enobarbus's description) a Cleopatra whom age cannot wither 'nor custom stale / Her infinite variety', one who 'makes hungry / Where most she satisfies' (2.2.245–8), a 'Royal queen' (5.2.36) whose 'Immortal longings' of loyalty to her 'husband' Antony are fulfilled in a noble suicide (5.2.275–81). We see this on stage along with much more: her teasing and lying, her erotic daydreaming, her pleasure in reminding the eunuch Mardian of his physical disability, her oriental despotism in dealing with messengers, and the like. Caesar, too, is both 'the fullest man, and worthiest / To have command obeyed', as Thidias praises him (3.13.89–90), and the cold practitioner of statecraft whose cynicism about women and about the plebeians seems to know no limit. Pompey speaks of himself as a republican idealist avenging the cause of his father and Brutus (2.6.10–23) but discovers he must enter into a pact with pirates and other 'discontents' (1.4.39) if he is to mount a persuasive challenge against the triumvirs. And so it goes.

In part, this is a divergence between how the characters think of themselves and how they in fact behave. Such a perception is often a wry, not a tragic one, and not surprisingly *Antony and Cleopatra* is one of the most ironic (along with some other Roman plays, like *Julius Caesar* and *Coriolanus*) of the major tragedies. Even Cleopatra, who is perhaps less prone to self-deception than Antony or Pompey, allows herself to be cajoled and flattered by ludicrously distorted accounts of her supposed rival, Octavia (3.3). Antony is intermittently capable of honesty with himself, but when he is in his manic mood he speaks with a hyperbole that at once collapses into bathos: 'The next time I do fight / I'll make Death love me, for I will contend / Even with his pestilent scythe' (3.13.196–8). As Enobarbus knows too well, this readiness to 'outstare the lightning' proceeds more from fury and 'A diminution in our captain's brain' than from manly resolution (3.13.199–202). Although this spectacle does not invite outright laughter, Antony's behaviour distances us and causes us to shake our heads in disbelief. Even his finest utterances, on hearing of the supposed death of Cleopatra (4.14.35 ff.), are undercut by 'a marked disjunction between the tragic grandeur of these speeches and the audience's awareness of the true situation', as A. P. Riemer puts it; the moment is at once Antony's 'achievement of the greatest self-knowledge' and the ironic result of another of Cleopatra's tricks. One is tempted 'to call the effect of this comic'.[1] This is the kind of irony that damages, in A. C. Bradley's eyes, the aura that should surround a tragic hero, but the point may be that Antony is in fact a tragic hero of a very different sort from Lear or Macbeth.

Shakespeare repeatedly allows Antony to be deflated by a humorous or ironic touch. Even before he comes on stage, Antony is characterised for us by Roman observers as a once-great captain now become 'the bellows and the fan / To cool a gipsy's lust', the 'triple pillar of the world transformed / Into a strumpet's fool'

[1] Riemer, *A Reading of Shakespeare's 'Antony and Cleopatra'*, p. 58. See also Robert Heilman, 'From mine own knowledge: a theme in the late tragedies', *Centennial Review* 8 (1964), 17–28, and Margery M. Morgan, '"Your crown's awry": *Antony and Cleopatra* in the comic tradition', *Komos* 1 (1968), 127–39.

2 Demetrius and Philo observe Antony, Cleopatra, and her train in Act 1, Scene 1, by C. Walter Hodges

(1.1.9–13). Cleopatra calls up blushes on Antony's cheeks and then ridicules his blushing as Caesar's 'homager' or else a token of shame 'When shrill-tongued Fulvia scolds' (33–4). She mocks him for playing the role of his enraged ancestor, Hercules (1.3.84–5). Caesar reports how Antony in his excessive revelry 'is not more manlike / Than Cleopatra, nor the queen of Ptolemy / More womanly than he' (1.4.5–7). In his summit meeting with Caesar in Rome, Antony is repeatedly forced to apologise or make excuses (2.2). Enobarbus recalls how, in Antony's first meeting with Cleopatra on the river of Cydnus, Antony embarrassingly found himself 'Enthroned i'th'market-place', sitting alone, 'Whistling to th'air', since the people had all been spellbound by Cleopatra's extraordinary spectacle. When his invitation to Cleopatra to supper was met by her counter-invitation, Antony, 'Whom ne'er the word of "No" woman heard speak, / Being barbered ten times o'er, goes to the feast' (2.2.225–6, 233–4).

These scenes in which Antony is humorously cut down to size tend to be clustered, as Ernst Honigmann notes, in the early part of the play. The snub is often administered by women, especially by Cleopatra, and Antony is given little opportunity to laugh back.[1] Little of this humour is in Plutarch; the comic deflation is Shakespeare's own emphasis. Later in the play, around the time of Actium and the fighting at Alexandria, we are more likely to see Antony reduced by the bathetic extravagance of his own rhetoric, as he disastrously accepts a challenge to fight Caesar at sea 'For that he dares us to't' (3.7.29), gives his followers ample reason to conclude that 'our leader's led, / And we are women's men' (3.7.69–70), and is 'unqualitied with very shame' at his ignominious flight from Actium in the wake of Cleopatra's vessels (3.11.43). He is obliged to humiliate himself in his negotiations with Caesar, flares into uncontrollable jealousy at the suspicion of Cleopatra's deserting him for Caesar, deals violently with Thidias, drowns all consideration in 'one other gaudy night' (3.13.187), is maudlin and self-pitying at one moment (4.2.11–37) and manically self-confident the next (4.2.37–46; and see 4.8.36–9). As Honigmann observes, we see Antony repeatedly in the play's latter half in scenes of farewell, scenes of hyperbole and bathos that culminate at last in the farewells to Eros and to Cleopatra.[2] The result, in A. L. French's view, is a kind of *bovarysme*; 'our mood is rather one of detachment, but a detachment that is more amused than censorious'.[3]

Although Antony does clearly enjoy both expertise and reputation in his military role, and is both physically courageous and capable at times of great leadership, Shakespeare takes pains to expose the more imperfect side of his career as well. Antony has lost at Modena, loses Actium, and loses his last battle; he has only one land victory to his credit.[4] Ventidius makes clear the disillusioning fact that both Antony and Caesar 'have ever won / More in their officer than person' (3.1.16–17). Antony (though he too can move quickly, as Pompey knows at 2.1.28 ff.) is amazed at Caesar's swiftness in crossing the Ionian Sea to arrive at Toryne, and indeed Antony is overmastered at every turn by Caesar in the movement of troops and the logistics of war. Antony's reliance on his own strength, 'sword against sword', is, in the context of this war, naïve. And for all his manliness, Antony's sense of self is heavily dependent on the good opinion of his friends and followers. His love for Cleopatra is in large part an extension of his engaging and

[1] E. A. J. Honigmann, *Shakespeare: Seven Tragedies: The Dramatist's Manipulation of Response*, 1976, pp. 150–69, esp. p. 151.

[2] *Ibid.*, pp. 153 ff.

[3] A. L. French, *Shakespeare and the Critics*, 1972, pp. 206–35, esp. p. 208. T. S. Eliot sees Antony as exhibiting *bovarysme*, 'the human will to see things as they are not' ('Shakespeare and the Stoicism of Seneca', in *Selected Essays*, 1951, p. 131).

[4] J. Leeds Barroll, 'Shakespeare and the art of character: a study of Anthony', *S.St.* 5 (1969), 159–235, and *Shakespearean Tragedy*, 1984, pp. 83–129, esp. p. 94.

debilitating self-regard; he loves something like himself in her.[1] In love and war, Antony is ultimately unable to resolve the potential absurdity of his self-defeating actions.[2]

Although Cleopatra is often discounted as a tragic protagonist,[3] surely she must be regarded as such, unless we are to take the whole of Act 5 as a kind of coda after the main action and Cleopatra herself as simply the object of Antony's wish-fulfilment. To regard Cleopatra as a co-protagonist with Antony is to face once again the problem of a comically wry perception, especially in the first half of the play. The comedy arises in this case not so much from self-deception on Cleopatra's part as from her self-professed expertise in guile, seduction, and putting men down. If male critics often betray their own unease by characterising her as typically womanly, they are saying no more than what the men in the play say about her. Antony sees her, intermittently to be sure, as an 'enchanting queen' (1.2.125). Enobarbus jests that their departure from Egypt will 'kill all our women', but is ready 'Under a compelling occasion' to 'let women die'; Cleopatra, chief among them, can 'die twenty times' in such circumstances and turn on the water-works as ably as Jove himself (1.2.130–46). The sexual double meaning of 'die' adds piquancy to Enobarbus's wryly misogynistic portrait of Cleopatra as the quintessential temptress.

Moreover, Cleopatra positively courts a reputation for prowess in matters of sexual conquest. She coaches Charmian in how to cross a man's desires with persistent frustration, and pities Charmian's lack of expertise in such matters: 'Thou teachest like a fool: the way to lose him' (1.3.10). Cleopatra asks for music, 'moody food / Of us that trade in love' (2.5.1–2), as though speaking on behalf of her sex, or at least those women who are not ashamed of their sexuality. She plays always to an audience, to her women, to the crowds along the shores of the Cydnus, to Thidias or Dolabella, to us in the theatre, and takes pleasure in her own performance. Like Antony, Cleopatra is intensely conscious of and preoccupied with her reputation as she goes about making a religion of erotic passion; her rhetoric, combining the imagery of feeding with that of theatre, is calculated to deify herself and Antony.[4] Cleopatra shows an indifferent attitude towards her children (as does Antony to his). She can laugh at her own perjuries in love, committed in 'My salad days, / When I was green in judgement' (1.5.76–7). She

1 Constance Brown Kuriyama, 'The mother of the world: a psychoanalytic interpretation of Shakespeare's *Antony and Cleopatra*', *ELR* 7 (1977), 324–51, argues that Antony regresses from the reality principle embodied in Roman ethics to the more archaic pleasure principle of oral and genital desire.

2 Terence Eagleton, *Shakespeare and Society*, 1967, p. 124. See also Knights, 'On the tragedy of Antony and Cleopatra', p. 320, on the play's 'sense of insubstantiality'.

3 Fitz, pp. 307 ff., aptly describes the male bias that denies Cleopatra tragic stature: the presumed hierarchy of political issues over those of personal emotion, the double standard whereby what is praiseworthy in Antony is damnable in her, etc., citing among others John F. Danby, *Poets on Fortune's Hill*, 1952, p. 146, and David Cecil, '*Antony and Cleopatra*', 1944, p. 21. Laurens J. Mills, *The Tragedies of Shakespeare's Antony and Cleopatra*, 1964, argues that the play features two tragedies, one for each protagonist.

4 John Alvis, 'The religion of eros: a re-interpretation of *Antony and Cleopatra*', *Renascence* 30 (1977/8), 185–98.

encourages her women to stroke her vanity. She enjoys being feared by her messengers and subjects, and her teasing the eunuch Mardian is not without its maliciously threatening suggestion (1.5.11–13). The remembrance of fooling Antony at fishing is dear to her because it reminds her of her skill in landing Antony himself: 'Aha! You're caught' (2.5.15). Her self-pity on hearing of Antony's marriage to Octavia is deliberately and comically overdramatised ('Pity me, Charmian, / But do not speak to me', 2.5.120–1), unlike Antony's self-pity, which is usually cloying and obsessive. If Cleopatra will not take herself seriously, how can we?

Increasingly in the later stages of the play her motives are complex and hard to fathom, and that very fact makes analysis of her as tragic protagonist difficult. If we are never entirely certain whether she intends to desert Antony or not, or whether she conceals her wealth from Caesar in order to deceive him, how are we to measure the interrelation of her character and her fate? Antony, however much he seems to forgive the betrayals he has suspected in her, seems convinced to the last that she will make an accommodation with Caesar (4.15.48). Cleopatra and Shakespeare alike exploit with gusto the notion that men commonly find women mysterious.[1]

Nowhere is deflation more evident than in Shakespeare's presentation of Caesar, or, more broadly, of the entire Roman world. This deflation is not, as it is with Antony, directed at self-delusion or hyperbole collapsing into bathos, nor is it, as it is with Cleopatra, directed at the incessant play-acting that is associated with a woman's capacity for creating deceitful illusion; it is more like the 'alienation effect' we associate with the name of Bertolt Brecht.[2] Caesar is presumably sincere in his dislike of Antony's riotous disregard of duty and in his passion for control; he is well-informed, realistically aware of what is possible, politically sagacious, efficient, and generous up to a point in his praise of Antony (perhaps because he wants to possess the virtues he identifies in Antony, even though he is aware that he cannot). Caesar knows himself and knows what he wants. At the same time, as Leeds Barroll observes, Caesar does seem remote and cold; the charges against him of being a machiavel cannot be shaken off.[3] His revulsion at Antony's Alexandrian revels seems motivated by personal rivalry and especially by uneasiness about any kind of emotional letting go. When drink washes his brain at the feast on board Pompey's ship, Caesar is appalled at the enervating surrender of masculine resolve: 'Strong Enobarb / Is weaker than the wine, and mine own tongue / Splits what it speaks. The wild disguise hath almost / Anticked us all'

1 Compare Fitz, pp. 314–16, who denies from a feminist perspective that Cleopatra's character is more ambiguous or unknowable than Antony's.

2 Dipak Nandy, 'The realism of *Antony and Cleopatra*', in Arnold Kettle (ed.), *Shakespeare in a Changing World*, 1964, pp. 172–94, esp. p. 190; Riemer, *A Reading of Shakespeare's 'Antony and Cleopatra'*, p. 47.

3 Several points in this paragraph and the following are indebted to J. Leeds Barroll, 'The characterization of Octavius', *S.St.* 6 (1970), 231–88, to Barroll's *Shakespearean Tragedy*, chap. 5, esp. pp. 195–6, and to Paul Cantor, *Shakespeare's Rome: Republic and Empire*, 1976, pp. 125–208, who stresses Caesar's unwillingness to tolerate any equals.

(2.7.117–20). He is not amused by stories of the Egyptian escapades of Julius Caesar or any mention of Caesarion, 'whom they call my father's son' (3.6.6); Octavius Caesar was himself regarded as Caesar's son and heir. Octavius Caesar appears to be the one male visitor to Egypt who is proof against Cleopatra's charms, and her knowing this to be true becomes a factor in her resolve to choose suicide rather than be captive to such a man. He is the voice inside the play for those male readers who cannot entertain the wholeness of Cleopatra and are threatened by the challenge she represents to a male desire for control.

Caesar's recollection of the Antony of former days, one who ate rude berries, tree bark, and even strange flesh, and 'didst drink / The stale of horses and the gilded puddle / Which beasts would cough at' to survive the rigours of campaign (1.4.62–8), expresses the ascetic Spartan ideal of soldiership in such overstated terms that we sense in his words the need to fend off in himself any urge to the contrary. His calculated desire to marry Antony to his sister Octavia, the one woman for whom he can care, is more than simply a matter of putting political necessity ahead of private affairs; we have every reason to suspect that he knows the marriage will not work, and that Octavia's misery will then afford him an excuse for war. In his cynical remark that 'want will perjure / The ne'er-touched vestal' (3.12.30–1) we see a glimpse of a personal need to demean women and control them because they are, in his mind, both inferior and dangerous. Surely his plan to take Cleopatra back to Rome at his chariot wheel for a triumphal entry is more than political in its intended gesture. The prospect of being laughed at (2.2.36–9), especially by a woman, does not please him, and yet that is precisely the revenge that Cleopatra has in store for him; she will 'call great Caesar ass / Unpolicied' (5.2.301–2). If Antony is a fool and Cleopatra the queen of folly, Caesar is one whose fear of being foolish goes well beyond the lack of a sense of humour. His sensitivity to being laughed at makes him vulnerable to the woman who increasingly realises this weakness in him.

Caesar's treatment of Lepidus is heartless, all the more so because Shakespeare has changed Plutarch's cunning and untrustworthy triumvir into a well-meaning, ineffectual older man who is arrested and removed from the triumvirate without substantial cause other than that Caesar has no more use for him. Caesar's approach to morality is utilitarian, never generous. In preparation for battle, as in sexual matters, he is Antony's foil in every way. Where Antony is generous to the point of recklessness, Caesar conserves his resources and only rarely consents to the 'waste' of feasting his soldiers (4.1.17). 'Want' is threatening to him. When Antony's soldiers desert him because of his unpredictability and caprice, Caesar places them 'in the van, / That Antony may seem to spend his fury / Upon himself' (4.6.9–11). He readily agrees to fight Antony at sea at the battle of Actium, entirely on Caesar's terms and to Antony's fatal disadvantage, but laughs at a challenge to single combat: 'Let the old ruffian know / I have many other ways to die' (4.1.4–5).[1] Antony wins his soldiers' hearts but cannot keep their loyalty at last

[1] See Susan Snyder, 'Ourselves alone: the challenge to single combat in Shakespeare', *SEL* 20 (1980), 201–16.

because of his erratic soldiership, winning one day and throwing it all away the next; Caesar is steady, remorseless, well briefed, able to move swiftly, never taking unnecessary chances, single-minded. Political power to him means control – of money, property, his followers, women. In the end he possesses everything – except, that is, what he most envies and yet hates, the life and spirit of Antony and Cleopatra.

Around Caesar, the Roman world of which he is the leader and symbol inevitably shares in his diminution. It is of course a world of splendour, of great events that determine the course of history, of conquests, of meetings between great personages, of trumpet calls and waving banners and mighty processions onstage. It is also pre-eminently what Charles Hallett calls the sublunar world,[1] a place of incessant flux and wavering. One scene that particularly captures the ironies of worldly power in constant turmoil is the drunken feast on board Pompey's galley.[2] Even the servants cannot help laughing at the spectacle of a triumvir, Lepidus, publicly 'called into a huge sphere' and yet not able 'to move in't' (2.7.13–14). When Lepidus is carried off drunk, Enobarbus takes wry delight in the perception that the servant who carries Lepidus 'bears / The third part of the world'. To Menas, this only proves that 'The third part, then, is drunk' (2.7.84–6). Menas, in the meantime, suggests privately to Pompey that they should cut the ship's cable and then slit the throats of their honoured guests, and is put off only because Pompey cannot allow such an unethical thing to be done with his knowledge and consent; if it had been done without asking, it would have been 'good service' (2.7.72). The decision spells the end of Pompey's brief-lived challenge to the triumvirs. *Sic transit gloria mundi.*

Pompey indeed epitomises the leader who is raised and then brought low by the unending vacillations of power in the Roman world – a condition of instability we find throughout the Roman plays. Despite his republican idealism on behalf of the Senate and its anti-tyrannical traditions, his emergence has more to do with the divisions between Antony and Caesar and the consequent restiveness all round the Mediterranean. Power, like Nature, abhors both a vacuum and an inert equipoise; as Antony explains to Cleopatra by way of justifying his departure, 'Equality of two domestic powers / Breed scrupulous faction' (1.3.47–8). Pompey does all he can to inherit the mantle of his father's reputation, but discovers that his strength lies not so much in republican devotion to the public weal as in the discontentedness 'of such as have not thrived / Upon the present state' (1.3.51–2). The way for Antony and Caesar to respond to this challenge is obvious: since their division has bred occasion for Pompey, they must now unite against him, however insincerely and temporarily. When Enobarbus characterises this strategy as borrowing 'one an other's love for the instant' and then returning it again 'when you hear no more words of Pompey' (2.2.110–13), he is rebuked for his plainness rather than for

[1] Charles Hallett, 'Change, fortune, and time: aspects of the sublunar world in *Antony and Cleopatra*', *JEGP* 75 (1976), 75–89.

[2] Harold C. Goddard, *The Meaning of Shakespeare*, 1951, II, 187–90; Paul J. Aldus, 'Analogical probability in Shakespeare's plays', *SQ* 6 (1955), 397–414.

having misrepresented the situation; as he himself ruefully says, 'That truth should be silent I had almost forgot' (2.2.115). Once Pompey has accepted the triumvirs' terms and has refused Menas's offer to cut the Gordian knot by slitting throats, he is done for and we scarcely hear of him again.

The fluctuations of political power and the absurdity of the idea of any stable base or vindication of political power in the 'popular will' are constantly brought to our attention, as they are generally in Shakespeare's Roman plays. Caesar likens the commoners to 'a vagabond flag upon the stream' that 'Goes to and back, lackeying the varying tide / To rot itself with motion' (1.4.45–7). In Cleopatra's view, the people of Rome are mere 'Mechanic slaves / With greasy aprons, rules, and hammers' whose offensive breaths are 'Rank of gross diet' (5.2.208–11).[1] Enobarbus pictures a world doomed to be worn down to nothing by the ceaseless clash of mighty antagonists: 'Then, world, thou hast a pair of chaps, no more; / And throw between them all the food thou hast, / They'll grind the one the other' (3.5.11–13).[2] Shakespeare's concept of fortune in this play, as Michael Lloyd has shown, places stress on 'chance', 'hazard', and 'luck' that are the very element of flux.[3] The wheel of Fortune elevates one favourite after another, producing in the narrative line a rising and falling pattern like that found in *Julius Caesar* and *Coriolanus*.[4] Antony is not lucky when he is near Caesar, as the Soothsayer points out to him (2.3.25–30). Caesar of course wins at last, but in the game he plays with Cleopatra, even Caesar turns out to be vulnerable. 'Not being Fortune, he's but Fortune's knave', she exults, and plays her trump card by doing 'that thing that ends all other deeds, / Which shackles accidents and bolts up change'. ''Tis paltry to be Caesar' (5.2.2–6).

The constant turmoil in the political sphere is matched on the human side, as David Kaula points out, by the instability of desire. 'Fundamental to the play's sense of time is the perception that the human heart, in ceaselessly riding the undulations of time, is unable to find a fixed locus of commitment in the enduring present, and so is forced to vacillate continually between future and past, anticipation and memory.'[5] The play is full of prognostications and omens, most of them foreboding. Time is no one's friend except perhaps Caesar's, and even he is cheated of what he especially desires. Constant temporal change generates a sense

1 Brents Stirling, *The Populace in Shakespeare*, 1965, esp. pp. 69–71.

2 Nandy, 'The realism of *Antony and Cleopatra*', p. 176, using a Marxist perspective, describes the Rome of this play as 'a basically corrupt society with a small entrenched ruling class, in which various groups jockey for position in a deadly struggle for survival, based on a large, ignorant and unstable populace. It is a society caught in a vicious circle of peace and prosperity, which breeds factions, leading to periodic wars, civil or imperialist, which in turn lead to a strong government and a corrupting peace, and so endlessly. There is neither progress nor development.'

3 Michael Lloyd, 'Antony and the game of chance', *JEGP* 61 (1962), 548–54. See also S. L. Goldberg, 'The tragedy of the imagination: a reading of *Antony and Cleopatra*', *Melbourne Critical Review* 4 (1961), 41–64, esp. p. 43, and Marilyn Williamson, 'Fortune in *Antony and Cleopatra*', *JEGP* 67 (1968), 423–9.

4 See John Velz, 'Undulating structure in *Julius Caesar*', *MLR* 66 (1971), 21–30.

5 David Kaula, 'The time sense of *Antony and Cleopatra*', *SQ* 15 (1964), 211–23. William Wolf, '"New heaven, new earth": the escape from mutability in *Antony and Cleopatra*', *SQ* 33 (1982), 328–35, similarly finds emotional fluctuation in the play to be as pervasive as political unrest.

of universal mutability, and because Antony cannot learn to adapt himself to the changing demands of time he is defeated. He tries without success to relive his own great past, and becomes a tragic figure best appreciated after he is dead, in memory, in a dream. The myth of an autonomous *virtus*, as Jonathan Dollimore shows, is discovered after Antony's death to be dead itself, surviving only as a legend; like all seekers after power in this play, Antony has been able to make history only in accord with the imperatives of what Antony calls 'The strong necessity of time' (1.3.42). *Virtus* and traditional ideas of honour have been erased by shifts in martial ideology towards imperialist consolidation, not unlike those shifts portrayed in *Richard II* and the Henriad. The conflict is all the more intense for Antony because it is at once personal and political, an ageing warrior's assertion of virility against his younger male rival.[1] Cleopatra meanwhile lives in a kind of continuous present that Roman sensibility can view only as idleness and sensual indulgence, though she is ultimately associated with a cyclical process of nature epitomised in the ebb and flow of the Nile that confutes the incessant fluctuation of historical time with a naturally undulating pattern of depletion and renewal, death and life.[2]

Transcending limits

Does the ironic gap discussed above limit our response to the play narrowly, trapping us merely in scepticism through an intensified awareness of the misalignment of word and deed? Is this all that the play has to offer us – a sense of a tragic disparity which has a very pointed appeal for the modern sensibility? For most audiences and viewers, this is not enough. The ending of *Antony and Cleopatra* compensates extraordinarily for all the failures of human action that have preceded it, to such an extent in fact that questions arise as to the play's artistic integrity. Is the Cleopatra of Act 5 inconsistent with the character we have seen before, and, more broadly, is Shakespeare asking poetry to do the work of drama, relying on the illusions of poetic sublimity to counter the impressions of a tragic distance from greatness? Are we being naïvely taken in if we embrace the dream of Antony and Cleopatra sporting in the Elysian Fields? Are we sentimentalising the tragedy, as Dryden did, if we accept the idea of 'the world well lost' for love, when in reality we have seen so much self-destructive behaviour in that love affair? Should we sceptically regard the vision of eternally blissful lovers as one last regressive self-delusion on their part?

Any attempt at answers to these questions must consider the remarkable way in which, as R. J. Dorius puts it, Antony 'is posthumously transfigured, and by the woman who helps to precipitate his worldly failure'.[3] Antony, alone among

[1] Jonathan Dollimore, *Radical Tragedy: Religion, Ideology, and Power in the Drama of Shakespeare and His Contemporaries*, 1984, pp. 204–17.

[2] Kaula, 'The time sense of *Antony and Cleopatra*', pp. 211–23.

[3] R. J. Dorius, 'Shakespeare's dramatic modes and *Antony and Cleopatra*', in Rudolf Hess *et al.* (eds.), *Literatur als Kritik des Lebens*, festschrift for Ludwig Borinski, Heidelberg, 1975, pp. 83–96, esp. p. 92.

Shakespeare's male tragic protagonists, is given more than a few lines after the catastrophe to dignify his fate. In a paradoxical vision of greatness, the relationship between the sexes is seen as at once doomed and triumphant. As Marilyn French observes, *Antony and Cleopatra* dares to present 'in a positive way the outlaw feminine principle embodied in a powerful female',[1] a female whose combination of sexuality and maturity is fully dramatised and made extraordinarily attractive, if also dangerous. The danger is unsurprising in a tragedy seemingly written after the devastating portrayals of sexual conflict in *Hamlet*, *Othello*, *Lear*, and *Macbeth*. What is surprising is the readiness of Antony to explore new territory in a mutual sexual relationship, to dare to break down traditional barriers between the sexes and thereby surrender part of his masculine protective sense of self.[2] Antony's involvement with Cleopatra can be seen, in Peter Erickson's view, as 'an attempt to reclaim the dark woman whom the poet of the *Sonnets* so consistently degraded'; although Antony never entirely escapes during his lifetime a negative view of role-reversal as emasculating, at his best he and Cleopatra are capable of participating in 'a gender-role exchange that enlarges but does not erase the original and primary sexual identity of each'.[3] The lovers are remarkably alike, as Ernest Schanzer has shown: they echo one another's sentiments and words ('Let Rome in Tiber melt', 1.1.35, 'Melt Egypt into Nile', 2.5.79), behave in similar ways towards messengers (2.5, 3.13), and describe each other in comparable terms of paradox (1.1.51–2, 1.5.62).[4]

Inevitably, in such an undertaking, in such a remarkable change of direction in middle life, Antony suffers the polarisation and loss of identity we today attribute to 'middle-age crisis'. He polarises women into saint and whore, like so many Shakespearean males before and after him – Claudio in *Much Ado*, Othello, Leontes. Octavia, however minor a figure in this play, does represent an important alternative for Antony as he attempts to satisfy the seemingly irreconcilable goals of duty and pleasure. What is different from Shakespeare's other tragic portrayals of sexual conflict is that Antony finally holds to a vision of wholeness in which he can be sustained by, and participate in, the feminine principle embodied in the Egyptian world and most of all in Cleopatra – the principle of life, the generative, erotic, fertile power of nature itself that encompasses both the slime and the sun, both life and death.

The paradox of failure and triumph is a part of everything Antony does. His greatness is, as Michael Goldman says, 'primarily a command over other people's imaginations',[5] including ours. The greatness of his command of language, his passion, his conflict, his physical energy, his suffering, his generosity vastly out-distance those of any other man in the play; he is, despite his manifest failures, the

1 Marilyn French, *Shakespeare's Division of Experience*, 1981, pp. 251–65, esp. p. 253.

2 As Dorius, 'Shakespeare's dramatic modes', p. 93, says, 'This is one of the few Renaissance plays that makes candid sexuality a field for the heroic.'

3 Peter Erickson, *Patriarchal Structures in Shakespeare's Drama*, 1985, pp. 125, 133.

4 Schanzer, *The Problem Plays of Shakespeare*, pp. 136 ff.

5 Michael Goldman, *Acting and Action in Shakespearean Tragedy*, 1985, pp. 112–39, esp. p. 113.

greatest man in the world, and he is paired with the greatest woman.[1] The greatness is a part of the whole and complex truth about the lovers, something that can be glimpsed and felt even at our moments of keenest scepticism. Antony's magnificence, both in the scale of his deeds and in his generosity to his followers, never fails him. No doubt his feasting of his soldiers and his sending chests and treasure after the deserting Enobarbus (4.5.12) are reckless things Caesar would never do, but they move even the sceptical Enobarbus to suicidal despair for having failed this 'mine of bounty' (4.6.33). We understand that Antony shows weak judgement in supposing that Caesar will accept his personal challenge, but we still admire the courage and the chivalric vision of a heroic encounter like that of Prince Hal and Hotspur in *1 Henry IV*, or, in a more problematic sense, that of Coriolanus and Aufidius. Cleopatra certainly admires this in Antony: 'That he and Caesar might / Determine this great war in single fight!' (4.4.36–7).

The world increasingly belongs to Caesar and hence is one in which such heroic gestures are seen as old-fashioned, even slightly ridiculous, but we are drawn to Antony for being as he is and sympathise with those very qualities of openness and extravagance that undo him. Better to be Antony and lose than to be Caesar and win. Even if the dialectic of the play gives ample consideration to the prudence of Caesar, it plainly offers admiration for those who, at whatever disastrous cost, take their chances in the name of commitment and integrity.[2] The sense of 'grace' or decorum that hovers about Antony even in defeat manifests itself in his liberality and in the aura of royalty he shares with Cleopatra.[3]

However much we may admire Antony's charisma and bounty, his sacrificing so much for Cleopatra cannot rank as noble unless she is really worth it. Shakespeare seems not content to rest with Plutarch's concession that she is obviously fascinating, infinite in her variety. This is only to allow, in Dr Johnson's terms, that she is a very high-class whore. Even the paradox of the Lucretian Venus, the paradox that somehow finds holiness in her even when she is riggish, is potentially a kind of deification of womanhood by the male anxious to assert his masculinity and prove his ability to stand up to a woman like this. Is Cleopatra worth what Antony loses for her?

Part of this play's intricacy in this regard is that we are left in a skilfully contrived uncertainty. Cleopatra's interview with Thidias gives Enobarbus good reason to fear that she is deserting a sinking ship (3.13.64–6), but a capable actress can deliver her responses to Thidias with an irony that suggests she has sized Caesar up already and can guess what he wants to hear her say: 'He is a god and knows / What is most right. Mine honour was not yielded, / But conquered merely' (3.13.61–3). Antony's jealous rage is at once plausible and overstated, and his quick capitulation to her professions of innocence ('I am satisfied', 3.13.171) is

[1] John Holloway, *The Story of the Night: Studies in Shakespeare's Major Tragedies*, 1961, pp. 99–120, sees the lovers as 'made on a grander and larger scale than average life', possessing a greatness that 'is inseparable from an incomparable physical energy'.

[2] Eagleton, *Shakespeare and Society*, p. 128.

[3] McAlindon, *Shakespeare and Decorum*, p. 201.

either a legitimately trusting acceptance of her word or a lapse into infatuation. Similarly, her plan to keep back some of her treasure from Caesar is for many critics a manifest ploy 'to throw the gullible Caesar off the track of her intention',[1] as in Plutarch, but a more sceptical reading sees that her extraordinary theatrical ability works both ways: she is fooling Caesar, certainly, but when can we be sure she ever stops 'acting'?[2]

The very point of these episodes may reside in their obscurity. Cleopatra is one of those Egyptians who love long life 'better than figs' (1.2.31), and it need not disillusion us to consider that she might take up with some Roman in Antony's place if he were a man in her terms. Caesar, however, is not such a man. Once she knows this, certain conclusions follow, and she has been studying how to die painlessly in case of need.[3] Among her many and complex motives for suicide, we should not eliminate the element of personal calculation, of wishing to avoid the disgrace of being led captive to Rome, and the like. Calculations such as these are perfectly human. If Cleopatra's greatness is to justify Antony's giving up so much for her, it must include rather than ignore the ways in which she, like Antony, is frail and mortal.

Cleopatra's abilities as an actress are at the heart of the matter. Even at her death she stages the scene with an eye to her audience and to posterity. She dresses for the part: 'Give me my robe. Put on my crown. I have / Immortal longings in me' (5.2.274–5). After Iras has died, Charmian attends to the matter of scenic display by adjusting Cleopatra's crown that has gone 'awry'. Several critics have noted that Cleopatra in effect restages her triumph at Cydnus ('I am again for Cydnus', 5.2.227), providing for our delectation a 'delayed presentation of Enobarbus' vision of her infinite variety'.[4] She is once again the jewel of a regal setting, attended to by her gentlewomen. No physical symptoms of death are permitted to deface the perfect beauty of the tableau. Caesar is understandably moved by this pictorial representation of 'high events'. In Cleopatra's death, says Duncan Harris, 'we are privileged to see at last what the poetry has made us desire for so long to believe'.[5] She has incorporated the roles of mother, wife, queen, and lover, as she hugs to her breast the asps and goes to meet the 'curlèd' Antony.

1 Goddard, *The Meaning of Shakespeare*, II, 201. J. Shaw, 'Cleopatra and Seleucus', *REL* 7.4 (1966), 79–86, and Derek R. C. Marsh, *Passion Lends Them Power: A Study of Shakespeare's Love Tragedies*, 1976, p. 177, are also convinced that Cleopatra is only play-acting.

2 Brents Stirling, 'Cleopatra's scene with Seleucus: Plutarch, Daniel, and Shakespeare', *SQ* 15.2 (1964), 299–311. Nandy, 'The realism of *Antony and Cleopatra*', p. 179, disagrees with Kenneth Muir's contention (*Shakespeare's Sources*, 1957, I, 205) that because Plutarch is unambiguous about Cleopatra's motives we are not meant to be puzzled by Shakespeare. Shakespeare could have followed his source in this or not. Fredson Bowers also sees intended ambiguity ('Shakespeare's dramatic vagueness', *VQR* 39 (1963), 475–84, esp. p. 478).

3 On the question of whether Cleopatra is unwaveringly determined to commit suicide from the moment of Antony's death or is capable of theatrical simulations of such a determination, see the contrasting arguments of MacCallum, pp. 423–8, and Honigmann, *Shakespeare: Seven Tragedies*, p. 165.

4 Duncan S. Harris, '"Again for Cydnus": the dramaturgical resolution of *Antony and Cleopatra*', *SEL* 17 (1977), 219–31. See also Thomas Van Laan, *Role-Playing in Shakespeare*, 1978, pp. 215–22.

5 Harris, '"Again for Cydnus"', p. 229.

We do not judge her in usual terms, but rather see an affirmation of all that she has stood for in the magnificent poetry and visualisations of the play. She is undeniably royal in speech and gesture, and we know that the myth of lovers' happiness, which has escaped her and Antony in much of their lives, will be true if only in story, in the art which the dramatist creates. The metamorphosis of her death, says Robert Ornstein, 'turns life into art'; hers is a death that is truly immortal, as the foolish Clown insists, because it is 'a death that lives in the artistic imagination'. Cleopatra stages her final scene with such care because she knows that 'her destiny is art'.[1]

Shakespeare's willingness to compare Cleopatra's use of theatrical illusion with his own illuminates the inherent contradictions of Cleopatra's charm and of art's magical power. *Antony and Cleopatra* offers both praise and blame for acting and theatre, as Sidney Homan and Michael Goldman show. Actors are perennially suspect for their self-indulgence, their purported freedom of personal life, their 'otherness', their glamour that often comes close to shoddiness – even, that is, for the very marginalisation that makes them so irresistible. The mutual resemblance of sex and drama in being able to lure and deceive exposes drama to the Platonic charge that art is chimerical in the worst sense.[2] Cleopatra's 'performance' at her death may remind us once again that art and imagination are often linked with something womanish, unreal, not to be trusted. Cleopatra's Egypt is, for better and worse, an illusory world in contrast to the apparent solidity and masculinity of the achievement-oriented world of Rome. Yet, as Phyllis Rackin urges, the very daring with which Cleopatra breaks theatrical illusion, derisively referring to the 'squeaking' juvenile actor who will 'boy' her 'greatness / I'th'posture of a whore' (5.2.219–20) on some future stage, thus reminding the Elizabethan audience that they are in fact watching a boy actor in the part, paradoxically makes the point that art's very limits are a means to its role of transforming nature.[3] Made aware that we are in the theatre, watching an impersonation, we come to realise that Cleopatra's life with Antony is only a sublunary approximation of the ideal vision that art seeks out for our sustenance. In Sir Philip Sidney's terms, art is neither history nor philosophy, but an imitation of an action transcending both: 'Only the poet, disdaining to be tied to any such subjection, lifted up with the vigour of his own invention, doth grow in effect another Nature, in making things either better than Nature bringeth forth or, quite anew, forms such as never were in Nature.'[4]

[1] Robert Ornstein, 'The ethic of the imagination: love and art in *Antony and Cleopatra*', in J. R. Brown and Bernard Harris (eds.), *Later Shakespeare*, 1966, pp. 31–46, esp. pp. 44–6. See also Walter C. Foreman, *The Music of the Close*, 1978, p. 199.

[2] Sidney R. Homan, 'Divided response and the imagination in *Antony and Cleopatra*', *PQ* 49 (1970), 460–8, and Goldman, *Acting and Action*, pp. 122–3.

[3] Phyllis Rackin, 'Shakespeare's boy Cleopatra, the decorum of nature, and the golden world of poetry', *PMLA* 87 (1972), 201–11. See also Sigurd Burckhardt, 'The king's language: Shakespeare's drama as social discovery', *AR* 21 (1961), 369–87, esp. p. 385, and Matthew N. Proser, *The Heroic Image in Five Shakespearean Tragedies*, 1965, pp. 171–235.

[4] Sidney, *Apology*, p. 156. Herbert B. Rothschild, Jr ('The oblique encounter: Shakespeare's confrontation of Plutarch with special reference to *Antony and Cleopatra*', *ELR* 6 (1976), 404–29) argues that Shakespeare is consciously concerned with the relation between drama and historiography in his refashioning of Plutarch.

Part of Cleopatra's greatness is that she understands this 'golden world' of art and seeks consolation in her belief that the Antony of her creation is 'past the size of dreaming' and 'Nature's piece 'gainst fancy, / Condemning shadows quite' (5.2.96–9) – that is, a creation (like Shakespeare's play) that in itself goes beyond mere imagination while reproducing something of which Nature alone is also incapable.

Cleopatra is thus the play's best spokesman for the transforming power of art, but she is also, with Antony, a tragic protagonist. The consolations of art that she applies to her own last scene of immolation atone for, but do not deny, her own suffering. She has indeed changed, or at least deepened, aware perhaps at last of how Antony is torn apart by her infinite charms and is now in need of something more sustaining and nurturing. Her eloquence on the emptiness of the world in Antony's absence (4.15.61–70) is Antony's best tribute, and her fainting on this occasion seems as genuine as her insistence that she is now 'No more but e'en a woman, and commanded / By such poor passion as the maid that milks / And does the meanest chares' (4.15.78–80). Her death makes similar use of this image of a simple and natural woman nursing a child at her breast, though the idea of unostentatious simplicity is at odds with the concurrent image of sublime royalty; she is not maternal as other women are, and even in her moment of simplest sincerity (as John Rees Moore observes) she is 'imposing her greatest artifice on us'.[1] In her determination to die 'after the high Roman fashion' (4.15.92), Cleopatra follows Antony not only in resolving to live no longer but in her very manner of ending her life; the double suicide, even though it is committed as they are apart and after Cleopatra has at least theoretically had a chance to consider other alternatives, is (as with Romeo and Juliet) the deed that unites them and makes them most alike. Cleopatra has become like Antony, internalising his Romanness even as he has dared to become like her.[2] As T. McAlindon puts it, their suicide is 'a triumphantly decorous act wherein they become what they should be', an act that transforms defect into perfection.[3] Caesar justly proclaims of Cleopatra that she deserves to 'be buried by her Antony. / No grave upon the earth shall clip in it / A pair so famous' (5.2.352–4).

Genre and structure

The emphasis in Act 5 on transformation of the lovers into another sphere, on the consolations of art, and on Cleopatra's outmanoeuvring of Caesar raises the question for some critics as to whether *Antony and Cleopatra* is really a tragedy after all.

[1] John Rees Moore, 'The enemies of love: the example of Antony and Cleopatra', *KR* 31 (1969), 646–74.

[2] Eva Buck, 'Cleopatra, eine Charakterdeutung', *SJ* 74 (1938), 101–22; Elias Schwartz, 'The shackling of accidents: *Antony and Cleopatra*', *CE* 23 (1967), 550–8; Shapiro, 'The varying shore of the world', pp. 18–32; Julian Markels, *The Pillar of the World: 'Antony and Cleopatra' in Shakespeare's Development*, 1968, p. 9; Michael Payne, *Irony in Shakespeare's Roman Plays*, 1974, pp. 56–85.

[3] McAlindon, *Shakespeare and Decorum*, pp. 184–6.

For some, the play is too genial for tragedy, ending as it does in an essentially lyric affirmation that transcends historical process and places the fate of the lovers beyond the reach of tragic failure.[1] A related response is to see the play's satiric insistence on delusion and folly as undercutting tragic effect through detachment and irony.[2] Bradley's perception that for a tragedy the play 'is not painful' is reinforced for such critics by the realisation that Shakespeare leaves no tragic abyss for us to discover.[3] These questionings of genre are compounded by the play's self-evident lack of 'regular' structure according to classical definition: the dual protagonists, the difficulty of ascribing *hamartia* or tragic flaw to either protagonist (since their manifest flaws are also part of their greatness), the ambiguity as to whether they suffer a tragic fall (since the ending raises them up), the number of episodes only tangentially connected to the main plot (such as Ventidius's conversation with Silius in 3.1 about the Parthian campaign), the mixing of comic and tragic, the blatant disregard of the so-called 'unities' of time and place, and so on.[4]

Attempts to identify the Aristotelian elements of tragedy do not seem wholly convincing or necessary. Are recognition and reversal (anagnorisis and peripeteia) to be located in the play's concluding action in Alexandria or earlier at the battle of Actium?[5] Are the terms really appropriate in any meaningful sense? Perhaps the desertion and death of Enobarbus, where the Aristotelian tragic model does come to eloquent fulfilment, serve by deliberate contrast to show the inadequacy of that model as a key to the destinies of Antony and Cleopatra.

Even if Aristotle does not provide the answer, however, a defence of the play as tragedy is possible in terms of other models. Walter Oakeshott argues that Shakespeare derived his concept of tragedy from Plutarch, and that he did so paradoxically in the very process of violating the classical rules of unity. In Plutarch, Shakespeare found an integral relationship between character and destiny more genuinely tragic than that allowed for by the providential moralisations and falls of princes in most English history and drama before Shakespeare, in which ultimate causality was ascribed to the inscrutable will of God. For Plutarch, as for Shakespeare, catastrophe grows 'out of the characters'; the tragic figures suffer for

[1] French, *Shakespeare and the Critics*, pp. 233–4; Arnold Stein, 'The image of Antony: lyric and tragic imagination', *KR* 21 (1959), 586–606.

[2] Brents Stirling, *Unity in Shakespearian Tragedy*, 1956, pp. 157–92; Riemer, *A Reading of Shakespeare's 'Antony and Cleopatra'*, pp. 98, 101; William Blissett, 'Dramatic irony in *Antony and Cleopatra*', *SQ* 18 (1967), 151–66; and Klaus Peter Jochum, *Discrepant Awareness*, 1979, pp. 192–5.

[3] Bradley, 'Shakespeare's *Antony and Cleopatra*'; Antony Caputi, 'Shakespeare's *Antony and Cleopatra*: tragedy without terror', *SQ* 16 (1965), 183–91.

[4] Mark Van Doren, *Shakespeare*, 1939, p. 273, concludes that *Antony and Cleopatra* has nothing Aristotle would have called a plot. Bethell, *Shakespeare and the Popular Dramatic Tradition*, p. 16, speaks of a 'rather haphazard story about a set of vaguely outlined and incredibly "stagey" characters', and sees the play as a success because of its poetry. See also Virgil Whitaker, 'Shakespeare the Elizabethan', *Rice Univ. Studies* 60 (1974), 141–8.

[5] Sylvan Barnet, 'Recognition and reversal in *Antony and Cleopatra*', *SQ* 8 (1957), 331–4, locates these elements in Act 5; Ruth Nevo, *Tragic Form in Shakespeare*, 1972, p. 324, places the peripeteia in Act 3.

some human reason. Their history, and the history of the world around them, is 'a record of events that develop out of character'. Antony, not Fortune, works his ruin, and we see his character as 'the inextricable mixture of good and bad which goes to make up the tragic figure'. Shakespeare enlarges upon Plutarch by ending his tragedy with the triumph of the tragic hero, but that triumphant ending does not gainsay the suffering and the tragic experience that have led to it.[1] The tragic destiny of the lovers is to confront a world they cannot change or conquer; their tragic greatness is to attempt the impossible nonetheless, and to find a means through Promethean self-destruction to shackle accident and bolt up change.[2] Shakespeare could have found suggestions of this view of humanity as responsible for its own fate in the Countess of Pembroke's *Antonie* and in Daniel's *Cleopatra*.[3]

As non-Aristotelian tragedy, *Antony and Cleopatra* establishes its own sense of genre – one in which, according to Dorothea Krook, the concept of tragedy is enriched and complicated by the concept of the heroic. Antony and Cleopatra are tragic in that they suffer (though in different ways) and acquire knowledge born of suffering. At the same time they are protagonists in a 'heroic' drama, not as the term is applied to Restoration tragedy or to French neo-classical tragedy but as it is applied to the tradition of heroic love in medieval Western culture. The play's sustained ambiguity is derived in large part from the contending values of the tragic and the heroic. On the one hand, the Plutarchan value-system of the pagan–heroic world deplores from its own perspective the self-destroying behaviour of Antony and Cleopatra, judging and condemning them by Aristotelian standards of honour, courage, and magnificence. On the other hand, because the medieval–Renaissance perspective takes sexual love seriously and can respond so vividly to the magic of uninhibited sensuality, a heroic vision emerges in which the lovers' doom is 'at once inescapable and willingly embraced'. The very genre of *Antony and Cleopatra* is thus a new creation by Shakespeare, fitted to his dual vision of self-destructive behaviour through which 'all losses are restored and sorrows end'.[4]

In its dramatic construction, too, *Antony and Cleopatra* can be regarded as Shakespeare's experimental and non-Aristotelian solution to the theatrical demands of the dramatist's material. Maynard Mack looks beyond Bradley's traditional formula of exposition, conflict, crisis, and catastrophe, arguing instead for a structure not tied solely to the integrity of plot and character but rather to elements inherent in Shakespeare's use of language and the visualising imagination: to antithesis, to hyperbole, to the processes of psychological change and self-discovery. The paired and opposing voices heard throughout the play offer an antiphonal pattern of thesis and antithesis, one that opposes accommodation to the community with the integrity of the heroic individual life. The play's essential structure ac-

[1] Walter Oakeshott, 'Shakespeare and Plutarch', in John Garrett (ed.), *Talking of Shakespeare*, 1954, pp. 111–25.

[2] Williamson, *Infinite Variety*, pp. 209–15, and Philip J. Traci, *The Love Play of Antony and Cleopatra*, 1970, p. 48.

[3] Riemer, *A Reading of Shakespeare's 'Antony and Cleopatra'*, pp. 12–13.

[4] Dorothea Krook, 'Tragic and heroic in Shakespeare's *Antony and Cleopatra*', in Ariel Sachs (ed.), *Scripta Hierosolymitana*, 1967, pp. 231–61.

cordingly juxtaposes comedy and seriousness (as in the Clown's visit to Cleopatra in Act 5). Mirroring scenes and recapitulation are essential to the play's design. The protagonists' characteristic hyperbole is offset by the deflating accents of 'foil' characters like Enobarbus, Demetrius, and Philo. Movement towards self-discovery takes the form of a symbolic journey, as in many of Shakespeare's tragedies. As Antony proceeds towards his destiny he is confronted with varieties of his own situation, as for example in Pompey's frustrated idealism and Enobarbus's dilemmas of loyalty. Antony's journey paradoxically brings him to the verge of madness (as in *King Lear*) even while he gropes for illumination and a manifestation of his better self. Cleopatra's journey of self-discovery is perhaps ambiguously delineated in terms of motivation, but she too gains a new perspective as she confronts her doom. Shakespeare's decision to include episodes and characters that may seem peripheral from a rigorously classical perspective is clarified once we are attuned to the structural requirements of antithesis and symbolic journeying.[1] An advantage of such a pragmatic definition of tragedy is that it deals in the materials of Shakespeare's story rather than seeking to impose a classical formula. Mack's argument is reinforced by critics like Hereward Price, Paul Aldus, and Thomas Stroup, who analyse in detail the rationale of mirror scenes, foreshadowings, and other devices of an English non-classical structure derived to an important extent from the medieval and Renaissance culture of Shakespeare's native land.[2]

R. J. Dorius accounts for the play's unique blend of tragedy, comedy, bitter satire, and romance by its affinity with other Shakespearean genres. In her role as the embodiment of the pleasure principle, Cleopatra invites comparison with Falstaff, while as the object of Antony's wish-fulfilment she ironically resembles Shakespeare's romantic heroines – the main difference being that Prince Hal in the *Henry IV* plays is permitted to enjoy both worlds of pleasure and responsibility, whereas the realm of tragic history cannot encompass the benevolent and restorative healing that Shakespeare's comic heroines provide.[3] The uniqueness of structure and genre in *Antony and Cleopatra* is thus best understood in terms of the

[1] Maynard Mack, 'The Jacobean Shakespeare: some observations on the construction of the tragedies', in J. R. Brown and Bernard Harris (eds.), *Jacobean Shakespeare*, 1960, pp. 11–41. Schanzer, *The Problem Plays of Shakespeare*, pp. 132–83, anticipates Mack to an extent by arguing that the play's essential structure resides in a series of parallels between Antony and Cleopatra and a series of contrasts between Egypt and Rome. Harley Granville-Barker, *Prefaces to Shakespeare*, 2nd ser., 1930, pp. 116–66, makes the point that Shakespeare's pragmatic theatrical experience vastly outweighs any theoretical commitment to five-act division.

[2] Hereward T. Price, 'Mirror-scenes in Shakespeare', in James G. McManaway *et al.* (eds.), *Joseph Quincy Adams Memorial Studies*, 1948, pp. 101–13; Paul J. Aldus, 'Analogical probability in Shakespeare's plays', *SQ* 6 (1955), 397–414; Thomas B. Stroup, 'The structure of *Antony and Cleopatra*', *SQ* 15.2 (1964), 289–98. See also David Bevington, *From 'Mankind' to Marlowe*, 1962.

[3] Dorius, 'Shakespeare's dramatic modes', pp. 83–96. See also Richard P. Wheeler, *Shakespeare's Development and the Problem Comedies*, 1981, pp. 154–79. The comparison between Cleopatra and Falstaff is pursued by Bradley, 'Shakespeare's *Antony and Cleopatra*', pp. 299–300, and Harold S. Wilson, *On the Design of Shakespearian Tragedy*, 1957, pp. 172–3. On the relation between *Antony and Cleopatra* and Shakespeare's history plays, see Markels, *The Pillar of the World*, pp. 11 ff. and 51 ff., and Simmons, *Shakespeare's Pagan World*, pp. 153 ff. and 168–96.

models that Shakespeare encountered in his native English theatre and in his own developing and flexible understanding of dramatic form.

Style

The extraordinary language of *Antony and Cleopatra* has received such careful attention that some of its interpreters have been charged with over-valuing the art of the play by seeming to claim that the poetry rather than the drama validates and even creates the noble visions the play reveals to us.[1] Despite such occasional excesses, however, New Criticism of this sort does provide us with remarkable insights into image patterns and recurrent metaphors, and therefore into the imaginative integrity and structural coherence of the play.

G. Wilson Knight argues, as we have seen, for an 'ascending scale' in the poetic vision of the whole.[2] He begins with the theme of the 'imperial magnificence' that Antony is to sacrifice for love. This splendour is manifest in empire imagery, in crowns and chairs of gold, and in glittering catalogues of proper names (Euphrates, Parthia, Labienus, Paphlagonia, Comagene, and so on). Like Caroline Spurgeon,[3] Knight notes the frequent recurrence of the words 'world' and 'earth'. The play's setting encompasses most of the Mediterranean, and, more broadly, the known universe. Cavalry and navies give evidence of the vast array of military might. Riches and gold testify to Antony's bounty and to Cleopatra's Eastern opulence. Cleopatra's barge, in Enobarbus's description (2.2), is a sensuous fabric of purple and gold, silver, divers-coloured fans, strange invisible perfume, and the like, in a sybaritic assault on all the physical senses at once. 'Rare', meaning 'excellent', is a favourite word, and anticipates other superlatives such as 'unparalleled' (5.2.310).

Themes of worldly magnificence are enriched by themes of physical and sensuous love, conveyed through images of 'lascivious wassails', of surfeiting and songs to Bacchus, and of the sun's ability to breed life from the 'dungy earth' of the Nile. Oppositions meet continually in paradoxical metaphors, as in the 'bellows and the fan' used to cool rather than heat a gipsy's lust (1.1.9–10). As Molly Mahood puts it, the 'blend of the mundane and the cosmic' constitutes the *feliciter audax* (in Coleridge's phrase) of Shakespeare's mature style.[4]

Worldly and erotic splendour suggests in turn a natural symbolism of elements that ascend from the material into the ethereal. Egypt teems with serpents (Cleopatra is the 'serpent of old Nile', 1.5.26), crocodiles, 'tawny-finned fishes', water-flies, sea birds, and animal life of all sorts. The earth is a place of foison and

[1] As S. L. Goldberg puts it, language-oriented critics too often 'conclude that the poetry somehow creates the *validity* of these inter-relations and these noble aspirations, as though imagery actually *makes* the relations, or "transcendent poetry" actually bestows transcendence on its meaning' ('The tragedy of the imagination', p. 45).

[2] Knight, *The Imperial Theme*, pp. 199–262. In a similar vein, Bethell (*Shakespeare and the Popular Dramatic Tradition*, pp. 116 ff.) and Markels (*The Pillar of the World*, pp. 153–70) stress the Brobdingnagian vastness of the play's cosmic imagery and its reaching for a 'transfiguration of life'.

[3] Caroline Spurgeon, *Shakespeare's Imagery and What It Tells Us*, 1935, pp. 349–54.

[4] M. M. Mahood, *Shakespeare's Wordplay*, 1957, p. 95.

blossoming, but it is also a place of weeds, of slime, and ooze; in the Nile's fertility, richness and decay are integral parts of the natural cycle. Melting and dissolution occur again and again. Water and land often meet in elemental conflict. Images of weeds or of swansdown feathers floating at full tide convey a sense of motionlessness, of hesitation and ambivalence. Fortunes are lost at sea, especially by Antony; repeatedly the sea is associated with Eastern femininity and softness, while the land is a place of Roman firmness and strength.[1] In the war of the elements, both Antony and Cleopatra are ready to let the water devour the land: 'Let Rome in Tiber melt' (1.1.35), 'Melt Egypt into Nile' (2.5.79), 'So half my Egypt were submerged and made / A cistern for scaled snakes' (2.5.96–7), 'Sink Rome' (3.7.15). In the final scenes especially, life is thought of as a dissolving: Antony speaks of clouds and vapours that 'mock our eyes with air' (4.14.7), while Cleopatra proclaims herself to be 'fire and air', having given her other elements to 'baser life' (5.2.283–93). Death is for her a soft dissolution, a 'transmigration', like that of the crocodile, into the higher elements.

Knight's fourth and last grouping, of spiritual and transcendental elements in the portrayal of love, lays stress on the ascent from water and land to air and fire. Heavenly bodies predominate. Fire conveys ideas of the ascent of the spirit, while the earth is left behind. As Morris Weitz puts it, 'a form of generation and corruption that destroys itself in its perfection' incorporates the essential paradox of a life 'that grows from itself and fully becomes itself at the very moment it becomes its opposite'.[2] Music marks a transition from martial feats (signalled by drum and trumpet) to the departure of the god from Antony's camp, with the ethereal effects of oboe music under the stage (4.3.12–17). The mingling of royalty and heroism in the early characterisation of Antony and Cleopatra gives way to a transcendental vision of coronation in Cleopatra's death scene. At her death she leaves behind the world as 'No better than a sty' (4.15.64) and seeks out an 'eternity' that transcendentally re-enacts the 'eternity' of 'lips and eyes' to which the lovers pledged themselves at the start (1.3.35). The images of fortune, meanwhile, decline from hopeful expectation (1.2.25–9) to disillusionment and rejection (4.15.46). Caesar is 'Fortune's knave', while death alone 'shackles accidents and bolts up change' (5.2.3–6). Images of sport, chance, and gaming, so essential in the earlier part of the play for suggesting amorous encounter and shifts in fortune, become at last the property of the lovers in their world of death and eternal reputation: Cleopatra gives Charmian leave to 'play till Doomsday' (5.2.231), and Charmian repeats the phrase when she says, of her dead queen, 'Your crown's awry; / I'll mend it, and then play' (312–13).

The image patterns analysed by other critics similarly reflect the oppositions and paradoxes in which the play abounds. Janet Adelman focuses on contrasting images of measure and overflow, fecundity and corruption, heroic past and tarnished present, myth and reality, boundedness and dissolution, time and death, mutability

[1] Wolfgang Clemen, *The Development of Shakespeare's Imagery*, 1951, pp. 159–67, explores the sea imagery of the play, along with the Nile and its creatures, heavenly bodies, and Fortune.

[2] Morris Weitz, 'Literature without philosophy: *Antony and Cleopatra*', *S.Sur.* 28 (1975), 29–36.

and eternal changelessness, seriousness and sport, the possible and the infinite.[1] Susan Snyder examines patterns of motion, of Roman fixity and speedy directness as opposed to Egyptian languor and seeming lack of purpose, of measured files of soldiers and unswerving pillars versus overflowing, bending, turning, and fanning, of efficiency versus prodigality and earth versus water, all generating an elemental conflict out of which Antony and Cleopatra opt at last for 'stillness over constant flux'.[2] To Charles R. Lyons, the play's ambiguity lies in the 'demonic' imagery of serpent, sun, and 'Nilus' slime', in the 'violent juxtaposition' of creation and decay, in the barrenness and sterile rot produced by the sun's copulation with the earth, in the emasculation and subjugation of sexual encounter.[3] Philip Traci too locates the play's elemental conflict in sexual imagery of horseriding, fishing, serpents and other water creatures, figs, dying, dung and slime, swords, the preparation and eating of food, and so forth.[4] Derek Traversi explores the 'balance between decay and fruitfulness' in images of sport and pleasure, poison, disintegration, and transcendence.[5] The imagery of eating and feeding, in Kenneth Muir's view, is expressive of a natural appetite which (like any other appetite) is liable to abuse.[6]

Iconographical sources offer a rich storehouse of pictorial representations for the verbal paradoxes found in the text. Even though we often cannot be sure that Shakespeare had seen a particular drawing or painting, he is likely to have been familiar with popular iconographical conventions. Certainly emblem books and other forms of illustration were widely disseminated in the Renaissance. The play's fascination with the story of Hercules and Omphale, for example, takes on an added pictorial dimension when we note that Henry Peacham presents his Hercules emblem in such a way as to emphasise certain standard tokens or attributes of this incident: Hercules throwing away his club and wearing a mantle in place of his lion's skin while he takes up the distaff and passes the day with Omphale and her maids.[7] The typological pairing of Mars and Venus has a no less detailed vocabulary of signs and attributes in Renaissance tradition, as in the emblem from Otho Vaenius's *Armorum Emblemata* (1608) depicting a cupid piercing an empty suit of armour with arrows in token of the truism that 'Nothing

[1] Adelman, *The Common Liar*, pp. 102–68.

[2] Susan Snyder, 'Patterns of motion in *Antony and Cleopatra*', *S.Sur.* 33 (1980), 113–22.

[3] Charles R. Lyons, 'The serpent, the sun, and "Nilus slime": a focal point for the ambiguity of Shakespeare's *Antony and Cleopatra*', *Revista di Litterature Moderne* 21 (1968), 13–34. See also Leo Kirschbaum, 'Shakspere's Cleopatra', *SAB* 19 (1944), 161–71, who points out a network of images equating Cleopatra with gourmandism, eroticism, nursing, and death, as contrasted with a Roman stress on abstinence; and Peter Berek, 'Doing and undoing: the value of action in *Antony and Cleopatra*', *SQ* 32 (1981), 295–304, who examines the verb *do* both as a euphemism for sexual activity and as conveying the paradoxical actions of this play.

[4] Traci, *The Love Play of Antony and Cleopatra*, pp. 62–95.

[5] Derek Traversi, *Shakespeare: The Roman Plays*, 1963, pp. 79–203, esp. pp. 95, 111, and 145–6.

[6] Kenneth Muir, 'The imagery of *Antony and Cleopatra*', *Kwartalnik Neofilologiczny* 8 (1961), 247–64. Muir arranges the play's images in four groups: (1) the world and heavenly bodies, (2) eating and feeding, (3) bodily movement, (4) melting and dissolution.

[7] Henry Peacham, *Minerva Britanna, or a Garden of Heroical Devices*, 1612, p. 95, cited in Raymond B. Waddington, 'Antony and Cleopatra: "What Venus did with Mars"', *S.St.* 2 (1966), 210–26. See illustration 1, p. 10 above.

3 The Entertainment at Elvetham, 1591. From John Nichols (ed.), *The Progresses, and Public Processions of Queen Elizabeth*, 3 vols., 1788–1805, III, 586–95

resisteth love.'[1] Religious iconography inspired by the Book of Revelation and the traditions of the *danse macabre* and the *memento mori* gave Shakespeare a wealth of material for his imagery of the paradoxical linking of death and love.[2] The iconography of royal pageants like that at Elvetham in 1591 may well have contributed directly to Enobarbus's description of Cleopatra on the river of Cydnus.[3] The juncture of the esoteric, the courtly, and the popular in such iconographical traditions finds a correlative in the mode and experience of the play as a whole, and is part of its largeness and almost baffling reach.

Style is essential not only to the play's imagery but to its individualisation and development of characters, thus contributing purposefully in yet another way to the overall coherence of design. As Robert Hume shows, the major characters are differentiated in terms of diction, rhythm, rhetorical patterns, wordplay, repetition, and the like. Lepidus, for example, continually beseeches and entreats in his role as ineffectual peacemaker. Pompey's dilemma of idealism and pragmatic ethics is

[1] *Armorum Emblemata*, 1608, pp. 22–3. Cited in Waddington, '"What Venus did with Mars"', p. 218. See Wind, *Pagan Mysteries*, 'Virtue reconciled with pleasure', pp. 81–96, and the discussion of Venus and Mars, p. 8 above.

[2] Seaton, pp. 219–24; Morris, pp. 252–62; Katherine Vance MacMullan, 'Death imagery in *Antony and Cleopatra*', *SQ* 14 (1963), 399–410; and Sheila Smith, '"This great solemnity": a study of the presentation of death in *Antony and Cleopatra*', *ES* 45 (1964), 163–76.

[3] Jean Wilson, *Entertainments for Elizabeth I*, 1980, pp. 96–118, esp. pp. 108 ff.; see also *Ant.* 2.2.200 ff. and Commentary. See illustration 3.

underscored by his vocabulary of 'honour' and 'justice' and its converse in his sarcasm. Caesar's speech lacks imagination; his occasional uses of metaphor deal practically in terms of 'hoop', 'fortress', and 'cement'.[1] Caesar is a rhetorician like Bolingbroke and his son Henry V,[2] though we must remember that Caesar is stirred at times to unusual imaginative activity – as in his tribute to the dead Antony.

All the Romans speak with a single tongue, as Michael Lloyd observes. They manifest dismay at Antony's reckless libidinal energy with demeaning metaphors ('He ploughed her, and she cropped', 2.2.238) and pejorative comparisons (gipsy, trull, ribaudred nag of Egypt). In their own lives they cloak matter-of-fact relationships under terms of exaggerated closeness, such as 'friend' and 'brother'. They are too prone to use speech cynically as a means of persuasion and manipulation. 'Try thy eloquence', Caesar tells Thidias as he dispatches him to win Cleopatra from Antony with any offer his 'invention' can devise (3.12.26–9).[3] Enobarbus, for all his witty incisiveness and wry perspective, is plain, blunt, and soldierly, even in his death. Language distinguishes Rome from Egypt: Rome is a place of words and voices where love and war are talked about, whereas Egypt is a place of actions and the body where love and war are made.[4] Antony's vacillation is reflected in the way he speaks, while Cleopatra's imagery is dual in the Egyptian sense. At the last, their language draws them to be more and more like each other.[5]

An essential figure of speech for the play is hyperbole, and, as Madeleine Doran shows, this trope helps mark the ascent of the lovers from failed protagonists to creators of their own imaginative destiny. Throughout, character is conceived of in terms of superlatives – the 'most', the 'best', the 'highest', or conversely the 'least', and so on. The chief value of history, according to Renaissance poetic theory, was that it furnished examples of greatness. Shakespeare found hyperbole in his sources, notably in Plutarch. Yet hyperbole is a trope that can be used to heighten or diminish, and we often see Shakespeare using it in both ways. When overreaching for effect falls into comic bathos, the result is reductive: we are disillusioned, for example, by the ludicrous drunken behaviour of the 'world-sharers' (especially Lepidus) on board Pompey's galley, or by Antony's ranting vow to contend with Death's own pestilent scythe (3.13.197–8). Yet the superlatives come true at last in a vital sense. Cleopatra's speeches in praise of the dead Antony are playful, witty, full of sheer virtuosity, and self-evidently exaggerated, but the superlatives are no less serious because we perceive they are true chiefly in the mind. At her death, Cleopatra has no need for hyperbole, for she and Antony are subsumed into what they dream; 'the thing and the idea are one'.[6]

1 Robert D. Hume, 'Individuation and development of character through language in *Antony and Cleopatra*', *SQ* 24 (1973), 280–300.
2 G. S. Griffiths, '*Antony and Cleopatra*', *E&S* 31 (1945), 34–67.
3 Michael Lloyd, 'The Roman tongue', *SQ* 10 (1959), 461–8.
4 Terence Hawkes, *Shakespeare's Talking Animals: Language and Drama in Society*, 1973, pp. 178–93.
5 Hume, 'Individuation and development', pp. 280–300. On Antony and Cleopatra's resembling one another in their language, see p. 26 above, and Schanzer, *Problem Plays*, pp. 136 ff.
6 Madeleine Doran, '"High events as these": the language of hyperbole in *Antony and Cleopatra*', *QQ* 72 (1965), 26–51.

A style that mediates between honest plainness and ostentatious hyperbole is, in Rosalie Colie's view, uniquely suited to *Antony and Cleopatra*. An 'Attic' or Roman style of direct simplicity is contrasted throughout with an 'Asian' or Egyptian style that is sensuous, self-indulgent, ornate. Renaissance debate comparing the merits of the Attic and Asian styles sometimes expressed itself in two views of Ciceronianism, as intelligible and adapted to its matter or as over-wrought and artificially formal; alternatively, 'Ciceronian' was used as a label in the Asian sense as opposed to 'Senecan' in the Attic sense. In Shakespeare's play, as Colie shows, Egypt is accused of the very excesses that were objected to in the 'Asian' style: of being as it were *inflatus* (blown up), *solutus* (dissolved), *tumens* (swollen), *superfluens*, *redundans*, *enervis* (idle), *inanus* (empty). Although Antony and Cleopatra speak 'excessively' and histrionically from the first, our pleasure in watching and listening is to see the play begin 'to live up to itself', to see 'the hyperbole coming true'. The grandiose play-acting, the bombastic claims of kinship to Venus and Mars or Isis, the resolve to die as heroes, all materialise in the poetry and spectacle of the play's end and are intensified, not destroyed, by our being reminded of what Omphale did with Hercules. Because the deaths of Antony and Cleopatra are both at once Roman and Egyptian, both resolute and ornate, what we remember of them is Antony's magnanimity and Cleopatra's magnificent poetry. By 'sinking the notions associated with the Asiatic style back into life itself', the lovers validate the claims that before had seemed so much like bombast.[1]

Shakespeare's style in this play is finally perceived, then, as one of wholeness fashioned out of antithetical elements. An idea of language is applied to the play as a whole even while allowing for the individuation of its characters. The style accommodates (in the phrase of George Hibbard) 'an astonishing union of the hyperbolical with the simple, the downright, and the direct'. Because Shakespeare is conscious of the new style he has created, he has the confidence to call attention to its hyperbole and even parody it, as at 3.2.6 ff. The play's 'heavenly mingle' of 'the elevated and grand with the simple and familiar' occurs everywhere in images and in paired words such as 'lass unparalleled' (5.2.310), in which Cleopatra is seen as somehow ordinary (a 'lass') and at the same time beyond the power of description ('unparalleled').[2] A style that so astonishingly combines spectacle, robustness, paradox, bombast, colour, light, motion, massiveness, spaciousness, sensuousness, plenitude, hyperbole, and grandeur essentially defies definition, but it is sometimes compared to the baroque in Renaissance art and music.[3]

[1] Rosalie Colie, *Shakespeare's Living Art*, 1974, pp. 168–207. S. C. Sen Gupta, *Aspects of Shakespearian Tragedy*, 1977, pp. 31–60, speaks similarly of a Roman 'packed' style deriving its strength from compression and clarity as opposed to an Egyptian style, redolent of Oriental opulence and mystery, that permits words to look beyond themselves into the erotic and ineffable. On Ciceronian and anti-Ciceronian, see Morris W. Croll, *'Attic' and Baroque Prose Style: The Anti-Ciceronian Movement*, ed. J. Max Patrick *et al.*, 1969, and George Williamson, *The Senecan Amble*, 1951.

[2] G. R. Hibbard, '*Feliciter audax: Antony and Cleopatra*, I, i, 1–24', in Philip Edwards *et al.* (eds.), *Shakespeare's Styles: Essays in Honour of Kenneth Muir*, 1980, pp. 95–109.

[3] Edith M. Roerecke, 'Baroque aspects of *Antony and Cleopatra*', in Gordon Ross Smith (ed.), *Essays on Shakespeare*, 1965, pp. 182–95, quotes Wylie Sypher, *Four Stages of Renaissance Style*, 1955, pp. 180–241, William Fleming, 'The element of motion in baroque art and music', *JAAC* 5 (1946),

It is through such devices of language, and especially through Shakespeare's use of Cleopatra as spokesman for the imagination, that, as Dolores Burton says, all of the traditional roles of the poet are affirmed of Cleopatra. She is given the power to dissemble and to evoke belief, to serve as a source of poetic life, with much the same fertility as she is associated with in the land of the Nile. *Antony and Cleopatra* is at last 'not about tawdry middle-aged lovers but about the power of imagination to place an Egyptian puppet and a drunken Antony on the stage and, by poetry, to make the audience forget their smaller-than-life reality. If Helen's beauty was a theme for honor's tongue, to see her beauty in a brow of Egypt and to communicate that vision was a theme for honor that would spur any poet of the Renaissance to emulate the ancients by creating a drama whose verbal opulence might wrest the laurel from the great classical master and give the story of Antony and Cleopatra its most felicitous expression.'[1]

Stagecraft

Shakespeare's defence of the poetic imagination in *Antony and Cleopatra* has so captivated a number of critics that they have tended to forget that Shakespeare wrote for the stage. The common assumption until recently, as we have seen, is that the play is loosely structured. The inability of nineteenth-century realistic staging conventions to deal with the play's many scenes and rapid shifts of locale (see pp. 51–6 below) also contributed to the neglect of its staging aspects. Today, we see a growing realisation that *Antony and Cleopatra* not only can be made to work in the theatre but that its greatness is essentially theatrical.

The magic of Shakespeare's stagecraft is especially evident in his juxtaposition of scenes. Consider, for example, the remarkable transition from the end of Act 2 to the beginning of Act 3, from the drinking scene on board Pompey's ship to *Enter Ventidius, as it were in triumph, the dead body of Pacorus borne before him.* Continuous acting reinforces a striking contrast, otherwise lost, between the world's rulers in their cups and soldiers speaking of the duty they perform in the name of their superiors, between the 'drunken halloos' of Enobarbus and Menas and sober reflection on the politics of war. The juxtaposition reminds us that '2.7' and '3.1' have no intrinsic meaning in Shakespeare's script; the act division was imposed probably by the Folio editors and here misrepresents the flow of Shakespeare's stage presentation. Since a change of scene in Shakespeare's theatre did not mean a change of scenery, as Harley Granville-Barker observes, 'there was no distracting of mind or eye, a unity of effect was kept, and the action flowed on unchecked'.[2] The properties and costumes used to distinguish one scene-setting from another did nothing to impede the fluidity of stage movement.

121–8, and René Wellek, 'The concept of baroque in literary scholarship', *JAAC* 5 (1946), 77–109. On *Antony and Cleopatra* and the Jacobean court masque, see Commentary at 5.2.79.

[1] Dolores M. Burton, *Shakespeare's Grammatical Style: A Computer-Assisted Analysis of 'Richard II' and 'Antony and Cleopatra'*, 1973, pp. 266–72.

[2] Granville-Barker, *Prefaces to Shakespeare*, 2nd ser., p. 122.

Interweaving of this sort occurs again in the movement from 3.2 to 3.3, from the seemingly cordial farewells when Antony and Octavia part from Caesar, to the fury of Cleopatra at the messenger who has dared to tell her of Antony's marriage to Octavia. Here the juxtaposition is comically reinforced by the dramatic irony of Cleopatra's ignorance of the political motives underlying the marriage. The play's movement back and forth from Rome to Egypt encourages this kind of ironic double vision. Multiplicity of viewpoint can take shape onstage within a single scene, too, as in the framing of Act 1, Scene 1: Demetrius and Philo, Roman soldiers, begin and end the scene, standing as commentators apart from the others, perhaps to one side or downstage (see illustration 2), where they can interpret for the audience the bantering conversation of Antony and Cleopatra.[1]

The notion of 'image' in a poetic drama needs to encompass more than the verbal images of the text; Shakespeare's language is given concrete expression onstage, and his own professional theatrical expertise encouraged him to pay attention to stage picture.[2] Maurice Charney examines *Antony and Cleopatra* in terms of three predominating themes that are both verbal and visual: sword and armour, vertical dimension, and dissolution.[3] Sword and armour are 'presentational' images, that is, visible in the theatre in Antony's actual costume. We see the buckles on the breast of this 'plated Mars' even while Philo describes him to us (1.1.1–8). Such tokens signify from the first Antony's might as a soldier and his claim to empire, but, as the play moves forward, they also serve as indexes to his loss of identity. In Egypt, the sword develops sexual connotations of 'ploughing' Cleopatra (2.2.238) and of surrender to her charms when she wears 'his sword Philippan' (2.5.23). Antony's unarming just before his suicide, dolefully reminiscent of the earlier scene (4.4) in which Cleopatra helped dress him for battle, is 'a formal dumbshow for his renunciation of Rome'. The persistent imagery of vertical movement reaches its tragic climax in the bearing aloft of Antony to Cleopatra in her monument; it is presentationally anticipated by, for example, Antony's sitting down in Cleopatra's presence, 'unqualitied with very shame', in the aftermath of his flight from Actium (3.11.24–45). Dissolution is, as we have seen, a favourite subject of poetic imagination in the final scenes of the play; it is also a vividly pictorial and auditory reality in the theatre, as when the soldiers on watch hear sounds 'i'th'air' and 'Under the earth' (4.3.16–17). As in much medieval religious drama, Shakespeare's stage here represents the world, with heaven above and hell beneath. The expansive world of empire, sun, moon, and all the rest is symbolised in the Elizabethan theatre on a raised platform with symbolically decorated 'heavens' above. Verbal imagery of appetite and sensual

[1] Adelman, *The Common Liar*, p. 31; Bernard Beckerman, 'Past the size of dreaming', in Mark Rose (ed.), *Twentieth Century Interpretations of 'Antony and Cleopatra'*, 1977, pp. 99–112; Mark Rose, *Shakespearean Design*, 1972, pp. 163–4.

[2] David Bevington, *Action is Eloquence: Shakespeare's Language of Gesture*, 1984, gives an overview.

[3] Charney, *Shakespeare's Roman Plays*, pp. 6 ff. Compare R. A. Foakes, 'Suggestions for a new approach to Shakespeare's imagery', *S.Sur.* 5 (1952), 85–6, who calls for a new definition of imagery that will enable criticism to realise 'the verbal image in dramatic terms'.

indulgence is visually confirmed in scenes of indolent luxury and drinking, and the hotness of Egypt takes particularised shape in the eunuchs who fan Cleopatra. The 'world theme' so pervasive in *Antony and Cleopatra* has its objective correlative in the theatre for which the play was written.[1]

That Shakespeare's stagecraft makes a virtue out of the play's often-deplored lack of the classical 'unities' of time and place can be seen in his use of messengers. They appear some thirty-five times and in virtually every scene of substantial length. A primary function is to remind us that distances are vast and that the play's setting embraces most of the Mediterranean world. Messengers help create a sense of the passage of time. They symbolise the royal authority of those whom they serve. Their reports tell us what people are saying about the major characters, what 'the common liar' thinks of Antony (1.1.62) or how Cleopatra 'is called in Rome' (1.2.102).[2] The reports of messengers often reveal more about the persons who receive the news than about the subject of the report; the audience usually knows the situation already and is primarily interested in how the news is taken.[3]

An important contrast, as Ray Heffner shows, is between the use and the abuse of messengers. We see Antony enquire seriously after bad news and urge the messenger to spare no unflattering details (1.2), whereas Cleopatra makes extravagant threats in 2.5 when she hears of Antony's marriage.[4] Messengers thus help clarify the contrast of two symbolic environments, Rome and Egypt. They are symptomatic of a breakdown in reliable communications; isolation, instability, and interruption are essential to the ironies and conflicts of the play, forming barriers in the face of which Antony and Cleopatra must try to find moments of quiet communication. The uncertainty of knowing whether messages are true provides moreover a key to the play's own ambiguity of meaning; we are drawn by this dramatic technique into the act of judging.[5]

Messengers are important to the play's sense of time. Between 2.5, when Cleopatra first hears of Antony's marriage to Octavia, and 3.3, when she receives the messenger again in a less threatening frame of mind, very little time can have elapsed in Egypt; Cleopatra needs to continue the interrupted conversation in order to set her heart at rest, and the messenger is still smarting from her blows. Yet in the intervening scenes, Antony and Caesar have settled matters with Pompey, and the latter has refused Menas's offer to cut the throats of the triumvirs on board his ship. Ventidius has triumphed over Pacorus in Parthia. Events such as these would require months. A similar use of discrepant time helps explain Antony's

[1] Compare Francis Fergusson's study of *Hamlet* in *The Idea of a Theatre*, 1949, pp. 98–142, and Goldman, *Acting and Action*, pp. 112–39, on how the actors of Antony and Cleopatra make us aware in the theatre that the play is about greatness.

[2] Marion Perret, 'Shakespeare's use of messengers in *Antony and Cleopatra*', *Drama Survey* 5 (1966), 67–72.

[3] Adelman, *The Common Liar*, p. 314, and Beckerman, 'Past the size of dreaming', p. 104.

[4] Ray L. Heffner, Jr, 'The messengers in Shakespeare's *Antony and Cleopatra*', *ELH* 43 (1976), 154–62.

[5] Adelman, *The Common Liar*, pp. 34–9, and Beckerman, 'Past the size of dreaming', pp. 99–112. See also Macdonald, 'Playing till Doomsday', pp. 78–99.

apparent hypocrisy towards Octavia, when he swears to be true to her (2.3.1–7), then determines to return to Egypt (2.3.38–40), and thereafter parts from her seemingly on the tenderest terms (3.2); however cynical these actions may appear when read strictly in sequence, we must realise that they involve the lapse of some months in historical time during which interval Antony's relationship with Cleopatra must follow the uninterrupted sense of time conveyed by her widely-separated but virtually continuous interviews with the messenger.[1] Shakespeare's use of messengers promotes a kind of dual time-structure like that sometimes identified in *Othello*.

Recovery of the staging methods originally used by Shakespeare's company is not always easy. How did the leading boy actor handle the role of Cleopatra? He must have been a boy of unusual ability, at the top of his form. Ernst Honigmann calls attention to all the implicit business requiring brilliance in the performance, such as when Cleopatra stages a fainting spell and cries out to have her lace cut, or threatens the messenger with bloody teeth, or calls for ink and paper, or (as verbal descriptions of her repeatedly suggest) dances, hops, pants, yawns, bites, pinches, and much more.[2] The conventional wisdom is that body contact between her and Antony was kept to a minimum as a sop to decorum between male actors, and it is true that Antony and Cleopatra are more often apart than together, like Romeo and Juliet.[3] It is also true that Cleopatra's charms are envisaged as much by description (especially in Enobarbus's speech) as by direct stage action. Still, Honigmann raises cogent questions when he asks if the kiss Antony requests and surely receives at 3.11.69–70 is the only one of its kind. Part of Cleopatra's infinite variety, even on Shakespeare's stage, may have been manifested in her fondling and embracing of Antony, along with her more coy frustration of his mood on other occasions. The lovers are certainly physically close in the scene of Antony's death, as Cleopatra attempts to 'Quicken' him with kissing (4.15.40).

Most problematic in terms of staging are the two scenes (4.15 and 5.2) in which Cleopatra appears in her monument. Hypotheses of an 'inner stage', in which Plutarch's visualisation of the action could be more or less literally reproduced, are now discredited, chiefly because the 'inner stage' itself can no longer be convincingly shown to have existed on Shakespeare's stage.[4] Instead, as Richard

[1] Markels, *The Pillar of the World*, pp. 30–1, and Heffner, 'The messengers', p. 157. See also Payne, *Irony in Shakespeare's Roman Plays*, pp. 76 ff., on the audience's linear time versus narrative time, and Arthur H. Bell, 'Time and convention in *Antony and Cleopatra*', *SQ* 24 (1973), 255–64, on our understanding Antony's very identity in terms of his various attempts to deal with the remorseless demands of calumniating time.

[2] Honigmann, *Shakespeare: Seven Tragedies*, p. 155–6.

[3] In *Romeo and Juliet*, the lovers are separated by the distance between window and garden for much of the time they are onstage together in 2.2.

[4] On the notion that Gallus's failure to reappear in 5.2 after having been deputed by Caesar in 5.1 to assist Proculeius in the arrest of Cleopatra was the result of two draft versions somehow having been included in the Folio in confused form, and that Shakespeare once intended to stage the scene in accordance with Plutarch's description, see Bernard Jenkin, '*Antony and Cleopatra*: some suggestions on the monument scenes', *RES* 21 (1945), 1–14. The textual uncertainty is now generally regarded as compositorial in origin.

Hosley has shown, the ending of the play works well in an Elizabethan theatre outfitted with a 'gallery' over the stage.[1]

Certainly the action in 4.15 must be aloft, for Cleopatra and her maids enter *aloft* in the Folio text. When the mortally wounded Antony is carried onstage by his guard, Diomedes' urging of Cleopatra to 'Look out o'th'other side your monument' (8) may mean simply that she turns one way and then the other; Diomedes is at one side of the stage while Antony is brought in by a door on the other side. When they *heave Antony aloft to Cleopatra* (stage direction at 38), Cleopatra and her maids assist in hoisting him to the gallery, and Cleopatra's words make much of the 'sport' of lifting so heavy a man (33–8). Hosley argues that a winch and pulley would be needed, and a kind of harness attached to the chair in which Antony was perhaps brought onstage, for this difficult operation, since the gallery was about fourteen feet above the level of the main stage.[2] For other possible arrangements, see illustration 4. In 5.2 Cleopatra is seemingly no longer 'aloft'; she and her maids come onstage as though to a room within the monument, whereupon Proculeius holds her in conversation while Roman soldiers enter from behind and rush upon her. Shakespeare has conflated matters in Plutarch, perhaps with a view to what was possible on his stage.

Antony and Cleopatra in performance

Presumably Shakespeare's play was staged in 1606 or 1607, although we have no direct evidence of this. The only authoritative text of *Antony and Cleopatra*, that printed in the First Folio, is of authorial origin rather than from the playhouse. The Lord Chamberlain's records for 1669 note that the play was 'formerly acted at the Blackfriars', without indication as to how often it was performed or whether it was acted publicly at the Globe. Information about the original staging can only be deduced from the text itself or surmised from contemporary illustrations, such as Henry Peacham's drawing of a composite scene from *Titus Andronicus*, and the masque designs of Inigo Jones. The Roman costuming was probably 'classical', though with plentiful allowance for contemporary Elizabethan costuming for ordinary citizens and walk-on parts.[3] The text calls for elaborate processions, musical fanfares for arriving or departing dignitaries, eunuchs with fans, a banqueting table and chairs for the scene on Pompey's ship, and the like. The sea battle at Actium was evidently rendered by musical signals and other offstage sounds, while persons onstage commented on what they saw afar. Land battles made use of alarums, signalled by drums and trumpets (4.7–8), and armies marching *over the stage*; see illustration 5.

Performance rights for *Antony and Cleopatra* and twenty other plays were assigned

[1] Richard Hosley, 'Shakespeare's use of a gallery over the stage', *S.Sur.* 10 (1957), 77–89.

[2] Richard Hosley, 'The staging of the monument scenes in *Antony and Cleopatra*', *LC* 30 (1964), 62–71.

[3] John Dover Wilson, '*Titus Andronicus* on the stage in 1595', *S.Sur.* 1 (1948), 17–22; W. M. Merchant, 'Classical costume in Shakespearian productions', *S.Sur.* 10 (1957), 71–6.

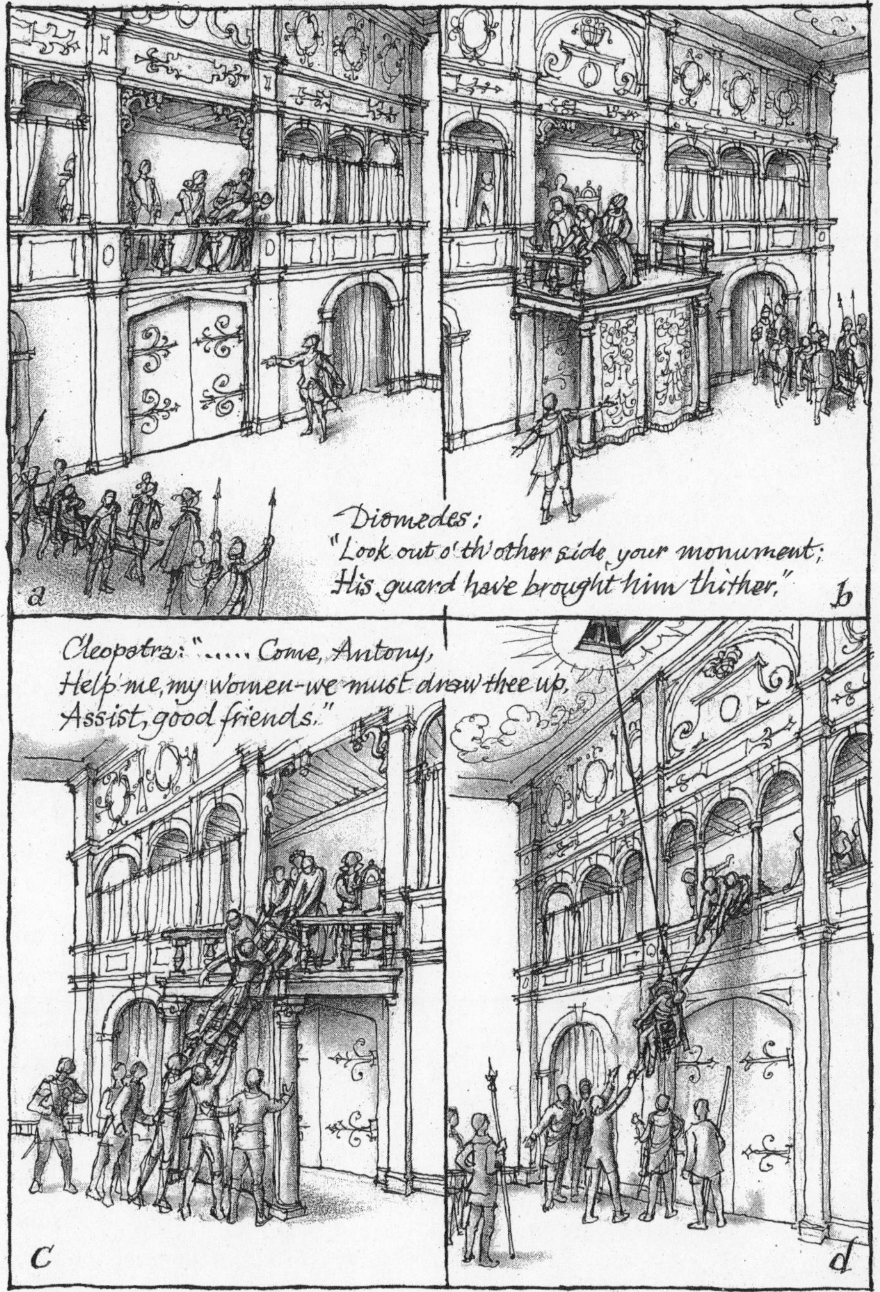

4 'Look out o'th'other side your monument.' Some possible stagings of Act 4, Scene 15, by C. Walter Hodges

a A solution with no added structures or machinery, as urged in this edition (see p. 44)

b, *c* Reconstructions by Walter Hodges, including an actual 'monument' built forward from the tiring-house wall

d A solution using a winch and pulley with harness, as described by Richard Hosley (see p. 44, nn. 1 and 2)

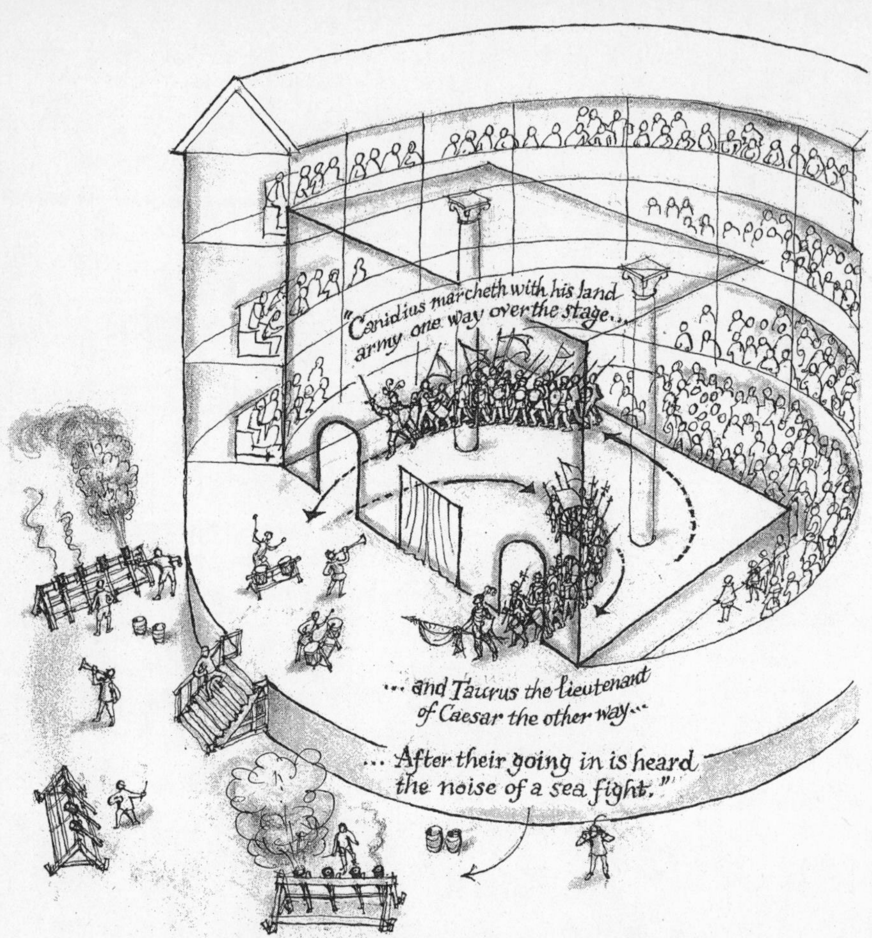

5 'Canidius marcheth with his land army one way over the stage.' A possible staging of Act 3, Scene 10, by C. Walter Hodges, showing a typical method of staging a quick succession of short warfare scenes. Sea fights were customarily represented by the sound of gunfire offstage, produced by drums and by the blank firing of small bombards or 'chambers'

or 'allowed' in 1669 to Thomas Killigrew's company, the King's Men, at the Theatre Royal in Bridges Street, but no record survives to demonstrate that the company availed itself of the exclusive right. Instead, Restoration acting companies and audiences seem to have preferred the heavily adapted versions of Charles Sedley and John Dryden. To us these classically 'correct' dramatisations seem pallid by comparison with Shakespeare's play, but we should remember the extraordinary dominance of the Senecan tradition before and after Shakespeare, both abroad and in England; his was the truly innovative interpretation. The Countess of Pembroke's *Antonie*, published in 1592 but never acted, is essentially a translation of Robert Garnier's Senecan *Marc Antoine*, published in 1578, which in turn owes much to Étienne Jodelle's *Cléopâtre captive* (1552). All three restrict the action to a small cast and a small number of scenes focusing on the last hours of the tragic story.[1] Samuel Daniel's *The Tragedy of Cleopatra* (1594), another closet drama, makes clear the author's deference to the Countess and the Sidney school: beginning the play after the death of Antony, as in Jodelle, it devotes the first act entirely to a soliloquy by Cleopatra, the second to Proculeius's recounting to Caesar the capture of Cleopatra, and the fifth chiefly to the Nuntius's description of Cleopatra's death. Samuel Brandon's *The Virtuous Octavia* of 1598 (following a lost play on the subject by Fulke Greville), though set in Rome and encompassing a larger historical period than its predecessors, is no less Senecan in its hostility to the popular stage. *The False One* by John Fletcher and Philip Massinger (*c.* 1620), while not a direct adaptation of Shakespeare's subject matter in that it deals with Cleopatra's affair with Julius Caesar, does echo his work in such a way as to illustrate the increasingly patrician and courtly vogue in the seventeenth century for symmetrical elaboration and heroic sentiment. So does Thomas May's *The Tragedy of Cleopatra, Queen of Egypt* (1626), with its rigorously classical five-act structure and its decision to keep Antony's death offstage. Sir Charles Sedley's *Antony and Cleopatra*, produced at the Duke's Theatre in 1677, begins after the battle of Actium and regularises the action in a studiously neo-classical manner, amplifying the theme of love versus honour in a number of subsidiary developments.

John Dryden's *All for Love, or, The World Well Lost*, acted next year, 1678, at the Theatre Royal with Charles Hart and Mrs Boutel in the title roles, is thus no isolated departure from Shakespeare. To be sure, Dryden is rather misleadingly eager to associate his genius with that of Shakespeare, one of the 'greatest wits of our nation' and a stylist especially worthy of imitation. Dryden even insists, in a prefatory essay, that he shares with Shakespeare and others a commitment to the story's didactic idea, 'the excellency of the moral'; for, says Dryden, 'the chief persons presented were famous patterns of unlawful love, and their end accordingly was unfortunate'. Nevertheless, the applicability of this description to Dryden's play rather than to Shakespeare's is evident when Dryden goes on to explain his conception of a 'middle course' in the portrayal of character. He has drawn the hero in Aristotelian fashion, he says, meaning that the hero must not be a character 'of perfect virtue', since his fall would then be unjustified, nor 'altogether wicked', since he could not then be pitied. Cleopatra too must be shown in as favourable a light as his sources will allow, though Dryden clearly does not regard her as a tragic heroine in the same sense that Antony is a tragic hero.

Dryden observes the unities of time and place by locating the scene at Alexandria throughout, and makes a great point of his unity of action: every scene in the

[1] Furness, pp. 507–83, provides information on and brief excerpts from the various dramatic versions of the tragedy of Antony and Cleopatra before and after Shakespeare. Giraldi Cinthio's *Cleopatra*, published in Italy in 1583, is not likely to have influenced Shakespeare.

tragedy is 'conducing to the main design, and every act concluding with a turn of it'. Shakespeare's cast of some thirty-four named roles is reduced to ten (besides some lesser speaking-parts for gentlemen and the like), with a preponderantly larger percentage of roles for women than in Shakespeare's play. The conflict of love and honour is schematically rendered in the opposed counsels of Alexas or Cleopatra (urging love) and Ventidius (urging honour). When Octavia and Cleopatra meet in Egypt, Antony's choice is all too perfectly clear, but he is irrationally swayed from his resolve to return to his marriage by a jealous fear that Cleopatra is faithless to him. In other ways as well, Dryden recasts his story to enhance the conflict between the lovers in terms of love and honour. Dryden's subtitle, *The World Well Lost*, plausibly indicates his own view that Antony is vindicated in his final choice of love. Cleopatra is ready to see Antony ruined if she cannot have him, but she is also a devoted woman whose situation evokes pathos and sympathy. She is not as amusing, as vital, or as erotic as Shakespeare's heroine, nor is she the spokesman for the artist's imagination. Dryden was not trying simply to redo what Shakespeare had accomplished, for his own tastes and those of his audience in terms of tragic decorum were such that Shakespeare could best be served (in Dryden's opinion) by an essentially new play in the heroic mould.

Though not especially successful at first, Dryden's version soon became an established play, while Shakespeare's text languished. Thomas Betterton, who had played Antony in Sedley's version, succeeded with Dryden's role in 1684 at Drury Lane. Between 1704 and 1706, according to John Downes, Drury Lane took its successful production to court, with Betterton as Antony and Elizabeth Barry as Cleopatra, where it was well received. A revival on 3 December 1718 at Drury Lane under the management of Colley Cibber, Robert Wilks, and Barton Booth starred Booth as Antony, Wilks as Dolabella, Cibber as Alexas, and Anne Oldfield as Cleopatra; it incurred an expense of nearly £600, 'a sum unheard of', says Cibber, 'for many years before, on the like occasion'.[1] The total eclipse of Shakespeare's play over such a prolonged period[2] helps us to understand the courage of David Garrick in mounting a production based on Shakespeare's text at Drury Lane in 1759.

Garrick saw a number of possible advantages in a revival of *Antony and Cleopatra*: it was full of spectacle and pageantry (currently much in vogue at Drury Lane and Covent Garden), and it offered something new, not having been produced since Shakespeare's own lifetime.[3] Still, Garrick was not so foolhardy as to suppose that he could produce the play intact and without scenic rearrangement.

[1] John Downes, *Roscius Anglicanus, or An Historical Review of the Stage*, 1708, pp. 46 ff.; Colley Cibber, *An Apology for the Life of Mr Colley Cibber*, 1740, II, 175–6.

[2] During this period, neo-classical plays in the vein of Jodelle and Garnier continued to appear on the continent, including those by Giovanni Delfino (a Venetian) in 1660, by Daniel Casper von Lohenstein (a German) in the same year, by de la Chapelle (a Frenchman) in 1682, by J. B. Robert Boistel d'Welles at Paris in 1741, and by Marmontel at the French court in 1750; see Furness, pp. 524–42.

[3] George Winchester Stone, Jr, 'Garrick's presentation of *Antony and Cleopatra*', *RES* 13 (1937), 20–38.

6 Mrs Yates as Cleopatra in a benefit performance of Dryden's *All for Love* at Covent Garden, 1768

Accordingly, the play's forty-plus scenes are reduced to twenty-seven, in a text prepared for Garrick by the well-known Shakespearean editor, Edward Capell, and shifts in locale are avoided where possible to facilitate the use of painted sets. Philo, Demetrius, Ventidius, and Scarus disappear, their lines reassigned to Thyreus (Shakespeare's Thidias) and Dolabella; Thyreus also delivers, in Scene 1, Enobarbus's Cydnus speech from Shakespeare's Act 2. Gallus, Menecrates, and Varrius are gone, along with some entire scenes, including 3.1, 3.4, and 4.1–3. Some 657 lines are cut in all. Bawdy double entendre is decorously excised. Pompey and Octavia are limited to one appearance each. Because the political exchanges among Antony, Caesar, and Pompey are given less prominence, Cleopatra's role, essentially uncut, emerges with particular splendour. The overall effect is to enhance the pageantry of the love story, divorced to a significant extent from its political context and its attendant ironies. Caesar is more humane, Enobarbus less blunt.

Yet with all the accommodations to eighteenth-century taste, and considerable expenditure on the scenery, the production was not a success. Garrick was not impressive in the role of Antony, and most observers simply preferred Dryden's 'soft flowing numbers' to the 'general language' of Shakespeare's Antony. Audiences went back to Dryden when they saw a play about Antony and Cleopatra at all.[1] A production at Drury Lane in 1788 with John Philip Kemble and Sarah Siddons as Antony and Cleopatra was noteworthy for its attention to historical accuracy in its depiction of ancient Rome and Egypt, but its text followed the Dryden tradition. Other revivals of Dryden's play took place at Covent Garden in 1790 and at Bath in 1818.[2]

Kemble seems nevertheless to have shared Garrick's dream of finding a way back to Shakespeare. Kemble himself may have compiled an acting-version for a production at Covent Garden in 1813 in which the announced aim was to rescue Shakespeare's play from 'the features which tend to render it unacceptable to the public' while at the same time redeeming Dryden's version from 'those weaknesses that have caused it to decline in popularity'. For all its odd excisions (including

[1] An anonymous critic, quoted in Stone, 'Garrick's presentation', p. 35, and in Furness, p. 587. Thomas Davies, *Dramatic Miscellanies*, 1783, II, 368–9, says that Garrick 'wanted one necessary accomplishment: his person was not sufficiently important and commanding to represent the part'. Davies admired Mrs Yates as Cleopatra, but found that Henry Mossop 'wanted the essential part of Enobarbus, humour'. After Garrick's attempt at Shakespeare, *All for Love* was revived at Drury Lane, under Garrick's management, in 1766 with Powell and Mrs Yates in the leading roles and in 1772 with Spranger Barry and Mrs Barry. Mrs Hartley appeared at Covent Garden in 1773 as Cleopatra. (An illustation of her in this role, published in 1778, is reprinted in Margery M. Morgan, 'Your crown's awry', *Komos* 1 (1968), 128.) Other revivals followed at Drury Lane or Covent Garden in 1775, 1776, and 1779. On the continent, classical tragedies on the theme continued to appear, including those by Vittorio Alfieri and Cornelius von Ayrenhoff; see Furness, pp. 542–69. Henry Brooke published his dramatic version of the story in 1778 in which, according to John Genest, *Some Account of the English Stage from the Restoration in 1660 to 1830*, 10 vols., VI, 63, he took 'one third, or perhaps one half, from Shakespeare', and wrote the remainder himself.

[2] James Boaden's comment on Sarah Siddons's 'delight in statuary' and 'severity of attitude' is quoted in Odell, II, 93, and in Merchant, 'Classical costume', p. 73. Furness, p. 584, gives further details on the performances in 1790 and 1818.

Enobarbus's description of Cleopatra) and its unhistorical additions from Dryden (including Octavia's visit to Egypt), Kemble's patchwork at least avoids any lines of his own invention and does include major segments from Shakespeare, especially from 3.6 to the defeat at Actium.[1] Moreover, Kemble seems also to have prepared another stage version based entirely on Shakespeare, in which the cast is reduced to twenty and many lines cut, but without significant additions and with relatively few transpositions.[2] Even if, as seems likely, this version was not performed, Kemble's interest in change suggests that the time for textual reform was at hand.

William Charles Macready, like Kemble, hesitantly toyed with textual restoration. His production at Drury Lane in 1833 still included a good deal of Dryden, even though it advertised itself as 'Shakespeare's Historical Play of *Antony and Cleopatra*'. The chief attraction appears to have been Clarkson Stanfield's beautiful painted scenery. The spectacle included 'a splendid hall in Cleopatra's palace', the 'garden of Cleopatra's palace', a 'portico attached to the house of Octavius Caesar, with the Capitol in the distance', 'a hall in the house of Lepidus', a locale 'near the promontory of Misenum', the 'promontory of Actium with a view of the fleets of Antony and Caesar', and still more.[3] Interest in historical reconstruction, evident already in the details of Kemble's seemingly unproduced version, was beginning to gain momentum. Macready's production did not succeed financially, but it may have contributed to the success that followed.

Samuel Phelps's production at Sadler's Wells in October 1849 managed at last to combine a Shakespearean text with stage spectacle in a way that audiences appreciated. The scenic effects rivalled those of Charles Kean in his revival of *King John* and other Shakespeare plays. As the *Illustrated London News* admiringly reported, the theatre managers did their best 'to put this "wonderful tragedy" of *Antony and Cleopatra* on the stage in the spirit in which it was composed. They have done their best to realise the past, and to bring the historical into actual presence. The Egyptian scenes are exceedingly *vraissemblable*; that on board Pompey's galley, with the banquetting sovereigns of the world as drunk as cobblers, is exceedingly life-like.' Phelps, the reviewer noted, 'aided the pictorial by his well-studied bacchanalian attitudes, some of which were exceedingly fine'. The illusion of Phelps's Antony 'was almost perfect'; the actor 'could scarcely be recognised through the disguise'. Isabel Glyn as Cleopatra elicited no less praise for her 'versatility of power', her 'grace and dignity', her 'classical' mannerisms and her 'poses' that were 'severely statuesque'. Her death was 'sublime'.[4] Phelps's interest in pictorial effects meant, of course, that he had to run together and transpose scenes in order to reduce the number of scenery changes. To be sure, at least one

[1] *Shakespeare's Tragedy of Antony and Cleopatra, with alterations and with additions from Dryden*, 1813, 'Advertisement' prefaced to the text. See Furness, p. 587. William Hazlitt, *A View of the English Stage*, 1818, p. 27, commented that the production still included 'considerable additions from Dryden's *All for Love*'.

[2] For John Genest's summary, see *Some Account of the English Stage*, VIII, 417–19.

[3] Odell, II, 176.

[4] *Illustrated London News*, 22 November 1849, p. 285, quoted in John Russell Brown (ed.), *Shakespeare: Antony and Cleopatra, A Casebook*, 1969, pp. 50–1. See illustration 7.

7 Isabel Glyn as Cleopatra in Samuel Phelps's production of *Antony and Cleopatra*, Sadler's Wells, 1849

reviewer held to the opinion that Shakespeare's play was irredeemably 'long-winded' and 'tedious', but even this sceptic found the production admirably mounted.[1]

Once Phelps had established the theatrical vitality of Shakespeare's text, it supplanted Dryden's as the basis of performance, but the trend towards further cutting of the text and further elaboration of the scenic effects was bound to continue. Sets became even more expensive and cumbersome in the search for opulence and realistic detail. An 1867 revival at the Princess's omitted some sixteen scenes from its text, no doubt to make as much as possible of 'the witchery of the blandishments, the Asiatic undulations of the form, the variety of the enchantments, the changes of mood, the impetuous passion, and in the end the noble resignation' of Glyn's performance.[2] The piece had become, in other words, a vehicle for a star performance. The scenic effects furnished by Thomas Grieve and Frederick Lloyds were no less appreciated, especially for the banqueting scene on board Pompey's ship.

Twelve scenes were thought sufficient for the entire play at Drury Lane in 1873, under F. R. Chatterton's management, in an abridgement by Andrew Halliday. The acting paled in comparison with the scenery. As the *Illustrated London News* put it, 'the stage architect and poet are brought into competition and the rivalry of the cognate arts gives birth to a picture worthy of the Shakespearean text'.[3] A pictorial illustration accompanying Enobarbus's description of the meeting of Antony and Cleopatra left the impression that the Cydnus River was in Egypt rather than in Cilicia. A Roman festival procession, complete with Amazons, thirty choirboys, and a ballet called the 'Path of Flowers' gave weight to the celebration of Antony's marriage to Octavia. At the battle of Actium, the crews of the contending galleys so alarmed the audience with their volleys of arrows that the manager had to offer his personal assurances that no spectator would be in danger. This production, as much as any other, gave substance to Chatterton's own managerial dictum that 'Shakespeare spelt ruin.'[4]

Not to be outdone, a revival at the Princess's Theatre in 1890 mounted a sumptuous production in which the relatively unimpressive performances of Charles Coghlan as Antony and Lily Langtry as Cleopatra were dwarfed by an 'Alexandrian festival', a 'triumphal reception of Antony by Cleopatra', and an allegorical ballet of 'the conflict between day and night'. Langtry was at least

[1] *Literary Review and Stage-Manager*, 25 October 1849, quoted in Brown, *Casebook*, p. 49. G. K. Dickinson played Caesar, Henry Marston Pompey, and George Bennett Enobarbus. Miss Glyn, in the best role of her career, acted Cleopatra again in 1855 at the Standard Theatre with Henry Marston as Antony and again in 1867 opposite Henry Loraine at the Princess's; see C. B. Young, 'The stage-history of *Antony and Cleopatra*', in Wilson, pp. xxxvii–xlvi, esp. p. xl.

[2] *The Athenaeum*, 18 May 1867, p. 669, quoted in Furness, p. 585.

[3] *Illustrated London News*, 27 September 1873, p. 290. A playbill for the first performance, in the Enthoven collection, Victoria and Albert Museum, speaks of 'new and magnificent scenery by William Beverley' and costumes 'designed by Mr E. C. Barnes from the splendid collection of Roman and Egyptian antiquities at the British museum'. Quoted in Merchant, 'Classical costume', pp. 75–6.

[4] Quoted in Furness, p. 585.

8 Herbert Beerbohm Tree as Antony, Basil Gill as Octavius Caesar, and Constance Collier as Cleopatra in Tree's production of *Antony and Cleopatra*, His Majesty's Theatre, 1906

allowed by the critics to have died in high style.[1] No less lavish were the productions by Frank Benson at Stratford-upon-Avon in 1898 and 1912, the first with Constance Benson as Cleopatra and the second with Dorothy Green, and at the Lyceum Theatre in 1900.[2]

The opulent traditions of Victorian and Edwardian staging culminated in Herbert Beerbohm Tree's production of the play at His Majesty's Theatre in 1906 and early 1907. A major theme was sexual infatuation. Tree minimised scenes of political negotiation in order that he (as Antony) and Constance Collier (as Cleopatra) might be 'given all the advantage of scenic magnificence and orchestral illustration'. To establish the point that Egypt was the hub of the action, a dissolving vision of

[1] Odell, II, 443, and Arthur Colby Sprague, *Shakespeare and the Actors*, 1944, p. 333, quoting *The Athenaeum*, 22 November 1890, pp. 707–8.

[2] M. C. Day and J. C. Trewin, *The Shakespeare Memorial Theatre*, 1932, p. 84; T. C. Kemp and J. C. Trewin, *The Stratford Festival: A History of the Shakespeare Memorial Theatre*, 1953, pp. 44–6. See Constance Benson, *Mainly Players: Bensonian Memories*, 1926, pp. 158–9, on the monument scene in the 1898 production, played with such realism that the leading lady found it 'no easy task' to lift Antony up to her even with her women's help. Two revivals are recorded in New York during this period, one in 1878 by Miss Rose Eytinge and the other in 1889 by Kyrle Bellew; see Furness, p. 594, and see Young, 'Stage-history', p. xlvi, for other American productions. Louis Calvert and Janet Achurch won considerable if qualified praise (from George Bernard Shaw (*Dramatic Opinions and Essays*, 1913, II, 214–20) and James Agate (*Brief Chronicles*, 1943, p. 175), among others) for their Antony and Cleopatra at the Queen's Theatre in Manchester, March 1897, and in May of that same year at the Olympic Theatre in London.

9*a* Alice Crawford as Charmian in Tree's production of *Antony and Cleopatra*, His Majesty's Theatre, 1906

the Sphinx opened and closed the production. Antony and Cleopatra made their first entries from a barge on the Nile that drew up to the steps of Cleopatra's palace. Weird oriental strains were audible, even in Rome; when Antony received a message from Cleopatra, he fell on a couch, murmuring 'Cleopatra' and day-dreaming of her to the faint sounds of Eastern music. The deck of Pompey's ship was a 'masterpiece' of stage carpentry and stage management, with fantastically-coloured lanterns in the poop and dancing-girls to entertain the triumvirs and then join them in a wild debauch. Cleopatra apparelled herself as the goddess Isis and sat upon a 'tribunal silvered', literalising in the theatre one of Shakespeare's descriptions of her (3.6.3 ff.), in order to celebrate with due splendour Antony's return to Egypt. In Act 5, Tree used a momentary black-out to make a transition from the exterior to the interior of Cleopatra's monument; at one moment Antony was seen being hoisted towards a window, while at the next glimpse he was being lifted inside through that same open window. Constance Collier, a dark-skinned and fiery woman, dominated the scene wherever she appeared, and proved with devastating conviction 'how close the tiger's cruelty lies under the sleek skin of the cultivated woman'.[1] Tree's Antony was a Samson caught by Delilah. The costumes were lauded as 'perfect' by one enthusiast, and those of Antony and Cleopatra especially 'beggared all description'.[2]

Reaction against nineteenth-century staging, with its ponderous realism and its cutting and rearranging of scenes, was already manifesting itself in productions of other Shakespeare plays by William Poel and by Harley Granville-Barker, but not until 1922 were audiences given a chance to discover, in a production by a Poel disciple, Robert Atkins, at the Old Vic, that *Antony and Cleopatra* was ideally suited to continuous performance. As with Harcourt Williams's Old Vic production of *Julius Caesar* at Sadler's Wells in 1930, the abandonment of 'realism' did not mean doing away with Roman costume, but it did mean a striving for a rapid sequence of events, almost kaleidoscopic in effect.[3] Atkins, with enthusiastic support from Granville-Barker, allowed himself only one interval. Wilfred Walter played Antony, Esther Whitehouse Cleopatra, Rupert Harvey Enobarbus, and Douglas Burbidge Caesar.

Antony and Cleopatra, now a proven success, was revived on several occasions in the early and mid 1920s.[4] Harcourt Williams's production of the play, at the Old Vic in 1930, starred John Gielgud as Antony, Dorothy Green as Cleopatra, and Ralph Richardson as Enobarbus in a nearly uncut version with costuming based (as in the Old Vic *Julius Caesar*) on paintings by Paul Veronese and Tiepolo.[5] Williams himself took the parts of the messenger sent to Cleopatra and the Clown

[1] *The Times*, 4 January 1907, and *Daily Telegraph*, 28 December 1906, quoted in Brown, *Casebook*, pp. 53–4.
[2] *The Athenaeum*, 5 January 1907, pp. 25–6, quoted in Furness, pp. 593–4.
[3] Merchant, 'Classical costume', p. 75.
[4] The play was revived in 1925 with Baliol Holloway as Antony, Edith Evans as Cleopatra, and Neil Porter as Enobarbus. Dorothy Green played Cleopatra a number of times at Stratford-upon-Avon, in 1921, 1924, and 1927. See Young, 'Stage-history', pp. xliii–xlv.
[5] Merchant, 'Classical costume', p. 75.

9*b* Dorothy Green as Cleopatra in Frank Benson's production of *Antony and Cleopatra*, Shakespeare Memorial Theatre, 1912

9c Randle Ayrton as Enobarbus in Benson's 1912 production

with the figs. The production did well, critically and financially. The play continued to be popular in the 1930s, with revivals and experimental versions.[1]

But for all its new success on modern stages, *Antony and Cleopatra* has proved extraordinarily difficult for its leading actors. It is probably fair to say that there have been no immortal performances of this play as there have been of *Hamlet* (Gielgud and others), *Othello* (Paul Robeson), *Richard III* (Olivier), and so on – performances that shape our very consciousness of those roles. David Garrick, as we have seen, did not succeed with Antony, and no nineteenth-century actress is remembered vividly as Cleopatra. Edmund and Charles Kean, Edwin Booth, Henry Irving, Sarah Bernhardt, Ellen Terry, Ada Rehan, and Lily Brayton all stayed away from the roles. Ellen Terry confessed her disappointment that Cleopatra, 'the most expressive of all Shakespeare's heroines', was so invariably 'idealized' in the theatre that 'the part does not hang together'.[2] Perhaps, as William Worthen argues, actors are defeated not by the roles so much as by the 'characters' as defined by others in the play.[3] Who can match, on stage, what Enobarbus says about Cleopatra's infinite variety? As the reviewer in *The Times* wrote in 1907, apropos of Constance Collier in Tree's production, 'It is a terribly exacting part for any actress. She must have beauty, of course, and, what is even more important, she must have glamour. She must be able to run at a rapid sweep through the whole gamut of emotion – from dove-like cooings to the rage of a tigress, from voluptuous languor to passion all aflame, from the frenzy of a virago to the calm and statuesque majesty of one of the noblest death-scenes in all Shakespeare.'[4] And what actor assigned the part of Antony can fully convince us, in his own person, that he is a 'triple pillar of the world', especially when Antony is so dismayed with his own behaviour? The actor is destined, by the very nature of the script, to come 'too short', in Philo's words, 'of that great property / Which still should go with Antony' (1.1.60–1).

A case in point is Glen Byam Shaw's revival at the Piccadilly Theatre in December 1946. Anthony Cookman, writing in the *Tatler and Bystander*, frankly took the view that Godfrey Tearle as Antony and Edith Evans as Cleopatra were miscast: 'there is as little in him of the reckless amorist as there is of the gipsy in her'. Yet the reviewer liked their performances, no doubt because they 'knew that they could not hope to represent directly the kind of love which Enobarbus described with soldierly

[1] Among others, there was a revival by Henry Cass in 1934 starring Wilfred Lawson as Antony, Mary Newcomb as Cleopatra, David Horne as Enobarbus, Maurice Evans as Octavius, and Leo Genn as Pompey; a Marlowe Society production at Cambridge by George Rylands in the same year and again in 1946; an experimental version at the New Theatre in 1936 by Theodore Komisarjevsky with Donald Wolfit as Antony, the Russian actress Leontovich as Cleopatra, and Leon Quartermaine as Enobarbus; a spectacular success in New York in 1947 (127 performances in the city and 73 more on tour) with Katherine Cornell and Godfrey Tearle; and a production in 1945 at Stratford-upon-Avon with Claire Luce and Anthony Eustrel.

[2] Quoted in Brown, *Casebook*, pp. 54–5.

[3] W. B. Worthen, '"The weight of Antony": staging "character" in *Antony and Cleopatra*', *SEL* 26 (1986), 295–308.

[4] *The Times*, 4 January 1907, quoted in Furness, pp. 591–2.

10 Baliol Holloway as Antony and Edith Evans as Cleopatra at the Old Vic, 1925

gusto and the vividness of the reporter *par excellence*'.[1] Intellectual comprehension of the limits of theatre gave a sense of completeness to their tragic dignity. The two leading performers relied on their mastery of classical Shakespearean acting and stage convention to give the audience an Antony and a Cleopatra paradoxically more convincing than an overly realistic attempt at sexiness and infatuation would have done. Anthony Quayle as Enobarbus and Michael Goodliffe as Caesar were effective as counterparts in the iconoclastic interpretations of the protagonists. By the same token, the ingenious permanent set incorporating the essential features of an Elizabethan stage (by Motley), the unrelenting pace, and the incidental music by Anthony Hopkins, all contributing to a kaleidoscopic change of scene and mood, proved more persuasive than nineteenth-century verisimilitude. Attempts at showing the first meeting of Antony and Cleopatra in sumptuous panorama,

[1] Anthony Cookman, *Tatler and Bystander*, 15 January 1947, quoted in Brown, *Casebook*, pp. 55–6.

11 Laurence Olivier as Antony and Vivien Leigh as Cleopatra at the St James's Theatre, 1951

directors were now realising, were not simply too costly and cumbersome; they violated the play's own awareness of the unbridgeable gulf between a verbal evocation of idealised life and a more complex perception of the way people, even great people, actually behave.

Still, what are the performers to do with this iconoclastic view of the performance itself? The most successful attempts have been made by those honestly aware of the problem, among whom Vivien Leigh and Laurence Olivier at the St James's Theatre, May 1951, rank as high as any. Ivor Brown, writing for the *Observer*, acknowledged the near impossibility of the task of equalling in performance the majesty of the characters' 'mighty utterance of desire, ecstasy, despair, and the brave end', but conceded that this production had done just that. Brown found Olivier's Antony to be missing 'the rich folly of the unlimited sensualist', but admirably witty in the scene of the Roman conference and 'infinitely tragic' in Antony's final dream of a lover's immortality.[1] Another reviewer noted the passionate vacillation as Olivier's Antony shifted 'from doting amorousness, through gusts of nervous optimism, to fierce despair'.[2] Olivier's cue was to be great in his versatility and stage presence while manifestly weak and inconstant as a man. Leigh, faced with an even greater challenge, managed also to be both wanton and marble-constant as she took advantage of her beauty and technical versatility to portray a woman at once cold, coquettish, intelligent, magnetic, emotional, and at last queenly in her dignity. The set, designed by Roger Furse, featured five dark stocky pillars to represent Rome, and, when the stage had been rotated, another set of slender Corinthian columns rising out of the burning sands to represent Egypt.

Another candidate for the most satisfying performance in the twentieth century might well be Glen Byam Shaw's production at Stratford-upon-Avon and at the Prince's Theatre, 1953, with Michael Redgrave and Peggy Ashcroft in the title roles and with Harry Andrews as Enobarbus and Marius Goring as Caesar. Once again, however, the ideal of 'definitive' was simply unattainable because the text asks for such greatness in the absence of noble action able to demonstrate that greatness. Redgrave has spoken well of his awareness of the problem: 'Antony is described as "noble" on no less than eight occasions. But, excepting for his generosity towards Enobarbus, and possibly in his death-scene, Antony is never *shown* to do one noble thing.'[3] All the same, no one was better suited than Redgrave to convey nobility simply by his stage presence, and the reviewers were warm in their praise for this portrayal 'full of splendid masculine strength, stirring in delivery, forthright in passion and deeply moving in fallen grandeur'.[4] The crux once again was Cleopatra, and, while Peggy Ashcroft moved some critics by her generosity of sacrifice to every passion, by her complex ability to be 'a gipsy, a

[1] Ivor Brown, *Observer*, 13 May 1951, p. 6, quoted in Brown, *Casebook*, p. 57.
[2] Harold Hobson, *Sunday Times*, 13 May 1951, quoted in Brown, *Casebook*, pp. 57–8.
[3] Michael Redgrave, *Mask or Face*, 1958, p. 79, quoted in Worthen, '"The weight of Antony"', pp. 295–308.
[4] A. E. Wilson, *Star*, 5 November 1953, quoted in Brown, *Casebook*, pp. 58–9.

12 Act 2, Scene 7: Marius Goring as Octavius Caesar refuses the wine offered by Antony (Michael Redgrave), in Glen Byam Shaw's production at the Shakespeare Memorial Theatre, Stratford-upon-Avon, in 1953. Harry Andrews as Enobarbus stands at the right, and Tony Britton (Pompey), John Bushelle (Agrippa), and Donald Eccles (Maecenas) sit in the foreground

child, a fury and a great and noble queen in her immortal longings',[1] at least one reviewer noted that Ashcroft had failed, like other fine actresses before her, to give 'completeness' to the 'many-sided character of the Egyptian enchantress'; her success was at last 'something of a triumph over the lack of that art which suggests Cleopatra's voluptuous guile, the beauty of a voice that should give music to gorgeous lines'.[2]

The reservations are much like those applied earlier to Vivien Leigh, whose intelligence and beauty were seen as having to compensate for the heat and duskiness that one finds in the Cleopatra of Shakespeare's imagination but not in Leigh herself. Similarly, Margaret Whiting as a twenty-three-year-old Cleopatra, opposite Keith Michell (aged thirty) in Robert Helpmann's production at the Old Vic in 1957, struck most reviewers as simply too young for the part, even if the producer attempted to justify his choice by observing in the programme notes that 'At the time of her death Cleopatra was thirty-eight, Mark Antony was fifty-three and

[1] 'E.F.', *News Chronicle*, 5 November 1953.
[2] A. E. Wilson, *Star*, 5 November 1953.

Octavius Caesar was thirty.' The casting difficulty was aggravated by costuming and make-up choices that did little to conceal the actress's youthful complexion. For different reasons Maggie Smith struck at least one reviewer as miscast, if fascinating, in Robin Phillips's production (with Keith Baxter as Antony) at Stratford, Ontario, in 1976.[1] Even more than with most other plays, the acting of this play is an art of illusion, one that calls attention to its own limits.

As the staging of *Antony and Cleopatra* moved into the 1960s and 70s, a trend towards a more political interpretation was perhaps the inevitable result of a new interest in 'relevance'. Whatever the distortions that might occasionally result, the new emphasis was at least a corrective to the minimising of political content so characteristic of nineteenth-century staging. Michael Langham, at Stratford, Ontario, in 1967, focused on the power struggles of the empire that influenced the lives of Antony (Christopher Plummer) and Cleopatra (Zoe Caldwell) as much as did their sexual passion.

The Antony of Trevor Nunn's production at Stratford-upon-Avon in 1972, played by Richard Johnson, dwelt on the painful realisation that his fall from greatness was the unavoidable consequence of his turning away from political ambition. Corin Redgrave's 'ice-floe' puritanism in the role of Caesar gave point to Antony's reflections on the Roman way of life and to Cleopatra's (Janet Suzman's) witty and calculating strategies of self-preservation. Suzman's Cleopatra was a selfish, greedy, frivolous, superficial, and controlling woman, more intelligent and cunning than charismatic and sensual, concerned chiefly with 'herself and the extent of her own power'.[2] The sense of an impersonal and irresistible political destiny was enhanced by the production of four Roman plays in sequence – *Coriolanus*, *Julius Caesar*, *Antony and Cleopatra*, and *Titus Andronicus* – with continuities in casting, each beginning with a crowd scene. The ironic view of Caesar's triumph thus generated was as relevant to the widespread disillusionment of the 1970s as it was justified by the text.

Tony Richardson's near-modern-dress production, at the Bankside Globe Playhouse in London in 1973, took disillusionment a step further: love itself was irrelevant and petty, while the world around the lovers appeared hopelessly destined to succumb to Caesar's imperial ambitions. Vanessa Redgrave as Cleopatra, appearing in the first scene as a girl in a wig from the 1920s, in long black silk, displayed her arrogance and fits of ill temper by throwing cola bottles at servants and messengers. Julian Glover as Antony revealed the temperament of a shallow narcissist whom everyone could walk over. Caesar, played by David Schofield, was a 'twitching psychopathic', according to one reviewer, a 'youthful, fascist saluting guy in dark

[1] Mary Clarke, *Shakespeare at the Old Vic*, 1957; Jules Aaron, *ETJ* 29 (1977), 114.

[2] Margaret Tierney, *Plays and Players* 20.1 (October 1972), 42–3; J. C. Trewin, *Illustrated London News* 260 (October 1972), no. 6891, p. 79; Peter Thomson, 'No Rome of safety: the Royal Shakespeare season 1972 reviewed', *S.Sur.* 26 (1973), 146–8. Ronnie Mulryne, '*Antony and Cleopatra*: penny plain or tuppence coloured', in M. T. Jones-Davies (ed.), *Du Texte à la scène: langages du théâtre*, 1983, pp. 93–109, stresses the sumptuous spectacle in the visual contrast between Egypt and Rome.

13 Janet Suzman as Cleopatra striking the Messenger (Joseph Charles) in Trevor Nunn's production for the Royal Shakespeare Company, Stratford-upon-Avon, 1972

glasses', while Lepidus (John Byron) was a cigar-smoking buffoon in a morning suit. Pompey's piracy scenes were 'out of Treasure Island'. Reviewers were for the most part not enchanted with the shrill relevance and some 'sheerly inadequate acting'.[1]

Peter Brook, too, in a deromanticised version staged at Stratford-upon-Avon in 1978 (and in 1979 at the Aldwych), saw the lovers (Glenda Jackson and Alan Howard) as self-indulgent and unable to extricate themselves from an unscrupulous world of political in-fighting. Tenderness and erotic feeling were generally absent; instead, as the reviewers noted, Jackson made full use of her uncompromising urchin haircut and her abrupt, stylised mannerisms – 'iciness of tone; the mouth stretched open in a rectangular shape, baring the teeth; angular gesture' – to play her role in a relationship dominated by political implications. The lovers were drawn to one another in complex psychological ways, not only by sexuality but above all by 'their increasing and moving dependence in the trauma – which is precisely how Brook treats it – of defeat'.[2] The permanent set featured a semi-

[1] Nicholas de Jongh, *Plays and Players* 21.1 (October 1973), 56–7; J. C. Trewin, *Illustrated London News* 261 (October 1973), no. 6903, p. 103.
[2] Russell Jackson, *Cahiers Élisabéthains* 16 (1979), 69–72; G. M. Pearce, *Cahiers Élisabéthains* 16 (1979), 72–3; Jeremy Treglown, *Plays and Players* 26.3 (December 1978), 18; Jack Kroll, *Newsweek*, 27 November 1978, p. 66; Richard Eder, *New York Times*, 19 August 1979, section D, p. 3.

circular pavilion serving as the centre of the lovers' universe, the small intimate world of their personal lives, with translucent panels through which the audience caught glimpses at the back of the stage of the frenetic, mindless exterior world of flux and carnage.

Toby Robertson's production for the Prospect Theatre Company, at the Old Vic Theatre, the Edinburgh Festival, and on tour in 1977, was on the whole a more traditional version, with costumes in Renaissance style inspired by Tiepolo. Yet this production too kept the world of politics very much in evidence, as indeed a responsible reading of an essentially uncut text demands. Dorothy Tutin as Cleopatra, wrote one reviewer, was no 'languorous, fly-blown, fleshly charmer', but 'a trim termagant, her passion in the end (and in Shakespeare's text) second to her political judgment'. Alec McCowen as Antony was accordingly no 'teased-out super-playboy' but rather 'a great man torn apart'. Derek Jacobi as Caesar, taking care to avoid the contemporary cliché of psychopathic obsession, was nonetheless able to 'cast a chill with the lift of an eyebrow'. Zöe Hicks and Suzanne Bertish as Charmian and Iras were 'bedizened middle-aged bitches', making the point that Cleopatra's Egypt was no exotic paradise for which the world might be well lost.[1] Perhaps uniquely in stage history, this *Antony and Cleopatra* played in repertory with Dryden's *All for Love*, the latter in Restoration décor of periwigs and flowing cloaks. Once again, as in Nunn's 1972 production and in so many before it, the reviewers complained of miscasting or even of deliberate casting against type; one reviewer suggested that the directors 'had put the wrong pair in each play', and that the 'expansive, passionate potential' of Barbara Jefford and John Turner in the Dryden version were just what Tutin and McCowen lacked.[2] This familiar litany of miscasting was levelled once again against McCowen and Tutin (and against Alan Howard and Glenda Jackson as well) in the context of a 1981 review in *The Times* of the new BBC *Antony and Cleopatra*, with Colin Blakely and Jane Lapotaire in the leading roles.[3] The reviewer, Michael Ratcliffe, thought Blakely and Lapotaire well suited to their roles in the television version, but I for one was not convinced by their performances; to me they seemed not psychically big enough for the greatness of their roles, and Jonathan Miller's intimate tone too scaled-down for the epic sweep of events.

Antony and Cleopatra has seen a number of productions in the 1980s, testifying at once to the play's increasing popularity and to the seeming impossibility of achieving in performance all that the play script seems to demand. The view of politics in the play has remained chiefly one of disillusionment. A production at the Nottingham Playhouse in 1982, with Ian McCulloch and Kate O'Mara in the lead roles, put so little emphasis on the pageantry and glamour of international politics and war that Rome and Egypt were virtually indistinguishable. Black costumes for all actors made their roles interchangeable and allowed for extensive doubling of parts,

[1] J. W. Lambert, *Sunday Times*, 28 August 1977, p. 31; J. C. Trewin, 'Shakespeare in Britain', *SQ* 29 (1978), 220; G. M. Pearce, *Cahiers Élisabéthains* 14 (1978), 106–7.

[2] Gerald M. Berkowitz, *ETJ* 30 (March 1978), 113–14.

[3] Michael Ratcliffe, *The Times*, 8 May 1981, p. 14.

14 Glenda Jackson as Cleopatra, Paola Dionisotti as Charmian, Juliet Stevenson as Iras, and Alan Howard as Antony in Peter Brook's production for the Royal Shakespeare Company, Stratford-upon-Avon, 1978

props were mimed throughout, and the set featured a sloping carpeted ramp leading up to a large screen on which was projected an unchanging cloudscape.[1] Adrian Noble's production of the same year, at The Other Place in Stratford-upon-Avon (later at the Barbican's Pit), chose also to be utterly simple in visual concept, with a bare stage and a single set. Egypt, as one reviewer remarked, was 'notably lacking in the emblems of egyptology'. Changes of location were 'subliminally' signalled, with a colder lighting for Rome and a warmer lighting for Egypt. The staging of an 'epic' play in studio space put the emphasis on character, and with considerable success. Noble made little attempt, until the end, to glorify the love of Antony and Cleopatra. Performance was generally low-key and conversational. Distinctions in ranks were de-emphasised in order to stress instead 'human beings in the human relationship'. Helen Mirren, as Cleopatra, excelled in volatility, socking the messenger in the jaw at one point and flying into hysterics, later besmirching her face with ashes and dirt in mourning for Antony, at last tragically majestic and serene. Michael Gambon as Antony was abrupt, unhinged, perfunctory in his relationships with everybody, a 'shambling bear' who was 'still hungry for passion and aware that time was running out'. The sybaritic feast on board Pompey's ship induced a good deal of homoerotic cuddling: a nearly naked

[1] Roger Warren, 'Shakespeare in England, 1982–83', *SQ* 34 (1983), 336–7.

15 Helen Mirren as Cleopatra and Michael Gambon as Antony in Adrian Noble's production at The Other Place, Stratford-upon-Avon, 1982

singer found companionship with Enobarbus, and a bare-chested Pompey embraced Antony. One could tell from this scene that 'narcissistic boorishness and political ambivalence' were at the heart of much that was diseased in the world surrounding the lovers. Throughout, Caesar (Jonathan Hyde) was impulsive, puritanical, and touchingly fond of his sister. Although, as Stanley Wells has observed, 'No production of *Antony and Cleopatra* seems ever to have provided a theatrical correlative to the text's poetic power', this nobly sparse one at least demonstrated that 'the text can be no less fascinating as chamber music than as grand opera'.[1]

On at least one recent occasion, the contemporary response to political disillusionment has been to dismiss politics from the play. Robin Phillips's production at the Chichester Festival Theatre in 1985, with Denis Quilley and Diana Rigg in the title roles, paid little attention to the framework of political and social conflict. The scene aboard Pompey's galley disappeared entirely, along with the Seleucus episode, Cleopatra's sending a false message of her death, and her cautious unwillingness

[1] Stanley Wells, *Times Educational Supplement*, 22 October 1982, p. 25; Nicholas Shrimpton, 'Shakespeare performances in Stratford-upon-Avon and London, 1982–3', *S.Sur.* 37 (1984), 173; Russell Jackson, *Cahiers Élisabéthains* 24 (October 1983), 108–9; Victoria Radin, *Observer*, 17 October 1982, p. 34; Robert Hewison, *Sunday Times*, 17 April 1983, p. 43; Roger Warren, 'Shakespeare in England, 1982–83', pp. 337–8.

to come down to the dying Antony. As a result, much of Cleopatra's waywardness and vulgarity were gone. 'Instead of Shakespeare's regal fishwife', wrote one reviewer, 'we get a spirited but well-mannered Englishwoman who's liable to fits of temper.' Only in Norman Rodway's Enobarbus and Philip Frank's Caesar was there much complexity of political and human motivation. Reviewers generally agreed that this experiment with non-political interpretation, so paradoxically reminiscent of the cut texts of the nineteenth century, was a failure.[1]

The Toby Robertson/Christopher Selbie production at the Theatre Royal, Haymarket (brought in from the Theatre Clwyd in Wales), 1986, attempted to make a virtue out of unorthodox casting. Vanessa Redgrave played Cleopatra as 'a large, fair-skinned, ungainly woman behaving like a middle-aged punk tomboy'; she wore ' a close-cropped, carrot-coloured wig' and projected a 'gauche, boyish, bony Englishness' that, in John Peter's estimation, 'directly contradicts everything that is said about her in the play'.[2] Instead of a gipsy's lust, Redgrave excelled in feminine cunning and a wide range of strategies in her various roles as lover, queen, betrayer, and noble suicide. She was gangling, intense, at her best in scenes of outrageous temperament and mocking awareness of her own jealousy, but constantly reminding the audience of an eccentric English bluestocking inexplicably propelled into the land of the Nile, a 'British matron gone wrong'. For some viewers, the countercasting achieved its own offbeat success; John Peter paid grudging tribute to 'a queen of shreds and patches, yes; but a queen, a queen'. Undoubtedly the show was hers. One reviewer at least found Timothy Dalton equally miscast, 'far too young and vigorous and alert for the part'.[3] The set, a two-tiered, partly decaying Roman mansion, seemed out of place in Egypt and did not come into its own until the monument scene. The overall effect was one of off-putting originality for some viewers, at odds both with the text and with any consistent view of greatness in the world of ancient Rome.

Anthony Hopkins and Judi Dench, as the leading actors in Peter Hall's valedictory production on the Olivier stage at the National Theatre in London in 1987, made paradoxical use of their physical and temperamental inadequacies for two such imposing roles: they saw themselves as mocking and witty lovers dwarfed by a world at war, their whole lives entangled in the larger chaos of history. Their interpretation eschewed predictable views of Antony as the lover and Cleopatra as the enchanting courtesan, providing instead a 'sense of outmanoeuvred heroism' on Antony's part and a Cleopatra who, though never in love with the Antony of real life, was enchanted with the 'colossal Antony' created by her own 'intoxicating magic of rhetoric and legend'. Tim Pigott-Smith as a 'superbly peevish' Caesar

[1] Michael Ratcliffe, *Observer*, 19 May 1985, p. 23; Sheridan Morley, *Punch*, 22 May 1985, p. 65; Roger Warren, 'Shakespeare in Britain, 1985', *SQ* 37 (1986), 119–20; John Peter, *Sunday Times*, 19 May 1985, p. 43.

[2] John Peter, *Sunday Times*, 1 June 1986, p. 49.

[3] Mary Harron, *Observer*, 1 June 1986, p. 21: Sheridan Morley, *Punch*, 11 June 1986, p. 58; John James, *Times Educational Supplement*, 4 July 1986, p. 25; Irving Wardle, *The Times*, 28 May 1986, p. 19; John Peter, *Sunday Times*, 1 June 1986, p. 49.

and Michael Bryant as Enobarbus helped to underscore the ironies of the two lovers' infatuation and a destiny chiefly beyond their control. Yet the production achieved a fine balance, too, between its manifest disillusionment and an ending in which the legend of the lovers' greatness offered some real compensation for their tragic falls.[1] This production perhaps shows contemporary staging of *Antony and Cleopatra* at its best, less insistent on star performances and on a romantic vision of the lovers than on a cohesiveness that can unify the play's irony and transcendence into something approaching a singleness of vision.

[1] Andrew Rissik, *Plays and Players*, June 1987, pp. 14–15.

NOTE ON THE TEXT

The copy-text for this edition is the First Folio of 1623 (F), which is probably based on Shakespeare's own manuscript or on some kind of transcript of it; see the Textual Analysis, p. 261 below. Spellings have been modernised in accordance with the practice of this series. Abbreviations are silently expanded, and characters' names have been regularised in the speech headings and stage directions. Vowels that would be elided today but are required for the metre in Shakespeare's text are marked with a grave accent: entertainèd, perfumèd; otherwise, *-ed* endings are assumed to be elided. In a few cases I have modernised where other editors might retain the original; for example, I read 'enough' for F's 'enow' at 1.4.11 and 'more' for F's 'moe' at 4.14.18 on the ground that Shakespeare's usage does not consistently support distinctions in meaning between these forms; such distinctions may therefore not be authorial. I have modernised 'vant' to 'van' at 4.6.9 because the F spelling is the old form of the same word and is not given a separate listing in the *OED*. So too with 'workaday' ('worky day'), 'bond' ('band'), 'doff' ('daff'), etc. On the other hand, an older spelling like 'huswife' (4.15.46) seems worth preserving because it catches some of the meaning of 'hussy' along with 'housewife'. Choices of this kind are explained in the Commentary. In the complicated matter of proper names, this edition preserves spellings like *Thidias* and *Antonio's* that appear to be authorial, but follows the spellings of North's Plutarch (*Ventidius* instead of F's *Ventigius*, *Canidius* instead of F's *Camidius* or *Camidias*) where the original reading may simply be a spelling variant or a minor inconsistency. See the Textual Analysis for further discussion.

In punctuation, this edition tries to give the text the pointing that will best clarify its meaning for contemporary readers, granting that such an editorial intervention is interpretative and that in some cases ambiguities cannot be resolved; for example, F's 'What was he sad, or merry?' at 1.5.53 may mean 'What, was he sad, or merry?' or 'What was he, sad or merry?', and no modern punctuation can leave open both interesting possibilities. Such ambiguous instances (compare 1.3.20 and 5.1.52) might be better served by retaining the original reading. In general, however, the F punctuation is so laden with error and so predominantly compositorial (because the compositors were presumably working with a sparsely pointed manuscript) that the editor can offer material assistance. I believe that the editor should accept the responsibility of making the wisest choices he or she can, remembering in all humility that one is offering an interpretation and that subsequent editors will find a better way for readers of another generation.

The same is true of emendation. I do not think this edition departs from the F text in a brash way, and certainly it introduces few emendations that have not been proposed before; as Dr Johnson insists, the editor's job is not to parade his or her ingenuity. At the same time, an editor who is well informed of the nature of the text, and can make logical choices as to where error is likeliest to appear and in what form, is presumably in a better position than most to make an educated guess about what word or words the author may have intended at a given point. Editors have usually tried to make sense of the original F reading at 3.13.26, for example, when Antony dares Caesar to 'lay his gay comparisons apart', but a consideration of Shakespeare's idiom suggests that he often uses 'gay' to modify clothes and that he may well have written 'caparisons' here. Compare also 'lessens' (F: 'lessons') at 3.12.13. Choices such as these are explained in the Commentary.

This edition is probably at its boldest in rejecting the way editorial tradition has too complacently linked half-lines of verse in such a way as to produce what seem to be whole lines of verse. Too often, in my view, the resulting verse is hypermetrical and unconvincing; at other times, three half-lines in succession are arbitrarily arranged so that two of the half-lines are linked with each other and the third left unattached. The Textual Analysis below gives several samples. I think we should remember that the original printed text (here the Folio) indents none of these verses to indicate linking; to do so is to venture into editorial intrusion, one that is justifiable only when the resulting versification can meet the remarkably high standard we find in Shakespeare's verse as a whole. Of course his verse is supple and varied, but it does not indulge in the wholesale use of four- and six-stress verse lines such as we routinely find in the inventions of editorial tradition. Those invented verse constructions are absent in this edition.

On the other hand, this edition is conservative in the marking of act and scene divisions. They are mainly a matter of editorial convenience in any case, useful for scholarly and critical reference; they are visually minimised in this edition in order to avoid the appearance of their being authorial. Since they are chiefly benchmarks for reference, it makes sense to preserve the divisions that have been used for that purpose since the late nineteenth century. Recent attempts to rationalise act and scene division into new standard schemes of reference lose that connection with critical history and are perhaps not likely to be universally adopted anyway, owing to the existence of conflicting plans and to the near impossibility of agreement as to what constitutes a 'scene' in the fluid movement of this play – especially in the battle scenes.

Editorial additions to the original stage directions appear in square brackets. The reader can then be assured that the stage directions not thus marked are in the language of the original text. On the infrequent occasions when F uses *Exit* to mean *Exeunt* (a normal Elizabethan usage), the wording in the present text is changed to *Exeunt* for clarity and the departure is noted in the collation, even though the change is not a substantive one.

The collation is selective. It records all substantive departures from F, with attribution to the first user of the adopted reading, and selectively mentions some other emendations that are worthy of serious consideration. Thus, at 1.1.52, 'whose] F2; who F; how *Ridley*' means that the F reading of line 52, 'who', has been replaced by 'whose', a reading that first occurs in the Second Folio, whereas M. R.

Ridley in the Arden Shakespeare emends instead to 'how'. Even when the F text is followed in this edition, a collation note may record an emendation proposed by a previous editor but not used here: 'now] F; new *Warburton*' at 1.1.49 means that this edition follows F but notes Warburton's interesting emendation. The notation *conj. Johnson* means that the reading in question was conjectured by Dr Johnson but not used by him; *Capell subst.* means that the reading is substantially that of Capell but varies in some non-substantive way. Variant spellings in F are collated where they seem significant or worthy. Emendations in punctuation are collated when they substantively affect meaning, and in such instances the absence of punctuation means that the punctuation is indeed missing in the text being quoted: 'Thou, eunuch] F; Thou eunuch, *Pope*' at 1.5.9 means that the F text, followed in this edition, has a comma after 'Thou' but none after 'eunuch', whereas Pope has emended by moving the comma to after 'eunuch'. Editors' names refer to the list of abbreviations found at the front of this volume.

Some collations record what this edition regards as spelling variants rather than as emendations. At 1.1.41, for example, 'On] F (One)' means that the F spelling, 'One', is regarded as a variant way of spelling 'On' and has been modernised accordingly. Some such F spellings may be Shakespearean and are analysed as such in the Textual Analysis below; hence the reason for the notation in the collation. When a substantive alternative may be involved, as at 1.3.36 ('brows' bent] *Capell;* browes bent F'), the change is treated as an emendation. Place and proper names have been collated as substantives throughout, though in some cases they may be only spelling variants; for example, Hirtius (F *Hirsius*), *Taurus* (*Towrus*), *Sicily* (*Cicilie*), *Lichas* (*Licas*), *Adullas* (*Adallas*).

An asterisk in the lemma of a note in the Commentary calls attention to the fact that a word or phrase has been emended in the text. Further information can be found in the collation.

Antony and Cleopatra

LIST OF CHARACTERS

MARK ANTONY, OCTAVIUS CAESAR, LEPIDUS — *triumvirs*

CLEOPATRA, *queen of Egypt*

CHARMIAN, IRAS, ALEXAS, MARDIAN, *a eunuch*, DIOMEDES, SELEUCUS, *Cleopatra's treasurer* — *Cleopatra's attendants*

OCTAVIA, *sister of Octavius Caesar and wife of Antony*

DEMETRIUS, PHILO, DOMITIUS ENOBARBUS, VENTIDIUS, SILIUS, CANIDIUS, SCARUS, EROS, DERCETUS — *Antony's friends and followers*

A SCHOOLMASTER, *Antony's* AMBASSADOR *to Caesar*

MAECENAS, AGRIPPA, TAURUS, THIDIAS, DOLABELLA, GALLUS, PROCULEIUS — *Octavius Caesar's friends and followers*

SEXTUS POMPEIUS *or* POMPEY

MENAS, MENECRATES, VARRIUS — *Pompey's friends*

MESSENGERS *to Antony, Octavius Caesar, and Cleopatra*

A SOOTHSAYER

Two SERVANTS *of Pompey*

SERVANTS *of Antony and Cleopatra*

A BOY
SOLDIERS, SENTRIES, GUARDSMEN *of Antony and Octavius Caesar*
A CAPTAIN *in Antony's army*
An EGYPTIAN
A CLOWN *with figs*

Ladies attending on Cleopatra, eunuchs, servants, soldiers, captains, officers, silent named characters (Rannius, Lucillius, Lamprius)

SCENE: *In several parts of the Roman empire*

Notes

A list of characters was first given by Rowe (1709). The present list differs substantially in the grouping of characters' names.

DEMETRIUS *and* PHILO Not named in the dialogue; on stage, they are anonymous Roman soldiers.

DOMITIUS ENOBARBUS The name Ahenobarbus means 'red-beard'.

SILIUS He is addressed by name at 3.1.11, but the speech headings refer simply to *Romaine* and *Rom.*, and the stage directions do not mention him.

SCARUS Perhaps to be identified with the Soldier at 3.7.60 ff., especially since the name 'Scarus' does not occur in the dialogue. M. Æmilius Scaurus, a half-brother of Sextus Pompeius, is not mentioned in Plutarch. See notes at 3.7.60 SD and 3.10.4 SD.

ANTONY AND CLEOPATRA

[1.1] *Enter* DEMETRIUS *and* PHILO

PHILO Nay, but this dotage of our general's
O'erflows the measure. Those his goodly eyes,
That o'er the files and musters of the war
Have glowed like plated Mars, now bend, now turn
The office and devotion of their view
Upon a tawny front. His captain's heart,
Which in the scuffles of great fights hath burst
The buckles on his breast, reneges all temper
And is become the bellows and the fan
To cool a gipsy's lust.

Act 1, Scene 1 1.1] *Actus Primus. Scœna Prima* F

Act 1, Scene 1

Location Egypt, presumably at court. At 1.4.3 we are told that the action set in Egypt takes place in Alexandria. On the use of this opening scene to establish multiple perspectives and competing value-systems, see p. 41 above.

1 **dotage** (1) infatuation, (2) the impaired intellect and judgement of old age.

1 **of our general's** i.e. of Antony's. The double genitive is not uncommon in Shakespeare; compare 1.2.167 below.

2 **measure** i.e. measuring cup or standard. The image appeals to the classical idea of the golden mean (Greek *medan agan*, nothing in excess), but also suggests the abundant overflowing of the Nile. Compare 2.7.16 ff. for allusions to measuring-scales and the idea of liquid excess providing fertility, and see pp. 34–5 above. Philo's name denotes judicious devotion as opposed to eros, passion (Marion Bodwell Smith, *Dualities in Shakespeare*, 1966, p. 207).

3 **files and musters** troops assembled in rows.

4 **like plated Mars** 'like the eyes of Mars when clad in plate armour and ready for the conflict' (Kittredge). 'Mars' could be genitive – Mars' – but other instances in the original Shakespearean texts print 'Marses' or 'Mars his' for the genitive even when, as in *Temp.* 4.1.98, the pronunciation called for is perhaps monosyllabic. On allusions to Mars and Venus as a feature of the hyperbolic mode of the play, see pp. 8 and 36–7 above.

5 'all their looks, as if they had no other duty to which to devote themselves' (Kittredge).

6 **tawny front** dark face (literally, brow) of an Egyptian ('gipsy', 10). Shakespeare equates 'a brow of Egypt' with a dark complexion in *MND* 5.1.11. Cleopatra calls herself 'black' at 1.5.29.

6 **captain's** Synonymous with 'general's' (1) (*OED* Captain *sb* 3).

8 **reneges all temper** renounces or denies all moderation and noble quality of self-restraint. 'Temper' also suggests that Antony's heart has lost the hardness and resiliency of good steel that it possessed in war (*OED* Temper *sb* 3, 5). It is a paradox here that excess of military energy is by implication seen as 'moderation'. 'Reneges' is sounded with a hard *g*.

9 **the bellows and the fan** Bellows are often used to blow up a fire, including (metaphorically) the fire of passion. As makers of wind they also 'cool', as suggested at 10; the image appears to be deliberately paradoxical, like the divers-coloured 'fans' in Enobarbus's description of Cleopatra's attendants 'whose winds did seem / To glow the delicate cheeks which they did cool' (2.2.213–14). Steevens's citation from John Lyly's *Midas* embodies the same paradox: 'methinks Venus and Nature stand with each of them a pair of bellows, the one cooling my low birth, the other kindling my lofty affections' (ed. Bond, 5.2.81–3). Antony's heart is now a bellows pouring forth sighs of love.

10 **gipsy's** Gipsies were widely thought to

Flourish. Enter ANTONY, CLEOPATRA, *her* LADIES [CHARMIAN *and* IRAS, *and*] *the train, with eunuchs fanning her*

Look where they come.
Take but good note, and you shall see in him
The triple pillar of the world transformed
Into a strumpet's fool. Behold and see.

CLEOPATRA If it be love indeed, tell me how much.
ANTONY There's beggary in the love that can be reckoned.
CLEOPATRA I'll set a bourn how far to be beloved.
ANTONY Then must thou needs find out new heaven, new earth.

Enter a MESSENGER

MESSENGER News, my good lord, from Rome.
ANTONY Grates me! The sum.
CLEOPATRA Nay, hear them, Antony.

10 SD *Charmian and Iras, and*] *Jones subst.; not in* F

have come from Egypt and had a reputation for cunning, fortune-telling, and loose behaviour. According to R. C. Hood, medieval laws in England made it a capital offence to be a gipsy, and gipsies were being hanged in York in 1570 for no other reason. Robert Greene speaks of Cleopatra as 'the black Egyptian' (*Ciceronis Amor* (1589), in *Works*, ed. Alexander Grosart, 1881–6, VII, 142), and in *Rom.* Cleopatra is but 'a gipsy', meaning that she is no match for the beauty of Rosaline (2.4.41).

10 SD ***Flourish*** A trumpet fanfare announcing the approach or departure of a person of distinction, as at 2.2.182 SD, 2.7.127 SD, etc.

10 SD ***train*** retinue; perhaps fairly sizeable in order to give the audience its first experience of Egyptian culture and to stress the rhythmic contrast, running throughout the play, between full and spare stages.

12 triple one of three (Latin *triplex*; compare *AWW* 2.1.108). North's Plutarch (984B) describes how the division of the Roman empire among the three triumvirs gave 'all the provinces eastward unto Antonius, and the countries westward unto Caesar, and left Africke unto Lepidus'.

13 fool dupe, plaything.

15 The love that can be counted or calculated is finite and therefore impoverished or valueless. Compare *Rom.* 2.6.32: 'They are but beggars that can count their worth.'

16 I'll...beloved i.e. 'I'll tell you how far your love stretches' (Wilson) or 'I'll establish an appropriate extent for your love of me.'

17 To do that, you must 'set the boundary of my love at a greater distance than the present visible universe affords' (Johnson). Noble, p. 238, cites a number of biblical passages: 'But we look for new heavens and a new earth, according to his promise' (2 Pet. 3.13, in the Genevan version; the Bishops' Bible reads 'heaven', closer to Shakespeare's language here, although, as Noble notes on pp. 75–6, Shakespeare clearly used both versions but tended towards the Genevan in his later years); 'And I saw a new heaven and a new earth' (Rev. 21.1 in the Genevan version); and 'For lo, I will create new heavens and a new earth' (Isa. 65.17 in the Genevan version).

17 SD ***Enter a*** **MESSENGER** The emendation to *Enter an Attendant*, introduced by Capell and followed by some other editors, is unnecessary, despite Cleopatra's urging at 31–4 to 'Call in the messengers'; we understand that other messengers are waiting at the door, as in 1.2.108 ff. Antony gruffly bids this messenger summarise his report at 19, and he would hardly do that if he were speaking to a mere attendant.

19 Grates me! The sum How irritating to be bothered by news from Rome! Be brief about it.

20 them i.e. the news.

Fulvia perchance is angry, or who knows
If the scarce-bearded Caesar have not sent
His powerful mandate to you, 'Do this, or this;
Take in that kingdom and enfranchise that;
Perform't, or else we damn thee.'
ANTONY How, my love?
CLEOPATRA Perchance? Nay, and most like.
You must not stay here longer; your dismission
Is come from Caesar. Therefore hear it, Antony.
Where's Fulvia's process? – Caesar's I would say. Both?
Call in the messengers. As I am Egypt's queen,
Thou blushest, Antony, and that blood of thine
Is Caesar's homager; else so thy cheek pays shame
When shrill-tongued Fulvia scolds. The messengers!
ANTONY Let Rome in Tiber melt and the wide arch

21 **Fulvia** North's Plutarch wryly describes Fulvia, whom Antony had married in 40 BC, as a woman who was 'not so basely minded to spend her time in spinning and housewifery, and was not contented to master her husband at home, but would also rule him in his office abroad, and command him' (975A). Cleopatra taunts Antony with being henpecked.

22 **scarce-bearded** In 40 BC, Antony was about 43 and Caesar 23; compare 3.13.17, 'the boy Caesar'. The simple disparity of age is elaborated during the course of the play to suggest irreconcilable modes of historical and emotional experience – almost a value-system in itself.

24 **Take in** Conquer, occupy.

24 **enfranchise** set free.

25 **we** The 'royal we' implies royal authority in addressing one who owes duty. Cleopatra's sarcasm simultaneously accuses Caesar of presumption and Antony of dependency.

25 **damn** condemn to death. The word recalls the proscriptions of *JC* 4.1.6: 'Look, with a spot I damn him.'

26 **How** What's that you say?

27 Cleopatra repeats her own word from 21 only to revise her estimate: 'Perchance, did I say? Nay, almost certainly.'

28 **dismission** (1) order to depart (as in *Cym.* 2.3.52), or (2) discharge from service (*OED* sv 3b).

29 **Therefore** 'Even in this word, there is a taunt' (Furness).

30 **process** summons; a writ ordering a person to appear in court.

30 **Both?** Having made, or pretended to make, a slip of the tongue, saying 'Fulvia's' when she meant 'Caesar's', Cleopatra adds wryly that *both* persons might well have reason to recall Antony to Rome (Jones).

33 **homager** vassal. Antony's blush confesses the truth of Cleopatra's barb, that Antony must obey Caesar's mandate.

33 **else so** or else. The only other possible explanation of Antony's blush, Cleopatra taunts, is that he is acknowledging the forcibleness of his wife's scolding.

35 **Let...melt** Compare Cleopatra's 'Melt Egypt into Nile' at 2.5.79 below. On the play's use of hyperbole, and its recurrent image of a relation between the solid and the amorphous, the shaped and the shapeless, see pp. 34–40 above. Antony is not proclaiming indifference to public life; as the rest of his speech shows, the love he seeks is itself a form of public life (Paul Cantor, *Shakespeare's Rome*, 1976, pp. 185–6).

35 **arch** The Roman empire is pictured as a vast arch reaching across its territories with the city as the keystone, or an arch supporting a structure as in the vault of a ceiling, or 'a fabric standing on pillars' (Johnson). Perhaps a triumphal arch is imagined, representing the city or realm, as it often did in pageants and civic festivities (Jones). But the suggestion of universal chaos and apocalypse may also be indebted to the Homilies 'Of Order and Obedience' and 'For Rogation Week' in the Book of Common Prayer, as invoked in Richard Hooker's eloquent appeal to the order of Nature: 'if the frame of that heavenly arch erected over our heads should loosen and dissolve itself...' (*Laws of Ecclesiastical Polity* (1594), quoted by Milward, p. 137).

Of the ranged empire fall! Here is my space.
Kingdoms are clay; our dungy earth alike
Feeds beast as man. The nobleness of life
Is to do thus, when such a mutual pair
And such a twain can do't – in which I bind,
On pain of punishment, the world to weet
We stand up peerless.

CLEOPATRA Excellent falsehood!
Why did he marry Fulvia, and not love her?
I'll seem the fool I am not. Antony
Will be himself.

ANTONY But stirred by Cleopatra.

41 On] F (One) 43 Why did] F; Why, did *conj. Ridley*

36 ranged (1) 'set in line, ranked' (*OED* sv *ppl adj*[1]); (2) 'orderly ranged; whose parts are now entire and distinct, like a number of well-built edifices' (Capell, *Notes*, I, 26); perhaps (3) with a sense of wide extent. Reuben Brower, *Hero and Saint*, 1971, p. 321, suggests that the word can also refer 'to the "ranges" (III.xiii.5) or files of Roman military formations or the "ranging" lines of buildings that compose the "wide arch"'.

36 my space space enough for me. (Antony may embrace, or gesture towards, Cleopatra.) Shakespeare may be recalling Marlowe and Nashe's *Dido, Queen of Carthage*: 'Stout love, in mine arms make thy Italy' (3.4.57), and 'This is the harbour that Aeneas seeks' (4.4.59; see Harrison, pp. 57–63).

37 Kingdoms are clay A biblical commonplace, as in Dan. 2.42: 'And as the toes of the feet were part of iron and part of clay, so shall the kingdom be partly strong and partly broken' (cited by Noble, p. 238). For 'Dungy earth', see Ps. 83.10 and Jer. 8.2 and 16.4 (Shaheen).

39 thus The stage direction inserted by Pope and many editors calling for an embrace or kiss offers a perfectly plausible option for the actor, as at 36 above, but Antony's 'thus' may refer more generally to the lovers' way of life and could be accompanied by an expansive sweep of the hand.

39 mutual equal in passion, well matched.

40–2 in which...peerless with respect to which love I compel the world, under penalty of punishment, to acknowledge that we are without peer. 'Weet' = 'know'; 'We stand up' = 'we declare ourselves'. The language is that of a public proclamation or proud challenge to the audience (Jones, Wilson), though ironically it serves in Antony's speech as an invitation to share a public irresponsibility.

43 and not if he did not; i.e. either way Antony is a hypocrite, having married Fulvia without love or having loved her whilst professing to love only Cleopatra.

44 I'll...not 'I'll play the trusting fool who believes your perjuries, though in fact I know better'; or, perhaps, a scornful protest – 'If I actually believed your professions, I'd look like the fool I'm certainly not.' Both are possible, and both may be involved. Performance would decide whether she still wants to resist Antony here or is simply resigned to the fact of him without illusions.

44–5 Antony...himself A commonplace expression, often suggesting in Shakespeare the idea of living up to an ideal image of royal or noble self-expression or command, as in King Henry IV's 'I will from henceforth rather be myself, / Mighty and to be fear'd' (*1H4* 1.3.5–6), and Prince Henry's later avowal to his father, 'I shall hereafter, my thrice-gracious lord, / Be more myself' (3.2.92–3). See Dent O64.1, and 3.10.26 below. Cleopatra speaks in double entendre, however, for her phrase can also mean 'Antony will be the fool he really is' or 'will be the deceiver he always is'.

45 But...Cleopatra Perhaps Antony parries her double entendres with double meaning of his own: (1) 'I will be my noble self only if inspired by Cleopatra', (2) 'I will play the fool if you like, but it's because I am stirred to my very soul by Cleopatra.' Or Antony may suggest 'I won't or can't change my nature, but my nature is susceptible to your influence.' Demetrius and Philo may hear something else: 'Antony will be himself unless stirred to base emotion by Cleopatra.'

Now, for the love of Love and her soft hours,
Let's not confound the time with conference harsh;
There's not a minute of our lives should stretch
Without some pleasure now. What sport tonight?

CLEOPATRA Hear the ambassadors.

ANTONY Fie, wrangling queen,
Whom everything becomes, to chide, to laugh,
To weep, whose every passion fully strives
To make itself, in thee, fair and admired!
No messenger but thine, and all alone
Tonight we'll wander through the streets and note
The qualities of people. Come, my queen,
Last night you did desire it. [*To the Messenger*] Speak not to us.

Exeunt [*Antony and Cleopatra*] *with the train,* [*Charmian, Iras, and eunuchs*]

DEMETRIUS Is Caesar with Antonius prized so slight?

PHILO Sir, sometimes when he is not Antony
He comes too short of that great property
Which still should go with Antony.

DEMETRIUS I am full sorry
That he approves the common liar, who
Thus speaks of him at Rome; but I will hope
Of better deeds tomorrow. Rest you happy!

Exeunt

49 now] F; new *Warburton* 52 whose] F2; who F; how *Ridley* 57 SD.1 *To the Messenger*] *Wilson subst.; not in* F 57 SD.2 *Antony and Cleopatra*] *Capell; not in* F 57 SD.3 *Charmian, Iras, and eunuchs*] *This edn; not in* F

47 **confound** spoil, waste; as at 1.4.28.

47 **conference** conversation.

48 **should stretch** that should be extended, prolonged.

50 **ambassadors** i.e. the messengers, who were not simply errand boys (see *OED* Messenger 1). Cleopatra is twitting Antony again with her 'exasperating parrot-cry' (Furness).

52 ***whose** This F2 reading is generally accepted in place of F's 'who', but F2 has no authority and Ridley proposes instead 'how' as graphically a little easier.

52 **passion** emotional mood. Antony is a conscious connoisseur or epicure of the range of her emotional behaviour; he admires, evokes, and sanctions her variety of moods. Compare 1.3.10.

54 **No messenger but thine** I will receive no messenger who does not come from you.

55 **wander through the streets** Compare North's Plutarch, 983C, for their further regular indulgence in this 'sport'.

56 **qualities** characteristics.

58 **with** by.

59 **is not Antony** fails to live up to his military greatness; compare 44–5 above.

60 **property** distinctive quality.

61 **still** always.

61 **Antony** i.e. the name and identity of Antony. This play is much occupied with the question of the relation between the names people have made for themselves and go by and their more essential selves.

62 **approves...liar** proves common gossip (usually malicious) in his case to be true indeed.

64 **Of** For.

64 **Rest you happy** May the gods prosper you.

[1.2] *Enter* ENOBARBUS, *Lamprius, a* SOOTHSAYER, *Rannius, Lucillius,* CHARMIAN, IRAS, MARDIAN *the Eunuch, and* ALEXAS

CHARMIAN Lord Alexas, sweet Alexas, most anything Alexas, almost most absolute Alexas, where's the soothsayer that you praised so to th'queen? O, that I knew this husband, which you say must charge his horns with garlands!
ALEXAS Soothsayer!
SOOTHSAYER Your will?
CHARMIAN Is this the man? – Is't you, sir, that know things?
SOOTHSAYER In nature's infinite book of secrecy
A little I can read.
ALEXAS [*To Charmian*] Show him your hand.
ENOBARBUS Bring in the banquet quickly; wine enough
Cleopatra's health to drink.
CHARMIAN [*Giving her hand to the Soothsayer*] Good sir, give me good fortune.
SOOTHSAYER I make not, but foresee.

Act 1, Scene 2 1.2] *Pope; no scene division in* F 1 Lord] *Johnson;* L. F 4 charge] *Theobald, conj. Warburton and Southern MS., cited in Cam.;* change F 9 SD] *Oxford; not in* F 12 SD] *Bevington subst.; not in* F

Act 1, Scene 2

Location As in Scene 1. According to Antony's later account at 2.2.83, it is 'next day' when he talks soberly to the messenger from Rome.

0 SD *Lamprius* Lamprius, Rannius, and Lucillius, who are Romans by their names and probably by their costume, are grouped in this scene with Enobarbus and visually contrasted with the four Egyptians present, but they are silent (unless Lamprius is the Soothsayer; the F direction is not clear on this point) and remain unidentified to the audience. Mardian too is mute in this scene but speaks later. Plutarch gives the name of 'Lampryas' to his grandfather and cites him as his authority for tales of wild banqueting in Egypt (982D) – a point of some relevance perhaps to the present banqueting. 'Lucillius' is a name in *JC* and *Tim.*; 'Rannius' appears nowhere in Shakespeare or his sources. The Soothsayer is not named 'Lamprius' in 2.3, where he appears eager to return to Egypt, but in this present scene he is not of the Egyptian party; he is named with the Romans, and must be summoned by the Egyptians at 2–6.

0 SD ALEXAS North's Plutarch reports that 'Alexas Laodician' was 'one of Cleopatra's ministers' who worked to win Antony to Cleopatra and to leave his wife Octavia, in return for which Alexas 'was in greater credit with him than any other Grecian' (1004E). Charmian's opening words reflect this status.

1 most anything Charmian speaks hyperbolically as though she cannot think of the right words to praise Alexas (Kittredge).

2 absolute perfect.

3–4 *this husband...garlands Evidently Alexas has been telling Charmian of a husband to be promised her by the Soothsayer, one who will wear the cuckold's horns of a deceived husband gaily decorated with flowers, like a sacrificial beast; he will be 'the champion cuckold of all Egypt' (Wilson). 'Charge' means 'lay as a load upon', but the F reading, 'change', is also possible in the sense of 'modify', 'alter'. (The expected meaning of 'change' in this construction, 'exchange', works against the F reading.) As Oxford notes, citing Sisson, *New Readings*, the same error may occur in *JC* 4.2.7.

8–9 In nature's...read The Soothsayer's use of verse throughout sets his manner in contrast to the frivolities of the others.

10–11 Bring in...drink Enobarbus may call out to servants within (i.e. offstage), or they may enter to receive his orders. The 'banquet', usually a light repast or dessert of wine, fruit, and sweetmeats, is for those present while Antony and Cleopatra entertain themselves more privately.

CHARMIAN Pray then, foresee me one.
SOOTHSAYER You shall be yet far fairer than you are.
CHARMIAN He means in flesh.
IRAS No, you shall paint when you are old.
CHARMIAN Wrinkles forbid!
ALEXAS Vex not his prescience. Be attentive.
CHARMIAN Hush!
SOOTHSAYER You shall be more beloving than beloved.
CHARMIAN I had rather heat my liver with drinking.
ALEXAS Nay, hear him.
CHARMIAN Good now, some excellent fortune! Let me be married to three kings in a forenoon and widow them all. Let me have a child at fifty, to whom Herod of Jewry may do homage. Find me to marry me with Octavius Caesar, and companion me with my mistress.
SOOTHSAYER You shall outlive the lady whom you serve.
CHARMIAN O, excellent! I love long life better than figs.

20 prescience] F; patience F3

16 far fairer The Soothsayer means 'much more fortunate', though Charmian (perhaps deliberately) mistakes him; see next note. The prophecy is fulfilled in an unforeseen sense by Charmian's unspotted, noble death.

17 in flesh plump, in good condition. Compare *AYLI* 1.1.12: 'they [the horses] are fair with their feeding'. Charmian glosses 'fairer' to apply to the body rather than to fortune.

18 No, the Soothsayer means you will hide your wrinkles of ageing with cosmetics.

20 his prescience Perhaps a mock title, like 'his worship' (Delius). The iambic pentameter regularity of this line is perhaps a parody of the incantatory gravity of the Soothsayer's lines, beginning 'You shall...You shall'.

22 more beloving than beloved Another enigmatic prediction of Charmian's death as an act of love for her mistress, one that will deprive her of the earthly love she admires in this scene.

23 heat...drinking As the organ where blood was thought to be manufactured, the liver was regarded as the seat of passionate desire and of courage. Charmian says she would rather heat her liver with drinking than with the unrequited love the Soothsayer appears to be promising, even if it might spoil her complexion.

25 Good now Come on, now.

26–7 three kings...Herod of Jewry The glancing reference to the birth of Christ, with the journey of the three Magi and the tyrannical rage of Herod the Great, King of Judaea (as portrayed in medieval religious drama), accentuates the ironic contrast between Charmian's vivacious hedonism and the sacred story to which she unconsciously alludes. Herod is portrayed in medieval drama as obsessed with the birth of a young king to whom he might owe homage; compare Alexas's picture of him at 3.3.3. For the biblical account, see Matt. 2.1–12. Cleopatra made an attempt to fascinate Herod the Great, who was her contemporary. Charmian's version of the holy story suits her temperament: a child at fifty would be a more attractive miracle for her than immaculate conception.

27 Find me i.e. in my palm. On 'me', compare 61 below and n.

28–9 companion...mistress make me equal with Cleopatra in having a husband of distinction.

30 This enigmatic prophecy of death sounds to Charmian like a promise of long life.

31 figs Figs are erotically suggestive, because of their genital appearance, and also because the fig-tree is 'more fruitful than other trees, for it beareth fruit three or four times in one year, and while one ripeth, another springeth anon...Figs do away rivels [i.e. wrinkles] of old men' (*Bartholomew* [*Berthelet*] (1535), Book XVII, para. 61, cited in Seager, p. 109). Compare the sexually allusive imprecation, 'fig me!' as in *2H4* 5.3.118. Among the other anticipations in this scene of the death of the women in Act 5, 'figs' anticipates the Clown and his basket of asps and fig-leaves.

SOOTHSAYER You have seen and proved a fairer former fortune
Than that which is to approach.

CHARMIAN Then belike my children shall have no names. Prithee, how many boys and wenches must I have?

SOOTHSAYER If every of your wishes had a womb,
And fertile every wish, a million.

CHARMIAN Out, fool! I forgive thee for a witch.

ALEXAS You think none but your sheets are privy to your wishes.

CHARMIAN Nay, come, tell Iras hers.

ALEXAS We'll know all our fortunes.

ENOBARBUS Mine, and most of our fortunes tonight, shall be – drunk to bed.

IRAS [*Giving her hand to the Soothsayer*] There's a palm presages chastity, if nothing else.

CHARMIAN E'en as the o'erflowing Nilus presageth famine.

IRAS Go, you wild bedfellow, you cannot soothsay.

CHARMIAN Nay, if an oily palm be not a fruitful prognostication, I cannot scratch mine ear. Prithee tell her but a workaday fortune.

SOOTHSAYER Your fortunes are alike.

IRAS But how, but how? Give me particulars.

SOOTHSAYER I have said.

IRAS Am I not an inch of fortune better than she?

37 fertile] *Theobald, conj. Warburton;* fore-tell F 44 SD] *Wilson subst.; not in* F 49 workaday] F (worky day)

32–3 You have...approach Again, the prophecy of death is misunderstood.

32 proved experienced.

34 belike probably.

34 have no names be illegitimate. Charmian jokes that her misfortune will be to remain unmarried but fecund.

35 wenches girls.

37 *fertile Wilson thinks that Shakespeare's 'fertill' may have been misread as 'fortell', the F reading (fore-tell); see collation.

38 Out An expression here of comic indignation.

38 I forgive...witch I absolve you of any accusation of witchcraft. ('For' means 'in the capacity of'.) Charmian either means 'I'll answer for your being no witch, if this is a sample of your skill' (Arden), or else laughingly forgives the free speech of one whose calling gives him licence. A witch could be male.

39 privy to in on the secret of. Alexas laughs that they all know about Charmian's secret longings.

41 all Emphatic: '*all* of us' (Kittredge).

46 Said ironically; the overflowing Nile is an image of abundance here and at 2.7.16–22.

47 wild wanton.

48 oily palm A sweaty or moist palm indicated a sensual disposition. To Othello, Desdemona's 'moist' hand 'argues fruitfulness and liberal heart; / Hot, hot, and moist' (*Oth.* 3.4.38–9). In *Venus and Adonis* a 'sweating palm' is 'president [precedent] of pith and livelihood' (25–6).

48 fruitful prognostication harbinger of fertility.

48–9 I cannot...ear I'm no true woman. To have itching ears is to enjoy the traditional female relish for hearing novelties (see *OED* Ear *sb*[1] 3d, citing 2 Tim. 4.3).

49 workaday ordinary; the opposite of 'holiday'.

52 I have said A set phrase suggesting emphasis and finality: 'I have no more to say on the subject' (Dent S118.1). Compare 2.6.106 and 3.2.34.

CHARMIAN Well, if you were but an inch of fortune better than I, where would you choose it?

IRAS Not in my husband's nose.

CHARMIAN Our worser thoughts heavens mend! Alexas – come, his fortune, his fortune! O, let him marry a woman that cannot go, sweet Isis, I beseech thee, and let her die too, and give him a worse, and let worse follow worse till the worst of all follow him laughing to his grave, fiftyfold a cuckold! Good Isis, hear me this prayer, though thou deny me a matter of more weight; good Isis, I beseech thee!

IRAS Amen, dear goddess, hear that prayer of the people! For, as it is a heart-breaking to see a handsome man loose-wived, so it is a deadly sorrow to behold a foul knave uncuckolded. Therefore, dear Isis, keep decorum, and fortune him accordingly!

CHARMIAN Amen.

ALEXAS Lo now, if it lay in their hands to make me a cuckold, they would make themselves whores but they'd do't.

Enter CLEOPATRA

ENOBARBUS Hush, here comes Antony.

57 Alexas – come] *Theobald; Alexas.* Come F (*treating / Alexas / as* SH)

54–6 inch...husband's nose Iras bawdily suggests that she can think of a fitter place for her husband to be thus endowed. At 1.3.40, Cleopatra says to Antony, 'I would I had thy inches.'

57 Our...mend May heaven purify our dirty minds! Charmian affects to be piously shocked (Wilson).

57 *Alexas – come See collation. Compositor B, evidently confused by the use of italics for proper names in the text as well as in speech headings, and barely having room for the word *Alexas* in his line after 'mend', began a new line with it and treated it as a speech heading, using, however, the full spelling instead of the usual abbreviation *Alex.* (Ridley).

58 cannot go (1) is lame, (2) cannot be pregnant (*OED* Go *v* 7; compare *LLL* 5.2.672–3: 'she is gone; she is two months on her way'), (3) is sexually incapable.

59 Isis The principal goddess of ancient Egypt, sister and wife of Osiris, identified with the moon and fertility. North's Plutarch mentions her (996C).

59–60 a worse i.e. one worse in another kind and in degree, one who will cuckold him.

61–2 hear me...weight Bawdy play continues: 'Give me this, even if you deny me the lovers I crave.' Compare 'weight' at 1.5.22.

61 hear me hear. 'Me', the so-called ethical dative, is colloquial, with some residual meaning of 'in my case', 'on my behalf'.

64 prayer of the people i.e. prayer of all (Egyptian) people assembled for worship (of Isis). A liturgical phrase (still part of the Book of Common Prayer), used here by Iras as mock piety.

66 foul ugly.

67 keep decorum observe a due fitness, use the gods' justice (in dealing with Alexas as a man without merit).

69–70 they would...do't they would even make themselves whores to cuckold me; they would stop at nothing. Alexas is also returning the insult, saying by implication 'I wouldn't touch either of them'; he will not let matters 'lay in their hands' (69).

71 here comes Antony Some editions (e.g. Arden) delay Cleopatra's entrance until after this remark, but Enobarbus may react impulsively to the commotion of an entrance before realising who has made it, or (as Furness suggests) he may speak with a 'veiled sneer', knowing well enough who it is. Jones argues that the mistake 'suggests Antony's loss of his former public identity'.

CHARMIAN Not he. The queen.
CLEOPATRA Saw you my lord?
ENOBARBUS No, lady.
CLEOPATRA Was he not here?
CHARMIAN No, madam.
CLEOPATRA He was disposed to mirth, but on the sudden
A Roman thought hath struck him. Enobarbus!
ENOBARBUS Madam?
CLEOPATRA Seek him and bring him hither. Where's Alexas?
ALEXAS Here at your service. – My lord approaches.

Enter ANTONY, *with a* MESSENGER

CLEOPATRA We will not look upon him. Go with us.
Exeunt [all but Antony and the Messenger]
MESSENGER Fulvia thy wife first came into the field.
ANTONY Against my brother Lucius?
MESSENGER Ay;
But soon that war had end, and the time's state
Made friends of them, jointing their force 'gainst Caesar,
Whose better issue in the war from Italy
Upon the first encounter drave them.
ANTONY Well, what worst?
MESSENGER The nature of bad news infects the teller.

73 Saw you my lord?] F2; Saue you, my Lord. F 80 Alexas] F2; *Alexias* F 81 SD MESSENGER] F; *Messenger and attendants / Rowe* 82 SD *all...Messenger*] *Capell subst.; not in* F

73 ***Saw** The F reading, 'Saue', is an easy error for 'Saw'. Compositor B mistakenly read the conventional greeting, 'Saue you, my lord', though it is plainly inappropriate here since it provides no question for Enobarbus to answer.

78 **A Roman thought** A thought worthy of Roman virtue, hence 'serious'; a thought of Rome. See pp. 16–25 above on competing sets of values between Rome and Egypt; it's interesting that Cleopatra recognises and employs this value-term.

80 **bring him hither** Enobarbus may start to exit, but then be spared further labour by Antony's arrival.

82 **We** Plural for singular; the style used by reigning monarchs. Cleopatra has been seeking Antony, but evidently sizes up the situation and concludes that the presence of the Messenger is unfavourable for her purposes. It is important that she see Antony (as the F placing of the stage direction indicates) before she sweeps out.

83–99 **Fulvia...Ionia** North's Plutarch provides the details of this report received by Antony in Alexandria: the falling out of Fulvia and Lucius, their joining forces against Octavius Caesar, and Labienus's success in Asia (983E). The verbal borrowings are especially evident in the place names and other proper names.

83 **field** battlefield.

86 **the time's state** the political and military necessities of the moment (like the practical considerations that later unite Antony and Caesar against Pompey).

87 **jointing** uniting.

88–89 **Whose...drave them** Whose better success in the war drove them (Fulvia and Lucius) from Italy upon the very first encounter.

91 **infects the teller** i.e. makes the messenger seem hateful, like the news he bears. Compare 2.5.86–7 – 'Though it be honest, it is never good / To bring bad news' – and the rest of that scene.

ANTONY When it concerns the fool or coward. On.
Things that are past are done, with me. 'Tis thus:
Who tells me true, though in his tale lie death,
I hear him as he flattered.
MESSENGER Labienus –
This is stiff news – hath with his Parthian force
Extended Asia; from Euphrates
His conquering banner shook, from Syria
To Lydia and to Ionia,
Whilst –
ANTONY Antony, thou wouldst say.
MESSENGER O, my lord!
ANTONY Speak to me home; mince not the general tongue.
Name Cleopatra as she is called in Rome;
Rail thou in Fulvia's phrase, and taunt my faults
With such full licence as both truth and malice
Have power to utter. O, then we bring forth weeds
When our quick minds lie still, and our ills told us
Is as our earing. Fare thee well awhile.
MESSENGER At your noble pleasure. *Exit Messenger*

Enter another MESSENGER[*; a third attends at the door*]

93 done, with me. 'Tis thus] F; done. With me, 'tis thus *Wilson* 106 minds] *Hanmer, conj. Warburton;* windes F 108 SD.1 *Exit Messenger*] F; *omitted Rowe* 108 SD.2 *a third attends at the door*] *This edn; not in* F

93 **Things...with me** A stoic acceptance that 'What's done is done', not, as is sometimes assumed, a rejection of past irresponsibility.

95 **as** as if.

95 **Labienus** Quintus Labienus, a supporter of Brutus and Cassius on the republican side of the civil wars, was sent by them to seek the aid of Parthia against Antony and Octavius. He is now overrunning the Roman provinces in the Middle East with a Parthian army under Pacorus, son of Orodes, and remains a threat until defeated by Antony's general Ventidius (3.1). See North's Plutarch, 985C. Parthia is in the area of modern-day Iraq and Iran.

97 **Extended** Seized upon; a legal term signifying the satisfaction of debt by seizure.

97 **Euphrates** Accented on the first syllable. ('Asia' is trisyllabic.)

101 **home** directly, bluntly.

101 **mince...tongue** do not mince words in reporting the common talk.

103 **Rail...phrase** Scold me as Fulvia would.

105–6 ***we bring...still** Proverbial (Dent W241); compare *2H4* 4.4.54: 'Most subject is the fattest soil to weeds.' The proverb tends to support Warburton's emendation of F's 'windes' to 'minds', correcting an easy minim error.

106 **quick** 'living, lively, – and so, "fertile"' (Kittredge).

106 **still** 'idle (like a fallow field). Our minds, like the earth, must always bring forth *something*. When they lie untilled, they produce weeds' (Kittredge). An interesting shift to a larger sense of fertility than that with which the scene opened.

106–7 **our ills...earing** being told our faults is like a ploughing to root out the weeds and prepare the ground for a true crop.

108 SD.2 ***Enter another*** **MESSENGER** This edition follows the Folio text for this entrance and for the speech headings of the messengers to 118, assuming however that the speech heading *1. Mes.* at 110 must mean the messenger now entering and not the messenger (unnumbered) who enters at 81 SD with Antony and exits at 108. Shake-

ANTONY From Sicyon, ho, the news! Speak there.
2 MESSENGER The man from Sicyon – is there such an one?
3 MESSENGER He stays upon your will.
ANTONY Let him appear. –
[*Exeunt Second and Third Messengers*]
These strong Egyptian fetters I must break,
Or lose myself in dotage.

Enter [a fourth] MESSENGER, *with a letter*

What are you?
4 MESSENGER Fulvia thy wife is dead.
ANTONY Where died she?
4 MESSENGER In Sicyon.
Her length of sickness, with what else more serious
Importeth thee to know, this bears.
[*He gives a letter*]
ANTONY Forbear me.
[*Exit Messenger*]
There's a great spirit gone! Thus did I desire it.

109 Sicyon, ho, the news!] *Collier*[3]; *Scicion* how the newes? F **110** SH 2 MESSENGER] *This edn; 1. Mes.* F; *Mes. / Rowe; 1 Attendant / Wilson* **111** SH 3 MESSENGER] *This edn; 2. Mes.* F; *Attend. / Rowe; 2 Attendant / Wilson* **111** SD] *Bevington*[2]; *not in* F **113** SD *a fourth*] *This edn; another* F **114** SH 4 MESSENGER] *This edn; 3. Mes.* F; *2 Mes. / Rowe* **116** SH 4 MESSENGER] *This edn; Mes.* F **118** SD.1 *He gives a letter*] *Johnson subst.; not in* F **118** SD.2 *Exit Messenger*] *Theobald subst.; not in* F

speare probably began numbering the messengers at this point in his manuscript rather than at 81, and so those designated as *1.*, *2.*, and *3. Mes.* are in effect the second, third, and fourth such persons to appear in this scene. Rowe and many subsequent editors (see collation) omit the stage direction at 108 and assign the speeches at 110 and 111 to attendants. As at 1.1.17 SD (see n.), the reassignment of speeches is unnecessary, and it ignores the Folio's plain intention that another messenger enter at 108. Antony, having spoken with one of several messengers waiting to report to him from various parts of the empire, wishes now to hear from Sicyon about Fulvia. He asks for this news from the entering messenger who, not in fact being from Sicyon, calls out in some confusion to those at the door if there is such a messenger waiting. Another messenger waiting at the door, knowing there to be such a one, answers in the affirmative, and the right man is summoned.

109 Sicyon A town in the Greek Peloponnesus (F 'Scicion') where Antony left Fulvia in 40 BC.

109 *ho The F reading, 'how', can be defended, but it is also plausibly regarded as a spelling variant of 'ho', and is not uncommon as a Shakespearean spelling; see 4.14.104.

111 stays upon your will awaits your pleasure, your orders.

112–13 These...dotage Aeneas expresses himself similarly in Marlowe and Nashe's *Dido, Queen of Carthage*: 'I may not dure this female drudgery' (4.3.55).

114 In North's Plutarch, this news reaches Antony considerably later than the report of war involving Lucius, Fulvia, and Octavius; in the interim, Antony undertakes a campaign against the Parthians (983E–984A). Shakespeare condenses his historical source.

118 Importeth Concerns.

118 Forbear me Leave me.

119–24 This remarkable revaluation testifies to Antony's sensitivity to and even obsession with other perspectives and sets of values. Compare Cleopatra in a similar vein at 77–8.

What our contempts doth often hurl from us,
We wish it ours again. The present pleasure,
By revolution lowering, does become
The opposite of itself. She's good, being gone;
The hand could pluck her back that shoved her on.
I must from this enchanting queen break off.
Ten thousand harms more than the ills I know
My idleness doth hatch. – How now, Enobarbus!

Enter ENOBARBUS

ENOBARBUS What's your pleasure, sir?

ANTONY I must with haste from hence.

ENOBARBUS Why then we kill all our women. We see how mortal an unkindness is to them; if they suffer our departure, death's the word.

ANTONY I must be gone.

ENOBARBUS Under a compelling occasion, let women die. It were

120 contempts doth] F; contempts doe F2; contempt doth *Staunton* **127** How now, Enobarbus!] *Placed as in Dyce; follows* SD *in* F; Ho now! Enobarbus *Collier*[3] **134** a compelling] *Rowe;* a compelling an F; as compelling an *anon. conj. in Cam.*; so compelling an *Nicholson, cited in Cam.*

120–1 What. . .again A proverbial reflection on the perversity of valuing something only when we have lost it or thrown it away (Dent W924 and G298.1). The sentiment recurs at 123 and 178–80 and in Caesar's observation at 1.4.41–4 that a political leader is never appreciated until he is gone. Antony and Caesar share this perception and are perhaps haunted by it as part of the complex problem of true recognition and valuation. The idea is common in the Roman plays; see 180 n. on *JC*, and compare *Cor.* 4.7.48–53.

122 By revolution lowering Being lowered in our estimation in due course of time (*OED* Revolution 2). 'Revolution' suggests the turning of a wheel, such as Fortune's wheel, as well as the alterations in our opinion over time. What is pleasure to us at one moment is pain later on, and vice versa. The language here is perhaps reminiscent of Daniel's *Cleopatra*: 'Thus doth the everchanging course of things / Run a perpetual circle, ever turning' (3.1; 555–6).

124 could would be willing to.

125 enchanting i.e. Circe-like (Wilson); holding men in her power as though by enchantment. This is part of the general association of Egypt with powerful and mysterious forces.

126–7 Ten thousand. . .hatch Idleness is proverbially the nurse of all ill; Dent I13. It probably has the further connotation here of 'lasciviousness' (Jones). It also reproduces, with a different metaphor from the natural world, the thought of 105–6 above.

127 *How now, Enobarbus This should probably be regarded as an exclamation of summons and thus should be placed as it is here before the entry of Enobarbus, but the F arrangement of placing the entry first (see collation) is also possible. Enobarbus is usually close at hand to Antony and might be expected to know that his presence is desired now that Antony has had a chance to consult with the messengers.

132 word watchword, motto.

134 *a compelling Some emendation of F's 'a compelling an' is necessary, and Rowe's suggestion, followed here, is often used by editors, but 'as compelling an' and 'so compelling an' are also plausible; see collation. Wilson regards this as a Shakespearean error in fair-copying his own manuscript (p. 125), but another copyist could have made the error as easily.

pity to cast them away for nothing, though between them and a great cause they should be esteemed nothing. Cleopatra, catching but the least noise of this, dies instantly; I have seen her die twenty times upon far poorer moment. I do think there is mettle in death, which commits some loving act upon her, she hath such a celerity in dying.

ANTONY She is cunning past man's thought.

ENOBARBUS Alack, sir, no, her passions are made of nothing but the finest part of pure love. We cannot call her winds and waters sighs and tears; they are greater storms and tempests than almanacs can report. This cannot be cunning in her; if it be, she makes a shower of rain as well as Jove.

ANTONY Would I had never seen her!

ENOBARBUS O sir, you had then left unseen a wonderful piece of work, which not to have been blest withal would have discredited your travel.

ANTONY Fulvia is dead.

ENOBARBUS Sir?

ANTONY Fulvia is dead.

ENOBARBUS Fulvia?

ANTONY Dead.

ENOBARBUS Why, sir, give the gods a thankful sacrifice. When it pleaseth their deities to take the wife of a man from him, it shows to man the tailors of the earth; comforting therein, that when old

150 travel] F (Trauaile)

137 noise rumour.

137 dies instantly The added bawdy suggestion of achieving sexual consummation is reinforced by Enobarbus's repeatedly playing upon the idea in this speech, and especially by the image of death as committing 'some loving act upon her' (139). In this erotic sense, Cleopatra 'dies' swiftly and often. The wordplay continues in Enobarbus's jest about her 'celerity in dying' (140).

138 upon far poorer moment on a matter of much less weight.

138 mettle vigour, spunk. Enobarbus plays on 'dying' in the sense of completing the sexual act. Wilson notes tragic irony in the image of Cleopatra flying to the embrace of Death as to that of a lover; compare 5.2.289–90.

143–4 We cannot...tears i.e. the words 'sighs' and 'tears' are inadequate to describe her passionate gusts and her flood of weeping.

145–6 Enobarbus denies Antony's allegation in 141 that Cleopatra is 'cunning', i.e. deceitful, but then allows her 'cunning' in the sense of skill, artifice; if she 'makes' her sighs and tears as things of artifice, we must allow her a skill in rain-making equal to Jupiter's (Kittredge). As Wilson notes, the tribute to Cleopatra is genuine despite the mockery.

146 Jove Jupiter (from *Jovis-pater*), god of the sky, of lightning and thunder, etc.

149–50 discredited your travel 'proved you a bad sight-seer' (Arden). Enobarbus is probably invoking a satiric literary tradition at the expense of contemporary fashion for travel and the notoriety of extravagant travellers' tales.

157 their deities An honorific title, like 'his worship'; compare 'his prescience' at 20.

158 the tailors In Enobarbus's metaphor, the gods are tailors because they repair loss or damage, fashioning a new wife to replace a worn-out one just as tailors fashion new garments.

158 therein in this respect.

robes are worn out, there are members to make new. If there were no more women but Fulvia, then had you indeed a cut, and the case to be lamented. This grief is crowned with consolation; your old smock brings forth a new petticoat, and indeed the tears live in an onion that should water this sorrow.

ANTONY The business she hath broachèd in the state
Cannot endure my absence.

ENOBARBUS And the business you have broached here cannot be without you, especially that of Cleopatra's, which wholly depends on your abode.

ANTONY No more light answers. Let our officers
Have notice what we purpose. I shall break
The cause of our expedience to the queen
And get her leave to part. For not alone
The death of Fulvia, with more urgent touches,
Do strongly speak to us, but the letters too

172 leave] *Pope;* loue F

159 members The bawdy play on 'sexual members' is followed up by double entendres on 'cut' and 'case' in 160–1, both suggesting the female sexual organs. See also 166 n. on 'business' and 'broached'. Tailors are associated with bawdry, e.g. in *Temp.* 2.2.53: 'Yet a tailor might scratch her where e'er she did itch'; and *2H4* 3.2.160 ff.: 'Prick the woman's tailor.'

160 no...Fulvia The notion of having only one woman to choose from in the whole world is proverbial; compare Dent W631.

160 cut blow; but with sexual double meaning as indicated in 159 n. above. In the light of the metaphor of fashioning new clothes, there may also be a play on 'shape' or 'fashion', as in *H8* 1.3.14: 'Their clothes are after such a pagan cut to't' (Thistelton, p. 9).

162 your old...petticoat Compare the proverbial formula, 'his old brass (etc.) will buy (make) you a new pan (etc.)' (Dent B607), and *Wiv.* 1.3.17: 'An old cloak makes a new jerkin.' The antithesis between 'old smock' and 'new petticoat' has several shades of meaning. A 'smock' can be quite plain; the word is used allusively to denote a woman or womankind, often in a defamatory or vulgar sense, and often suggestive of loose conduct or immorality (*OED* Smock *sb* 1c, 3b). A 'petticoat', also a metonymy for a female or the female sex, is more suggestive of feminine character and attractiveness, with an idea also of female control over men (*OED* Petticoat *sb* 4a, b).

162–3 tears live in an onion More proverbial lore (Dent O67 and P391; see also 4.2.36 below). Enobarbus's jest that an onion would be needed to produce tears for the death of Fulvia recalls what he has just said about Cleopatra's skill in the artifice of water-works.

164 broachèd set abroach, started. Compare 83–9 above.

166 business you have broached Enobarbus repeats Antony's words with bawdy equivocation, suggesting in 'broached' something that has been opened and entered by Antony. See 159 above and n.

167 that of Cleopatra's On the double genitive, see 1.1.1 and n.

168 abode staying.

169 light indelicate; Antony has not missed Enobarbus's bawdy suggestions.

169 our The royal plural, continued in 'we' (170), 'us' (174, 176), and 'our' (178, 187, 189). Compare Cleopatra's falling back on her dignity at 82 above.

170 break disclose (*OED* sv *v* 22).

171 expedience hasty departure; as in *1H4* 1.1.33.

172 *leave to part permission to depart – either as a gesture of courtesy or as intending to confirm Antony's dependence. Wilson suggests that Shakespeare's manuscript read 'leue', easily misread by the compositor as 'loue' (see collation).

173 more urgent touches 'things that touch me more sensibly, more pressing motives' (Johnson).

Of many our contriving friends in Rome
Petition us at home. Sextus Pompeius
Hath given the dare to Caesar and commands
The empire of the sea. Our slippery people,
Whose love is never linked to the deserver
Till his deserts are past, begin to throw
Pompey the Great and all his dignities
Upon his son, who – high in name and power,
Higher than both in blood and life – stands up
For the main soldier; whose quality, going on,
The sides o'th'world may danger. Much is breeding,
Which, like the courser's hair, hath yet but life
And not a serpent's poison. Say our pleasure,
To such whose place is under us, requires
Our quick remove from hence.

ENOBARBUS I shall do't.

[*Exeunt*]

177 Hath] F2; Haue F 186 hair] *Rowe;* heire F 188 whose…requires] F2*;* whose places vnder vs, require F*;* who've places under us, requires *conj. Mason;* whose places under us require, *Ridley* 190 SD] F2*; not in* F

175 Of…friends From many friends making plans in my interest.

176 Petition us at home Beg me to come home.

176–8 Sextus Pompeius…sea See North's Plutarch (984C) and 1.3.45–6 and 1.4.36–40 below. This younger son of Pompey the Great escaped after the defeat of himself and his brother Gnaeus by Caesar at Munda in southern Spain (45 BC), took command of the republican fleet after Caesar's death, and conducted a piratical career that gave him control of Sicily and the ability to interrupt Rome's grain supply.

177 *Hath The correction of F's 'Haue' to 'Hath' has been followed by virtually all editions since F2, in accord with Shakespeare's usage elsewhere.

180 throw bestow, confer (with a suggestion of 'without good judgement'). The fickle commoners, who in *JC* 1.1.36–51 are described as having shown ingratitude and forgetfulness towards the once-idolised Pompey the Great, now confer their veneration of the father upon the son. Compare 120–1 above and n., also 1.3.48–52 and Caesar's similar lament at 1.4.40–7.

183 blood and life mettle and spirit, vital energy.

183–4 stands up…soldier lays claim to being the greatest soldier – a challenge to which Antony, 'the greatest soldier of the world' (1.3.38), is especially sensitive. Perhaps 'main' also means 'sea', since Pompey's strength is at sea (Jones).

184–5 whose quality…danger whose aspiring nature and condition, if permitted to go on unchecked, may endanger the whole frame or body of the Roman empire. On the distinctive sense of a global architecture and its possible collapse, which is a recurring image in this play, compare 1.1.35 and n.

186–7 the courser's hair…poison 'It is believed…that an horse hair laid in a pail full of the like water [i.e. stagnant water] will in short time stir and become a living creature' (William Harrison, *The Description of England*, in Raphael Holinshed's *Chronicles* (1586), I, iii, 224A, 52–4). The phenomenon, as Coleridge notes, is not imaginary: the horsehairs attract microscopic creatures and appear to wriggle like tiny eels. Antony likens such a horsehair to a breeding serpent, not yet dangerous but destined to be so, like the 'serpent's egg' to which Brutus compares Caesar in *JC* 2.1.32–3.

187–8 *Say our…requires Of the various emendations proposed for this crux (see collation) F2 offers perhaps the best; as Wilson conjectures, 'places' in F may be a copyist's error for 'place is'. Ridley's emendation is a conservative reading of F and is possible.

[1.3] *Enter* CLEOPATRA, CHARMIAN, ALEXAS, *and* IRAS

CLEOPATRA Where is he?
CHARMIAN I did not see him since.
CLEOPATRA [*To Alexas*]
See where he is, who's with him, what he does.
I did not send you. If you find him sad,
Say I am dancing; if in mirth, report
That I am sudden sick. Quick, and return.
[*Exit Alexas*]
CHARMIAN Madam, methinks if you did love him dearly,
You do not hold the method to enforce
The like from him.
CLEOPATRA What should I do I do not?
CHARMIAN In each thing give him way. Cross him in nothing.
CLEOPATRA Thou teachest like a fool: the way to lose him.
CHARMIAN Tempt him not so too far. I wish, forbear;
In time we hate that which we often fear.

Enter ANTONY

But here comes Antony.
CLEOPATRA I am sick and sullen.
ANTONY I am sorry to give breathing to my purpose –
CLEOPATRA Help me away, dear Charmian, I shall fall.

Act 1, Scene 3 1.3] *Capell; no scene division in* F 2 SD] *Jones; not in* F 2 who's] F (Whose) 5 SD] *Capell; not in* F 11 I wish] F; I wis *Wilson, anon. conj. in Cam.*

Act 1, Scene 3

Location As in Scenes 1 and 2, and following soon afterwards. 'Cleopatra returns to discover what keeps Antony so long in talk' (Wilson).

1 **since** lately.

3 **I did not send you** i.e. do not let him know I sent you.

3–5 **If...sick** Cleopatra's perversity is a popular truth applied. Compare the proverb, 'When the husband is sad (merry) the wife will be merry (sad)' (Dent H839). 'Sad' = 'serious'.

5 SD Of the named persons present, Alexas is the most likely to obey Cleopatra's orders, and editors have accordingly assumed, as here, that he must exit. Conceivably an unnamed attendant or attendants are at hand as an alternative, though the opening stage direction in F does not indicate this.

7 **hold the method** pursue the right course.

8 **I do not** that I am not doing. This debate on how to please a lover has a precedent in, for example, Ovid's *Ars Amatoria*, esp. II, 13 ff.

11 **Tempt** Try, vex.

11 **I wish** I wish you would. Some editors emend to 'iwis', meaning 'certainly', 'trust me'.

12 Compare the proverb, 'He cannot love me that is afraid of me' (Dent L556), of which Dent gives no examples before Shakespeare.

13 **I am sick and sullen** To be 'sick of the sullens' is a commonplace (Dent S964). 'Sullen' here means 'melancholy, in low spirits', not 'sulking'.

14 **breathing** utterance.

It cannot be thus long; the sides of nature
Will not sustain it.

ANTONY Now, my dearest queen –

CLEOPATRA Pray you, stand farther from me.

ANTONY What's the matter?

CLEOPATRA I know by that same eye there's some good news.
What, says the married woman you may go?
Would she had never given you leave to come!
Let her not say 'tis I that keep you here.
I have no power upon you; hers you are.

ANTONY The gods best know –

CLEOPATRA O, never was there queen
So mightily betrayed! Yet at the first
I saw the treasons planted.

ANTONY Cleopatra –

CLEOPATRA Why should I think you can be mine, and true,
Though you in swearing shake the thronèd gods,
Who have been false to Fulvia? Riotous madness,
To be entangled with those mouth-made vows,
Which break themselves in swearing!

ANTONY Most sweet queen –

20 What, says...go?] F4 *subst.* (What! saies...go?); What sayes the married woman you may goe? F; What says the marry'd Woman? you may go; *Rowe* **25** first] F2; fitst F

16 It cannot be thus long i.e. I cannot last long at this rate.

16 the sides of nature my bodily frame, my human strength. Compare 1.2.185, 4.14.39, and *TN* 2.4.93–4: 'There is no woman's sides / Can bide the beating of so strong a passion.'

18 stand farther from me i.e. give me air.

20 * This line, without any commas in F, can be variously read: 'What, says the married woman you may go?' or 'What says the married woman – you may go?' or 'What says the married woman? You may go!', though the antithetical idea of 21 makes the last of these alternatives seem least likely. 'The married woman' is Fulvia. Th. Zielinski, 'Marginalien', *Philologus* 64 (1905), 1–26, points out that 20–1 are probably based on Ovid's *Heroides*, VII, 139, in which Dido addresses Aeneas by verse epistle as follows: '"But", you say, "the god orders you to go." I wish he had forbidden you to come' ('"Sed iubet ire deus." vellem, vetuisset adire'). Zielinski sees further parallels to Ovid's *Heroides* in Cleopatra's twitting Antony about his treatment of Fulvia, as at 27–9, 63–5, and 75–8; compare *Heroides*, VII, 81–4, in which Dido reproaches Aeneas as follows: 'omnia mentiris, neque enim tua fallere lingua / incipit a nobis', 'You lie in everything you say, nor am I the first to be deceived by your tongue', etc. Aeneas's desertion of Dido to attend his destiny at Rome is an event that Shakespeare must have had in mind, especially as told by Virgil in the *Aeneid*, Book IV; the story of these famous lovers returns at 4.14.53. See p. 7 above. Some of these parallels may have come to Shakespeare by way of Marlowe and Nashe's *Dido, Queen of Carthage*; see 92 n. below.

28 'Cleopatra alludes hyperbolically to the notion that when Jupiter, king of the gods, swore an oath, the whole of Olympus shuddered to its foundations' (Jones). On hyperbole, see pp. 38–9 above.

29 Who i.e. you who.

29 Riotous madness 'It was raving madness on my part' (Kittredge).

30 mouth-made made of words only, not heartfelt.

31 in swearing even while they are being sworn.

CLEOPATRA Nay, pray you, seek no colour for your going,
But bid farewell and go. When you sued staying,
Then was the time for words. No going then.
Eternity was in our lips and eyes,
Bliss in our brows' bent; none our parts so poor
But was a race of heaven. They are so still,
Or thou, the greatest soldier of the world,
Art turned the greatest liar.

ANTONY How now, lady?

CLEOPATRA I would I had thy inches. Thou shouldst know
There were a heart in Egypt.

ANTONY Hear me, queen:
The strong necessity of time commands
Our services awhile, but my full heart
Remains in use with you. Our Italy
Shines o'er with civil swords; Sextus Pompeius
Makes his approaches to the port of Rome;
Equality of two domestic powers

36 brows' bent] *Capell;* browes bent F 43 services] F2; Seruicles F

32 colour pretext.

33 sued staying begged to stay. Cleopatra retrieves a sense of her authority in asserting her lack of it; compare 23 above.

35 Eternity 'Immortal pleasures' (Kittredge).

35 our i.e. my (the royal plural). Cleopatra reminds Antony of the praises he has offered to her beauty; she is quoting back at him some of his 'mouth-made vows'.

36 Bliss 'The joy of heaven' (Kittredge).

36 our brows' bent the arch or curve of my eyebrows.

36 none our parts so poor none of my features, however poor.

37 a race of heaven divine in origin and descent, godlike; or perhaps 'having a smack or flavour of heaven'. (As Johnson explains, 'the *race* of wine is the taste of the soil'.)

40 inches (1) height, (2) manly strength, with perhaps a bawdy suggestion, especially in light of the wordplay on 'inches' at 1.2.53–6.

41 a heart i.e. courage, resolution (to stand up to or reprove with proper vigour Antony's perjuries).

41 Egypt the Queen of Egypt.

43 Our...my Antony shifts from the royal 'we' of his public image to 'my' when he speaks as Cleopatra's lover (Kittredge).

43 *services Perhaps F's 'Seruicles' is a misprint for 'Seruicies'.

44 in use with you for your use and enjoyment, or in trust with you. Johnson's gloss, 'The poet seems to allude to the legal distinction between the *use* and *absolute possession*', implies a sense of limitation on Antony's commitment to her, which may or may not be appropriate (compare 'full heart' at 43). The financial metaphor of usury may simply suggest that Antony's full heart 'remains increasingly indebted to you'. Compare 'use' in Sonnets 2, 4, 6, 20, etc.

45 Shines...swords Glitters everywhere with the light reflected from swords drawn in civil war (*OED* Shine *v* 2b).

45 Sextus Pompeius See 1.2.176–8 and n., and 1.4.36–40.

46 the port of Rome the gate of Rome (Dyce, glossary), or more probably the harbour of Rome, Ostia, at the mouth of the Tiber (Arden). At 4.4.23, 'port' appears to mean 'gate', but here Pompey is approaching by sea.

47–8 Equality...faction The even division of strength in the Roman world (between Antony and Octavius, or else between Pompey and the triumvirs) breeds factional squabbling over trifles. 'Breed' is plural by the attraction of the plural noun 'powers' (Abbott 412).

Breed scrupulous faction; the hated, grown to strength,
Are newly grown to love; the condemned Pompey,
Rich in his father's honour, creeps apace
Into the hearts of such as have not thrived
Upon the present state, whose numbers threaten;
And quietness, grown sick of rest, would purge
By any desperate change. My more particular,
And that which most with you should safe my going,
Is Fulvia's death.

CLEOPATRA Though age from folly could not give me freedom,
It does from childishness. Can Fulvia die?

ANTONY She's dead, my queen.
[*He offers letters*]
Look here, and at thy sovereign leisure read
The garboils she awaked; at the last, best,
See when and where she died.

CLEOPATRA O most false love!
Where be the sacred vials thou shouldst fill
With sorrowful water? Now I see, I see,
In Fulvia's death how mine received shall be.

ANTONY Quarrel no more, but be prepared to know

59 SD] *Jones subst.; not in* F 63 vials] F (Violles)

48–9 the hated...to love those who were hated or neglected (like Pompey; see 1.2.176–82, and 180 n.), having now grown to strength, are newly received into popular favour.

49–50 Pompey...honour Sextus Pompeius, richly inheriting the honour once bestowed on his father, Pompey the Great (see 1.2.180–2). Pompey had been 'condemned' or proscribed, i.e. declared an outlaw, by the Roman Senate.

50 creeps stealthily insinuates (with no sense of slowness).

52 state government (of the triumvirate).

52 whose i.e. those supporting Pompey.

53 quietness...purge The image of peace as a corrosive disease to be cured by periodic bloodletting of the body politic, a commonplace of Elizabethan thought, is found in *Ham.* 4.4.27–9, *1H4* 4.2.29–30, *2H4* 4.1.54–66, and elsewhere. 'Purge' means to cleanse or purify by vomiting, evacuation, or bloodletting to be rid of sickness. The F punctuation, with a comma after 'threaten', allows, according to R. C. Hood, for a slightly different reading, with 'purge' as a transitive verb and 'quietness' as its object: 'whose numbers threaten and – grown sick of rest – would purge quietness by any desperate change'. 'Quietness' in this reading is ironically a diseased condition.

54 particular personal concern. Compare 4.9.20, 'in thine own particular'.

55 safe make safe, remove any sense of threat in. Compare 4.6.27, 'Best you safed the bringer.'

57–8 Though...childishness i.e. though the supposed wisdom of age has not freed me from foolish behaviour (especially in loving you), I am not so childish as to hope that you might be free of your wife.

58 Can Fulvia die? An expression of incredulity, perhaps with erotic double meaning. Either mere hyperbole or implying 'Will I ever be free from cause of jealousy?'

61 garboils disturbances, commotions. Antony uses the word again in referring to Fulvia at 2.2.73.

61 at the last, best i.e. last and best news of all.

63 sacred vials 'Alluding to the lachrymatory vials, or bottles of tears, which the Romans sometimes put into the urn of a friend' (Johnson).

The purposes I bear, which are, or cease,
As you shall give th'advice. By the fire
That quickens Nilus' slime, I go from hence
Thy soldier, servant, making peace or war
As thou affects.

CLEOPATRA Cut my lace, Charmian, come!
But let it be; I am quickly ill, and well,
So Antony loves.

ANTONY My precious queen, forbear,
And give true evidence to his love which stands
An honourable trial.

CLEOPATRA So Fulvia told me.
I prithee, turn aside and weep for her,
Then bid adieu to me, and say the tears
Belong to Egypt. Good now, play one scene
Of excellent dissembling, and let it look
Like perfect honour.

ANTONY You'll heat my blood. No more.

CLEOPATRA You can do better yet; but this is meetly.

80 blood. No more.] *Rowe subst.;* blood no more? F

67 **bear** (1) hold, (2) bring.

67 **which are, or cease** which will proceed or not (but stated hyperbolically: 'which live or die').

68 **advice** judgement. Antony gives Cleopatra the right (as sovereign) to pronounce sentence of life or death on his purposes.

68 **fire** i.e. sun. The image, suggesting the divine principle of Osiris conflated with Horus, is appropriate to Antony's purpose throughout this scene in deliberately recreating the status of Cleopatra as a supreme authority.

69 **quickens** brings to life. Compare 2.7.25–6.

69 **Nilus' slime** The fertile mud deposited annually by the overflowing Nile. J. A. K. Thomson (*Shakespeare and the Classics*, 1952, p. 148) thinks the image may have been suggested by *The Faerie Queene*, I, i, 21, 1–3: 'As when old father *Nilus* gins to swell...His fattie waues do fertile slime outwell...'; and perhaps too by Ovid's *Metamorphoses*, I, 498–9 (Golding's translation): 'And that the fat and slimy mud in moorish grounds begun / To swell through warmth of Phoebus' beams' ('aetherioque recens exarcit sidere limus').

71 **thou affects** you desire.

71 **lace** i.e. the lacing of Cleopatra's bodice or stays. Cleopatra pretends she is fainting, but quickly recovers (Kittredge). Queen Elizabeth in *R3* (4.1.33) and Paulina in *WT* (3.2.173) similarly ask that their lace be cut in situations of emotional stress.

72 **well** well again.

73 **So** Provided that; or perhaps Cleopatra means that Antony's love is as changeable as her fluctuating mood, with 'so' meaning 'thus'.

73 **forbear** i.e. stop this kind of talk.

74–5 **give...trial** bear true witness to the love of one who is ready to sustain any honourable test.

75 **So Fulvia told me** i.e. so I've learned from your behaviour towards Fulvia. If Antony wants a true witness of his faithfulness in love, Cleopatra taunts him, perhaps Fulvia can give testimony.

78 **Belong to Egypt** Are shed for the Queen of Egypt.

78 **Good now** An expression denoting entreaty or expostulation, as in *Ham.* 1.1.70: 'Good now, sit down.'

80 **heat my blood** anger me, make me lose my temper.

81 **meetly** i.e. pretty well acted. Cleopatra speaks mockingly as though in praise of a feigned display of emotion, the kind of artifice for which Enobarbus praises *her* at 1.2.142–6. Contrast her later resistance to the idea of bad performance.

ANTONY Now by my sword –
CLEOPATRA And target. Still he mends.
But this is not the best. Look, prithee, Charmian,
How this herculean Roman does become
The carriage of his chafe.
ANTONY I'll leave you, lady.
CLEOPATRA Courteous lord, one word.
Sir, you and I must part, but that's not it;
Sir, you and I have loved, but there's not it;
That you know well. Something it is I would –
O, my oblivion is a very Antony,
And I am all forgotten.
ANTONY But that your royalty
Holds idleness your subject, I should take you
For idleness itself.
CLEOPATRA 'Tis sweating labour
To bear such idleness so near the heart
As Cleopatra this. But sir, forgive me,

82 by my] F2; by F

82 *by my sword F's 'by Sword' is an easy error of compressing 'by my' into one word. The F2 emendation has been universally adopted.

82 target shield, buckler. 'This makes it a swashbuckler's oath' (Wilson, comparing *1H4* 1.3.230). Sword and target, masculine and feminine symbols respectively, may suggest the physical gestures that accompany this interchange (Terence Hawkes, *Shakespeare's Speaking Animals*, 1973, p. 185).

82 mends improves (in his 'scene / Of excellent dissembling').

84–5 How this...chafe i.e. how admirably this Roman, who claims descent from Anton, son of Hercules (see North's Plutarch, 971F, and 4.3.21 and 4.12.44 below), plays the role of a furious man. Antony's role is that of Hercules Furens, whom Hera maddened and goaded into killing his wife and children – a role that invites histrionic bluster. 'Herculean' is accented on the second syllable. 'Carriage of his chafe' = 'bearing or demeanour of his fury'. Many dramatic and literary archetypes might have fuelled this idea of the braggart soldier.

86 I'll leave you, lady 'i.e. lest I lose control of myself' (Wilson). Antony may bow as he prepares to leave, thus prompting the response of 'Courteous lord'.

90 would wished to say.

91 my oblivion is a very Antony i.e. my forgetful memory, like Antony, is deserting me, as though 'Antony' were synonymous with forgetfulness itself.

92 I am all forgotten (1) I have completely forgotten what I was going to say, (2) I am entirely forgotten. Shakespeare's likely debt to Marlowe and Nashe's *Dido, Queen of Carthage*, 'What did I say? / Something it was that now I have forgot' (3.4.29–30), is noted, along with other parallels, by Harrison, pp. 57–63.

92–3 But that...subject i.e. if I weren't perfectly aware that you could control your frivolous ways as easily as you command your own subjects. 'Idleness' = 'foolishness', 'folly' (*OED* sv 3). Antony's metaphor also suggests that Cleopatra is the queen of foolishness, able to command this kingdom of trifling for her own purposes.

94–6 'Tis...this Quibbling on 'labour' and 'idleness', as Wilson notes, Cleopatra compares herself with unnerving accuracy to a woman undergoing the pains of childbirth. What Antony calls 'idleness', she insists, is to her intensely passionate.

Since my becomings kill me when they do not
Eye well to you. Your honour calls you hence;
Therefore be deaf to my unpitied folly,
And all the gods go with you! Upon your sword
Sit laurel victory, and smooth success
Be strewed before your feet!

ANTONY Let us go. Come;
Our separation so abides and flies
That thou, residing here, goes yet with me,
And I, hence fleeting, here remain with thee.
Away!

Exeunt

[1.4] *Enter* OCTAVIUS [CAESAR], *reading a letter,* LEPIDUS, *and their train*

CAESAR You may see, Lepidus, and henceforth know,
It is not Caesar's natural vice to hate
Our great competitor. From Alexandria
This is the news: he fishes, drinks, and wastes
The lamps of night in revel; is not more manlike
Than Cleopatra, nor the queen of Ptolemy
More womanly than he; hardly gave audience, or
Vouchsafed to think he had partners. You shall find there

Act 1, Scene 4 1.4] *Capell; no scene division in* F 0 SD CAESAR] *Rowe; not in* F 3 Our] *Singer, conj. Heath and Johnson;* One F 8 Vouchsafed] *Johnson;* vouchsafe F; did vouchsafe F2

97 my becomings (1) even those qualities that become me, (2) my changes. (Perhaps a recollection of Antony's tribute to her, 'Whom everything becomes', 1.1.51.)

98 Eye Appear.

100–2 The image is of a triumphal procession.

103 so abides and flies mingles staying and going in such a paradoxical way.

Act 1, Scene 4

Location Rome. A busy council scene, distinctively Roman in perspective.

2 natural i.e. unprovoked.

3 *Our F's 'One' is an easy error for 'Our', perhaps (as Wilson suggests, p. 126) misreading the contraction 'o^r^' as 'on', and the emendation has been generally accepted.

3 competitor partner (as at 2.7.66 and 5.1.42); but perhaps also with a suggestion of rivalry.

4–5 Compare North's Plutarch, 983B–D, and 2.5.10–18 below.

4 wastes extravagantly (and profitlessly) consumes.

6 Ptolemy Cleopatra's younger brother, to whom she had been nominally married in accordance with Egyptian custom (and at Julius Caesar's command), and whom she is reported to have poisoned. See 17 below. Cleopatra is called 'Egypt's widow' at 2.1.38.

7 gave audience i.e. received the messengers from Rome, as shown in Scenes 1 and 2.

8 *Vouchsafed F reads 'vouchsafe'. Compare 'dumbed' (1.5.52) for a similar mistaking of *d* for *e* by Compositor B.

8 there i.e. in this letter (which Caesar may or

A man who is the abstract of all faults
That all men follow.
LEPIDUS I must not think there are
Evils enough to darken all his goodness.
His faults in him seem as the spots of heaven,
More fiery by night's blackness, hereditary
Rather than purchased, what he cannot change
Than what he chooses.
CAESAR You are too indulgent. Let's grant it is not
Amiss to tumble on the bed of Ptolemy,
To give a kingdom for a mirth, to sit
And keep the turn of tippling with a slave,
To reel the streets at noon, and stand the buffet
With knaves that smells of sweat. Say this becomes him –
As his composure must be rare indeed
Whom these things cannot blemish – yet must Antony
No way excuse his foils when we do bear

9 the] F3 *subst.* (the'); th' F 9 abstract] F2; abstracts F 11 enough] F (enow) 21 smells] F (smels); smell F2 24 foils] F (foyles); soils *Malone*

may not hand to Lepidus; the gesture provides a nice bit of stage business by which to gauge our response to Caesar and our understanding of the role of Lepidus).

9 ***abstract** epitome. F's 'abstracts' may have picked up the unwarranted plural from 'faults'.

11 **Evils** Faults.

11 **enough** F reads 'enow'. Some scholars argue for an Elizabethan distinction between 'enough' as used of quantity and 'enow' as used of numbers, similar to that between 'more' and 'moe', but Shakespeare's text heavily supports 'enough' in both senses and provides some 331 usages as against 10 for 'enow'. Such one-sided and arbitrary distinctions may not be authorial.

12–13 **His...blackness** 'His faults are made more conspicuous by his goodness, as the stars by night's blackness' (Arden). 'Faults' are thus like 'stars' only in terms of contrast with what surrounds them; more commonly, evils are associated with darkness and virtue with light, as in *MV* 5.1.91: 'So shines a good deed in a naughty world', or *Ham.* 5.2.256–7. Caesar may mean, as Capell suggests, that Antony's faults seem all the more glaring when set against the dark background of the turbulent state of affairs in the Roman empire (*Notes*, I, 30).

14 **purchased** acquired.

16 **Let's grant** i.e. just for the sake of argument. Caesar's merely rhetorical concession is caught up by 'yet' in 23.

16 **is** Possibly a scribal or compositorial addition (R. C. Hood).

18 **for a mirth** as reward for some idle jest or diversion.

19 **keep the turn of tippling** take turns drinking toasts. Compare 19–20 with North's Plutarch, 983B.

20 **stand the buffet** endure the blows, engage in fisticuffs.

21 **smells** This F reading is a possible plural; compare 50 below and Abbott 333. It would also be an easy error for 'smell', and the plural form may have been influenced by 'knaues'.

22 **As** i.e. and.

22 **his composure** a person's disposition or character.

24 **foils** disgraces, stigmas (*OED* Foil *sb*[2] 2b); traits that defile or pollute Antony's better qualities; compare *Temp.* 3.1.44–6.

24–5 **when we...lightness** when we have to bear the heavy burden imposed by his levity. The metaphor is that of scales in which one pan sinks as the other rises.

So great weight in his lightness. If he filled
His vacancy with his voluptuousness,
Full surfeits and the dryness of his bones
Call on him for't. But to confound such time
That drums him from his sport and speaks as loud
As his own state and ours, 'tis to be chid
As we rate boys who, being mature in knowledge,
Pawn their experience to their present pleasure
And so rebel to judgement.

Enter a MESSENGER

LEPIDUS Here's more news.

MESSENGER Thy biddings have been done, and every hour,
Most noble Caesar, shalt thou have report
How 'tis abroad. Pompey is strong at sea,
And it appears he is beloved of those
That only have feared Caesar. To the ports
The discontents repair, and men's reports
Give him much wronged. [*Exit*]

CAESAR I should have known no less.
It hath been taught us from the primal state
That he which is was wished until he were;

30 chid] *Capell;* chid: F **40** SD] *This edn; not in* F

26 His vacancy Merely his leisure time.

27–8 Full surfeits...for't Stomach disorders and the symptoms of venereal disease would call him to account. Hollow or aching bones are a consequence of syphilis in *MM* 1.2.56–7 and *Tro.* 5.10.50. On dry bones, compare Prov. 17.22 and Ezek. 37.11 (Shaheen).

28 confound waste; as at 1.1.47.

29 drums summons as with a military call to arms.

29–30 speaks...ours 'i.e. proclaims the fate of the whole triumvirate at stake' (Wilson).

30 'tis to be chid deserves to be reprimanded.

31 rate berate.

31 mature in knowledge 'old enough to know their duty' (Johnson).

32 'sacrifice to their present pleasure the experience they have had of the ill consequences which will certainly follow from such indulgence' (Heath, p. 451).

33 to judgement against sound judgement.

34–6 The contrast of the bustle and eager reception of reports here with Antony's earlier treatment of messengers from Rome gives reinforcement to Caesar's remarks at 7–9.

37 of by.

38 That...Caesar That have obeyed Caesar only out of fear, not love.

39 The discontents The malcontents, the discontented.

40 Give him Represent him as, declare him to be.

41 It has been a constant lesson since the first commonwealth that ever existed, since the primeval state of society.

42 That the man now in power was desired (by the populace) until, and only until, he obtained that power. 'Caesar glances at his own loss of popular favour' (Arden). On the proverbial perversity of valuing someone only after the person is gone, see 1.2.120–1 and n., and Dent M1015.

And the ebbed man, ne'er loved till ne'er worth love,
Comes deared by being lacked. This common body,
Like to a vagabond flag upon the stream,
Goes to and back, lackeying the varying tide
To rot itself with motion.

[*Enter a second* MESSENGER]

MESSENGER Caesar, I bring thee word
Menecrates and Menas, famous pirates,
Makes the sea serve them, which they ear and wound
With keels of every kind. Many hot inroads
They make in Italy; the borders maritime
Lack blood to think on't, and flush youth revolt.
No vessel can peep forth but 'tis as soon
Taken as seen; for Pompey's name strikes more

44 deared] *Theobald, conj. Warburton;* fear'd F 46 lackeying] *Theobald, conj. Warburton;* lacking F 47 SD] *Capell subst.; not in* F 49 Menecrates] F4 *(following North's Plutarch); Menacrates* F 50 Makes] F; Make F4

43 **ebbed** decayed in fortune.

43 **ne'er worth love** no longer able to confer (or withhold) actual rewards. The contrast is between the attraction of the man who can only hold out the *prospect* of power, and disenchantment with or alienation from the man who can offer *actual* favour.

44 ***Comes deared** Becomes loved, acquires popularity at last. The F reading, 'fear'd', might mean 'revered', but the opposition of 'beloved' and 'feared' in 37–8 suggests a meaning for 'feared' that is inappropriate in 44 and tends to confirm the emendation of Theobald.

44 **This common body** The populace.

45 **vagabond** 'At once shifty and rascally' (Wilson).

45 **flag** In early use, any reed or rush; later an iris (*OED* sv *sb*[1] 1, 2).

46 ***lackeying** 'like a page or lackey at his master's heels' (Theobald). The F reading, 'lacking', is probably influenced by 'lacked' in 44 (Wilson).

47 **rot itself with motion** Kittredge compares *Ham.* 1.5.32–3: 'the fat weed / That rots itself in ease on Lethe wharf' ('rots' is the F reading; Q1 and Q2 read 'roots').

47 SD* F provides no stage direction for this entry, but the Messenger here speaks as though bringing fresh news, and Caesar's previous speech of reflective commentary might seem awkward if it interrupted the delivery of news from one messenger (Capell, Arden). In terms of dramatic design, the scene should be bustling with messengers.

49–56 **Menecrates...resisted** The information and diction here are closely based on Plutarch, 984C–D. Compare 'Menecrates and Menas, famous pirates' with Plutarch's 'Two notable pirates, Menas and Menecrates', 'the sea...which they ear and wound' (50) with 'who so scoured all the sea thereabouts', 'Many hot inroads / They make in Italy' (51–2) with 'made many an inroad into Italy', and 'No vessel can peep forth' (54) with 'none durst peep out with a sail'. The 'keels of every kind' (51) are elaborated by North's Plutarch as 'a great number of pinnaces and other pirate's ships'. See pp. 2–3 above.

49 **famous** notorious.

50 **Makes** A plural, as at 3.6.91, though F4 'Make' is also possible.

50 **ear** plough; as at 1.2.107.

51 **keels** i.e. ships; metonymy, the part for the whole.

51 **hot inroads** fierce forays, hostile incursions.

52 **borders maritime** coastal territories.

53 **Lack blood** Turn pale.

53 **flush youth revolt** vigorous young men join the pirates.

55–6 **strikes...resisted** is more threatening than his forces would be if war were declared; or 'causes you more loss than armed resistance would' (Ridley).

Than could his war resisted. [*Exit*]

CAESAR Antony,
Leave thy lascivious wassails. When thou once
Was beaten from Modena, where thou slew'st
Hirtius and Pansa, consuls, at thy heel
Did famine follow, whom thou fought'st against,
Though daintily brought up, with patience more
Than savages could suffer. Thou didst drink
The stale of horses and the gilded puddle
Which beasts would cough at. Thy palate then did deign
The roughest berry on the rudest hedge.
Yea, like the stag when snow the pasture sheets,
The barks of trees thou browsèd. On the Alps
It is reported thou didst eat strange flesh,
Which some did die to look on. And all this –
It wounds thine honour that I speak it now –
Was borne so like a soldier that thy cheek
So much as lanked not.

LEPIDUS 'Tis pity of him.

CAESAR Let his shames quickly
Drive him to Rome. 'Tis time we twain
Did show ourselves i'th'field, and to that end
Assemble we immediate council. Pompey
Thrives in our idleness.

56 SD] *Oxford; not in* F **57** wassails] *Pope;* Vassailes F **58** Was] F*;* Wert F2*;* Wast *Steevens* **58** Modena] *Johnson (following North's Plutarch); Medena* F **59** Hirtius] F4*; Hirsius* F *(North's Plutarch / Hircius)* **59** Pansa] F2*; Pausa* F **67** browsèd] brows'd F*;* browsedst F2 **77** we] F2*;* me F **77** council] F (counsell)

57 *wassails carousals, revels. Caesar's contrasting of wanton luxury with spare diet suggests that this emendation is preferable to F's 'Vassailes', i.e. vassals.

57–72 When thou...lanked not As at 49–56, North's Plutarch (977E–978A) provides many specific details: the location at Modena, Antony's slaying of the consuls Hirtius and Pansa, the famine, the drinking of 'puddle water', the eating of 'wild fruits and roots' and 'the barks of trees' and 'such beasts as never man tasted of their flesh before' as Antony's army passed the Alps, etc. Hirtius and Pansa were sent by the Roman Senate in 43 BC to drive Antony out of Italy, following the assassination of Julius Caesar. At the battle of Mutina (Modena), Antony was forced to retire westward across the Alps, but the consuls were killed. On the nature and place of this eulogy within Caesar's overall political strategy and its importance to our sense of both men and to the developing design of the play, see p. 22 above.

60 whom i.e. famine.

61–2 with patience...suffer 'with more fortitude than savages could show in suffering' (Jones).

63 stale urine.

63 gilded covered with iridescent scum. Compare 'filthy-mantled' (*Temp.* 4.1.182) and 'cream and mantle like a standing pond' (*MV* 1.1.89).

64 deign not disdain.

72 lanked not did not grow thin.

73 of him about him.

75 we twain i.e. Caesar and Lepidus.

77 *we This F2 emendation (F: 'me') is suggested by 'we twain' in 75 and 'our' in 78. Caesar is not contemptuous of Lepidus as he is later, though he is here giving the orders for their departure.

LEPIDUS Tomorrow, Caesar,
I shall be furnished to inform you rightly
Both what by sea and land I can be able
To front this present time.
CAESAR Till which encounter,
It is my business too. Farewell.
LEPIDUS Farewell, my lord. What you shall know meantime
Of stirs abroad, I shall beseech you, sir,
To let me be partaker.
CAESAR Doubt not, sir, I knew it for my bond.
Exeunt [separately]

[1.5] *Enter* CLEOPATRA, CHARMIAN, IRAS, *and* MARDIAN

CLEOPATRA Charmian!
CHARMIAN Madam?
CLEOPATRA Ha, ha! Give me to drink mandragora.
CHARMIAN Why, madam?
CLEOPATRA That I might sleep out this great gap of time
My Antony is away.
CHARMIAN You think of him too much.
CLEOPATRA O, 'tis treason!
CHARMIAN Madam, I trust not so.
CLEOPATRA Thou, eunuch Mardian!
MARDIAN What's your highness' pleasure?
CLEOPATRA Not now to hear thee sing. I take no pleasure
In aught an eunuch has. 'Tis well for thee

86 knew] F; know *Dyce*[2], *conj. Walker* 86 SD *separately*] *Bevington subst.; not in* F **Act 1, Scene 5** 1.5] *Capell; no scene division in* F 3 mandragora] *Johnson; Mandragoru* F 5 time] *Rowe* (time,); time: F 9 Thou, eunuch] F; Thou eunuch, *Pope*

80 be able be capable of mustering.

81 front confront, meet face to face.

84 stirs stirrings, happenings.

86 knew knew already, needed no reminder. The emendation to 'know', adopted by some editors, is plausible but perhaps less subtle; the tone of F suggests 'I don't need to be reminded.'

86 bond bounden duty.

Act 1, Scene 5

Location Egypt, as in Scenes 1–3.

3 Ha, ha! 'A yawn of ennui' (Kittredge).

3 mandragora juice of the mandrake (a narcotic). Compare *Oth.* 3.3.330–1: 'Not poppy, nor mandragora, / Nor all the drowsy syrups of the world...'

10 to hear thee sing Mardian is the official singer, here and at 2.5.2 SD (Ridley). Perhaps he has started to sing until Cleopatra cuts him off. In *TN* 1.2.55–9, Viola resolves to take the disguise of a eunuch and singer to Duke Orsino.

11 aught an eunuch has Cleopatra loves to jest with Mardian about his physical inability to please her, and he plays up the defective role expected of him. Compare 2.5.4–9.

11–12 'Tis...That You are fortunate in that. Cleopatra ironically compliments the eunuch for being free of the sexual longings that make her

That, being unseminared, thy freer thoughts
May not fly forth of Egypt. Hast thou affections?

MARDIAN Yes, gracious madam.

CLEOPATRA Indeed?

MARDIAN Not in deed, madam, for I can do nothing
But what indeed is honest to be done.
Yet have I fierce affections, and think
What Venus did with Mars.

CLEOPATRA O Charmian,
Where think'st thou he is now? Stands he, or sits he?
Or does he walk? Or is he on his horse?
O happy horse, to bear the weight of Antony!
Do bravely, horse, for wot'st thou whom thou mov'st?
The demi-Atlas of this earth, the arm
And burgonet of men. He's speaking now,
Or murmuring 'Where's my serpent of old Nile?'
For so he calls me. Now I feed myself

17 indeed] F2; in deede F

wish to be elsewhere, with Antony. Cleopatra's words can also be read in the threatening sense of 'it's just as well for you that, being a eunuch, you do not think of leaving Egypt (as Antony has done)'. Mardian at least is a man she can control.

12 **unseminared** castrated.

13 **of** from.

13 **affections** passions, desires.

15–16 ***Indeed? Not in deed** Mardian plays on Cleopatra's question, 'Really?', in the literal sense of 'not in deed', not through physical act. As a eunuch he can 'do nothing' of the sort she suggests. Compare 'Do' at 23. The F spellings of 'Indeed' and 'in deed' underscore the wordplay.

17 ***indeed** Captures both senses: (1) truly, (2) in act (F: 'in deede').

17 **honest** chaste (as well as the ordinary modern sense).

19 **What...Mars** This mythic story of sexual play is central to *Antony and Cleopatra*; see p. 8 above.

22 **O happy horse** The association of horse-riding with sexual intercourse is found, for example, in Ovid's *Amores*; compare 3.7.7–9 below, and Shakespeare's *Venus and Adonis*, 595–600. The suggestion is one of unabashed 'natural' physicality and does not hint at bestiality (as it does in *H5* 3.7.44 ff.).

23 **Do bravely** Move with a proud spirit; but with a hint of sexual meaning, as at 15–16 and n. Compare *MM* 1.2.87–8: 'What has he done? – A woman', and *Tit.* 4.2.76: 'I have done thy mother.'

23 **wot'st thou** do you know.

24 **demi-Atlas** one who holds up half of Atlas's load, the weight of the whole world. At 1.1.12, 'triple pillar of the world' conveys a similar image. If Cleopatra has the leaders of the world in mind here, she disregards Lepidus. Frank Kermode argues that 'demi-Atlas' means 'the substitute of Atlas' (*Renaissance Essays*, 1973, pp. 98–9). In Daniel's *Cleopatra*, the queen refers to Antony as 'My Atlas and supporter of my pride' (1; 15).

24–5 **the arm...men** i.e. the complete soldier, equipped for offence with his own strong arm (or weapon) and for defence with a light steel helmet (named from its Burgundian origin) offering efficient protection to the wearer (Arden). Antony is the mighty leader and defender of men, contrasted with the picture of him as the braggart soldier at 1.3.82–5.

With most delicious poison. Think on me,
That am with Phoebus' amorous pinches black
And wrinkled deep in time. Broad-fronted Caesar,
When thou wast here above the ground I was
A morsel for a monarch. And great Pompey
Would stand and make his eyes grow in my brow;
There would he anchor his aspect, and die
With looking on his life.

Enter ALEXAS *from Antony*

ALEXAS Sovereign of Egypt, hail!
CLEOPATRA How much unlike art thou Mark Antony!
Yet coming from him, that great med'cine hath
With his tinct gilded thee.
How goes it with my brave Mark Antony?
ALEXAS Last thing he did, dear queen,
He kissed – the last of many doubled kisses –
This orient pearl. His speech sticks in my heart.

30 time.] F; time? *Capell* 35 SD *from Antony*] *Collier MS.*; *from Caesar* F 42 kissed – the...kisses –] *Theobald subst.*; kist the...kisses F

28 delicious poison The notion of love as sweet poison is proverbial (Dent P456.1). Cleopatra's self-administered poison is the flattering thought that Antony is thinking of her.

28 Think on me i.e. why should I suppose he thinks about me. Capell adds a question mark after 'time' at 30, but it is not necessary. Furness believes Cleopatra is apostrophising the absent Antony, as she does Julius Caesar at 30.

29 amorous pinches Compare 5.2.289: 'The stroke of death is as a lover's pinch.' Cleopatra 'includes both the sun and death among her lovers' (Ridley). In her world of erotic violence, love pinches and bruises.

29 black i.e. tanned by the rays of Phoebus, the sun. Considered unhandsome by English tastes; compare 'tawny', 1.1.6 and n.

30 Broad-fronted With broad forehead. This, along with the aquiline Roman nose, is standard in iconographic tradition.

30 Caesar i.e. Julius Caesar. North's Plutarch names 'Julius Caesar and Cneius [Gnaeus] Pompey, the son of Pompey the Great', as among Cleopatra's former lovers (981C). Compare 2.6.64 ff.

32 A morsel At 3.13.119–20, Antony speaks bitterly of Cleopatra as 'a morsel cold upon / Dead Caesar's trencher'.

32 great Pompey Shakespeare appears to conflate Pompey the Great with his elder son Gnaeus; see 30 and n., and 1.2.181–2 above. At 3.13.120–1, Antony speaks of Cleopatra as 'a fragment / Of Cneius Pompey's'; see Th. Zielinski, 'Marginalien', *Philologus* 64 (1905), 26, and Waino S. Nyland, 'Pompey as the mythical lover of Cleopatra', *MLN* 64 (1949), 515–16.

33 make...brow i.e. plant his eyes there, rivet them on my face.

34 aspect look, gaze (accented on second syllable).

34 die i.e. suffer in extremity the pangs of love. The erotic connotations so often associated with dying in this play are confirmed by 'stand' and 'grow' in 33.

35 his life that which he lived for.

38 that great med'cine i.e. the philosopher's stone or alchemist's elixir of life by which it was hoped to turn all base metals into gold and bestow immortality on those who possessed its secret (*OED* Medicine *sb*[1] 3).

39 tinct (1) colour, (2) the universal tincture or elixir of life (*OED* Tincture *sb* 6). 'Even Alexas has grown "gilded" by gazing upon the elixir, Antony' (Wilson).

40 brave splendid in every way.

43 orient shining, lustrous; applied to pearls and precious stones of superior value and bril-

CLEOPATRA Mine ear must pluck it thence.
ALEXAS 'Good friend', quoth he,
'Say the firm Roman to great Egypt sends
This treasure of an oyster; at whose foot,
To mend the petty present, I will piece
Her opulent throne with kingdoms. All the East,
Say thou, shall call her mistress.' So he nodded,
And soberly did mount an arm-gaunt steed,
Who neighed so high that what I would have spoke
Was beastly dumbed by him.
CLEOPATRA What, was he sad, or merry?
ALEXAS Like to the time o'th'year between the extremes
Of hot and cold, he was nor sad nor merry.
CLEOPATRA O well-divided disposition! Note him,
Note him, good Charmian, 'tis the man; but note him.
He was not sad, for he would shine on those
That make their looks by his; he was not merry,

52 dumbed] *Theobald;* dumbe F 53 What, was he sad,] *Rowe subst.;* What was he sad, F; What was he, sad *Wilson, conj. Furness*

liance as coming anciently from the East (*OED* Orient *adj* 2), or 'because of the clearness which resembles the colour of the clear air before the rising of the sun' (William Harrison, *The Description of England*, in Raphael Holinshed's *Chronicles* (1586), I, iii, 240A, 20–1).

45 **firm** constant, resolute.

45 **Egypt** the Queen of Egypt.

47–8 **To mend...kingdoms** To improve upon the trivial or ordinary state of things as they are at present, I will augment her realm with kingdoms so as to make it truly opulent (Kittredge). The image of all this wealth laid at the foot of Cleopatra is so striking as to suggest an iconographic source; Alexas also presents Antony here in a highly pictorial way.

47 **piece** piece out, enrich.

48 **All the East** Caesar complains at 3.6.9–11 that Antony has made Cleopatra queen of Egypt, lower Syria, Cyprus, and Lydia.

50 **arm-gaunt** made trim and hard by service in armour. The negative connotations of 'gaunt' have struck many editors as inappropriate here, and emendations have been proposed, including 'arm-girt' (Hanmer), 'termagaunt' (Mason), 'war-gaunt' (Jackson, pp. 286–8), 'arrogaunt' (Singer, conj. Boaden), 'rampaunt' (Lettsom), and 'armigerent' (John Sampson, *TLS*, 30 April 1920, p. 272). See Cam., p. 435, n. 48, and Arden, Appendix 1. Nevertheless, *OED* Gaunt *adj* 1 provides favourable or neutral senses of the word as well as negative. 'Arm-gaunt' may also suggest 'fierce-looking in armour' or 'hungry for battle'.

52 ***Was beastly dumbed by him** i.e. was drowned out by the neighing. 'Beastly' plays on two senses: (1) as done by a beast or animal, (2) brutishly, rudely. 'Dumbed' corrects F's 'dumbe'; the mistaking of *d* for *e* is easy in working from manuscript ('dumbd'), as at 1.4.8, 'Vouchsafed'.

53 ***What...merry** The F reading, with no comma after 'What', can be interpreted as 'What, was he sad, or merry?' or 'What was he, sad or merry?'

55 **nor sad** neither sad.

56 **well-divided disposition** well-balanced temperament.

57 **'tis the man** that's just like him, just what he is like.

57 **but** do but, just.

58 **would** wished to.

59 **make their looks by his** fashion their demeanour with him as their model. Compare the emphasis on the importance of being observed here with the later resistance to the idea of being seen in humiliation. The relation between being regarded, regard, and reputation is strong here as elsewhere in Shakespeare (e.g. *Othello*).

Which seemed to tell them his remembrance lay
In Egypt with his joy; but between both.
O heavenly mingle! Be'st thou sad or merry,
The violence of either thee becomes,
So does it no man else. – Met'st thou my posts?

ALEXAS Ay, madam, twenty several messengers.
Why do you send so thick?

CLEOPATRA Who's born that day
When I forget to send to Antony
Shall die a beggar. Ink and paper, Charmian.
Welcome, my good Alexas. Did I, Charmian,
Ever love Caesar so?

CHARMIAN O, that brave Caesar!

CLEOPATRA Be choked with such another emphasis!
Say, 'the brave Antony'.

CHARMIAN The valiant Caesar!

CLEOPATRA By Isis, I will give thee bloody teeth
If thou with Caesar paragon again
My man of men.

CHARMIAN By your most gracious pardon,
I sing but after you.

CLEOPATRA My salad days,
When I was green in judgement, cold in blood,
To say as I said then. But come, away,
Get me ink and paper.

64 man] F2; mans F **74** again] F2; againe: F

62 mingle Used as a noun also at 4.8.37, not elsewhere in Shakespeare (Arden). Abbott 451 discusses Elizabethan freedom in converting one part of speech into another. The idea here of 'well-divided disposition', which might suggest 'measure', breaks down later into a violent extremity of each half, demonstrating an instability with which the play is concerned.

63 thee becomes is becoming to you. Cleopatra returns the compliment offered to her by Antony at 1.1.51–3 (Arden).

64 So As.

64 *man The F reading, 'mans', is an easy error for 'man' in a line also containing 'do's' and 'else'. The F2 emendation has been generally followed.

64 posts messengers.

65 several separate, distinct.

66 thick in rapid succession.

66 Who's Anyone who is.

68 Shall die a beggar i.e. that day will be ill-omened. 'Cleopatra means to say that no such day shall ever dawn' (Kittredge).

70 Caesar Julius Caesar.

70 brave splendid; as at 40.

74 paragon match, compare.

76 salad days 'i.e. before she took to strong meat' (Wilson) or 'explained by *green* in the next line' (Kittredge). See North's Plutarch: 'Caesar and Pompey knew her when she was but a young thing, and knew not then what the world meant' (981C–D).

77 cold in blood lacking in passionate warmth.

He shall have every day a several greeting,
Or I'll unpeople Egypt.

Exeunt

[2.1] *Enter* POMPEY, MENECRATES, *and* MENAS, *in warlike manner*

POMPEY If the great gods be just, they shall assist
The deeds of justest men.
MENAS Know, worthy Pompey,
That what they do delay they not deny.
POMPEY Whiles we are suitors to their throne, decays
The thing we sue for.
MENAS We, ignorant of ourselves,
Beg often our own harms, which the wise powers
Deny us for our good; so find we profit
By losing of our prayers.
POMPEY I shall do well.
The people love me, and the sea is mine;

Act 2, Scene 1 2.1] *Rowe; no act or scene division in* F 2,5 SH MENAS] *Wilson, conj. Capell, Johnson; Mene.* F; *Menecrates / most eds.*

80 several distinct; as at 65.

81 I'll unpeople Egypt 'by sending out messengers' (Johnson) or perhaps with a flamboyant hint of something more menacing, something like 'Or I'll lay waste my kingdom'; a consciously exaggerated expression of her loving Antony beyond all other concerns. Since she has been dealing in the hyperbole of impossibilities at 66–8, her 'Or' may simply signal the preposterous: 'Egypt is so prolific in population that it can't be exhausted' (compare the idiom 'Or I'm a Dutchman').

Act 2, Scene 1

Location Indeterminate; perhaps Sicily, since that place is identified as Pompey's centre of operations in North's Plutarch, 984C–D, and at 2.6.7, 2.6.35, 2.6.45, and 3.6.25 below.

1 shall will certainly (Abbott 315).

2, 5 SH MENAS See supplementary note, p. 259 below.

3 what...deny i.e. a delayed answer to a petition is not a refusal. (A proverbial sentiment; compare Dent D198.1.)

4–5 Whiles...sue for 'while we are praying, the thing for which we pray is losing its value' (Johnson). This is perhaps significantly a more modest address to the gods than the invocations of Antony and Cleopatra in Act 1.

5–8 We...prayers This sentiment was widely known in Elizabethan England, as reflected for example in Rom. 8.26 and in the next-to-last offertory collect of the Communion Service in the Book of Common Prayer ('Almighty God, the fountain of all wisdom, which knowest our necessities before we ask and our ignorance in asking...', 1606 edn, sig. B3^v, cited by Wilson), and need not be derived from Juvenal's Satire X, 346–52, as argued by Theobald and by J. Churton Collins, *Studies in Shakespeare*, 1904, p. 29.

5 ignorant of ourselves 'Know thyself' is proverbial wisdom (Dent K175); compare Antony's confession at 2.2.97–8 that 'poisoned hours had bound me up / From mine own knowledge'.

My powers are crescent, and my auguring hope
Says it will come to th'full. Mark Antony
In Egypt sits at dinner, and will make
No wars without doors. Caesar gets money where
He loses hearts. Lepidus flatters both,
Of both is flattered; but he neither loves,
Nor either cares for him.

MENAS Caesar and Lepidus
Are in the field. A mighty strength they carry.

POMPEY Where have you this? 'Tis false.

MENAS From Silvius, sir.

POMPEY He dreams. I know they are in Rome together
Looking for Antony. But all the charms of love,
Salt Cleopatra, soften thy waned lip!
Let witchcraft joined with beauty, lust with both,
Tie up the libertine in a field of feasts,
Keep his brain fuming. Epicurean cooks,
Sharpen with cloyless sauce his appetite,

16, 18, 39 SH MENAS] *Malone, conj. Capell; Mene.* F **21** waned] *Steevens*[3], *conj. Percy;* wand F; wan *Pope* **22** joined] *This edn, conj. Ridley;* ioyne F

10 powers armed forces. Contrast the 'wise powers' of 6. An element of hubris creeps in here.

10 crescent on the increase.

10 auguring prophesying.

11 it i.e. Pompey's fortunes, imagined as a crescent moon becoming full. Compare also the moon metaphor in 'the sea is mine', 'crescent', and 'come to th'full' at 9–11 – an unconsciously attempted possession of Cleopatra's unstable goddess.

12 sits at dinner On the suggestive connection between eating and sexual pleasure, see 1.5.32, 'A morsel for a monarch,' 2.1.23–7 and 34, 2.2.230–6 and 246–8, 2.6.63–5 and 123; and 3.13.119–23 (Jones).

13 without doors outdoors; i.e. on the field of battle, rather than (as conventionally in Elizabethan love poetry) in the amorous encounters of love. The flat conventionality of Pompey's assessment generally in 11–16 is in interesting contrast to the richer experience of Egypt we have already been offered.

15 Of By.

15 neither loves loves neither. ('Neither' is not paired with 'nor' in 16.)

17 A mighty...carry They command a mighty army.

20 Looking for Awaiting (rather than 'expecting').

20 charms spells.

21 Salt Lustful, wanton. See also 26–7 n. below.

21 *waned faded, withered, as in the waning of the moon (see 10–11 and n.), or perhaps 'made wan'. 'Soften' confirms the idea of 'withered and dry'. F 'wand' could signify 'wann'd', as in *Ham.* 2.2.554: 'all the visage wann'd'.

22 *joined F 'ioyne' may well represent the common *e:d* error for 'ioynd' (Ridley). 'Joined' makes best sense of F's punctuation, preserved here, and makes clear what Pompey is addressing in 'Tie up the libertine...' He is not asking Cleopatra to do these things, but the agencies of amorous surfeiting. The F reading and punctuation can also yield the same sense if the forms are cumulative: 'Let witchcraft, beauty, and lust join forces and all tie up...', etc., but the idiom of that construction is less typically Shakespearean.

23 i.e. tether him in a rich pasture of delights from which he will not wish to stray.

24 fuming The fumes of wine were thought to ascend to the brain, thus causing drunkenness. (Kittredge cites *Mac.* 1.7.63–7 as a parallel.)

25 cloyless that will never satiate.

That sleep and feeding may prorogue his honour
Even till a Lethe'd dullness –

Enter VARRIUS

How now, Varrius?

VARRIUS This is most certain that I shall deliver:
Mark Antony is every hour in Rome
Expected. Since he went from Egypt 'tis
A space for farther travel.

POMPEY I could have given less matter
A better ear. Menas, I did not think
This amorous surfeiter would have donned his helm
For such a petty war. His soldiership
Is twice the other twain. But let us rear
The higher our opinion, that our stirring
Can from the lap of Egypt's widow pluck
The ne'er-lust-wearied Antony.

MENAS I cannot hope
Caesar and Antony shall well greet together.
His wife that's dead did trespasses to Caesar;
His brother warred upon him, although, I think,
Not moved by Antony.

POMPEY I know not, Menas,
How lesser enmities may give way to greater.
Were't not that we stand up against them all,
'Twere pregnant they should square between themselves,

39 ne'er] F (neere) 40 greet] F; gree *conj. Furness* 42 warred] F2 (warr'd); wan'd F 44–5 greater. / Were't...all,] *Rowe;* greater, / Were't...all: F

26–7 **may prorogue...dullness** i.e. may suspend the operation or thought of honour until he is too sunk in lethargy and oblivion to respond to it. It is difficult in 23–6 to distinguish between the literal and figurative notions of eating. The image of eating even gives some credence to the idea of 21 as referring to salted or preserved meat more appetisingly reconstituted.

27 **Lethe'd** All-forgetting. From the river in Hades, the waters of which produced forgetfulness of the past in those who drank.

28 **deliver** report.

30–1 **'tis...travel** there has been time enough for an even longer journey (i.e. he could easily have arrived already).

32 **less** less weighty.

36 **rear** raise.

37 **our opinion** i.e. of ourselves.

38 **Egypt's widow** i.e. Cleopatra, widow of the young King Ptolemy; compare 1.4.6, 17.

39 **hope** expect.

40 **well greet together** meet amicably, settle their differences.

42 **brother** i.e. Lucius Antonius. See 1.2.84 ff., 2.2.48–52.

42 ***warred** The F reading, 'wan'd', probably represents a minim error (Wilson).

43 **moved** encouraged.

44 **lesser...greater** Compare the proverb, 'The greater (one) grief (sorrow) drives out the less (another)' (Dent G446).

46 **pregnant** ripe with potential, very likely.

46 **square** quarrel; as at 3.13.41.

For they have entertainèd cause enough
To draw their swords. But how the fear of us
May cement their divisions and bind up
The petty difference, we yet not know.
Be't as our gods will have't! It only stands
Our lives upon to use our strongest hands.
Come, Menas.

Exeunt

[2.2] *Enter* ENOBARBUS *and* LEPIDUS

LEPIDUS Good Enobarbus, 'tis a worthy deed,
And shall become you well, to entreat your captain
To soft and gentle speech.
ENOBARBUS I shall entreat him
To answer like himself. If Caesar move him,
Let Antony look over Caesar's head
And speak as loud as Mars. By Jupiter,
Were I the wearer of Antonio's beard,
I would not shave't today.
LEPIDUS 'Tis not a time for private stomaching.

Act 2, Scene 2 2.2] *Rowe; no scene division in* F 7 Antonio's] F *(Anthonio's)*; Antonius' *Steevens*

47 **entertainèd** maintained, received (from each other).

49 **cement** Accented on the first syllable.

51–2 **It only...hands** Our very lives depend upon our using our utmost strength. The rhyming couplet gives a sense of completion to the scene, as often elsewhere in this and other of Shakespeare's plays.

Act 2, Scene 2

Location Rome (see 30). Furniture seems to be required for Antony and Caesar to sit. Capell and others specify the house of Lepidus, but Lepidus's role as peacemaker is appropriate to his status as triumvir and does not require him to be host as well. Shakespeare is responsible for conceiving and realising the detail of personal and political tensions here; North's Plutarch tells us simply that 'when Antonius landed in Italy, and that men saw Caesar asked nothing of him, and that Antonius on the other side laid all the fault and burden on his wife Fulvia, the friends of both parties would not suffer them to unrip any old matters...' (984A).

4 **like himself** i.e. in a manner commensurate with his greatness. Compare 1.1.44–5 and n.

4 **move him** i.e. to anger.

5 **look over Caesar's head** i.e. treat Caesar as a man of small stature (Jones). Antony is physically the more imposing and mature.

6 **as loud as Mars** i.e. in an aggressively warlike manner.

7 **Antonio's** This F reading may give a familiar form of address, here and at 2.5.26, though F could also represent an easy compositorial error in reading Shakespeare's manuscript.

8 **I would not shave't** i.e. I would provocatively give Caesar the opportunity of insultingly plucking my beard if he dared. Only Cleopatra will barber Antony (234 below). The insult of plucking or shaking a beard occurs in *Lear* 3.7.36 and 76–7, *Ham.* 2.2.573, *1H6* 1.3.44, and elsewhere. See also *AYLI* 5.4.69–82.

9 **stomaching** resentment, taking offence; compare 'Stomach', 3.4.12.

9–19 Lineation in this edition follows F, in contrast to editorial tradition, which generally

ENOBARBUS Every time serves for the matter that is then born in't.
LEPIDUS But small to greater matters must give way.
ENOBARBUS Not if the small come first.
LEPIDUS Your speech is passion; but pray you stir
No embers up. Here comes the noble Antony.

Enter ANTONY *and* VENTIDIUS [*in conversation*]

ENOBARBUS And yonder Caesar.

Enter CAESAR, MAECENAS, *and* AGRIPPA [*by another door, also in conversation*]

ANTONY If we compose well here, to Parthia.
Hark, Ventidius.
[*They confer apart*]
CAESAR I do not know, Maecenas. Ask Agrippa.
LEPIDUS Noble friends:
That which combined us was most great, and let not
A leaner action rend us. What's amiss,
May it be gently heard. When we debate
Our trivial difference loud, we do commit
Murder in healing wounds. Then, noble partners,
The rather for I earnestly beseech,
Touch you the sourest points with sweetest terms,
Nor curstness grow to th'matter.

14 SD *in conversation*] *Wilson subst.; not in* F 15 SD *by another door, also in conversation*] *Wilson subst.; not in* F 17 SD *They confer apart*] *This edn; not in* F

divides as follows: '...a time / ...Every time / ...born in't. / ...give way. / ...passion; / ...Here comes / ...Caesar. / ...Parthia. / ...not know, / ...friends:' In the F arrangement, Enobarbus speaks at 10 and perhaps what follows in prose whereas he has spoken previously in verse, but his medium elsewhere in the play is generally prose, and the staccato rhythms of the F arrangement throughout this present passage convey a better sense of the taut meeting of two quarrelling leaders than do the fabricated verse lines of editorial tradition. That tradition also unnecessarily divides lines at 9, 13, 14, and 18 when they are plausible pentameter lines in F. 'Passion' in 13 is pronounced in three syllables, as often in Shakespeare.

16 **compose** come to an agreement.

17 **Hark, Ventidius** Antony confers privately with his senior officer (see 3.1), not yet acknowledging Caesar, who in his turn does not acknowledge Antony until Lepidus brings them together. On the possibility of Ventidius's exiting at this point, see 182 SD n.

21 **A leaner action rend us** A slighter cause divide us.

21 **What's** Whatever is.

24 **healing** i.e. attempting to heal. Aggressive discussion destroys the hope of reconciliation it is meant to promote.

25 **The rather for** All the more because.

26 **Touch** (1) touch upon, speak of (*OED* sv *v* 18), (2) probe a wound, apply some substance lightly (*OED* sv *v* 6d, continuing the medical metaphor of 24).

27 **Nor...matter** (1) And do not let quarrelsomeness be added to the matter we

ANTONY 'Tis spoken well.
Were we before our armies, and to fight,
I should do thus.

Flourish

CAESAR Welcome to Rome.
ANTONY Thank you.
CAESAR Sit.
ANTONY Sit, sir.
CAESAR Nay, then.

[*They sit*]

ANTONY I learn you take things ill which are not so,
Or, being, concern you not.
CAESAR I must be laughed at
If or for nothing or a little, I
Should say myself offended, and with you
Chiefly i'th'world; more laughed at that I should
Once name you derogately, when to sound your name
It not concerned me.
ANTONY My being in Egypt, Caesar, what was't to you?
CAESAR No more than my residing here at Rome
Might be to you in Egypt. Yet if you there
Did practise on my state, your being in Egypt
Might be my question.

34 SD] *Jones; not in* F

discuss, (2) And do not irritate or inflame the existing poison and so produce a deadly gangrene (continuing the medical metaphor of 24, and using 'matter' in the sense of 'pus', *OED* Matter *sb*[1] 4).

28 Were we Even if we were.

28 to about to.

29 thus Antony may exchange a handshake or embrace with Caesar. The *Flourish* is suggestive of some ceremonial action (Furness). On the other hand, Antony's words may simply mean that he would speak temperately as Lepidus urges under any circumstances (Arden). Compare Antony's 'thus' at 1.1.39 and n. Antony and Caesar do shake hands later over the marriage agreement (158); their present grudging conversation does not indicate a readiness to shake yet. No flourish greets their ceremonial handshaking at 158. Perhaps it is used in the present instance to signal the commencement of their meeting, or possibly Caesar pauses momentarily over Antony's words and then signals for the flourish, thereby giving himself the edge in the politics of the situation.

34 Nay, then 'Well, then – since you insist' (Kittredge). Caesar sits first, putting an end to their bandying of civilities, and Antony no doubt soon after.

36 being being so; i.e. even if they are.

37 or...or either...or.

39 i'th'world of all people. Caesar would look foolish, he says, to quarrel over straws with his fellow triumvir. Caesar deftly combines compliment and reproach in this reference to Antony as triumvir.

40 Once Under any circumstances, at all.

40 derogately disparagingly.

40–1 when...concerned me i.e. if, as you say, it were none of my business.

45 practise on my state plot against my imperial power.

46 question business.

ANTONY How intend you, ‘practised’?
CAESAR You may be pleased to catch at mine intent
By what did here befall me. Your wife and brother
Made wars upon me, and their contestation
Was theme for you; you were the word of war.
ANTONY You do mistake your business. My brother never
Did urge me in his act. I did enquire it,
And have my learning from some true reports
That drew their swords with you. Did he not rather
Discredit my authority with yours,
And make the wars alike against my stomach,
Having alike your cause? Of this, my letters
Before did satisfy you. If you'll patch a quarrel,
As matter whole you have to make it with,
It must not be with this.

51 your] F; the *Hanmer* 54–7 you. Did...cause?] F3; you, did...cause. F 59 you have to make] F; you haue to take F2; you've not to make *Rowe;* you'd have to make *Sisson*

46 practised ‘Emphatic. The word has an offensive suggestion’ (Kittredge).

48 wife and brother See 1.2.83–9 and 2.1.42.

50 Was theme for you Had you for its theme, was something that concerned you, was conducted on your behalf. The hypothesis that ‘Theame’ in F is a misreading of ‘Thenne’ in Shakespeare's manuscript, involving only a minim error, is also possible (Deighton, *Old Dramatists*, 2nd ser., 1898, p. 41).

50 word watchword; as at 3.1.32. ‘They made war in your name’ (Kittredge).

51 You...business You are mistaken. (Hanmer reads ‘the’ in place of ‘your’, and Oxford follows, reasoning that ‘y^{e}’ may have been misread as ‘y^{r}’.)

52 urge me in his act capitalise on my name to justify his acts (of war).

52 enquire enquire into.

53 reports reporters.

54 drew their swords with you i.e. fought in your army.

54–7 Did he...cause i.e. he injured both my authority and yours, giving us equal offence since our interests were identical.

56 stomach inclination.

57 Having alike your cause I having just as much cause to be displeased as you (at Lucius's action).

58 did satisfy you gave you complete information.

58–60 If you'll...with this i.e. if you want to piece together a quarrel and press it as though it were a complete substantial one (or ‘as though you had all the material for doing so’), you'll have to find something more plausible than this. Perhaps there is a combination of both senses, taking ‘patch’ to mean (1) bring together bits and pieces, and (2) use a sufficient piece of material to cover the hole. In both meanings, ‘as’ = ‘as though’. Alternatively, ‘as’ could mean ‘whereas’ or ‘although’ (see *OED* As *adv* 8d, and *Ham.* 5.2.336–7, ‘Had I but time – as this fell sergeant, Death, / Is strict in his arrest’, proposed by Ridley), in which case the passage could mean, ‘if you insist on manufacturing a quarrel out of shreds and patches, even though you do have other substantial matter to make it with, you cannot do it with this unsubstantial charge’. Such a reading supposes Antony to hint here at his one substantial failure, that of neglecting to send arms and aid as requested, which he does apologise for in 96–105. Many editors accept Rowe's emendation of 59, ‘As matter whole you've not to make it with’, reading this line to mean ‘you will have to invent an occasion for quarrelling with me, since you have no really substantial material to make a quarrel with’.

CAESAR You praise yourself
By laying defects of judgement to me, but
You patched up your excuses.
ANTONY Not so, not so.
I know you could not lack – I am certain on't –
Very necessity of this thought, that I,
Your partner in the cause 'gainst which he fought,
Could not with graceful eyes attend those wars
Which fronted mine own peace. As for my wife,
I would you had her spirit in such another;
The third o'th'world is yours, which with a snaffle
You may pace easy, but not such a wife.
ENOBARBUS Would we had all such wives, that the men might go to wars with the women!
ANTONY So much uncurbable, her garboils, Caesar,
Made out of her impatience – which not wanted
Shrewdness of policy too – I grieving grant
Did you too much disquiet. For that you must
But say I could not help it.
CAESAR I wrote to you
When rioting in Alexandria; you
Did pocket up my letters, and with taunts
Did gibe my missive out of audience.

66 graceful] F; grateful *Pope* 76 disquiet. For...must] *Theobald subst.;* disquiet, for...must, F 77–8 to you / When rioting in Alexandria; you] *Steevens*[2] *subst.;* to you, when rioting in Alexandria you F; to you / When, rioting in Alexandria, you *Oxford*

60–2 You praise...excuses i.e. you make yourself look good by claiming that I have misinterpreted or overreacted, but at the time your excuses were (to use your own word) patched together. The repetition of Antony's word 'patched' is coldly insulting (Kittredge).

63–7 I know...peace I know you must have realised that as your partner in the cause against which Lucius fought I could not condone any military action that was therefore against my interests too. 'Fronted' in 67 means 'opposed, confronted' (*OED* Front *v*[1] 3b). Compare 'To front this present time' (1.4.81).

66 *with graceful eyes attend favourably regard, condone. F's 'grateful' represents an easy *c:t* error (Ridley).

68 I wish you had a wife like her so that you could understand my difficulties. On 'her spirit', see North's Plutarch, 975A–B.

69 snaffle A bridle bit, with less restraining power than a bit provided with a curb. To 'ride with a snaffle' is to guide with a light hand (*OED* Snaffle *sb*[1] 1c).

70 pace train or exercise in pacing, manage.

72 with (1) along with, (2) doing battle with. Enobarbus's wry remark, an aside, does not interrupt Antony's argument, though it does affect the audience's sense of the gravity and tone of the exchange.

73–6 So much...disquiet She being so very unmanageable, Caesar, I regretfully concede that her commotions, brought on by her impatience (at my being in Egypt) but not lacking in keenness of stratagem (calculated to bring me back from Egypt), caused you too much disquiet.

73 uncurbable Continues the metaphor of managing horses in 69–70: even a 'curb bit' (as contrasted with a 'snaffle') would not hold Fulvia (Kittredge).

73 garboils disturbances; as at 1.3.61.

80 missive messenger. The audience has seen what Caesar refers to, at 1.1.18 ff.

ANTONY Sir, he fell upon me ere admitted, then;
Three kings I had newly feasted, and did want
Of what I was i'th'morning. But next day
I told him of myself, which was as much
As to have asked him pardon. Let this fellow
Be nothing of our strife; if we contend,
Out of our question wipe him.

CAESAR You have broken
The article of your oath, which you shall never
Have tongue to charge me with.

LEPIDUS Soft, Caesar!

ANTONY No, Lepidus, let him speak.
The honour is sacred which he talks on now,
Supposing that I lacked it. But on, Caesar –
The article of my oath.

CAESAR To lend me arms and aid when I required them,
The which you both denied.

ANTONY Neglected, rather;
And then when poisoned hours had bound me up
From mine own knowledge. As nearly as I may
I'll play the penitent to you, but mine honesty
Shall not make poor my greatness, nor my power
Work without it. Truth is that Fulvia,
To have me out of Egypt, made wars here,
For which myself, the ignorant motive, do

81 admitted, then;] F *subst.;* admitted: then *Rowe* 98 knowledge.] *Rowe subst.;* knowledge, F

81 ere admitted, then F's punctuation deserves to be restored from Rowe's 'ere admitted: then'. 'Then' is contrasted with 'next day' (83) when the messenger was admitted in proper form (Ridley).

82–3 did want...morning was not at my best as I had been earlier in the day.

84 told him of myself i.e. told him the condition I was in before.

86 Be nothing of Have no part in, be irrelevant to.

87 question contention.

88 article precise terms.

90 Soft Gently, take it easy.

92–3 The honour...lacked it i.e. my honour, which Caesar impugns, positing or implying that I lacked it entirely, is in fact sacred to me. (Antony knows that he is vulnerable to criticism for what he did, but will insist that he did not violate honour since he acted neglectingly rather than with intent to defraud.)

95 required requested.

97 bound me up drugged or paralysed me.

98 From mine own knowledge So that I didn't know what I was doing. A similar appeal to the proverbial wisdom of knowing oneself (Dent K175) occurs earlier at 2.1.5.

99–101 mine honesty...without it my honesty (in admitting this) shall not detract from my authority, nor will that authority be dishonestly or dishonourably used.

102 To...Egypt North's Plutarch reports that Fulvia 'purposely raised this uproar in Italy, in hope thereby to withdraw him from Cleopatra' (984A).

103 motive moving or inciting cause (*OED* sv *sb* 4b).

So far ask pardon as befits mine honour
To stoop in such a case.

LEPIDUS 'Tis noble spoken.

MAECENAS If it might please you to enforce no further
The griefs between ye; to forget them quite
Were to remember that the present need
Speaks to atone you.

LEPIDUS Worthily spoken, Maecenas.

ENOBARBUS Or, if you borrow one another's love for the instant, you may, when you hear no more words of Pompey, return it again. You shall have time to wrangle in when you have nothing else to do.

ANTONY Thou art a soldier only. Speak no more.

ENOBARBUS That truth should be silent I had almost forgot.

ANTONY You wrong this presence, therefore speak no more.

ENOBARBUS Go to, then; your considerate stone.

CAESAR I do not much dislike the matter, but
The manner of his speech; for't cannot be
We shall remain in friendship, our conditions
So differing in their acts. Yet if I knew
What hoop should hold us staunch, from edge to edge
O'th'world I would pursue it.

105 noble] F; Nobly F3 **108** remember that the present need] F (remember: that the present neede,) **114** soldier only. Speak] *Theobald subst.;* Souldier, onely speake F **122–3** staunch, from...world I] *Rowe subst.;* staunch from...world: I F **123** O'th'world] F (Ath'world)

104 honour honourable position, dignity.

105 noble Abbott 1 gives many instances of adjectives used as adverbs.

106 enforce press home, urge (*OED* sv *v* 4). Maecenas's remarks, like those of Agrippa at 124 and following, suggest that Caesar's lieutenants have been well briefed; they begin to conduct the negotiations according to prearranged signal, while the protagonists rest. Enobarbus is not so well briefed, if indeed at all.

107 griefs grievances.

109 atone reconcile.

114 a soldier only i.e. not a statesman. There is no implication of 'common soldier' (Kittredge).

115 Enobarbus wryly recalls the proverb, 'All truths must not be told' (Dent T594). Compare *Lear* 1.4.111: 'Truth's a dog must to kennel.'

116 presence august company.

117 Go to, then A remonstrance of mild protest: All right, then, I get the point.

117 your considerate stone Once again Enobarbus varies a proverbial phrase, 'as still as a stone' (Dent S879). 'Considerate' means 'considering, thinking'. I will be silent, since you wish it, says Enobarbus, but I'm still thinking. 'That the phrase sounds like the respectful conclusion of a letter adds to the suggestion of finality' (Wilson).

120 conditions dispositions, temperaments.

122 hoop i.e. a hoop about a cask, holding it 'staunch' or water-tight (with a suggestion also of 'loyal, unwavering'), as in *2H4* 4.4.43: 'A hoop of gold to bind thy brothers in', and *Ham.* 1.3.63. Rowe's comma after 'staunch', adopted by many editions including this one, is not incontrovertible; since a hoop for the triumvirs would encircle the whole world, one could punctuate, 'staunch from edge to edge / O'th'world, I would pursue it'. Dennis Mitchell, *Explicator* 35.1 (1976), 22–4, defends the F reading. The image of the hoop recalls the notion of a frame collapsing or melting or dissolving, as in 1.1.35 ff. See pp. 34–5 above.

AGRIPPA Give me leave, Caesar.
CAESAR Speak, Agrippa.
AGRIPPA Thou hast a sister by the mother's side,
Admired Octavia. Great Mark Antony
Is now a widower.
CAESAR Say not so, Agrippa.
If Cleopatra heard you, your reproof
Were well deserved of rashness.
ANTONY I am not married, Caesar. Let me hear
Agrippa further speak.
AGRIPPA To hold you in perpetual amity,
To make you brothers, and to knit your hearts
With an unslipping knot, take Antony
Octavia to his wife, whose beauty claims
No worse a husband than the best of men,
Whose virtue and whose general graces speak
That which none else can utter. By this marriage
All little jealousies, which now seem great,
And all great fears, which now import their dangers,

128 not so,] *Rowe;* not, say F 129 Cleopatra] F (*Cleopater*) 129 reproof] *Hanmer;* proofe F; approof *Theobald*

126–80 Here Shakespeare relies considerably on North's Plutarch, 984B–C.

126 by the mother's side Caesar had an elder half-sister on his father's side and a younger full sister, both called Octavia. In North's Plutarch (984B), Antony is said to have married the former ('the eldest sister of Caesar, not by one mother'), though he actually married the latter. Shakespeare's error does not agree with Plutarch's, but the errors do at least have in common the idea of a half-sister.

128 *Say not so F's 'Say not, say' is easy to explain as an error caused by the repetition of the first 'Say'. Although not proposed until Rowe, the emendation has been generally adopted since then.

129–30 *your reproof...rashness your rash speech would well deserve the reprimand you would get. 'Of' = 'for'. F's 'your proofe' is an easy compositorial error if Compositor E misread 'your reproof' as 'yourre proof'.

131 I am not married North's Plutarch says: 'Antonius had been widower ever since the death of his wife, Fulvia. For he denied not that he kept Cleopatra, but so did he not confess that he had her as his wife' (984B). Shakespeare uses this material to produce a barbed exchange between Caesar, who is growingly obsessed with Antony's profligacy (see 1.4.1–10), and the older man, who would like to insist that his love life is his own business (2.2.42) but who is forced to see the relevance of it now that marriage is proposed.

133–6 To hold...wife Wilson notes the verbal parallels in these lines to the Countess of Pembroke's *Antonie* (1592), from 'The Argument': 'Antonius, who for *knitting a straiter bonde of amitie* betweene them had *taken to wife* Octavia' (italics supplied by Wilson). The knot, like the hoop in 122 above, is a metaphor for that which makes secure the essentially separate.

138–9 Whose...can utter Whose virtuous qualities declare themselves as they do in no other woman; i.e. she is a woman of evident and unique virtue. Or possibly, 'whose virtues speak for themselves; no one's words can do justice to them'.

140 jealousies misunderstandings, suspicions.

141 import carry with them.

Would then be nothing. Truths would be tales,
Where now half tales be truths. Her love to both
Would each to other and all loves to both
Draw after her. Pardon what I have spoke,
For 'tis a studied, not a present thought,
By duty ruminated.

ANTONY Will Caesar speak?

CAESAR Not till he hears how Antony is touched
With what is spoke already.

ANTONY What power is in Agrippa
If I would say, 'Agrippa, be it so',
To make this good?

CAESAR The power of Caesar, and
His power unto Octavia.

ANTONY May I never
To this good purpose, that so fairly shows,
Dream of impediment! Let me have thy hand
Further this act of grace; and from this hour
The heart of brothers govern in our loves
And sway our great designs!

CAESAR There's my hand.

[*They clasp hands*]

A sister I bequeath you whom no brother
Did ever love so dearly. Let her live
To join our kingdoms and our hearts; and never
Fly off our loves again!

LEPIDUS Happily, amen!

142–3 Truths...truths] F (Truth's...truth's) **155–6** hand / Further] F; hand; / Further *Theobald* **158** SD] *Collier² subst.; not in* F

142–3 Truths...be truths i.e. even true reports (no matter how disturbing) would be trustingly dismissed as mere rumours, whereas at present half-true reports are taken as the whole truth (and thus cause mistrust).

146 present on the spur of the moment. Agrippa's very language is composed and comes across as 'rehearsed'. See 106 n.

148–9 touched With affected by.

154 so fairly shows looks so promising.

155 impediment Compare Sonnet 116: 'Let me not to the marriage of true minds / Admit impediments.' Wilson writes: 'Both probably derive from the Marriage Service in the Book of Common Prayer.' The image draws attention to the conflation here of the political and the 'sacramental' in an ironic way that is further underscored by 'grace' in the next line and by the grotesque irony of their joining hands as though in celebration of a political 'marriage'. (Their marriage feast is delayed until 2.7.)

155–6 hand Further Theobald's semicolon after 'hand' is widely adopted, but (as Ridley observes) misses the meaning of the F punctuation: 'Give me your hand in furtherance of this act of reconciliation.'

159 bequeath bestow upon.

161–2 never...again may our amity never desert us again. Compare *Lear* 2.4.90: 'The images of revolt and flying off'.

ANTONY I did not think to draw my sword 'gainst Pompey,
For he hath laid strange courtesies and great
Of late upon me. I must thank him only,
Lest my remembrance suffer ill report;
At heel of that, defy him.
LEPIDUS Time calls upon's.
Of us must Pompey presently be sought,
Or else he seeks out us.
ANTONY Where lies he?
CAESAR About the Mount Misena.
ANTONY What is his strength by land?
CAESAR Great and increasing;
But by sea he is an absolute master.
ANTONY So is the fame.
Would we had spoke together! Haste we for it.
Yet, ere we put ourselves in arms, dispatch we
The business we have talked of.
CAESAR With most gladness,
And do invite you to my sister's view,
Whither straight I'll lead you.
ANTONY Let us, Lepidus, not lack your company.

171 Mount Misena] *Sisson (following North's Plutarch)*; Mount-Mesena F; Mount-Misenum *Rowe* 172–3 by land? / CAESAR Great] F; *Caes.* By land great *Hanmer*

164 strange remarkable. At 2.6.44–6 and in North's Plutarch, 984D, we learn that Sextus Pompeius courteously received Antony's mother in Sicily when she fled out of Italy with Fulvia.

165 only at least. The thanks will ring hollow at best under the circumstances; Antony sees the irony but cannot avoid it.

166 i.e. lest I be called an ingrate, forgetful of favours done.

167 At heel of Close on the heels of, immediately after.

168 Of By.

168 presently at once.

171 Misena F 'Mesena' may be an error based on North's 'Misena' (984D). Rowe and others correct to 'Misenum', but Shakespeare did not write this. Wilson suggests that 'Misena' may derive from Amyot's 'Misene'. The place is in south Italy, on the bay of modern Naples, and is not to be confused with Messina, Sicily, where Pompey's operations are presumably based.

172 by land Hanmer and some other editors assign this phrase to Caesar as part of his next speech, arguing that Antony would not ask for information about land armies only, but the argument is too subjective in view of F's clarity. Antony may intend to ask about land forces first and then proceed to estimates of naval strength.

175 So is the fame So it is reported.

176 Would...together Sometimes interpreted as 'would we had exchanged blows, joined battle!' (Schmidt sv 'speak'; Case compares 'speak' at 2.6.25), or 'if only *you and I* had taken counsel together (instead of quarrelling) this disaster (Pompey's mastery of the sea) would never have happened' (Wilson); but more probably Antony simply wishes that the preliminary talk with Pompey were over (Kittredge). Antony envisages negotiations before battle at 165–7 above, and the parley actually occurs in 2.6.

178 most the greatest (Abbott 17).

179 do I do.

179 to my sister's view to see my sister.

180 straight straightway.

LEPIDUS Noble Antony, not sickness should detain me.

Flourish. Exeunt [Caesar, Antony, Lepidus, and Ventidius]. Enobarbus, Agrippa, Maecenas remain

MAECENAS Welcome from Egypt, sir.

ENOBARBUS Half the heart of Caesar, worthy Maecenas! My honourable friend Agrippa!

AGRIPPA Good Enobarbus!

MAECENAS We have cause to be glad that matters are so well digested. You stayed well by't in Egypt.

ENOBARBUS Ay, sir, we did sleep day out of countenance, and made the night light with drinking.

MAECENAS Eight wild boars roasted whole at a breakfast, and but twelve persons there. Is this true?

ENOBARBUS This was but as a fly by an eagle. We had much more monstrous matter of feast, which worthily deserved noting.

MAECENAS She's a most triumphant lady, if report be square to her.

ENOBARBUS When she first met Mark Antony, she pursed up his

182 SD] F *subst.* 188 digested] F (disgested)

182 SD *and Ventidius* Ventidius's one function in this scene is to be engaged in private conversation with Antony as they enter at 14. Antony speaks to him in 16–17, after which Ventidius takes no part in the scene and has no lines at all. Possibly he is meant to exit at 17, after having been given his orders by Antony; but the conditional nature of what Antony then says to him, along with the unmotivated nature of such an abrupt departure almost immediately after entry, suggests that Ventidius silently remains to learn how the negotiations come out. Antony has no 'train', but his general needs to know whether peace is agreed upon or not.

184 Half...Caesar i.e. you who are someone very dear to Caesar (referring to the proverbial idea of 'one soul, heart, or mind in bodies twain', Dent B503.1), or else meaning that Maecenas is one half of Caesar's heart, Agrippa the other. North's Plutarch, 986B, refers to Maecenas and Agrippa as Octavius Caesar's 'two chief friends', thus supporting the second reading here.

188 digested i.e. arranged, settled. F's 'disgested' is an alternative form common in the early seventeenth century.

188 stayed well by't i.e. kept at your swilling, stuck to it. Once the leaders have left, the conversation at once shifts from the political to 'clubman' talk.

189 we did...countenance i.e. we disconcerted day by sleeping right through it (so that we could revel all night). 'To be put out of countenance' is a common expression for being embarrassed or discomforted (Dent C705).

190 light (1) bright with artificial illumination, (2) debauched, (3) light-headed from drink (Arden).

191–2 Eight...there Plutarch says he heard this tale from his grandfather Lampryas, who got it in turn from one Philotas, a physician (982D). Shakespeare heightens the comedy by changing the time from evening to breakfast and allowing the impression to stand that this sort of thing happened all the time (MacCallum, p. 324). Enobarbus naturally plays up the story in response to his listeners' expectations. This comedy does nothing to undermine our sense that Egypt is a place of physical as well as verbal and emotional extravagance and hyperbole.

193 a fly by an eagle A commonplace standard of vast discrepancy; compare Dent E1.

193 by beside, compared with.

194 which...noting Enobarbus sounds as though he is parodying the language and manner of the traveller's tale.

195 triumphant magnificent.

195 square just.

196 pursed up pocketed up, put in her purse (perhaps with bawdy suggestion).

heart upon the river of Cydnus.

AGRIPPA There she appeared indeed, or my reporter devised well for her.

ENOBARBUS I will tell you.
The barge she sat in, like a burnished throne
Burned on the water. The poop was beaten gold;
Purple the sails, and so perfumèd that
The winds were lovesick with them. The oars were silver,
Which to the tune of flutes kept stroke, and made
The water which they beat to follow faster,
As amorous of their strokes. For her own person,
It beggared all description: she did lie
In her pavilion – cloth of gold, of tissue –
O'erpicturing that Venus where we see

197 Cydnus] F2 *(following North's Plutarch)*; Sidnis F **204** lovesick with them. The] *Capell subst.*; Loue-sicke. / With them the F *(or* Loue-sicke *may be followed by a defective comma)*; love-sick with 'em; the *Pope*

197 upon the river of Cydnus Not in Egypt, but in Cilicia, at Tarsus, near the Mediterranean coast in south-eastern modern-day Turkey. The actual meeting did not take place on the river (see 229 ff. below), but the seductive image of Cleopatra begins its work there; throughout the play she is closely associated with water. The historical date is the summer of 41 BC. Shakespeare has in mind a water pageant. For an analogue, see the account of the entertainment at Elvetham, 1591, in Jean Wilson, *Entertainments for Elizabeth I*, 1980, pp. 96–118, esp. pp. 108 ff., and illustration 3 (p. 37 above).

198 appeared indeed 'made a truly magnificent appearance' (Kittredge) – unless something is missing from the text.

198 devised feigned, invented (*OED* Devise *v* 7b).

200–36 Many details in this famous passage are taken from North's Plutarch, 981D–982B, but the idea of presenting it all through the admiring scepticism of Enobarbus as entertainment for his duty-bound but spellbound Roman acquaintances is all Shakespeare's (see pp. 2–3 above). The barge burning on the water is reminiscent, as Arden notes, of a representation of the battle of Actium in Edward Fairfax's translation of Tasso's *Jerusalem Delivered* under the English title *Godfrey of Bulloigne* (1600), Book XVI, stanza 4: 'The waters *burnt* about their vessel good, / Such flames the gold therein enchasèd threw...' Peter Dronke (*N&Q* 225, ns 27 (1980), 172–4) offers an intriguing parallel passage in the late-twelfth-century epic of Troy by Joseph of Exeter, printed some seven times between 1541 and 1608, wherein Joseph describes the ship outfitted by Paris for his expedition to abduct Helen; its brow is clothed in Tyrian purple, the poop is gold, the winds rival one another to see which can swell the sails, and so on. Barges in Shakespeare's day were often used for ceremonial official visits rather than for towing merchandise. Some details, such as the water playing with the oars and the cupids with fans, may have been coloured by Shakespeare's recollection of Marlowe and Nashe's *Dido, Queen of Carthage* 3.1.118–19 and 4.4.48–9; see Harrison, pp. 57–63.

207 As...strokes As if desiring to be beaten with loving strokes. Enobarbus's wordplay on 'strokes' suggests (1) blows (enlarging on the image of 'beat' in 206), (2) caresses, (3) the pulsing stroke of the oars. The close relation between the erotic and the violent or cruel is seen as typically Egyptian.

207 For As for.

209 cloth of gold, of tissue coloured silk interwoven with threads of gold. 'Tissue' means that it was woven of twisted rather than plain thread, being thus of doubly rich texture (Linthicum, pp. 114, 117–18). The phrase occurs in North's Plutarch, 981E. See p. 3 above.

210 O'erpicturing that Venus Surpassing the picture or statue of Venus. Whether Shakespeare had a particular work in mind is unknown. Pliny's *Natural History* (Book XXXV,

The fancy outwork nature. On each side her
Stood pretty dimpled boys, like smiling Cupids,
With divers-coloured fans, whose wind did seem
To glow the delicate cheeks which they did cool,
And what they undid did.

AGRIPPA O rare for Antony!

ENOBARBUS Her gentlewomen, like the Nereides,
So many mermaids, tended her i'th'eyes,
And made their bends adornings. At the helm
A seeming mermaid steers. The silken tackle
Swell with the touches of those flower-soft hands,
That yarely frame the office. From the barge
A strange invisible perfume hits the sense
Of the adjacent wharfs. The city cast
Her people out upon her; and Antony,
Enthroned i'th'market-place, did sit alone,
Whistling to th'air, which, but for vacancy,

214 glow] *Rowe;* gloue F **215** undid did] F; did, undid *conj. Johnson* **216** gentlewomen] F2; Gentlewoman F

chap. 10, trans. Philemon Holland (1601), p. 539B) mentions a famous picture by Apelles, 'Venus Anadyomene' or Venus Rising from the Sea – a subject also painted by Botticelli, and seemingly alluded to in John Lyly's *Sappho and Phao* (1584), 3.3.86 ff. Harold Fisch (*S.Sur.* 23 (1970), 60) argues that this whole scene on the Cydnus 'naturally recalls the most famous scene associated in mythology with the goddess Venus, *viz.*, her riding on a sea-shell wafted by Zephyrs to the foot of mount Cythera. On that occasion she was accompanied by Nereids, Cupids, and Graces.'

211 The fancy The artist's imagination. Compare what Cleopatra says about nature, art, and imagination at 5.2.95–9. Throughout the play, the main characters strive to make themselves works of art. See pp. 28–30 above.

212 like 'in the guise of – not merely resembling' (Kittredge). Also at 216 below and 3.6.44.

214 *glow make glow. On the paradox of cooling and heating, compare 'the bellows and the fan / To cool a gipsy's lust', 1.1.9–10 and n. F 'gloue' is probably a minim error.

216 Nereides Sea nymphs of the Aegean, the fifty daughters of Nereus and Doris, human in shape.

217 So many As if they were so many.

217–18 tended her...adornings i.e. attended to her every glance or nod, and made their graceful bowings lovely to behold, as in a work of art, providing adornment to Cleopatra as the central figure in a tableau. 'I'th'eyes' suggests also that they are not menial servants relegated to the background, but personal attendants, as in *MND* 3.1.165: 'Hop in his walks and gambol in his eyes' (Kittredge, Arden). Paul Chipchase suggests there is a nautical play on words: the gentlewomen exquisitely attending to Cleopatra's wants are imagined in terms of sailors doing delicate rope-work of the kind one can still see decorating sailing ships, where the 'eye' is the loop of a cord and the 'bend' is a knot.

219 A seeming mermaid One of the attendants in mermaid's guise.

219 tackle Refers collectively to sails, ropes, etc. (Arden).

220 Swell i.e. the sails billow as the gentlewomen gracefully handle the lines. The word suggests an erotic sub-text.

221 yarely frame the office readily and nimbly perform their nautical duties.

223 wharfs banks.

226 but for vacancy except that this would have created a vacuum (something that Nature proverbially abhors; Dent N42).

Had gone to gaze on Cleopatra too,
And made a gap in nature.

AGRIPPA Rare Egyptian!

ENOBARBUS Upon her landing, Antony sent to her,
Invited her to supper. She replied,
It should be better he became her guest,
Which she entreated. Our courteous Antony,
Whom ne'er the word of 'No' woman heard speak,
Being barbered ten times o'er, goes to the feast,
And for his ordinary pays his heart
For what his eyes ate only.

AGRIPPA Royal wench!
She made great Caesar lay his sword to bed;
He ploughed her, and she cropped.

ENOBARBUS I saw her once
Hop forty paces through the public street,
And having lost her breath, she spoke, and panted,
That she did make defect perfection
And, breathless, power breathe forth.

MAECENAS Now Antony must leave her utterly.

ENOBARBUS Never. He will not.
Age cannot wither her, nor custom stale
Her infinite variety. Other women cloy
The appetites they feed, but she makes hungry

227 Cleopatra] F (*Cleopater*) **233** heard] F (hard) **236** ate] F (eate) **242** breathless,] *Hanmer;* breathlesse F

227 Had Would have.

231 should might (Abbott 326).

235 ordinary meal, supper at a public table in a tavern or other gathering place where each person pays his share. A humorous choice of term here, that goes of course with the comic picture of Antony whistling to the air, getting barbered ten times over, and so forth. The comedy doesn't puncture the image of Cleopatra herself, unless there is a suggestion that she is the tavern-keeper, as in the double perspective of Agrippa's shift from 'Rare Egyptian' to 'Royal wench'.

236 ate F 'eate' is an old form of the past indicative, like 'et'.

237 great Caesar Julius Caesar; as in North's Plutarch, 981C.

237–8 sword...ploughed Caesar is made to turn his sword into a ploughshare. The phallic image of ploughing is at least as old as Sophocles' *Antigone*, first chorus.

238 cropped bore fruit. North's Plutarch notes that Cleopatra's son Caesarion 'was supposed to be the son of Julius Caesar' (996B). The fact is mentioned also in North's translation of 'The Life of Julius Caesar' (787B). Caesarion is mentioned at 3.6.6 and 3.13.166.

241 That In such a way that.

242 power breathe forth did breathe forth charm. Her breathlessness is charming.

245 stale make stale. Enobarbus may be playing on the proverbial phrase, 'As stale as custom' (Dent C930). Both 'custom' and 'stale' may have risible suggestions of prostitution; see 'custom-shrunk', *MM* 1.2.84, and *OED* Stale *sb*[3] 4.

246 infinite variety More proverbial wisdom from Enobarbus; compare 'Variety takes away satiety' (Dent V18).

246–8 cloy...satisfies The imagery reinforces the association of love and food as at

Where most she satisfies. For vilest things
Become themselves in her, that the holy priests
Bless her when she is riggish.

MAECENAS If beauty, wisdom, modesty can settle
The heart of Antony, Octavia is
A blessèd lottery to him.

AGRIPPA Let us go.
Good Enobarbus, make yourself my guest
Whilst you abide here.

ENOBARBUS Humbly, sir, I thank you.

Exeunt

[2.3] *Enter* ANTONY, CAESAR, OCTAVIA *between them*

ANTONY The world, and my great office, will sometimes
Divide me from your bosom.

OCTAVIA All which time
Before the gods my knee shall bow my prayers
To them for you.

ANTONY Good night, sir. My Octavia,
Read not my blemishes in the world's report.
I have not kept my square, but that to come

248 vilest] F (vildest) Act 2, Scene 3 2.3] *Capell; no scene division in* F

1.5.32, 2.5.1–2, and throughout the play; see pp. 34–6 above.

249 Become themselves Make themselves becoming, attractive.

249 that so that.

250 riggish lustful, wanton. The paradox of holy amorousness (as in the worship of the Venus Verticordia) reappears in the invocation of Cleopatra as 'eastern star', i.e. Venus, at 5.2.302.

251 beauty, wisdom, modesty Octavia, says North's Plutarch, had 'grace, wisdom, and honesty, joined unto so rare a beauty' (984C).

253 lottery prize, gift of fortune.

Act 2, Scene 3

Location Rome. Caesar has invited Antony in the previous scene 'to my sister's view, / Whither straight I'll lead you' (2.2.179–80), and editors since Capell have generally assumed the present scene to be at Caesar's house, but Antony's conversation with the Soothsayer and his summoning of Ventidius are less well suited to such specific location. Shakespeare exploits a fluid sense of place.

5 Don't interpret my blemishes according to what people say.

6 kept my square kept my life in good order, on a straight course. Compare 'if report be square to her', 2.2.195. *OED* Square *sb* 2 cites Thomas Wright, *Passions of the Mind in General* (1604), I, iii, 13: 'To govern the body...by the square of prudence and rule of reason'. 'By th'rule' (7) also plays on the idea of a carpenter's square and ruler. The image is part of the series of metaphors from building and architecture used in the play; it is transferred here from the world itself to individual behaviour. Compare also the images of hoop and knot in the previous scene (2.2.122 and 135 and nn.).

Shall all be done by th'rule. Good night, dear lady.
OCTAVIA Good night, sir.
CAESAR Good night.

Exit [*with Octavia*]

Enter SOOTHSAYER

ANTONY Now, sirrah: you do wish yourself in Egypt?
SOOTHSAYER Would I had never come from thence, nor you thither!
ANTONY If you can, your reason?
SOOTHSAYER I see it in my motion, have it not in my tongue; but yet hie you to Egypt again.
ANTONY Say to me, whose fortunes shall rise higher,
Caesar's or mine?
SOOTHSAYER Caesar's.
Therefore, O Antony, stay not by his side.
Thy daemon – that thy spirit which keeps thee – is
Noble, courageous, high unmatchable,
Where Caesar's is not. But near him thy angel
Becomes afeard, as being o'erpowered; therefore
Make space enough between you.
ANTONY Speak this no more.
SOOTHSAYER To none but thee; no more but when to thee.

8 SH OCTAVIA] F2; *not in* F 9 SD.1 *with Octavia*] *Rowe subst.; not in* F 11 thither] F; Gone thither *Oxford* 14 to Egypt again] F; again to *Egypt / Capell* 20 high unmatchable] F; high, unmatchable F3 22 afeard,] *Collier²*, *conj. Upton;* a feare: F 24 thee; no more...thee.] *Theobald subst.;* thee no more but: when to thee, F

8 SH *OCTAVIA F omits the speech heading, thus assigning this 'Good night, sir' to Antony, but Antony has already said good night to Caesar, and Octavia surely must respond to her husband's farewell.

10–38 Now, sirrah...at odds The details borrowed from North's Plutarch (985A–B) are numerous: the comparing of Antony's fortune with Caesar's, Antony's daemon or angel being afraid, Antony's losing at dice and at drawing lots for pastime as well as at cockfighting and quail-fighting, etc. The passage also consolidates the force of superstition in the play; the preternatural, which Enobarbus's death perhaps confirms, is more than just a fancy throughout.

10 sirrah A form of address to servants and inferiors.

11 nor you thither i.e. would you had never gone to Egypt in the first place.

13 I...tongue 'I feel it but can't express it' (Wilson); 'motion' = a movement of the soul or mind, intuition, inward prompting.

19 daemon Synonymous with 'angel' (21). North's Plutarch explains: 'thy Daemon, said he [the Soothsayer], that is to say the good angel and spirit that keepeth thee, is afraid of his' (985A–B).

19 that thy spirit that spirit of yours. Compare 4.14.79: 'that thy honest sword'.

20–1 courageous...is not Compare North's Plutarch, 985B: 'being courageous and high when he is alone'. 'Where' = 'wherever', not 'whereas'.

22 *afeard F 'a feare' is sometimes defended as meaning 'a thing frightened or terrified', but *OED* offers no support for such a definition. The common *e:d* error seems likely in view of North's Plutarch: 'is affraied of his' (985B), and Shakespeare's 'Is all afraid' (29 below). North's Plutarch also uses the word 'fearful', but it hardly suggests 'a feare'. The form 'afeard' recurs at 2.5.82.

If thou dost play with him at any game,
Thou art sure to lose; and of that natural luck
He beats thee 'gainst the odds. Thy lustre thickens
When he shines by. I say again, thy spirit
Is all afraid to govern thee near him;
But, he away, 'tis noble.

ANTONY Get thee gone.
Say to Ventidius I would speak with him.

Exit [*Soothsayer*]

He shall to Parthia. – Be it art or hap,
He hath spoken true. The very dice obey him,
And in our sports my better cunning faints
Under his chance. If we draw lots, he speeds;
His cocks do win the battle still of mine
When it is all to naught, and his quails ever
Beat mine, inhooped, at odds. I will to Egypt;
And though I make this marriage for my peace,
I'th'East my pleasure lies.

Enter VENTIDIUS

O, come, Ventidius.
You must to Parthia; your commission's ready.
Follow me and receive't.

Exeunt

30 away,] *Pope;* alway F 31, 40 Ventidius] F2; *Ventigius* F *(and throughout scene)* 31 SD *Soothsayer*] *Rowe; not in* F 40 SD] *Placed as in Dyce; after 40 in* F

26 of out of, in consequence of (Abbott 168).

27 thickens grows dim and obscured.

28 by nearby.

28–9 I say...near him Compare North's Plutarch: 'becometh fearful and timorous when he cometh near unto the other' (985B).

30 *away F's 'alway' is an easy error, and the sense seems to require this generally accepted emendation.

32 art or hap prophetic skill or mere chance, luck.

34 cunning skill.

35 chance luck.

35 speeds wins.

36 still always.

36 of from.

37 When...naught When the odds are everything to nothing (in my favour).

38 inhooped confined within a hoop (to make them fight). Quail fighting, well known to the ancients and mentioned in North's Plutarch (985B), was not common in Elizabethan England, but cockfighting was, and Shakespeare appears to have embellished North from his own observation. Arden cites an epigram of Sir John Davies of Hereford (*Works*, ed. Alexander Grosart, 1869–76, II, 'Upon English Proverbs', p. 47, no. 287): 'For cocking in hoops is now all the play', and a reproduction and description by Francis Douce (*Illustrations of Shakspeare*, 1807, II, 86–7), of a Chinese miniature painting in which quails are 'actually *inhoop'd*' within a hoop, a small, low circular enclosure, set on a table, for the amusement of ladies.

38 at odds against the odds.

41 commission i.e. as commander in Parthia (as is shown in 3.1). On the management of the time scheme, by which the urgency of 2.2.176 is maintained alongside the suggestion of an extended time frame in which the Parthian campaign might have taken place, see pp. 42–3 above.

[2.4] *Enter* LEPIDUS, MAECENAS, *and* AGRIPPA

LEPIDUS Trouble yourselves no further. Pray you hasten
Your generals after.
AGRIPPA Sir, Mark Antony
Will e'en but kiss Octavia, and we'll follow.
LEPIDUS Till I shall see you in your soldiers' dress,
Which will become you both, farewell.
MAECENAS We shall,
As I conceive the journey, be at th'Mount
Before you, Lepidus.
LEPIDUS Your way is shorter;
My purposes do draw me much about.
You'll win two days upon me.
MAECENAS, AGRIPPA Sir, good success!
LEPIDUS Farewell.
Exeunt

[2.5] *Enter* CLEOPATRA, CHARMIAN, IRAS, *and* ALEXAS

CLEOPATRA Give me some music; music, moody food
Of us that trade in love.
ALL The music, ho!

Act 2, Scene 4 2.4] *Capell; no scene division in* F 6 at th'] *This edn;* at the F2; at F 9 SH MAECENAS, AGRIPPA] *Capell; Both.* F **Act 2, Scene 5** 2.5] *Pope; no scene division in* F 0 SD CLEOPATRA] F *(Cleopater)* 2 SH ALL] F *(Omnes)*

Act 2, Scene 4

Location Rome. The designation of 'a street' in most editions is too specific.

1 Trouble...further A courteous dismissal: Maecenas and Agrippa need assist Lepidus no further or attend on his journey, he says.

6 *th'Mount i.e. Mount Misenum (or 'Misena'), where the conference with Pompey is to take place. See 2.2.171 above and North's Plutarch, 984D. F's omission of the definite article is probably a simple error of omission, but may be metrically suggestive; hence, this edition reads 'th'Mount' where most editions read 'the Mount'.

8 draw me much about take me the long way round.

Act 2, Scene 5

Location Alexandria, as in Scenes 1–3 and 5 of Act 1.

1 moody melancholy. Compare *TN* 1.1.1: 'If music be the food of love, play on.'

2 trade engage (but with a suggestion of majestic whoring).

2 The music, ho Mardian's entrance in response to this command makes clear that he is the court singer, as at 1.5.10.

Enter MARDIAN *the eunuch*

CLEOPATRA Let it alone. Let's to billiards. Come, Charmian.
CHARMIAN My arm is sore. Best play with Mardian.
CLEOPATRA As well a woman with an eunuch played
As with a woman. Come, you'll play with me, sir?
MARDIAN As well as I can, madam.
CLEOPATRA And when good will is showed, though't come too short,
The actor may plead pardon. I'll none now.
Give me mine angle; we'll to the river. There,
My music playing far off, I will betray
Tawny-finned fishes. My bended hook shall pierce
Their slimy jaws, and as I draw them up
I'll think them every one an Antony
And say, 'Aha! You're caught.'
CHARMIAN 'Twas merry when
You wagered on your angling, when your diver
Did hang a salt fish on his hook, which he
With fervency drew up.
CLEOPATRA That time? – O times! –
I laughed him out of patience; and that night
I laughed him into patience, and next morn,

3 billiards] F (Billards) 10–11 river. There, / My...off,] F4 *subst.;* Riuer there / My...off. F 12 Tawny-finned] *Theobald;* Tawny fine F 12 fishes. My] *Capell subst.;* fishes, my F

3 **billiards** Shakespeare may have taken the notion of billiards as an Egyptian game played by ladies from George Chapman's *The Blind Beggar of Alexandria* (1598), iv.12–13: 'Send for some ladies to go play with you / At chess, at billiards...' (A. A. Adee, *Literary World*, 21 April 1883, p. 131, cited by Furness).

5 **played** With sexual suggestion.

7 **As well as I can** Mardian offers up his physical deficiency for humour as he did at 1.5.16: 'Not in deed, madam'.

8 **when good will is showed** Cleopatra continues her bawdy witticisms at Mardian's expense (see 1.5.9 ff.) by varying the proverbial phrase, 'to take the will for the deed' (Dent W393). 'Will' has the connotation of 'sexual desire', as in Sonnet 135 and elsewhere. 'Come too short' is a dig at Mardian's emasculation and inability to achieve sexual completion.

9 **I'll none now** I won't play billiards after all. (Compare 'Let it alone' (3), i.e. never mind about the music.)

10 **angle** fishing rod; with suggestion of a phallic preoccupation, as with billiard cues. (The imaginative shift to the river nicely echoes Enobarbus's description of her at 2.2.200 ff., with variation of tone.) The words 'angle', 'pierce', and 'jaws' (10–13) all occur in the Genevan text of Job 40.21, referring to the Leviathan: 'Canst thou pierce his jaws with an angle?' (Shaheen).

12 ***Tawny-finned** F 'Tawny fine' represents another *e:d* error, as at 1.4.8 and 1.5.52.

15–18 **'Twas merry...drew up** North's Plutarch tells this tale, adding that Antony had recently ordered his men to put real fish on his line in order that he might impress Cleopatra with his fishing (983C–D). In other words, he asked for it. Shakespeare changes this into a wager between them.

17 **salt** preserved in salt. North's Plutarch: 'some old salt fish' (983D). Stockfish were often associated with sexual impotence, as in the joking about 'Poor John' in *Rom.* 1.1.30–1.

Ere the ninth hour, I drunk him to his bed;
Then put my tires and mantles on him, whilst
I wore his sword Philippan.

Enter a MESSENGER

O, from Italy!
Ram thou thy fruitful tidings in mine ears,
That long time have been barren.

MESSENGER Madam, madam –

CLEOPATRA Antonio's dead! If thou say so, villain,
Thou kill'st thy mistress; but well and free,
If thou so yield him, there is gold, and here
My bluest veins to kiss – a hand that kings
Have lipped, and trembled kissing.

MESSENGER First, madam, he is well.

CLEOPATRA Why, there's more gold. But, sirrah, mark, we use
To say the dead are well. Bring it to that,
The gold I give thee will I melt and pour
Down thy ill-uttering throat.

MESSENGER Good madam, hear me.

CLEOPATRA Well, go to, I will.

23 SD] *Placed as in Collier; after 23 in* F 26 Antonio's] F *(Anthonyo's);* Antonius *Delius* 28 him, there] *Pope*[2]; him. / There F

21 the ninth hour 9 a.m., as in *JC* 2.4.23, though in Roman reckoning the ninth hour would be 3 p.m.

21 drunk drank. (Abbott 339 gives other past indicative forms with *u*.)

22 tires headdresses; but the word can also mean 'attire'. As Warburton notes, Cleopatra's actions recall those of Omphale, the Amazonian Queen of Lydia who enslaved Hercules (Antony's mythical ancestor; see 4.12.44), attiring him in her garments and obliging him to spin while she wore his lion's skin. Propertius refers to the story in his *Elegies*, Book III, Elegy 11. On the kind of bisexuality that enables Antony and Cleopatra to incorporate aspects of each other, see pp. 26–30 above and illustration 1 (p. 10).

23 Philippan i.e. Philippian. So named for the victory over Brutus and Cassius at the battle of Philippi, 42 BC. The victor at Philippi is now vanquished by a woman. Naming swords after a victory (or a mistress) is found in medieval romances; historically, Antony had no such named sword (Theobald).

24–5 Ram...barren The extraordinary vigour of the sexual imagery here calls to mind the Roman empress who is supposed to have lamented the fact that the female anatomy has only seven orifices.

26 Antonio's The F reading is here retained as a familiar form of address, but the emendation to 'Antonius' is also possible; see 2.2.7.

27 free i.e. not captive to Caesar; see 45.

28 yield (1) grant, allow (*OED* sv *v* 10b); (2) report (*OED* sv *v* 12b).

32 sirrah A form of address to servants and inferiors, as at 2.3.10.

33 the dead are well i.e. well out of it, in heaven. A euphemism often used in Shakespeare to soften the blow of unwelcome news, as when Balthasar speaks of the seemingly dead Juliet in *Rom.* 5.1.17: 'Then she is well and nothing can be ill.' See also *Mac.* 4.3.177, and 2 Kings 4.26 in the Bishops' Bible (Noble, p. 240).

33 Bring it to that If it comes to *that*.

37 go to all right then (pettishly or apologetically or remonstratingly, as the actress decides); as at 2.2.117.

But there's no goodness in thy face, if Antony
Be free and healthful – so tart a favour
To trumpet such good tidings! If not well,
Thou shouldst come like a Fury crowned with snakes,
Not like a formal man.

MESSENGER Will't please you hear me?

CLEOPATRA I have a mind to strike thee ere thou speak'st.
Yet if thou say Antony lives, is well,
Or friends with Caesar, or not captive to him,
I'll set thee in a shower of gold and hail
Rich pearls upon thee.

MESSENGER Madam, he's well.

CLEOPATRA Well said.

MESSENGER And friends with Caesar.

CLEOPATRA Thou'rt an honest man.

MESSENGER Caesar and he are greater friends than ever.

CLEOPATRA Make thee a fortune from me.

MESSENGER But yet, madam –

CLEOPATRA I do not like 'But yet'; it does allay
The good precedence. Fie upon 'But yet'!
'But yet' is as a gaoler to bring forth
Some monstrous malefactor. Prithee, friend,
Pour out the pack of matter to mine ear,
The good and bad together: he's friends with Caesar,
In state of health, thou say'st, and, thou say'st, free.

MESSENGER Free, madam? No! I made no such report.
He's bound unto Octavia.

38 face, if] F2; face if F 44 is] *Capell, conj. Tyrwhitt;* 'tis F 53 But] F2; Bur F

39 tart a favour sour a face.

40 trumpet As in sounding a triumphal flourish.

41 like in the shape of. In Aeschylus's *The Eumenides*, the Erinyes (Furies) are represented as having snakes twined in their hair. Cleopatra alludes to snakes repeatedly in this scene, at 80 and 97; see also 118.

42 like a formal man in ordinary human form (as contrasted with the Furies).

46–7 I'll...upon thee Probably an allusion to the story of Danaë, a princess of Argos imprisoned by her father in a brazen tower where she was visited by Zeus in the form of a shower of gold. Cleopatra characteristically expresses her largesse and power in an image of amorous encounter.

48 honest worthy.

51–2 does...precedence qualifies and abates the good news that preceded it. 'Allay', to put down (*OED* sv v^1), is historically confused with 'allay' (*OED* sv v^2) or 'alloy', to mix with base metal. Cleopatra does not like to see the pure gold of the Messenger's good news debased with 'But yet'.

55 pack As if the Messenger were a pedlar. Cleopatra returns to this metaphor at 106–7 (Arden).

CLEOPATRA For what good turn?
MESSENGER For the best turn i'th'bed.
CLEOPATRA I am pale, Charmian.
MESSENGER Madam, he's married to Octavia.
CLEOPATRA The most infectious pestilence upon thee!
Strikes him down
MESSENGER Good madam, patience.
CLEOPATRA What say you?
Strikes him
Hence,
Horrible villain, or I'll spurn thine eyes
Like balls before me! I'll unhair thy head!
She hales him up and down
Thou shalt be whipped with wire, and stewed in brine,
Smarting in ling'ring pickle!
MESSENGER Gracious madam,
I that do bring the news made not the match.
CLEOPATRA Say 'tis not so, a province I will give thee
And make thy fortunes proud. The blow thou hadst
Shall make thy peace for moving me to rage,
And I will boot thee with what gift beside
Thy modesty can beg.
MESSENGER He's married, madam.
CLEOPATRA Rogue, thou hast lived too long! *Draw a knife*
MESSENGER Nay then, I'll run.
What mean you, madam? I have made no fault. *Exit*
CHARMIAN Good madam, keep yourself within yourself.
The man is innocent.
CLEOPATRA Some innocents scape not the thunderbolt.
Melt Egypt into Nile, and kindly creatures

59 good turn good purpose. Taking the Messenger's word 'bound' in the sense of 'obliged', she asks what favour Octavia has done Antony (Kittredge).

60 turn feat, piece of work, spell or bout; here with a sexual suggestion, as in the modern American use of the word 'trick'. The Messenger presumably doesn't mean to be coarse, but doesn't know how else to answer the question.

64 spurn kick. She will make footballs of his eyes. As before, the hyperbole of invective is as impressive as that of compliment and reward.

65 SD ***hales*** drags (by the hair).

67 pickle pickling solution.

71 make thy peace atone, compensate.

72 boot thee with give you as well ('to boot' = 'in addition', 'into the bargain'); or 'enrich you with' (*OED* Boot *v*[1] 4), 'make amends to you with'.

72 what whatever.

73 Thy modesty i.e. a man of your modest expectations. A request that would seem enormous to him would be a trifle to her.

76 keep...within yourself contain yourself. 'The opposite of "beside yourself"' (Wilson).

79 Melt Egypt into Nile Compare 'Let Rome in Tiber melt' (1.1.35), and p. 26 above.

79 kindly possessing good natural qualities, goodly (*OED* sv *adj* 4).

Turn all to serpents! Call the slave again.
Though I am mad, I will not bite him. Call!

CHARMIAN He is afeard to come.

CLEOPATRA I will not hurt him.

[*The Messenger is sent for*]

These hands do lack nobility, that they strike
A meaner than myself, since I myself
Have given myself the cause.

Enter the MESSENGER *again*

Come hither, sir.
Though it be honest, it is never good
To bring bad news. Give to a gracious message
An host of tongues, but let ill tidings tell
Themselves when they be felt.

MESSENGER I have done my duty.

CLEOPATRA Is he married?
I cannot hate thee worser than I do
If thou again say 'Yes'.

MESSENGER He's married, madam.

CLEOPATRA The gods confound thee, dost thou hold there still?

MESSENGER Should I lie, madam?

CLEOPATRA O, I would thou didst,
So half my Egypt were submerged and made
A cistern for scaled snakes! Go, get thee hence.
Hadst thou Narcissus in thy face, to me
Thou wouldst appear most ugly. He is married?

82 SD] *Bevington; not in* F 85 SD] *Placed as in Arden; after 85 in* F 98 face, to me] F2; face to me, F

81 Though...him Cleopatra plays on the word 'mad' = (1) furious, (2) insane – like the proverbial mad dog that bites its master (Dent M2.2).

82 SD Most editors have Charmian exit here and return with the Messenger at 85, but she need do no more than go to the door; perhaps she looks out of the door as she says, 'He is afeard to come', seeing him cowering there. (Ridley offers a similar reading.)

84 meaner one of lower station.

84–5 I myself...the cause i.e. I am the one to blame, having loved Antony so infatuatedly.

87 gracious pleasing.

88–9 let...be felt i.e. let bad news tell itself by being felt rather than pronounced; let the unfortunate event announce itself.

94 confound destroy.

94 hold there still stick to that story.

96 So Even if. Half Egypt would not be too great a price to pay to have the report prove false. It's as though Cleopatra is prepared to let the fertilising Nile become merely destructive.

98 Narcissus A youth of Greek mythology, so beautiful that he fell in love with his own reflected image (Ovid, *Metamorphoses*, III, 428, ff., Golding's translation). The nymph Echo fell in love with Narcissus, but offended Hera and was punished by being condemned to use her tongue only to repeat whatever was said to her – a plight of the unhappy lover which is perhaps echoed here in Cleopatra's plaintive refrain: 'Is he married?' 'He is married?' 'He is married?' in answer to the Messenger's 'He's married, madam', 'He's married to Octavia' (91–103).

MESSENGER I crave your highness' pardon.
CLEOPATRA He is married?
MESSENGER Take no offence that I would not offend you;
To punish me for what you make me do
Seems much unequal. He's married to Octavia.
CLEOPATRA O, that his fault should make a knave of thee,
That art not what thou'rt sure of! Get thee hence.
The merchandise which thou hast brought from Rome
Are all too dear for me. Lie they upon thy hand,
And be undone by 'em!
[*Exit Messenger*]
CHARMIAN Good your highness, patience.
CLEOPATRA In praising Antony, I have dispraised Caesar.
CHARMIAN Many times, madam.
CLEOPATRA I am paid for't now. Lead me from hence;
I faint. O Iras, Charmian! – 'Tis no matter.
Go to the fellow, good Alexas. Bid him
Report the feature of Octavia, her years,
Her inclination. Let him not leave out
The colour of her hair. Bring me word quickly.
[*Exit Alexas*]
Let him for ever go! – Let him not, Charmian.
Though he be painted one way like a Gorgon,
The other way's a Mars. [*To Mardian*] Bid you Alexas

105 art] F; act *Oxford; variously emended by many eds. (e.g.* That say'st but what thou'rt sure of *Hanmer;* That art – not what? – Thou'rt sure on't *Johnson)* **108** SD] *Rowe; not in* F **116** SD] *Capell; not in* F **119** SD] *Capell; not in* F

100 I crave…pardon i.e. I'm sorry that I cannot answer as you would have me.

101 Don't be offended that I am hesitant to offend you (by repeating the bad news).

103 much unequal most unjust.

104–5 O, that…sure of i.e. it's regrettable that Antony's fault should make you seem a villain in my eyes, you who are not yourself hateful like the fact you're so sure of. (The line troubles editors and is often emended; see collation.)

107 dear expensive (but with a play on 'lovable' in reference to Antony).

107–8 Lie they…by 'em May the merchandise remain in your possession unsold, and may you be ruined by it. Perhaps a reference to the idea of wealth as a curse. The merchandising metaphor recalls the 'pack of matter' in 55, said as though the Messenger were a pedlar, and Cleopatra's amused reference to 'us that trade in love' (2). See Joseph S. Stull, 'Cleopatra's magnanimity: the dismissal of the messenger', *SQ* 7 (1956), 73–8.

112 I faint A poignant reprise of Cleopatra's earlier tactical fainting, 1.3.15–17, and an anticipation of her fainting at the death of Antony, 4.15.71–7.

114 feature physical appearance.

115 inclination disposition.

117 him i.e. Antony (in both instances).

118–19 painted one way…a Mars Antony is like the type of picture known as a perspective, constructed so as to create an optical illusion whereby dissimilar images are to be perceived from different points of view, as in *H5* 5.2.320–1: 'you see them perspectively: the cities turn'd into a maid'; also *R2* 2.2.18 ff., and *TN* 5.1.217.

118 Gorgon At the sight of the Gorgon Medusa – her head crowned with snakes like the Fury in 41 – a viewer was turned to stone.

Bring me word how tall she is. – Pity me, Charmian,
But do not speak to me. Lead me to my chamber.
Exeunt

[2.6] *Flourish. Enter* POMPEY [*and*] MENAS *at one door, with Drum and Trumpet; at another,* CAESAR, LEPIDUS, ANTONY, ENOBARBUS, MAECENAS, AGRIPPA, *with Soldiers marching*

POMPEY Your hostages I have, so have you mine,
And we shall talk before we fight.
CAESAR Most meet
That first we come to words, and therefore have we
Our written purposes before us sent,
Which if thou hast considered, let us know
If 'twill tie up thy discontented sword
And carry back to Sicily much tall youth
That else must perish here.
POMPEY To you all three,
The senators alone of this great world,
Chief factors for the gods: I do not know

Act 2, Scene 6 2.6] *Pope; no scene division in* F 0 SD.1 *and* MENAS] *Placed as in Rowe; named in* F *after / Agrippa* 7, 35, 45 Sicily] F2 *(following North's Plutarch);* Cicelie F 10 gods: I] *Arden;* Gods. I F; Gods, – I *Theobald*

Act 2, Scene 6

Location Near 'Mount Misena', or Misenum, in the vicinity of modern Naples; at 2.4.6 Maecenas and the rest are leaving Rome to meet Pompey there (see also 2.2.171). North's Plutarch reports that 'they met all three together by the mount of Misena, upon a hill that runneth far into the sea', with Pompey's ships hard by at anchor and the triumvirs' armies on the shore (984D). The historical date is 39 BC.

0 SD *and MENAS F's order of entry, naming Menas after Agrippa, is possible if those who do not speak during the negotiations are grouped here at the end of the stage direction and thus relegated to the background (Ridley), but since the armies are followed by their officers and soldiers, and since the two sides enter from different stage doors (signifying that they are encountering one another, not that they are indoors), an entry by Menas from the second door would seem to place him in the wrong camp. Wilson speculates that Shakespeare may have added Menas's name later when he came to write the prose epilogue to this scene. In support of Wilson's view, it may be significant that Pompey in 1 speaks of 'I' rather than the 'we' one might expect if he were originally teamed with Menas here.

0 SD *Drum and Trumpet* Drummer and trumpeter.

2 meet fitting.

4 purposes propositions (*OED* Purpose *sb* 4).

7 tall brave.

9 senators alone i.e. sole leaders of the state; but the choice of words implies a criticism that the triumvirs have supplanted the senators of Rome, whose republican traditions Pompey purports to represent.

10 factors agents; but with overtones of 'perpetrators', 'partisans' (*OED* Factor 1, 2). The sarcasm continues. Compare *1H4* 3.2.147–8, for the suggestion of presumption.

10–14 I do...for him I cannot see why my father should lack avengers, having me his son and other friends or relatives, just as Julius Caesar (who appeared as a ghost to the worthy Brutus at the battle of Philippi) had you for his avengers there. 'Since' in 12 also implies a more

Wherefore my father should revengers want,
Having a son and friends, since Julius Caesar,
Who at Philippi the good Brutus ghosted,
There saw you labouring for him. What was't
That moved pale Cassius to conspire? And what
Made th'all-honoured, honest Roman, Brutus,
With the armed rest, courtiers of beauteous freedom,
To drench the Capitol, but that they would
Have one man but a man? And that is it
Hath made me rig my navy, at whose burden
The angered ocean foams, with which I meant
To scourge th'ingratitude that despiteful Rome
Cast on my noble father.

CAESAR Take your time.

ANTONY Thou canst not fear us, Pompey, with thy sails.
We'll speak with thee at sea. At land thou know'st
How much we do o'ercount thee.

POMPEY At land indeed
Thou dost o'ercount me of my father's house;
But since the cuckoo builds not for himself,
Remain in't as thou mayst.

16 Made th'] *This edn;* Made F; Mad the F2; Made the F3 **16** honest Roman, Brutus] F2 *subst.;* honest, Romaine *Brutus* F **19** is] F2; his F

direct causality: since Julius Caesar brought down my father, Pompey the Great, and since you furthered Caesar's cause against the republicans who assassinated Caesar, it follows that I and my friends should avenge Pompey the Great by warring on the triumvirs. This second meaning introduces what Pompey says next. On 'Philippi' and 'ghosted', see *JC* 4.3.275–87.

15 pale Cassius Caesar mistrusted the pale looks of Cassius (North's Plutarch, 'The Life of Julius Caesar', 792E; compare the 'lean and hungry look' of Cassius in *JC* 1.2.194), but Pompey is speaking admiringly, and perhaps uses the word to suggest earnestness of purpose.

16 *Made th'all-honoured F's omission of the definite article is probably accidental, but may be metrically suggestive; hence, this edition reads 'th'all-honoured' where most editions read 'the all-honoured'. Compare 2.4.6, 'th'Mount'.

16 honest honourable.

17 courtiers i.e. freedom is their only monarch.

18 drench drown (in blood).

19 Have one man but a man i.e. prevent one man, Julius Caesar, from being crowned, lest he thus 'become a god' (*JC* 1.2.116).

19 *is F's 'his' is an easy error. The F2 emendation is universally accepted.

24 fear frighten.

25 speak with thee encounter you. Antony's readiness to fight at sea, where Pompey is acknowledged 'absolute master' (2.2.174), anticipates his bravado towards Caesar at Actium (3.7.27 ff.).

26 o'ercount outnumber. But at 27 'o'ercount' = 'overreach', 'cheat'. North's Plutarch reports that when Pompey the Great's house was put up for open sale (after having been confiscated by the government), Antony bought it but then balked at payment, and proceeded to offend many people by his riotous living in the house of a man noted for his temperate life (975A, 979B, 984E). Pompey taunts Antony also with wordplay on 'at land' (25–6): (1) on land, where armies fight, (2) in terms of landed estate.

28–9 since the cuckoo . . . thou mayst i.e. since like the cuckoo, which lays its eggs in other birds' nests, you have taken a house that does not

LEPIDUS Be pleased to tell us –
For this is from the present – how you take
The offers we have sent you.
CAESAR There's the point.
ANTONY Which do not be entreated to, but weigh
What it is worth embraced.
CAESAR And what may follow
To try a larger fortune.
POMPEY You have made me offer
Of Sicily, Sardinia; and I must
Rid all the sea of pirates; then, to send
Measures of wheat to Rome. This 'greed upon,
To part with unhacked edges and bear back
Our targes undinted.
CAESAR, ANTONY, LEPIDUS That's our offer.
POMPEY Know then
I came before you here a man prepared
To take this offer. But Mark Antony
Put me to some impatience. Though I lose
The praise of it by telling, you must know,
When Caesar and your brother were at blows,
Your mother came to Sicily, and did find
Her welcome friendly.
ANTONY I have heard it, Pompey,
And am well studied for a liberal thanks
Which I do owe you.
POMPEY Let me have your hand.
[*They shake hands*]
I did not think, sir, to have met you here.

30 For...present – how you take] *Theobald subst.;* (For...present how you take) F **39** SH CAESAR...LEPIDUS] *Capell; Omnes.* F **42–3** impatience. Though...telling,] *Theobald;* impatience: though...telling. F **48** SD] *Collier² subst.; not in* F

belong to you, remain in it as long as you can. (Pompey implies a threat.)

30 from the present digressing from the business at hand.

32–3 Which do not...embraced Do not regard this as an entreaty; simply consider what it is worth to you if you accept it.

34 To try a larger fortune i.e. 'if you reject our offer and try what the fortune of war can do for your ambitions'; or 'if you join with us to share a greater fortune'. Caesar offers a veiled threat or a promise.

34–9 You have...undinted The particular terms of the treaty are in North's Plutarch, 984D.

36 to send I am to send.

38 To part We are to part company.

38 edges swords.

39 targes shields.

42–3 Though...telling It is a proverbial idea that praise of oneself is self-defeating (Dent M476, P547).

43 you must know I would have you know.

44 your brother Lucius. (See 1.2.84 ff.)

45 Your mother See 2.2.164 and n., and North's Plutarch, 984D, for an account of Pompey's generosity on this occasion.

47 well studied for fully prepared to deliver.

ANTONY The beds i'th'East are soft; and thanks to you,
That called me timelier than my purpose hither,
For I have gained by't.
CAESAR Since I saw you last,
There's a change upon you.
POMPEY Well, I know not
What counts harsh fortune casts upon my face,
But in my bosom shall she never come
To make my heart her vassal.
LEPIDUS Well met here.
POMPEY I hope so, Lepidus. Thus we are agreed.
I crave our composition may be written
And sealed between us.
CAESAR That's the next to do.
POMPEY We'll feast each other ere we part, and let's
Draw lots who shall begin.
ANTONY That will I, Pompey.
POMPEY No, Antony, take the lot. But, first or last,
Your fine Egyptian cookery shall have
The fame. I have heard that Julius Caesar
Grew fat with feasting there.
ANTONY You have heard much.
POMPEY I have fair meanings, sir.

54 casts] F (cast's) 58 composition] F2; composion F 67 meanings] *Malone, conj. Heath;* meaning F

50 thanks to you my thanks to you (for being the occasion of my leaving the indulgent pleasure of Egypt). Antony does not mean that it is 'thanks to you' the beds in the East are soft.

51 timelier than my purpose earlier than I would otherwise have resolved.

54 counts tally marks. From the practice of 'casting accounts' by means of marks or notches on a tally stick.

58 composition agreement. Compare 'compose', 2.2.16.

59 sealed between us affixed with an official seal by each co-signer. Compare 3.2.3, where the triumvirs are 'sealing' their agreements.

61 Draw lots Shakespeare follows North's Plutarch (984D): 'Now, after they had agreed that Sextus Pompeius should have Sicily and Sardinia...one of them did feast another, and drew cuts who should begin.'

61 That will I i.e. I will begin, will host the first feast.

62 take the lot i.e. draw lots with the rest of us – no doubt an ominous suggestion to Antony in view of his being so susceptible to ill luck in Caesar's presence (2.3.33–8). (In fact, it is Pompey who begins the feasting, 82.)

62 first or last whether you go first (by the lottery) or last.

63–4 have The fame 'have a chance to do justice to its reputation' (Kittredge), or 'have all the glory'. If Pompey means to smooth a ruffled Antony by praising his Egyptian cookery, he manages in fact to irritate him further.

67 *fair meanings Pompey somewhat disingenuously denies the innuendo in his remark about Julius Caesar that Antony has implied in 66. The topic is a bit delicate with Octavius Caesar present, reflecting as it does upon Julius Caesar's 'unlawful issue' supposedly begotten in his affair with Cleopatra (to which Octavius Caesar bitterly refers in 3.6.6–7), and it touches Antony as well by suggesting that he has taken up with a famous whore. The F reading, 'faire meaning', is sometimes retained, but would be a

ANTONY And fair words to them.
POMPEY Then so much have I heard.
And I have heard Apollodorus carried –
ENOBARBUS No more of that. He did so.
POMPEY What, I pray you?
ENOBARBUS A certain queen to Caesar in a mattress.
POMPEY I know thee now. How far'st thou, soldier?
ENOBARBUS Well,
And well am like to do, for I perceive
Four feasts are toward.
POMPEY Let me shake thy hand.
I never hated thee. I have seen thee fight
When I have envied thy behaviour.
ENOBARBUS Sir,
I never loved you much, but I ha' praised ye
When you have well deserved ten times as much
As I have said you did.
POMPEY Enjoy thy plainness;
It nothing ill becomes thee.
Aboard my galley I invite you all.
Will you lead, lords?
CAESAR, ANTONY, LEPIDUS Show's the way, sir.
POMPEY Come.
Exeunt. Enobarbus and Menas remain

71 of that] F3; that F; o'that *Collier MS.* 83 SH CAESAR . . . LEPIDUS] *Capell; All.* F 83 SD] F *subst.*

simple error for 'fair meanings', and 'them' in 68 clearly points to a plural. The Concordance affords no other example in which 'meaning' takes on a plural sense.

68 **fair** elegant, smooth – too smooth, perhaps. Antony's response, taking up Pompey's word 'fair', is perhaps intended to claim a gracious indifference to the insult.

69 **Then. . . heard** i.e. that's all I meant to say I had heard, that Caesar literally grew fat with feasting. Pompey's repeated denial of innuendo conveys the sense of 'That's all right, then.' But he continues in the next line, saying 'And I've heard as well', with another story that, as Enobarbus makes plain, goes straight back to the matter causing the social tension. Whether Pompey is blundering or being disingenuous is hard to tell. He may have assumed, inadequately of course, that Antony would be ready to engage in 'clubman' talk.

70–2 **Apollodorus. . . mattress** North's Plutarch, 'The Life of Julius Caesar', relates how Cleopatra, secretly sent for by Julius Caesar, came with Apollodorus in a boat to the foot of the castle, and there 'laid herself down upon a mattress or flockbed, which Apollodorus, her friend, tied and bound up together like a bundle with a great leather thong, and so took her up on his back and brought her thus hampered in this fardel unto Caesar in at the castle gate' (786D–E). This was the beginning of their romance.

71 ***of that** F's 'that' is metrically and substantively unsatisfactory, and the emendation has been universally accepted.

75 **toward** coming up.

80 **Enjoy thy plainness** Give free rein to your blunt speech.

81 **nothing** not at all.

MENAS [*Aside*] Thy father, Pompey, would ne'er have made this treaty. – You and I have known, sir.

ENOBARBUS At sea, I think.

MENAS We have, sir.

ENOBARBUS You have done well by water.

MENAS And you by land.

ENOBARBUS I will praise any man that will praise me, though it cannot be denied what I have done by land.

MENAS Nor what I have done by water.

ENOBARBUS Yes, something you can deny for your own safety: you have been a great thief by sea.

MENAS And you by land.

ENOBARBUS There I deny my land service. But give me your hand, Menas. If our eyes had authority, here they might take two thieves kissing.

MENAS All men's faces are true, whatsome'er their hands are.

ENOBARBUS But there is never a fair woman has a true face.

MENAS No slander, they steal hearts.

ENOBARBUS We came hither to fight with you.

MENAS For my part, I am sorry it is turned to a drinking. Pompey doth this day laugh away his fortune.

ENOBARBUS If he do, sure he cannot weep't back again.

MENAS You've said, sir. We looked not for Mark Antony here. Pray you, is he married to Cleopatra?

84 SD] *Johnson; not in* F

85 have known have been acquainted (Abbott 382). The wary ritual of this greeting between Menas and Enobarbus is a parody of that between Caesar and Antony in 2.2.16 ff.

96 There...service (1) as regards that, I deny being a robber as you are a pirate, (2) I claim exemption from military service. (In *2H4* 1.2.135, Falstaff is shrewd in avoiding 'the laws of this land-service'.)

97 authority i.e. to make arrests, like a constable.

97 take apprehend.

97–8 two thieves kissing (1) our two thieving hands clasping, (2) two thieves putting their heads together, fraternising.

99–101 Men's faces are true indexes of their thoughts, whatever their actions may be. – Fair women's faces, on the other hand, are always dishonest because they use cosmetics. – What you've said is not entirely slanderous because fair women are thieves in their own way; they use deceptive looks to steal men's affections. Unless Menas also means in 99 that men's faces always look honest however deceitful their actions, his statement about the transparency of men's faces reinforces the irony of his behaviour in the next scene, 2.7.33 ff.

105 i.e. plaintive regrets certainly won't restore prospects lightheartedly abandoned ('laughed away').

106 You've said, sir What you've said is undeniable. Compare 1.2.52 and n., and 3.2.34.

ENOBARBUS Caesar's sister is called Octavia.

MENAS True, sir. She was the wife of Caius Marcellus.

ENOBARBUS But she is now the wife of Marcus Antonius.

MENAS Pray ye, sir?

ENOBARBUS 'Tis true.

MENAS Then is Caesar and he for ever knit together.

ENOBARBUS If I were bound to divine of this unity, I would not prophesy so.

MENAS I think the policy of that purpose made more in the marriage than the love of the parties.

ENOBARBUS I think so, too. But you shall find the band that seems to tie their friendship together will be the very strangler of their amity: Octavia is of a holy, cold, and still conversation.

MENAS Who would not have his wife so?

ENOBARBUS Not he that himself is not so, which is Mark Antony. He will to his Egyptian dish again. Then shall the sighs of Octavia blow the fire up in Caesar, and, as I said before, that which is the strength of their amity shall prove the immediate author of their variance. Antony will use his affection where it is. He married but his occasion here.

MENAS And thus it may be. Come, sir, will you aboard? I have a health for you.

ENOBARBUS I shall take it, sir. We have used our throats in Egypt.

MENAS Come, let's away.

Exeunt

111 **Pray ye, sir?** i.e. say that again. Do you really mean what you've said?

114 **divine of** prophesy about.

116 **made more** played more of a role.

117 **the love of the parties** Either (1) the love between Antony and Octavia or (2) genuine affection between Caesar and Antony as parties to the marriage. Enobarbus's reply tends to confirm the second meaning.

120 **still conversation** silent demeanour.

123–4 **sighs . . . fire up** An echo of the bellows and the fan (1.1.9, 2.2.213–15), one that reinforces a comparison and contrast between Octavia and Cleopatra. Later, in 3.4.10–32 and 3.6.63–81, Octavia does try to cool the fire of antagonism, though her unhappiness produces the effect on Caesar that Enobarbus anticipates.

125–6 **author of their variance** agent of their falling out.

126 **use . . . it is** indulge his passion where it is now engaged (i.e. in Egypt).

127 **his occasion** to suit his immediate need.

129 **health** toast.

[2.7] *Music plays. Enter two or three* SERVANTS *with a banquet*

1 SERVANT Here they'll be, man. Some o'their plants are ill-rooted already; the least wind i'th'world will blow them down.

2 SERVANT Lepidus is high-coloured.

1 SERVANT They have made him drink alms-drink.

2 SERVANT As they pinch one another by the disposition, he cries out, 'No more', reconciles them to his entreaty, and himself to the drink.

1 SERVANT But it raises the greater war between him and his discretion.

2 SERVANT Why, this it is to have a name in great men's fellowship. I had as lief have a reed that will do me no service as a partisan I could not heave.

1 SERVANT To be called into a huge sphere, and not to be seen to

Act 2, Scene 7 2.7] *Pope; no scene division in* F 1–13 SH] *Expanded by Rowe from* 1 *and* 2 *in* F 1 their] F2; th'their F 3 high-coloured] F2 *subst.;* high Conlord F 8 greater] F2; greatet F 11 lief] *Capell;* liue F; lieve F3

Act 2, Scene 7

Location On board Pompey's galley, off Misenum. A table and stools are brought on.

0 SD *banquet* A dessert with wine, as at 1.2.10. The guests have already been dining and drinking.

1 **Here they'll be** i.e. they are coming here for the after-dinner 'banquet'. Compare *2H4* 2.4.1–21, where servants are preparing a room (complete with music) for Falstaff and Doll Tearsheet, due to arrive any moment from 'the room where they supp'd'.

1 **plants** (1) planted trees, here about to be uprooted, (2) soles of the feet; Latin *planta* (Johnson). As usual in Shakespeare, the servants' perspective on the doings of the great is iconoclastically revealing.

4 **alms-drink** *OED* defines as 'the remains of liquor reserved for alms-people' (Alms 4b), but with this Shakespearean usage as the only example, and a more likely meaning suggests itself in the present scene. As the second servant explains in the next speech, the bickering of his companions repeatedly obliges Lepidus to raise a toast in the way of peacemaking; his drinking is an act of charity. Moreover, the custom of emptying the cup every time one is drunk requires Lepidus to drink deep whenever Pompey toasts him – at 28–30, 36, and 79. So Lepidus drinks to keep the peace, and his efforts are ironically rewarded as the distinguished company jests at his expense and meanly plies him with more drink. He is the charitable scapegoat, and his alms is drink. Some editors, on ill-defined authority, explain 'alms-drink' as drinking in someone else's place during a round of drinking, but this is clearly an inappropriate definition here.

5 **pinch...disposition** take the opportunity of irritating one another according to their differing temperaments.

6 **No more** i.e. no more quarrelling.

6–7 **reconciles...drink** i.e. when every effort at peacemaking leads inevitably to another round of toasts in pledge of friendship, Lepidus accepts the necessity of another drink.

6 **his entreaty** i.e. that they stop quarrelling.

10 **a name** a name only.

11 **as lief** as soon. F's 'as liue' is an old form.

11 **a reed...service** a useless reed, i.e. no weapon at all.

11 **partisan** A long-handled two-edged spear.

13–15 **To be...cheeks** To be called to greatness and then be seen as unable to fulfil that great position is like having eye sockets without eyes – a defect that would pitifully disfigure the countenance, lead to a 'loss of face', and call to mind the conventional emblem of the death's head. The underlying image is of a heavenly body that cannot circle properly in its fixed concentric sphere. Eyes are often compared with stars in Shakespeare, and 'disaster' is an astrological term meaning 'to strike with calamity', since as a noun the word signifies 'an unfavourable aspect of a star or planet' (*OED* sv *sb* 1).

move in't, are the holes where eyes should be, which pitifully disaster the cheeks.

A sennet sounded. Enter CAESAR, ANTONY, POMPEY, LEPIDUS, AGRIPPA, MAECENAS, ENOBARBUS, MENAS, *with other Captains* [*and a* BOY]

ANTONY [*To Caesar*] Thus do they, sir: they take the flow o'th'Nile
By certain scales i'th'Pyramid; they know,
By the height, the lowness, or the mean if dearth
Or foison follow. The higher Nilus swells,
The more it promises; as it ebbs, the seedsman
Upon the slime and ooze scatters his grain,
And shortly comes to harvest.

LEPIDUS You've strange serpents there.

ANTONY Ay, Lepidus.

LEPIDUS Your serpent of Egypt is bred now of your mud by the operation of your sun; so is your crocodile.

ANTONY They are so.

POMPEY Sit – and some wine. A health to Lepidus!
[*They sit and drink*]

LEPIDUS I am not so well as I should be, but I'll ne'er out.

ENOBARBUS Not till you have slept; I fear me you'll be in till then.

LEPIDUS Nay, certainly, I have heard the Ptolemies' pyramises are

15 SD.3 *and a* BOY] *Jones; not in* F 16 SD] *Capell; not in* F 28 SD] *Bevington; not in* F

15 SD ***sennet*** A trumpet call signalling the ceremonial arrival of a distinguished person or persons.

15 SD ***and a* BOY** See 104 n. below.

16 **take the flow** calculate the height of the annual flooding.

17 **By...Pyramid** By graduated markings on the Pyramid. Pliny, *Natural History*, Book V, chap. 9, describes how the height of the Nile is calculated 'by marks and measures taken of certain pits' in order to predict famine or abundance (trans. Philemon Holland (1601), p. 98H). Shakespeare may have thought of a pyramid as rather like an obelisk; compare 5.2.60 below in which Cleopatra thinks of a 'high pyramides' as a 'gibbet', and *Mac.* 4.1.57–8, where pyramids might topple like castles or palaces (W. Watkiss Lloyd, *N&Q* 7th ser., 11 (1891), 283).

18 **mean** middle.

19 **foison** plenty.

23 **strange serpents** 'Shakespeare gives tipsy Lepidus plenty of sibilants to slur' (Wilson).

25 **Your serpent** i.e. this serpent people talk about (the colloquial indefinite 'your'; Abbott 221). In his cups, Lepidus assumes an off-hand manner as though thoroughly familiar with the subject (Kittredge).

25–6 **the operation of your sun** A common belief, as in *Ham.* 2.2.181: 'For if the sun breed maggots in a dead dog'.

29 **not so well** Lepidus responds with serio-comic literalness to Pompey's 'A health'.

29 **I'll ne'er out** i.e. I'll never refuse a toast, never quit. See 4 and n.; Pompey plays his trick of obliging Lepidus to drink up when he is toasted.

30 **be in** i.e. be in liquor, in your cups; playing on the opposite phrase, to 'be out'. Enobarbus does not say this for Lepidus to hear.

31 **pyramises** (F reads 'Pyramisis'.) This plural is the comical result of Lepidus's drunken speech (contrast the normal 'pyramides', 5.2.60), but 'pyramis' is in fact the Greek singular form of the word, and was common in Shakespeare's time.

very goodly things. Without contradiction I have heard that.

MENAS [*Aside to Pompey*] Pompey, a word.

POMPEY [*Aside to Menas*] Say in mine ear, what is't?

MENAS (*Whispers in's ear*) Forsake thy seat, I do beseech thee, captain, And hear me speak a word.

POMPEY [*Aside to Menas*] Forbear me till anon. – This wine for Lepidus!

LEPIDUS What manner o'thing is your crocodile?

ANTONY It is shaped, sir, like itself, and it is as broad as it hath breadth. It is just so high as it is, and moves with it own organs. It lives by that which nourisheth it, and the elements once out of it, it transmigrates.

LEPIDUS What colour is it of?

ANTONY Of it own colour too.

LEPIDUS 'Tis a strange serpent.

ANTONY 'Tis so, and the tears of it are wet.

CAESAR Will this description satisfy him?

ANTONY With the health that Pompey gives him, else he is a very epicure.

[*Menas whispers again*]

POMPEY [*Aside to Menas*] Go hang, sir, hang! Tell me of that? Away!

33 SD.1 *Aside to Pompey*] *Rowe subst.; not in* F 33 SD.2, 36 SD *Aside to Menas*] *Capell subst.; not in* F 34 SD *Whispers in's ear*] *Placed as in Wilson; opposite 36,* Forbeare me till anon, *in* F 48 SD *Menas whispers again*] *Wilson; not in* F 49 SD *Aside to Menas*] *Johnson subst.; not in* F

33–79 Pompey...more Shakespeare follows North's Plutarch (984E) in some detail: Menas's whispering in Pompey's ear in the midst of general merriment, the offer to cut the cable (67) and make Pompey lord of the whole empire of Rome (58), Pompey's answer pleading the constraints of honour, and so on.

34 SD ***Whispers in's ear** This stage direction, opposite 'Forbeare me till anon' in F, may apply to Menas's speech here, since Pompey has just said, 'Say in mine ear'; but this speech at 34 must of course be audible to the audience, and the direction could refer, as Oxford argues, to an inaudible whispering that continues from 37 to 48. It is also possible, as Wilson proposes, that Pompey turns his attention to his drinking companions until Menas whispers to him again at 48. See next note.

36 **Forbear me** Let me alone. Pompey is enjoying the feast too much. (This line tends to support Wilson's staging in the previous note.)

39, 43 **it own** its own. 'It' is an early provincial form of the old genitive (Abbott 228).

40 **the elements** The vital principle, the subtle union of the four elements (earth, air, fire and water) without which life was assumed to be impossible. Compare *TN* 2.3.9–10: 'Does not our lives consist of the four elements?' (Kittredge).

41 **transmigrates** A comically lofty conclusion for Antony's description, alluding to the doctrine of the transmigration of souls or passage of the soul at death into another body; but probably without any reference to Egyptian beliefs or worship of the crocodile.

45 **the tears of it are wet** Antony caps his mocking description with a proverbial allusion to 'crocodile tears' (Dent C831).

48 **epicure** (1) glutton (taking 'satisfy' (46) in a physical sense), (2) atheist. Only a confirmed unbeliever would drink as much as Lepidus and not believe what he is told. (Wilson quotes Hugh Latimer, *Seven Sermons before Edward VI*...*1549*, ed. Edward Arber, 1869, p. 54, end of the first sermon: 'believe (as the Epicures do) that after this life there is neither hell nor heaven'.)

49 **Go hang** i.e. 'be damned', 'go to hell'. A form of the common curse, 'Farewell (come away) and be hanged' (Dent H130.1).

49 **Tell me of that?** i.e. are you still harping on that?

Do as I bid you. – Where's this cup I called for?
MENAS [*Aside to Pompey*] If for the sake of merit thou wilt hear me,
Rise from thy stool.
POMPEY [*Aside to Menas*] I think thou'rt mad.
[*He rises, and they walk aside*]
The matter?
MENAS I have ever held my cap off to thy fortunes.
POMPEY Thou hast served me with much faith. What's else to say? –
Be jolly, lords.
ANTONY These quicksands, Lepidus,
Keep off them, for you sink.
[*Menas and Pompey speak aside*]
MENAS Wilt thou be lord of all the world?
POMPEY What say'st thou?
MENAS Wilt thou be lord of the whole world? That's twice.
POMPEY How should that be?
MENAS But entertain it,
And, though thou think me poor, I am the man
Will give thee all the world.
POMPEY Hast thou drunk well?
MENAS No, Pompey, I have kept me from the cup.
Thou art, if thou dar'st be, the earthly Jove.
Whate'er the ocean pales or sky inclips
Is thine, if thou wilt ha't.
POMPEY Show me which way.
MENAS These three world-sharers, these competitors,
Are in thy vessel. Let me cut the cable,
And when we are put off, fall to their throats.
All there is thine.
POMPEY Ah, this thou shouldst have done

51 SD *Aside to Pompey*] *Johnson subst.; not in* F 52 SD.1 *Aside to Menas*] *Johnson subst., not in* F 52 SD.2 *He rises, and they walk aside*] *Johnson subst.; not in* F 56 SD] *This edn; not in* F 69 All there] F; All then *Pope (from Southern MS. notes in* F4)

51 merit i.e. my merits, my past services (Kittredge).

53 held my cap off showed respect or deference.

54 faith faithfulness.

55 quicksands Probably a reference to the wine, or the philosophical discussion.

59 But entertain it Only accept my offer or suggestion.

64 pales fences in, encircles.

64 inclips embraces, encloses.

66 competitors partners (as at 1.4.3, 5.1.42).

67 the cable 'the gables [= cables] of the ankers' (North's Plutarch, 984E).

68 are put off have left the land. (A nautical term; *OED* Put v^1 45n.)

69 All there i.e. all that 'these three world-sharers' possess. Menas gestures towards the triumvirs. Pope's 'All then' is sometimes adopted by editors, especially since, as Wilson notes (p. 126), minim errors involving *r* and *n* are common, but the F reading can be defended.

And not have spoke on't! In me 'tis villainy;
In thee't had been good service. Thou must know,
'Tis not my profit that does lead mine honour;
Mine honour, it. Repent that e'er thy tongue
Hath so betrayed thine act. Being done unknown,
I should have found it afterwards well done,
But must condemn it now. Desist, and drink.

[*He returns to the feast*]

MENAS [*Aside*] For this, I'll never follow thy palled fortunes more.
Who seeks and will not take when once 'tis offered
Shall never find it more.

POMPEY This health to Lepidus!

ANTONY Bear him ashore. I'll pledge it for him, Pompey.

ENOBARBUS Here's to thee, Menas!

[*They drink*]

MENAS Enobarbus, welcome!

POMPEY Fill till the cup be hid.

ENOBARBUS There's a strong fellow, Menas.

[*He points to the Servant who carries off Lepidus*]

MENAS Why?

ENOBARBUS A bears
The third part of the world, man; see'st not?

MENAS The third part, then, is drunk. Would it were all,

76 SD *He returns to the feast*] *Bevington; not in* F **77** SD *Aside*] *Capell; not in* F **81** SD *They drink*] *This edn; not in* F **83** SD *He...Lepidus*] *Steevens subst.; not in* F **85** part, then, is] *Rowe subst.;* part, then he is F

70 on't of it.

71 Thou must know Let me tell you; as at 2.6.43. Pompey's ironic observations about honour, sometimes read as an isolated cynicism, represent only one level or shade of cynicism evident or implicit in this scene and its context.

73 Mine honour, it Rather it is my honour that must come before my profit.

73 Repent Regret.

77 palled waned, decayed, darkened.

78–9 Who seeks...it more Proverbial wisdom sententiously applied: 'He that will not when he may, when he would he shall have nay' (Dent N54). Compare *JC* 4.3.218 ff.: 'There is a tide in the affairs of men.'

80 Bear...for him i.e. I'll drink the toast for Lepidus, who is too far gone to drink and must be carried ashore. See 4 and n. on one's obligation to empty the cup whenever one is toasted.

83 SD ***He...Lepidus*** Perhaps the two servants who began this scene exit at this point with Lepidus, even though Enobarbus mentions only one bearer. They have probably been onstage during the drinking scene, filling the cups, cleaning up the vomit, and so on. Lepidus will need help getting ashore at this point (80). On the other hand, one or more servants may be wanted onstage until the feast itself is over at 123, and the image of bearing a third part of the world is visually stronger if one servant can cope with Lepidus.

83 A He; also at 128 and elsewhere.

84 third part of the world Compare 'triple pillar of the world', 1.1.12.

85 *is F's 'he is' can make sense if the line is read, 'The third part? Then he is drunk', a reading to which the F punctuation also lends support, but the F reading could be an easy error, and the conclusion of the line makes better sense if Rowe's emendation is accepted.

That it might go on wheels!
ENOBARBUS Drink thou; increase the reels.
MENAS Come.
POMPEY This is not yet an Alexandrian feast.
ANTONY It ripens towards it. Strike the vessels, ho!
Here's to Caesar.
CAESAR I could well forbear't.
It's monstrous labour when I wash my brain
And it grow fouler.
ANTONY Be a child o'th'time.
CAESAR Possess it, I'll make answer;
But I had rather fast from all, four days,
Than drink so much in one.
ENOBARBUS [*To Antony*] Ha, my brave emperor,
Shall we dance now the Egyptian Bacchanals,
And celebrate our drink?
POMPEY Let's ha't, good soldier.
ANTONY Come, let's all take hands,
Till that the conquering wine hath steeped our sense
In soft and delicate Lethe.
ENOBARBUS All take hands.

93 grow] F; growes F2 96 SD] *Capell; not in* F

86 That. . .wheels A proverbial expression meaning 'to go fast and easily', as in *TGV* 3.1.315–16: 'Then may I set the world on wheels, when she [my prospective wife] can spin for her living.' See Dent W893 and Arden for contemporary examples. The play on 'wheel' in the sense of 'reel' (*OED* Wheel *v* 1c) leads to Enobarbus's reply (Wilson).

87 Drink. . .reels Drink up, and you will (1) increase the number of those who are reeling or staggering, (2) increase the revels (*OED* Reel sb^2 1b).

89 an Alexandrian feast i.e. such as you would have in Egypt. Roman feasting, with no women present, seems able only to parody iconoclastically the sort of feast we might expect Egypt to supply.

90 Strike the vessels Broach the casks, open more bottles. Antony, dared by Pompey to match the proportions of an Egyptian orgy, calls for more wine even though he is not the host.

91 I could well forbear't Caesar is reluctant to fulfil his obligation to drink up in response to Antony's toast.

92 monstrous unnatural.

92 wash my brain A common jocular expression (*OED* Wash *v* 5c) for wine-drinking.

93 grow Possibly a subjunctive, dependent on a conditional sense of 'when' (Ridley). Some editors emend to 'grows'. Case and Oxford argue instead that 'And' is a form of 'An', meaning 'if'.

94 Possess. . .answer Usually taken as 'My reply is, "Be master of the time"', though, given the following line, it might mean merely, 'Drink it off, I'll drink in return.'

95 fast. . .days abstain altogether for four days in a row.

96 brave noble, splendid.

97 Bacchanals A drunken dance to Bacchus, god of wine (*OED*'s first citation, under Bacchanal *sb* 5).

98 celebrate (1) consecrate as though by religious rites (see *OED* sv *v* 2), or (2) extol, honour with observances.

102 Lethe i.e. forgetfulness. (Literally, the river of oblivion in Hades.)

Make battery to our ears with the loud music,
The while I'll place you; then the boy shall sing.
The holding every man shall bear as loud
As his strong sides can volley.
Music plays. Enobarbus places them hand in hand

The Song

BOY [*Sings*] Come thou monarch of the vine,
Plumpy Bacchus with pink eyne!
In thy fats our cares be drowned,
With thy grapes our hairs be crowned.
ALL Cup us till the world go round,
Cup us till the world go round.
CAESAR What would you more? Pompey, good night. Good brother,
Let me request you off. Our graver business
Frowns at this levity. Gentle lords, let's part;
You see we have burnt our cheeks. Strong Enobarb
Is weaker than the wine, and mine own tongue
Splits what it speaks. The wild disguise hath almost
Anticked us all. What needs more words? Good night.
Good Antony, your hand.
POMPEY I'll try you on the shore.

105 bear] *Theobald;* beate F **107** SH BOY] *Collier MS.; not in* F **109** fats] F (Fattes) **111** SH ALL] *Staunton; not in* F **114** off. Our] *Rowe subst.;* of our F **118** Splits] F (Spleet's)

103 Make battery to Assault.

104 the boy His entrance is not marked in F. Seemingly he is brought on at 15 to sing the song (Wilson). Solo singing is reserved for professionals, as with Mardian at 1.5.8–10 and 2.5.2.

105 holding refrain.

105 *bear carry, sing. F's 'beate' could easily be an error for 'beare', but Oxford retains the F reading. 'Beat' could mean 'labour, hammer at, thresh out' (*OED* Beat v^1 8).

106 volley utter rapidly, fire a return. The military metaphor from 103 is continued. This is a soldiers' occasion.

108 pink eyne having small, narrow, or half-closed eyes; to 'pink' (*OED* v^2 1) is 'to peep or peer with half-closed eyes; to blink or wink in a sleepy or sly manner'. Kyd's *Soliman and Perseda* (ed. Boas, 5.3.7) alludes to 'The mightie *pinckanyed* [pinky-ey'd] brand-bearing God'. Bacchus's eyes are sometimes referred to as red, perhaps as a result of drinking (Arden).

109 fats vats.

111 Cup us...round Compare the proverbial expression, '(To drink until) the world goes round' (Dent W885.1).

113 brother i.e. brother-in-law.

114 *off to come away. The F reading, 'of our' (for 'off. Our'), requires emendation, and omitted punctuation is not uncommon; 'of' is a normal spelling of 'off'.

118 Splits F 'Spleet's' is a Shakespearean spelling.

118 wild disguise (1) licentious masque (i.e. the Egyptian Bacchanals just danced), (2) disorderly drunkenness making us appear unlike our sober selves.

119 Anticked us (1) Made dancers of us, (2) Made us grotesque.

120 try you i.e. in a drinking bout. Antony offered before to fight with Pompey at sea, where he is strong (2.6.25); now Pompey challenges Antony to a contest on shore in which Antony is reported mighty. It is on the shore, 'At land', as Pompey recalls, that Antony has cheated him of his father's house (2.6.25–9).

ANTONY And shall, sir. Give's your hand.
POMPEY O Antony,
You have my father's house. But what? We are friends.
Come down into the boat.
ENOBARBUS Take heed you fall not.
[*Exeunt all but Enobarbus and Menas*]
Menas, I'll not on shore.
MENAS No, to my cabin.
These drums, these trumpets, flutes! What!
Let Neptune hear we bid a loud farewell
To these great fellows. Sound and be hanged, sound out!
Sound a flourish, with drums
ENOBARBUS Hoo! says a. There's my cap.
[*He flings his cap in the air*]
MENAS Hoo! Noble captain, come.
Exeunt

122 father's] F2; Father F **123–4** fall not. / Menas, I'll] *Capell;* fall not *Menas*: Ile F; fall not, / *Men.* I'll *Rowe;* fall not, *Menas. / Men.* I'll *Pope* **123** SD] *Capell subst.; not in* F **124** SH MENAS] *Capell; not in* F **126** a loud] *Rowe*[2]; aloud F **128** SD *He flings his cap in the air*] *Wilson subst.; not in* F

122 *father's The F reading, 'Father', is an easy error, and F2's emendation has been generally followed.

123 into the boat Shakespeare changes North's Plutarch, where Pompey 'built a bridge of wood to convey them to his galley from the head of Mount Misena' (984E). Pompey here seems to be escorting his guests down into a boat that will take them ashore from his galley, or possibly he intends to go with them. The motivation is unclear, and Shakespeare's main dramatic concern may have been to provide a coda to the scene after the departure of the world leaders.

123 Take...not Said perhaps as a comment on the departing guests, rather than for them to hear.

124 *The F reading (see collation), assigning the dialogue up to 127 to Enobarbus, is unsatisfactory, since the cabin in 124 cannot be his. Presumably a speech heading for Menas has been lost because Compositor E mistook '*Men.*' for a vocative or else eliminated one of two '*Men.*'s from his copy thinking it to be duplicatory, but editors disagree as to how the speech should be divided. Pope's solution ('Take heed you fall not, Menas.' *Menas*: 'I'll not on shore') is possible, but Enobarbus's line 'Take heed you fall not' seems more plausibly directed at those who are in fact stepping down into the boat (see previous gloss) than to Menas, who has no intention of leaving, and 'No, to my cabin' makes better sense as a response to Enobarbus's announced resolution not to go ashore than as a second thought by Menas himself. In Pope's arrangement, 'I'll not on shore' would seem to mean that Menas, wishing to argue with Enobarbus's suggestion that Menas watch his step getting down into the boat, counters by saying 'No, I'm not going anywhere.' But why should Enobarbus imply that Menas is about to depart, or Menas need to defend his staying, when Menas has his own cabin at hand?

125 These drums...What A ceremonial visit at sea or in port would require a fanfare for the departing honoured guests, and, as Alexander Falconer (*Shakespeare and the Sea*, 1964, p. 19) proposes, Menas may speak here as officer of the watch recalling the musicians (present from the start of the scene) sharply to their duty. The *flourish* at 127 SD is the carrying out of his order. The guests have already departed; Menas would hardly refer to them familiarly as 'these great fellows' if they had not already left the stage.

[3.1] *Enter* VENTIDIUS, *as it were in triumph* [*with* SILIUS, and other *Romans, Officers, and Soldiers*], *the dead body of Pacorus borne before him*

VENTIDIUS Now, darting Parthia, art thou struck, and now
Pleased Fortune does of Marcus Crassus' death
Make me revenger. Bear the king's son's body
Before our army. Thy Pacorus, Orodes,
Pays this for Marcus Crassus.

SILIUS Noble Ventidius,
Whilst yet with Parthian blood thy sword is warm,
The fugitive Parthians follow. Spur through Media,
Mesopotamia, and the shelters whither
The routed fly. So thy grand captain, Antony,
Shall set thee on triumphant chariots and
Put garlands on thy head.

VENTIDIUS O Silius, Silius,
I have done enough. A lower place, note well,
May make too great an act. For learn this, Silius:
Better to leave undone than by our deed
Acquire too high a fame when him we serve's away.

Act 3, Scene 1 3.1] *Rowe; no act or scene division in* F 0 SD *with* SILIUS...*Soldiers*] *Capell subst.; not in* F 1 struck] F3 (strook)*;* stroke F 4 army. Thy] F2 (Army,thy)*;* Army thy F 4 Orodes] *Rowe (following North's Plutarch); Orades* F 5 SH SILIUS] *Theobald; Romaine* F *(and similarly / Rom. / at 28 and 35)* 8 whither] F (whether)

Act 3, Scene 1

Location The Middle East. The Parthian empire includes present-day Iraq. Ventidius is urged (7–8) to pursue the defeated Parthians through Media (eastern Iran) and Mesopotamia, in the valley of the Tigris and Euphrates (present-day Iraq). As Paul Cantor points out, the defeat of the Parthians means the elimination of the last external threat to Rome and hence the end of the last external enemy that could force Rome to unite for the common good (*Shakespeare's Rome*, 1976, p. 133).

1 **darting Parthia** At 2.3.41, Antony commissioned Ventidius against the Parthians, as reported in North's Plutarch (984F). Plutarch reports later how (in 38 BC) Ventidius overcame Pacorus, the son of Orodes, King of Parthia. The Parthians were much feared for their tactic of flinging their darts and then discharging a 'Parthian shot' of arrows as they retreated or appeared to retreat. Compare 4.14.70.

1 **struck** i.e. struck in turn. 'Thou whose darts have so often struck others, art struck now thyself' (Johnson).

2 **Marcus Crassus' death** Marcus Licinius Crassus, member of the first triumvirate with Pompey the Great and Julius Caesar, was utterly defeated by the Parthians and treacherously slain by Orodes in Mesopotamia in 53 BC. North's Plutarch describes Ventidius's victory over Pacorus as 'a full revenge to the Romans of the shame and loss they had received before by the death of Marcus Crassus' (985D).

7 **The fugitive Parthians follow** Follow the fleeing Parthians.

10 **chariots** The plural may suggest a procession (Wilson). Roman 'triumphs' (see stage direction at opening of scene), often emulated in the Renaissance, were entrances of a victorious commander with his army in solemn procession into Rome, and required many chariots. See 4.12.35 and 5.2.108.

12 **I have done enough** 'Ventidius durst not undertake to follow them any further, fearing lest he should have gotten Antonius' displeasure by it' (North's Plutarch, 985D).

12 **A lower place** i.e. a subordinate.

Caesar and Antony have ever won
More in their officer than person. Sossius,
One of my place in Syria, his lieutenant,
For quick accumulation of renown,
Which he achieved by th'minute, lost his favour.
Who does i'th'wars more than his captain can
Becomes his captain's captain; and ambition,
The soldier's virtue, rather makes choice of loss
Than gain which darkens him.
I could do more to do Antonius good,
But 'twould offend him, and in his offence
Should my performance perish.

SILIUS Thou hast, Ventidius, that
Without the which a soldier and his sword
Grants scarce distinction. Thou wilt write to Antony?

VENTIDIUS I'll humbly signify what in his name,
That magical word of war, we have effected:
How with his banners and his well-paid ranks
The ne'er-yet-beaten horse of Parthia
We have jaded out o'th'field.

SILIUS Where is he now?

VENTIDIUS He purposeth to Athens, whither, with what haste
The weight we must convey with's will permit,
We shall appear before him. – On, there; pass along!

Exeunt

37 with's will permit,] *Rowe*[3] *subst.;* with's, will permit: F

16–19 Caesar...renown 'They [Antonius and Caesar] were alway more fortunate when they made war by their lieutenants than by themselves. For Sosius, one of Antonius' lieutenants in Syria, did notable good service' (North's Plutarch, 986A). This iconoclastic view of the world leaders is perhaps what Shakespeare wished to convey in this odd but telling scene of almost choric commentary; see 22–4 n. below. It has often been cut from production.

18 of my place of the same rank as I.

18 his lieutenant i.e. the commanding officer acting for Antony.

20 by th'minute each minute, rapidly and continually.

22–4 ambition...darkens him ambition, albeit a soldierly virtue (that would normally cause him to seek glory), prompts him (the field commander) to accept loss rather than a gain which will bring him into disfavour with his superior. 'Darkens him' can equally mean 'darkens the renown of his superior'. Or the whole can refer to the superior, like Antony, who through merely personal ambition might sometimes prefer to see his lieutenant lose rather than win and thereby steal his superior's glory. In any reading the sentiment radically challenges the idea of military heroism.

26 his offence his being offended thus.

28–30 that...distinction i.e. discretion, without which a soldier can scarcely be distinguished from the sword he uses.

30 Grants scarce Scarcely admits of.

32 word of war watchword; as at 2.2.50.

34 horse cavalry.

35 jaded driven exhausted like jades, inferior horses.

37 with's with us.

[3.2] *Enter* AGRIPPA *at one door,* ENOBARBUS *at another*

AGRIPPA What, are the brothers parted?
ENOBARBUS They have dispatched with Pompey; he is gone.
The other three are sealing. Octavia weeps
To part from Rome; Caesar is sad; and Lepidus
Since Pompey's feast, as Menas says, is troubled
With the green-sickness.
AGRIPPA 'Tis a noble Lepidus.
ENOBARBUS A very fine one. O, how he loves Caesar!
AGRIPPA Nay, but how dearly he adores Mark Antony!
ENOBARBUS Caesar? Why, he's the Jupiter of men.
AGRIPPA What's Antony? The god of Jupiter.
ENOBARBUS Spake you of Caesar? How, the nonpareil!
AGRIPPA O Antony, O thou Arabian bird!
ENOBARBUS Would you praise Caesar, say 'Caesar', go no further.
AGRIPPA Indeed, he plied them both with excellent praises.
ENOBARBUS But he loves Caesar best; yet he loves Antony:
Hoo! Hearts, tongues, figures, scribes, bards, poets, cannot
Think, speak, cast, write, sing, number, hoo!

Act 3, Scene 2 3.2] *Rowe; no scene division in* F 10 SH AGRIPPA] *Rowe; Ant.* F 10 Antony? The god of Jupiter.] *Johnson; Anthony,* the God of Iupiter? F 11 Spake] F*;* Speak F3 16 figures] *Hanmer;* Figure F

Act 3, Scene 2

Location Rome, soon after 2.7; Lepidus is still ill from drinking (4–6).

1 **brothers parted** brothers-in-law departed, or parted company.

2 **dispatched** concluded the business (with a suggestion of having got Pompey out of the way).

3 **sealing** affixing seals to their agreements. Since Pompey is gone, there are presumably further agreements among the triumvirs. Compare 2.6.59 and *1H4* 3.1.80 and 265, where the rebels' indentures or contracts are 'sealed interchangeably'.

4 **sad** serious.

6 **green-sickness** A kind of anaemia supposed to affect young women, especially those who are lovesick. The metaphor is doubly appropriate: to Lepidus's greenish hue after so much drinking and to his almost girlish fawning on Caesar and Antony.

6 **'Tis** The pronoun 'it' is condescending; one might speak thus of a child, as in *Rom.* 1.3.32: 'To see it teachy [tetchy] and fall out wi'th'dug'.

7 **A very fine one** Enobarbus puns on the meaning of *lepidus* in Latin, 'fine, elegant' (Ridley).

7–13 **O, how...further** Enobarbus and Agrippa mock and exaggerate Lepidus's flattering of Antony and Caesar.

11 **How** Perhaps a Shakespearean spelling of 'Ho!' (Wilson), or 'Hoo!' (16–17).

12 **Arabian bird** i.e. the fabled phoenix. Only one was thought to exist at a time; it recreated itself by arising from its own ashes.

16–18 **Hearts...Antony** Scribes' hearts cannot think and write, bards' tongues cannot speak and sing, poets' figures cannot cast and number, his love for Antony. This *tour de force* is parodically put in the form of a rhetorical figure, following the crassly vulgar parody of Lepidus's hyperbole in 7–13. The casting of figures is a complex idea here, partly rhetorical and partly astrological; see *OED* Figure *sb* 9–12 and 14, and Cast *v* 38–9. 'Number' suggests both 'reckon' and 'write metrically, versify'.

His love to Antony. But as for Caesar,
Kneel down, kneel down, and wonder.

AGRIPPA Both he loves.

ENOBARBUS They are his shards, and he their beetle.
[*Trumpets within*]
So;
This is to horse. Adieu, noble Agrippa.

AGRIPPA Good fortune, worthy soldier, and farewell.

Enter CAESAR, ANTONY, LEPIDUS, *and* OCTAVIA

ANTONY No further, sir.

CAESAR You take from me a great part of myself;
Use me well in't. – Sister, prove such a wife
As my thoughts make thee, and as my farthest bond
Shall pass on thy approof. – Most noble Antony,
Let not the piece of virtue which is set
Betwixt us as the cement of our love
To keep it builded, be the ram to batter

20 beetle. So;] *Theobald subst.;* Beetle, so: F **20** SD] *Capell; not in* F **26** bond] F (Band)

20 shards Probably the pats of dung on which Lepidus feeds (*OED* Shard *sb*[2]), but the meaning is uncertain. Since Johnson's perhaps misguided speculation about 'shard-born' in *Mac.* 3.2.42 (F reads 'shard-borne'), the sense 'wings or wing-cases which support him' has found favour. However, 'shard' and 'sharded' are not applied to beetles' wings or wing-cases until the eighteenth century, unless Shakespeare's problematic uses here and in *Cym.* 3.3.20 are exceptions. The shard beetle is so named because it is commonly found in dung. *OED* cites the present passage in *Ant.* and that in *Mac.* as referring to dung. Enobarbus suggests that Lepidus feeds off his fellow tribunes in a most unattractive way.

21–2 Adieu...farewell The two officers say farewell to each other, but are probably not about to exit when the dignitaries enter; Enobarbus knows he is to go with Antony, Agrippa with Caesar, and that departure on separate ways is imminent. Enobarbus's 'So; / This is to horse' (i.e. 'this means we're off') may well signify that he can tell from trumpet signals or other commotion that Caesar and the rest are approaching. The staff officers stand aside during the expected formalities of farewell among their superiors, and comment on the scene to one another at 51–60.

23 No further, sir i.e. (1) you need not go on urging your point; or (2) you need accompany me no further.

26–7 as my farthest...approof 'as I will venture the greatest pledge of security on the trial of thy conduct' (Johnson). To 'pass on' is to pass verdict; 'approof' is proved worthiness. Caesar uses a commercial metaphor of a 'bond' or promissory note according to which, in Elizabethan views of the marriage contract, he vouches (in place of Octavia's father) for her integrity and chastity (though not her virginity, since she is a widow). Marriage involves the transfer of the woman as property from one man to another, and it is essential that she be a 'piece of virtue' (28). Caesar goes on to make plain that Octavia is the essential property in a contract that will get Antony into trouble if he violates it.

28 piece of virtue A set phrase (Dent P291.1). Compare *Temp.* 1.2.56: 'Thy mother was a piece of virtue.' 'Piece' means 'masterpiece', but with connotations of 'object', 'possession', and even slangier meanings; see 26–7 n. Wilson notes also that 'piece' means to join, unite (*OED* sv *v* 2).

29 cement Accented on the first syllable, like the verb at 2.1.49 above. The metaphor is again that of architectural security and collapse; see 1.1.35 n. on 'arch', and 2.2.122 and 133–6 nn. on 'hoop' and 'knot'.

The fortress of it; for better might we
Have loved without this mean, if on both parts
This be not cherished.

ANTONY Make me not offended
In your distrust.

CAESAR I have said.

ANTONY You shall not find,
Though you be therein curious, the least cause
For what you seem to fear. So the gods keep you,
And make the hearts of Romans serve your ends!
We will here part.

CAESAR Farewell, my dearest sister, fare thee well.
The elements be kind to thee, and make
Thy spirits all of comfort! Fare thee well.

OCTAVIA My noble brother! [*She weeps*]

ANTONY The April's in her eyes; it is love's spring,
And these the showers to bring it on. – Be cheerful.

OCTAVIA [*To Caesar*] Sir, look well to my husband's house; and –

CAESAR What, Octavia?

OCTAVIA I'll tell you in your ear.
[*She whispers to Caesar*]

ANTONY Her tongue will not obey her heart, nor can

42 SD] *Jones subst.; not in* F 46 SD] *Capell subst.; not in* F

32 mean (1) intermediary, or (2) means – as at 4.6.36.

34 distrust distrusting.

34 I have said i.e. I stand by what I have said. Compare 1.2.52 and 2.6.106 and nn.

35 curious (1) minutely enquiring, or (2) touchy.

40 The elements i.e. the heavens (*OED* Element *sb* 10b); perhaps also the forces of nature that make up life.

43–4 The April's...bring it on Antony uses the proverb 'April showers bring May flowers' (Dent S411). Antony's tender language raises questions of sincerity in view of his earlier admission that he intends to return to his 'pleasure' in Egypt after having made this marriage only for his 'peace' (2.3.38–40), and in view of the choric cynicism privately expressed in this scene by Enobarbus and Agrippa (51–60). The issue is delicately balanced; the cynicism of the choric observers need not represent the whole truth of the matter, and we are left to imagine that it is possible to be genuinely tender within an overall pragmatism. At the same time we cannot deny the immediate context of political expediency, nor the larger context in which any expression of sentiment is suspect.

45 my husband's house Antony's house; as at 2.7.123.

46 tell you in your ear Caesar's response at 60–2 suggests that she simply asks him to write and not forget her.

47–50 Her tongue...inclines Octavia's tongue cannot express her conflicting emotions, and her heart is too full to direct her speech, so that her state of mind is like a swansdown feather floating at full tide in the pause between flow and ebb, moving neither up nor down stream. The 'swell' (49) occurs at high water, at the period of motionlessness known as the 'stand'.

Her heart inform her tongue – the swansdown feather,
That stands upon the swell at the full of tide,
And neither way inclines.

ENOBARBUS [*Aside to Agrippa*] Will Caesar weep?

AGRIPPA [*Aside to Enobarbus*] He has a cloud in's face.

ENOBARBUS [*Aside to Agrippa*]
He were the worse for that were he a horse,
So is he being a man.

AGRIPPA [*Aside to Enobarbus*] Why, Enobarbus,
When Antony found Julius Caesar dead,
He cried almost to roaring; and he wept
When at Philippi he found Brutus slain.

ENOBARBUS [*Aside to Agrippa*]
That year, indeed, he was troubled with a rheum;
What willingly he did confound, he wailed,
Believe't, till I wept too.

CAESAR No, sweet Octavia,
You shall hear from me still; the time shall not
Outgo my thinking on you.

ANTONY Come, sir, come,
I'll wrestle with you in my strength of love.
Look, here I have you [*Embracing him*]; thus I let you go,

49 at the full] F; at full F2 51, 52, 53, 54, 58 SD] *Capell; not in* F 54 Enobarbus,] *Collier; Enobarbus:* F; *Enobarbus?* / *Rowe* 60 wept] *Theobald;* weepe F 64 SD] *Hanmer; not in* F

49 at the full This F reading is open to suspicion of a repeated 'the' from 'the swell', and Abbott 90 supports the F2 emendation of 'at full', but F is not plainly wrong and is perhaps metrically felicitous following a semi-caesura after 'swell'.

53 were he a horse Enobarbus plays on Agrippa's word 'cloud', that which promises rain. A horse with 'a cloud in's face' (52), according to *OED*, has a dark spot on its face thought to be indicative of undesirable traits (Cloud *sb* 6b, citing this as its earliest example but with others from 1675). According to Madden, p. 255, a 'cloud' is simply the lack of a white star, a mark of excellence in a horse. On the assumption of viciousness in a horse altogether without white markings, see *TNK* 5.4.50–3 (Arden).

55–7 When...slain Antony does weep for Caesar in *JC* 3.1.282–5, but at 5.5.68 ff. in the same play there are no tears for Brutus, nor are any suggested in 3.11.38 below.

58 rheum running at the eyes. (Literally, any secretion of nose, eyes, mouth, etc., or a catarrh.)

59 confound destroy.

59 wailed bewailed. Enobarbus wryly points out the contradiction in Antony's weeping for one he has killed; his tears are 'crocodile tears' (see 2.7.45). Enobarbus has good reason to be wary of emotion in Antony, which is both life-giving and life-destroying whether it is accepted or rejected, but in so far as Antony defeats the kind of logic Enobarbus applies here, the implied criticism cannot be seen as definitive.

60 *wept F's 'weepe' is possible: 'Believe my words until I weep too – which will be never', but Enobarbus is compassionate towards Antony and capable of tears.

61 still continually.

61–2 the time...on you (1) time itself will not outlast my thinking of you, or (2) my thought of you will keep pace with the passage of time (Arden). See 46 and n.

63 wrestle with you i.e. (1) in an embrace of friendship, (2) in a rivalry of mutual good will (Arden).

And give you to the gods.

CAESAR Adieu. Be happy!

LEPIDUS Let all the number of the stars give light
To thy fair way!

CAESAR Farewell, farewell!

Kisses Octavia

ANTONY Farewell!

Trumpets sound. Exeunt [in separate groups]

[3.3] *Enter* CLEOPATRA, CHARMIAN, IRAS, *and* ALEXAS

CLEOPATRA Where is the fellow?

ALEXAS Half afeard to come.

CLEOPATRA Go to, go to.

Enter the MESSENGER *as before*

Come hither, sir.

ALEXAS Good majesty,
Herod of Jewry dare not look upon you
But when you are well pleased.

CLEOPATRA That Herod's head
I'll have; but how, when Antony is gone,
Through whom I might command it? – Come thou near.

MESSENGER Most gracious majesty!

CLEOPATRA Didst thou behold Octavia?

MESSENGER Ay, dread queen.

CLEOPATRA Where?

67 SD.2 *in separate groups*] *Oxford subst.; not in* F **Act 3, Scene 3** 3.3] *Rowe; no scene division in* F 2 SD] *Placed as in Arden; after* Come hither sir *in* F

Act 3, Scene 3

Location Egypt. The scene is virtually continuous with 2.5, ignoring for the moment the interval required for the intervening scenes (Kittredge).

2 **Go to** i.e. nonsense, nonsense. An expression of impatience, though it might also admit a sense of deserved reproach – 'that's enough'.

3 **Herod of Jewry** i.e. even the notorious tyrant who slaughtered the innocent children. See 1.2.26–7 and n.

4 **That Herod's head** Antony beheaded Antigonus, King of the Jews (North's Plutarch, 986D), but the allusion here more probably allies Cleopatra with Amazonian women, like the Scythian Tomyris, who slew Cyrus the Great and had his head placed in a wineskin filled with blood (see *1H6* 2.3.6), or Salome, daughter of Herodias, who demanded of Herod Antipas the head of John the Baptist (Matt. 14.3–12, Mark 6.17–29). Herod Antipas (also known as Herod the Tetrarch) and his father Herod the Great were universally confused. Herod the Great was ruler of Judaea at the time of the events in this play.

MESSENGER Madam, in Rome.
I looked her in the face, and saw her led
Between her brother and Mark Antony.
CLEOPATRA Is she as tall as me?
MESSENGER She is not, madam.
CLEOPATRA Didst hear her speak? Is she shrill-tongued or low?
MESSENGER Madam, I heard her speak. She is low-voiced.
CLEOPATRA That's not so good. He cannot like her long.
CHARMIAN Like her? O Isis! 'Tis impossible.
CLEOPATRA I think so, Charmian. Dull of tongue, and dwarfish. –
What majesty is in her gait? Remember
If e'er thou look'st on majesty.
MESSENGER She creeps:
Her motion and her station are as one.
She shows a body rather than a life,
A statue than a breather.
CLEOPATRA Is this certain?
MESSENGER Or I have no observance.
CHARMIAN Three in Egypt
Cannot make better note.
CLEOPATRA He's very knowing,
I do perceive't. There's nothing in her yet.
The fellow has good judgement.
CHARMIAN Excellent.
CLEOPATRA Guess at her years, I prithee.
MESSENGER Madam,
She was a widow –
CLEOPATRA Widow? Charmian, hark.
MESSENGER And I do think she's thirty.
CLEOPATRA Bear'st thou her face in mind? Is't long or round?
MESSENGER Round, even to faultiness.

17 Remember] F; Remember, *Theobald* 18 look'st] F; look'dst *Pope*

14 **not so good** i.e. not so good for her.

17 **Remember** Editors often follow this word with a comma, yielding a plausible meaning, 'Remember, if you have any previous experience in seeing majesty to judge it by', but the F reading, preserved here, can mean 'Remember whether' in the sense 'Remember that you *have* looked on majesty.'

18 **look'st** looked'st, didst look.

19 **station** manner of standing. Octavia walks stiffly, as the Messenger goes on to explain.

20 **shows** appears to be.

21 **breather** living being.

28 **thirty** Shakespeare pointedly gives Cleopatra, who is well past her own 'salad days', no comment on this detail.

CLEOPATRA For the most part, too, they are foolish that are so. –
Her hair, what colour?

MESSENGER Brown, madam, and her forehead
As low as she would wish it.

CLEOPATRA There's gold for thee.
Thou must not take my former sharpness ill.
I will employ thee back again; I find thee
Most fit for business. Go make thee ready;
Our letters are prepared.

[*Exit Messenger*]

CHARMIAN A proper man.

CLEOPATRA Indeed, he is so. I repent me much
That so I harried him. Why, methinks, by him,
This creature's no such thing.

CHARMIAN Nothing, madam.

CLEOPATRA The man hath seen some majesty, and should know.

CHARMIAN Hath he seen majesty? Isis else defend,
And serving you so long!

CLEOPATRA I have one thing more to ask him yet, good Charmian –
But 'tis no matter; thou shalt bring him to me
Where I will write. All may be well enough.

CHARMIAN I warrant you, madam.

Exeunt

[3.4] *Enter* ANTONY *and* OCTAVIA

ANTONY Nay, nay, Octavia, not only that –

37 SD] *Hanmer; not in* F **Act 3, Scene 4** 3.4] *Rowe; no scene division in* F

31 **they are...so** 'The head very round' argues one 'to be forgetful and foolish' (Thomas Hill, *Pleasant History* (1613), p. 218, first printed in 1571 as *The Contemplation of Mankind*, cited by Steevens[3] and others).

33 **As low...wish it** i.e. such that she would not wish it any lower. A colloquial understatement; high foreheads like that of Rosaline (*Rom.* 2.1.18) were accounted beautiful; see also *TGV* 4.4.193.

37 **proper** worthy, excellent.

39 **harried** maltreated.

39 **by him** according to his report.

40 **no such thing** nothing much.

42 **else defend** forbid that it be otherwise. (An interjection.)

47 **warrant** assure.

Act 3, Scene 4

Location Athens. Antony intends to go there, we are told at 3.1.36, and Octavia thinks he is still there when she joins her brother at 3.6.66. According to North's Plutarch, Antony was actually at Tarentum, preparing to fight with Caesar, when 'his wife Octavia, that came out of Greece with him, besought him to send her unto her brother; the which he did' (986B). Shakespeare has considerably condensed historical time to focus dramatically on the rupture between Antony and Caesar. It was eight years from Antony's marriage to the preparations for war in 32 BC. See p. 4 above for details of the condensation.

1 **Nay, nay** Antony is in the midst of complaining to Octavia about Caesar.

That were excusable, that and thousands more
Of semblable import – but he hath waged
New wars 'gainst Pompey, made his will and read it
To public ear, spoke scantly of me.
When perforce he could not
But pay me terms of honour, cold and sickly
He vented them, most narrow measure lent me;
When the best hint was given him, he not took't,
Or did it from his teeth.

OCTAVIA O my good lord,
Believe not all, or, if you must believe,
Stomach not all. A more unhappy lady,
If this division chance, ne'er stood between,
Praying for both parts.
The good gods will mock me presently,
When I shall pray, 'O, bless my lord and husband!',
Undo that prayer by crying out as loud,
'O, bless my brother!' Husband win, win brother,
Prays and destroys the prayer; no midway
'Twixt these extremes at all.

5–9 of me. / When...honour,...them,...measure lent me;...him,] *Rowe subst.*; of me, / When... Honour:...then...measure:lent me,...him: F 9 took't] *Theobald, conj. Thirlby*; look't F

3 **semblable** similar.

4 **New wars 'gainst Pompey** Antony's complaint is that Caesar, having made war 'with Sextus Pompeius to get Sicilia into his hands' and 'having spoiled Sextus Pompeius in Sicily', 'did not give him his part of the isle' (North's Plutarch, 986D, 996C). See 3.6.25–8.

4–5 **read...ear** North's Plutarch reports that Caesar demanded custody of Antony's will, and, noting 'certain places worthy of reproach', read it before the assembled Senate (997E–F). Shakespeare's changes no doubt reflect Antony's reading of Julius Caesar's will in *JC* 3.2.129 ff. (Kittredge), for Octavius Caesar's intention in *Ant.* is clearly to win popular support by showing the people what benefits they might expect from him. Antony is no doubt galled to have a trick he had employed in *JC* now turned against him.

5 **scantly** slightingly.

8 ***vented them** uttered the terms of honour (*OED* Vent v^2 3a). F's 'then' can perhaps be defended, since *OED* supplies intransitive meanings for 'vent' (*OED* sv v^2 11, 12), but those meanings apply to exhalations, liquids, confined spaces, etc., and only figuratively to persons, and convey a sense of finding a way of escape rather than of uttering.

8 **narrow measure lent me** gave me a minimal amount of praise.

9 **hint** occasion (to praise Antony).

10 **from his teeth** i.e. with a professed respect only; through clenched teeth, not from the heart. A conventional phrase (*OED* Tooth *sb* 8b and Dent T423).

12 **Stomach** Resent.

12–20 **A more...at all** In North's Plutarch, Octavia's touching description of herself as 'the most wretched and unfortunatest creature of all other', who 'can be but most miserable still' no matter 'on which side soever victory fall', is addressed not to Antony but to Octavius Caesar and his friends Maecenas and Agrippa (986B–C). Octavia pacifies the antagonists for a time. It is only thereafter in Plutarch that Antony leaves with Caesar his wife and the children begotten of her and goes to Egypt, falling there under Cleopatra's spell. Shakespeare condenses history, omitting a further scene in which Octavia journeys to Athens to meet with Antony (995).

13 **chance** occur.

15 **presently** instantly.

17 **Undo** (1) And then undo, or (2) I shall undo.

18–19 **Husband...prayer** To pray that husband win and that brother win also is to pray and then undo the prayer.

ANTONY Gentle Octavia,
Let your best love draw to that point which seeks
Best to preserve it. If I lose mine honour,
I lose myself; better I were not yours
Than yours so branchless. But, as you requested,
Yourself shall go between's. The meantime, lady,
I'll raise the preparation of a war
Shall stain your brother. Make your soonest haste;
So your desires are yours.

OCTAVIA Thanks to my lord.
The Jove of power make me, most weak, most weak,
Your reconciler! Wars 'twixt you twain would be
As if the world should cleave, and that slain men
Should solder up the rift.

ANTONY When it appears to you where this begins,
Turn your displeasure that way, for our faults
Can never be so equal that your love
Can equally move with them. Provide your going;
Choose your own company and command what cost
Your heart has mind to.

Exeunt

24 yours] F2; your F **30** Your] F2; You F **38** has] F2; he's F

21–2 Let...preserve it i.e. give your dearest love to him who does most to preserve it and you. 'Point' = (1) place to which your love resorts or joins (*OED* Draw *v* 71), or (2) point on the compass to which the needle draws.

24 branchless pruned (of honours), lopped.

24 as you requested Wilson argues, perhaps rightly, that 'Antony attempts to justify himself in his own eyes and Octavia's by throwing the blame of her departure upon her', but it is worth noting that Octavia insists that the departure was at her request when she explains the matter to her brother in 3.6.56–61. Whatever her reasons, Antony is scarcely blameless.

25 between's between us (as a moderator).

26 the preparation of a war i.e. an armed force.

27 Shall stain your brother Which will throw your brother's preparedness into the shade. To 'stain' is to deprive other luminaries of their lustre – an astrological image (*OED* Stain *v* 1b).

28 So...yours 'So you have what you want' (taking 'So' to mean 'thus'); or perhaps 'Granted that this is what *you* want, and not something that your brother has instigated you to want' (Ridley). Alternatively, Wilson interprets 'So' to mean 'so that', suggesting that Octavia is to make haste in order to achieve her desires.

32 Should Would be needed to. Such a large war will require many deaths. The metaphor of cleaving and soldering is part of the general pattern of architectural solidity and collapse; see 3.2.29 n. on 'cement'.

33 where this begins who started this quarrel.

34–6 for our...them i.e. you will have to judge between our faults and choose. 'Spoken resentfully, it seems, these words are his own condemnation, and he knows it', Wilson argues, rightly enough, though the fact does not confirm that Antony has forced Octavia to go; he rather takes advantage of her inclination.

36 Provide Make arrangements for.

[3.5] *Enter* ENOBARBUS *and* EROS, [*meeting*]

ENOBARBUS How now, friend Eros?
EROS There's strange news come, sir.
ENOBARBUS What, man?
EROS Caesar and Lepidus have made wars upon Pompey.
ENOBARBUS This is old. What is the success?
EROS Caesar, having made use of him in the wars 'gainst Pompey, presently denied him rivality, would not let him partake in the glory of the action; and, not resting here, accuses him of letters he had formerly wrote to Pompey; upon his own appeal seizes him. So the poor third is up, till death enlarge his confine.
ENOBARBUS Then, world, thou hast a pair of chaps, no more;
And throw between them all the food thou hast,
They'll grind the one the other. Where's Antony?
EROS He's walking in the garden – thus – and spurns
The rush that lies before him; cries, 'Fool Lepidus!'

Act 3, Scene 5 3.5] *Capell; no scene division in* F 0 SD *meeting*] *Capell; not in* F 11 world, thou hast] *Hanmer subst.;* would thou hadst F 11 chaps, no more] *Theobald;* chapsn o more F 13 the one the other] *Capell, conj. Johnson;* the other F

Act 3, Scene 5

Location As in the previous scene.

1 **Eros** Eros is mentioned only later in North's Plutarch as a trusted servant of Antony's (see 4.4.2 SD and n.).

4 **wars upon Pompey** Antony complained of these 'new wars 'gainst Pompey' at 3.4.4. Caesar, with Lepidus as an untrustworthy partner, defeated Pompey in 36 BC.

5 **success** (1) sequel (*OED* sv *sb* 1), or (2) outcome, result, as in *AWW* 3.6.79.

6 **him** i.e. Lepidus. In North's translation of 'The Life of Marcus Antonius' by Plutarch, Caesar concedes that he deposed Lepidus, but did so 'because he did overcruelly use his authority' (996D) – an allusion to Lepidus's treachery that is more fully revealed in Simon Goulart's translation of 'The Life of Octavius Caesar Augustus' (first included in the 1603 edition of North's Plutarch and reprinted in 1612). Shakespeare plainly knew Caesar's side of the quarrel, since he paraphrases it at 3.6.33–5, but in Act 3, Scene 5 he presents the fall of Lepidus as the ruthless elimination of an innocent bumbler and thus gives Antony seemingly just cause for resentment against Caesar.

7 **presently** at once.

7 **rivality** the rights of a partner.

8 **not resting here** not stopping with this.

8–9 **accuses...Pompey** This may reflect matter from 'The Life of Octavius Caesar Augustus', where Lepidus is said to have behaved treacherously towards Caesar in the campaign against Pompey (Plutarch, trans. Goulart, 1612 edn, pp. 1166–7).

9 **upon his own appeal** with no further warrant than Caesar's own accusation (*OED* Appeal *sb* 1).

10 **up** shut up (in prison).

10 **enlarge his confine** set him free.

11 ***world** F's 'would' is an easy minim error (see Wilson, p. 126), and the emendation is widely accepted.

11 **a pair of chaps** two jaws, chops.

11 **no more** i.e. no more than two, no third partner.

13 ***They'll...other** i.e. the jaws will continue to grind against each other and thus grind each other down. F's omission of 'the one' is an easy error of eyeskip, and the emendation is generally accepted.

14 **thus** Eros imitates Antony's angry walk, and 'spurns' (= kicks) the rushes on the stage.

And threats the throat of that his officer
That murdered Pompey.

ENOBARBUS Our great navy's rigged.

EROS For Italy and Caesar. More, Domitius:
My lord desires you presently. My news
I might have told hereafter.

ENOBARBUS 'Twill be naught,
But let it be. Bring me to Antony.

EROS Come, sir.

Exeunt

[3.6] *Enter* AGRIPPA, MAECENAS, *and* CAESAR

CAESAR Contemning Rome, he has done all this and more
In Alexandria. Here's the manner of't:
I'th'market-place, on a tribunal silvered,
Cleopatra and himself in chairs of gold
Were publicly enthroned; at the feet sat
Caesarion, whom they call my father's son,

Act 3, Scene 6 3.6] *Capell; no scene division in* F 5 the] F; their *Collier MS.*

16 that his officer that officer of his. 'The Life of Octavius Caesar Augustus' describes how Antony's lieutenant, Titius, found the means after Pompey's defeat in 36 BC 'to lay hands upon Sextus Pompeius' and to put him to death 'by Antonius' commandment, for which fact he was so hated of the people of Rome that, though he had given them the pastime of certain plays at his own cost and charges, they drave him out of the theatre' (Plutarch, 1612 edn, trans. Goulart, p. 1167). Shakespeare says nothing of Antony's having ordered the assassination or of the popular outcry, choosing instead to suggest that Antony is furious at his officer's officiousness. Perhaps Antony is only attempting to shift blame in much the same way as Bolingbroke rebukes Exton in *R2* for killing Richard, but the matter is uncertain; Antony is here given real cause for outrage and frustration; see also 6 n. above.

18 More I have more to say.

20 naught i.e. something ill-advised and disastrous, as at 3.10.1: 'Naught, naught, all naught!'

Act 3, Scene 6

Location Rome.

1 Contemning Disdaining.

3–39 I'th'market-place...in this Shakespeare follows North's Plutarch (996A–D) closely, with many verbal borrowings: the assembling in the 'show-place' (see 12), the 'high tribunal silvered', the two 'chairs of gold', the lower chairs for his children, the 'establishing' of Cleopatra as Queen of Egypt, lower Syria, Cyprus, and Lydia, the various awards to Alexander and Ptolemy, the apparelling of Cleopatra like 'the goddess Isis' (see 17), the accusations against Caesar for 'having spoiled Sextus Pompeius in Sicily' without giving Antony 'his part of the isle' (see 25–7), the other charges of lent ships being detained and Lepidus 'deposed' (see 28–30), Lepidus's revenues 'retained' (compare 'detain' in 30), and Caesar's answers, including his willingness to share what he has conquered if Antony will 'let him have his part of Armenia' (see 36). These events took place in 34 BC.

3 tribunal platform.

6 Caesarion Reputedly the son of Julius Caesar and Cleopatra; see 2.2.238 and n., and 3.13.166.

6 my father's Julius Caesar had adopted his grand-nephew Octavius in his will.

And all the unlawful issue that their lust
Since then hath made between them. Unto her
He gave the stablishment of Egypt, made her
Of lower Syria, Cyprus, Lydia,
Absolute queen.

MAECENAS This in the public eye?

CAESAR I'th'common show-place, where they exercise.
His sons he there proclaimed the kings of kings:
Great Media, Parthia, and Armenia
He gave to Alexander; to Ptolemy he assigned
Syria, Cilicia, and Phoenicia. She
In th'habiliments of the goddess Isis
That day appeared, and oft before gave audience –
As 'tis reported – so.

MAECENAS Let Rome be thus informed.

AGRIPPA Who, queasy with his insolence already,
Will their good thoughts call from him.

CAESAR The people knows it, and have now received
His accusations.

AGRIPPA Who does he accuse?

CAESAR Caesar, and that having in Sicily
Sextus Pompeius spoiled, we had not rated him
His part o'th'isle. Then does he say he lent me
Some shipping, unrestored. Lastly, he frets
That Lepidus of the triumvirate
Should be deposed, and, being, that we detain
All his revenue.

13 he there] *Johnson;* hither F 13 kings of] *Rowe (following North's Plutarch);* King of F 18–19 audience – / As 'tis reported – so] F2 *subst.;* audience, / As 'tis reported so F 23 knows] F; know F3 25 Sicily] F2; Cicilie F *(North's Plutarch / Sicile)* 29 triumvirate] F (Triumpherate) 30 and, being, that] *Arden;* And being that, F

9 **stablishment** settled possession, rule.

12 **exercise** Exercise in the 'common show-place' would probably be vulgar entertainments, exhibitions, sports, etc. (*OED* Exercise *sb* 8b, 9), rather than ceremonial functions (*OED* sv *sb* 4). The annoyance of Caesar seems typically twofold: (1) the public demonstration, (2) the vulgarity of it.

13 ***he there** F 'hither' is perhaps derived from 'he ther' in Shakespeare's manuscript (Wilson).

17 **Isis** See 1.2.59 n. on this Egyptian goddess of the moon and fertility.

21 **queasy** nauseated, 'fed up'.

22 Will withdraw their favour and support from him.

23 **knows** An old plural form. 'People' cannot be regarded as a collective singular, since it is followed by 'have now received' (Arden).

26 **spoiled** despoiled.

26 **rated him** assigned to Antony (*OED* Rate v^1 1).

28 **unrestored** i.e. which I did not return to him.

29 **of** from.

30 **being** being deposed.

31 **revenue** Accented on the second syllable.

AGRIPPA Sir, this should be answered.
CAESAR 'Tis done already, and the messenger gone.
I have told him Lepidus was grown too cruel,
That he his high authority abused
And did deserve his change. For what I have conquered,
I grant him part; but then in his Armenia
And other of his conquered kingdoms I
Demand the like.
MAECENAS He'll never yield to that.
CAESAR Nor must not then be yielded to in this.

Enter OCTAVIA *with her train*

OCTAVIA Hail, Caesar, and my lord! Hail, most dear Caesar!
CAESAR That ever I should call thee castaway!
OCTAVIA You have not called me so, nor have you cause.
CAESAR Why have you stol'n upon us thus? You come not
Like Caesar's sister. The wife of Antony
Should have an army for an usher and
The neighs of horse to tell of her approach
Long ere she did appear. The trees by th'way
Should have borne men, and expectation fainted,
Longing for what it had not. Nay, the dust
Should have ascended to the roof of heaven,
Raised by your populous troops. But you are come
A market maid to Rome, and have prevented
The ostentation of our love, which, left unshown,
Is often left unloved. We should have met you

40 lord!] F3; L. F; lords! *Ridley*

33 **cruel** A specific charge of cruelty seems unprepared for, and indeed contradicts all that we have seen of Lepidus. See 3.5.6 n. on Shakespeare's reworking of Plutarch to minimise Caesar's justification for proceeding against Lepidus as he did. In the present passage, Shakespeare makes use of Plutarch's report that Lepidus 'did overcruelly use his authority' in Sicily (996D), but in view of Lepidus's earlier kindly ineffectuality the rhetorical effect here is to suggest that Caesar is exaggerating or even lying in order to justify his conduct.

35 **For** As for.

40 ***lord** F's abbreviation 'L' could stand for 'lord' or 'lords'. Ridley argues that Octavia would wish to greet Maecenas and Agrippa along with Octavius, but most editors take the view that her attention is on her brother. The rest of the line tends to support the singular reading.

41 **castaway** In *Tit.* 5.3.75, and *The Rape of Lucrece*, 744, as Wilson notes, a 'castaway' is a ruined woman, and *OED* gives the primary meaning as one who is cast away or rejected, a reprobate. Caesar doesn't seem particularly surprised to see her.

44 **Like** In a fashion or manner appropriate to.

46 **horse** Plural, as at 3.7.7.

52 **prevented** forestalled (by your too early arrival).

53 **ostentation** ceremonial display.

53–4 **which...unloved** i.e. 'which, if given no proper outward display, is often unappreciated or ceases to exist'. (One of Caesar's concerns may be to have a public display in order to generate popular sympathy.)

By sea and land, supplying every stage
With an augmented greeting.

OCTAVIA Good my lord,
To come thus was I not constrained, but did it
On my free will. My lord, Mark Antony,
Hearing that you prepared for war, acquainted
My grievèd ear withal, whereon I begged
His pardon for return.

CAESAR Which soon he granted,
Being an abstract 'tween his lust and him.

OCTAVIA Do not say so, my lord.

CAESAR I have eyes upon him,
And his affairs come to me on the wind.
Where is he now?

OCTAVIA My lord, in Athens.

CAESAR No, my most wrongèd sister, Cleopatra
Hath nodded him to her. He hath given his empire
Up to a whore, who now are levying
The kings o'th'earth for war. He hath assembled
Bocchus, the King of Libya; Archelaus,
Of Cappadocia; Philadelphos, King
Of Paphlagonia; the Thracian king, Adallas;
King Manchus of Arabia; King of Pont;
Herod of Jewry; Mithridates, King

62 abstract] F; Obstruct *Theobald* **73** Adallas] *Rowe (following North's Plutarch); Adullas* F **74** Manchus] *Alexander (following North's Plutarch); Mauchus* F; *Malchus / Theobald*

55–6 supplying...greeting providing a more elaborate welcome at every stage of your journey.

57 was I not constrained See 3.4.24 n. Octavia may mean what she says, even if she has allowed Antony to presume on her selfless sense of duty, or she may be concealing an element of constraint out of tact and embarrassment.

61 pardon for permission to

62 Since your return to Rome has removed the obstacle between him and the gratification of his desire, has provided the readiest way for him to fulfil his lust. 'Abstract' is an abridgement (of distance). 'Obstruct' is a possible emendation, requiring 'you' rather than 'your return' as the understood subject of 'Being'.

69 who i.e. and they, Antony and Cleopatra.

71–7 Bocchus...Lycaonia The names are taken from North's Plutarch (999B) with some omissions, rearrangements, and minor confusions. For example, 'Polemon, King of Pont' emerges in Shakespeare's text as 'King of Pont' and, two lines later, 'Polemon', King of 'Mede'. Shakespeare does not distinguish between those who were present in person and those who, according to Plutarch, sent their armies. He thereby gives the scene a more impressive gathering of rulers. The historical date is 31 BC. The picture of the kings of the earth making ready for war may recall medieval traditions of the Antichrist based on Rev. 17.1–2 and 19.19; see, for example, the Antichrist plays in the Chester cycle of mystery plays (Seaton, p. 223, and Shaheen, pp. 179–80).

74 *Manchus F 'Mauchus' seems an obvious misprint for 'Manchus', as it appears in North (999B). In Plutarch it is 'Malchus'.

74 Pont Pontus.

Of Comagene; Polemon and Amyntas,
The Kings of Mede and Lycaonia,
With a more larger list of sceptres.

OCTAVIA Ay me most wretched,
That have my heart parted betwixt two friends
That does afflict each other!

CAESAR Welcome hither.
Your letters did withhold our breaking forth
Till we perceived both how you were wrong led
And we in negligent danger. Cheer your heart;
Be you not troubled with the time, which drives
O'er your content these strong necessities,
But let determined things to destiny
Hold unbewailed their way. Welcome to Rome,
Nothing more dear to me. You are abused
Beyond the mark of thought, and the high gods,
To do you justice, makes his ministers
Of us and those that love you. Best of comfort,
And ever welcome to us.

AGRIPPA Welcome, lady.

MAECENAS Welcome, dear madam.
Each heart in Rome does love and pity you;
Only th'adulterous Antony, most large
In his abominations, turns you off

76 Comagene] *Rowe;* Comageat F *(North's Plutarch / Comagena)* 76 Polemon] *Theobald (following North's Plutarch);* *Polemen* F 77 Lycaonia] F2 *(following North's Plutarch);* Licoania F 83 wrong led] F*;* wrong'd *Capell* 91 makes his] F*;* make his F2*;* make their *Theobald;* make them *Capell*

77 **Mede** Media, as it is spelt at 3.1.7 and 3.6.14.

81 **does** Either an old northern form of the plural (*OED* Do *v* A 2d), or an error for 'do'. It refers to 'friends'.

82 **withhold our breaking forth** restrain my rapid advance (to battle). Caesar uses the royal plural in 'our'.

84 **negligent danger** danger through negligence or inaction.

85 **Be you...the time** Compare the proverb 'never grieve for that you cannot help' (Dent G453).

85–6 **drives O'er** The metaphor is of driving a team of animals or a vehicle over Octavia's 'content' or happiness, trampling it underfoot.

87–8 **let determined...way** let predestined events go unlamented to their certain conclusion.

90 **mark** reach, range.

90–2 **the high gods...love you** i.e. the high gods (here a single concept) make us and those who love you their instruments of justice in your cause. Compare Rom. 13.4, 6 (Shaheen). 'Makes' is also a possible plural; compare 'does' (81), and 'Makes' (1.4.50). In that case 'his' in 91 should perhaps read 'their', and Oxford emends accordingly, following Theobald, but in view of the uncertainty as to what reading should be taken ('make their' and 'make them' have also been proposed), the passage is perhaps best read as in F with 'high gods' as a single concept.

92 **Best of comfort** i.e. my best of comfort be yours.

97 **large** unrestrained.

98 **abominations** The F spelling, 'abhominations', reveals the false but illuminating etymological meaning: unnatural acts.

98 **turns you off** rejects you.

And gives his potent regiment to a trull
That noises it against us.

OCTAVIA Is it so, sir?

CAESAR Most certain. Sister, welcome. Pray you
Be ever known to patience. My dear'st sister!

Exeunt

[3.7] *Enter* CLEOPATRA *and* ENOBARBUS

CLEOPATRA I will be even with thee, doubt it not.

ENOBARBUS But why, why, why?

CLEOPATRA Thou hast forspoke my being in these wars,
And say'st it is not fit.

ENOBARBUS Well, is it, is it?

CLEOPATRA If not denounced against us, why should not we
Be there is person?

ENOBARBUS [*Aside*] Well, I could reply.
If we should serve with horse and mares together,
The horse were merely lost; the mares would bear
A soldier and his horse.

CLEOPATRA What is't you say?

ENOBARBUS Your presence needs must puzzle Antony,

Act 3, Scene 7 3.7] *Capell; no scene division in* F 4 it is] F2; it it F 5 If not denounced] *Boswell, conj. Malone;* If not, denounc'd F; Is't not denounc'd *Rowe* 6 SD] *Johnson; not in* F

99 regiment government, rule.

99 trull harlot.

100 noises it is clamorous.

102 known to patience patient, calm.

Act 3, Scene 7

Location Actium, on the western coast of Greece, in the Roman province of Epirus, 'where the city of Nicopolis standeth' (North's Plutarch, 999E), or present-day Préveza. North's Plutarch reports that Antony 'rode at anchor, lying idly in harbour at the head of Actium', while Caesar advanced quickly towards him. The historical date is September, 31 BC.

3 forspoke spoken against. North's Plutarch (996E) tells how Antony, 'through the persuasions of Domitius, commanded Cleopatra to return again into Egypt, and there to understand the success of this war', until Cleopatra bribed Canidius to speak with Antony on her behalf. This sentence in North is one of the few hints on which Shakespeare based the role of Enobarbus (called Domitius at 3.5.18 and 4.2.1). Historically the business takes place some time before Actium, at Ephesus; Shakespeare has compressed time and place.

5 If...us i.e. even if the war were not declared against me (as you well know it is). Many editors prefer Rowe's 'Is't not denounc'd'.

7 horse Plural, as at 3.6.46, and here signifying male horses.

8 were merely lost would be utterly lost to service (since they would be mounting the mares). 'Bear' has the sexual connotation of supporting the male. Gordon N. Ross, 'Enobarbus on horses', *SQ* 31 (1980), 386–7, suggests a pun on 'merely' and 'marely'.

10 puzzle confound, distract.

Take from his heart, take from his brain, from's time
What should not then be spared. He is already
Traduced for levity, and 'tis said in Rome
That Photinus, an eunuch, and your maids
Manage this war.

CLEOPATRA Sink Rome, and their tongues rot
That speak against us! A charge we bear i'th'war,
And as the president of my kingdom will
Appear there for a man. Speak not against it;
I will not stay behind.

Enter ANTONY *and* CANIDIUS

ENOBARBUS Nay, I have done.
Here comes the emperor.

ANTONY Is it not strange, Canidius,
That from Tarentum and Brundusium
He could so quickly cut the Ionian Sea

14 Photinus, an eunuch] *Delius; Photinus* an eunuch F 19 SD CANIDIUS] *Rowe (following North's Plutarch); Camidias* F 20, 27, 57, 80 Canidius] *Rowe; Camidius* F 21 Brundusium] F2 *(following North's Plutarch);* Brandusium F

14 ***Photinus, an eunuch** In North's Plutarch (998E), Caesar (not Enobarbus) offers his opinion that 'Mardian the eunuch, Photinus, and Iras', along with Charmian, rule Antony's affairs. It is not clear if Shakespeare intends the phrase 'an eunuch' to be in apposition with 'Photinus' or not. F provides no comma after 'Photinus'. Delius urges the necessity of distinguishing the eunuch from Photinus, but it seems odd for Enobarbus to refer to Mardian, so well known to him and Cleopatra, as 'an eunuch' while naming Photinus. Moreover, Photinus (or Pothinus, as he is called in Plutarch's original 'The Life of Marcus Antonius' and also in North's translation of 'The Life of Julius Caesar', 786F), was a eunuch. He was the cause of Pompey the Great's murder, and later plotted in Egypt against Julius Caesar, for which, Plutarch reports, Caesar 'slew the eunuch Pothinus himself', though he is then reported alive at the time of Actium.

15 **Sink...rot** Let Rome sink, and may their tongues rot.

16 **charge** responsibility, including a financial one. In North's Plutarch, 996F, Canidius tells Antony on Cleopatra's behalf that 'there was no reason to send her from this war, who defrayed so great a charge'.

19 SD ***CANIDIUS** The F spelling is *Camidias*; at 20 it is *Camidius*. It is elsewhere spelt *Camidius* except for *Camindius* at 4.6.16; the speech heading is generally *Cam.* A case can be made for retaining *Camidius*, the most common F spelling, and Oxford adopts this reading. In view, however, of Compositor B's uncertainty, and the ease of a minim error in transcribing *ni* or *mi* (*Camindius* suggests the ease of such an error), there is a real possibility that Shakespeare knew the name as *Canidius*, as in his printed text of North's Plutarch, and that the varied F spelling is compositorial. F's *Brandusium* in the next line is usually corrected (by the Oxford editors as well) to North's and Plutarch's *Brundusium*, and F's *Troine* at 23 is similarly corrected by most editors, following North's Plutarch, to *Toryne*. See also *Actium* (F reads *Action*) at 51. B's repeated difficulty with unfamiliar proper names renders suspect his preference for *Camidius*, even if he generally stuck to this spelling once he had tentatively decided how the word was spelt. A similar tendency on the part of Compositor B may be evident at 4.14.104 SD, *Dercetus*; see n.

22 **the Ionian Sea** i.e. the Adriatic Sea between the 'boot' of Italy and Toryne (near Actium) on the shore of western Greece. Tarentum (present-day Taranto) and Brundusium (present-day Brindisi) (21) are on the 'boot' of Italy. The place names and events are closely based on North's Plutarch, 999D–E.

And take in Toryne? – You have heard on't, sweet?
CLEOPATRA Celerity is never more admired
Than by the negligent.
ANTONY A good rebuke,
Which might have well becomed the best of men,
To taunt at slackness. Canidius, we will fight
With him by sea.
CLEOPATRA By sea, what else?
CANIDIUS Why will
My lord do so?
ANTONY For that he dares us to't.
ENOBARBUS So hath my lord dared him to single fight.
CANIDIUS Ay, and to wage this battle at Pharsalia,
Where Caesar fought with Pompey. But these offers,
Which serve not for his vantage, he shakes off,
And so should you.
ENOBARBUS Your ships are not well manned.
Your mariners are muleteers, reapers, people
Ingrossed by swift impress; in Caesar's fleet
Are those that often have 'gainst Pompey fought.
Their ships are yare, yours heavy. No disgrace
Shall fall you for refusing him at sea,
Being prepared for land.
ANTONY By sea, by sea.
ENOBARBUS Most worthy sir, you therein throw away

23 Toryne] F2 *(following North's Plutarch);* Troine F 28 SH CANIDIUS] *Rowe; Cam.* F *(and so throughout)* 35 muleteers] F2 (Muliters)*;* Militers F

23 **take in** conquer; as at 1.1.24 and 3.13.85.

24 **admired** wondered at (envyingly).

26 **becomed** i.e. become (as also in *Cym.* 5.5.406). Antony praises Cleopatra for speaking manfully in rebuking him; it shows she is fit for command.

29 **he dares us to't** North's Plutarch reports that 'for Cleopatra's sake' Antony 'would needs have this battle tried by sea' (999C). Shakespeare seems to wish to emphasise Antony's own *Ate* or infatuated blindness. In other particulars here he is very close to North's Plutarch; 30–2, for example, rephrase Antony's offer to fight in single combat or 'in the fields of Pharsalia, as Julius Caesar and Pompey had done before' (999D–E).

35 ***muleteers** F 'Militers' represents a minim error for 'Muliters'. The common Elizabethan form, 'muleters' or 'muletters', signifies those who drive mulets or mules. Compare North's Plutarch, 'muletters, reapers, harvest men, and young boys' (999C).

36 **Ingrossed** Rounded up wholesale.

36 **impress** capture, conscription. North's Plutarch (999C) reports that Antony's officers did 'press by force all sorts of men out of Greece'. The muleteers and reapers (i.e. migrant crop-gatherers) mentioned at 35 were especially vulnerable to press-gang conscription because they were itinerants.

38 **yare** dexterous, manoeuvrable. The details of the contrast are taken from North's Plutarch, 999C–D. Compare 'yarely' and 'yare' at 2.2.221, 3.13.134, and 5.2.277.

39 **fall** befall.

The absolute soldiership you have by land,
Distract your army, which doth most consist
Of war-marked footmen, leave unexecuted
Your own renownèd knowledge, quite forgo
The way which promises assurance, and
Give up yourself merely to chance and hazard
From firm security.

ANTONY I'll fight at sea.

CLEOPATRA I have sixty sails, Caesar none better.

ANTONY Our overplus of shipping will we burn,
And with the rest full-manned, from th'head of Actium
Beat th'approaching Caesar. But if we fail,
We then can do't at land.

Enter a MESSENGER

Thy business?

MESSENGER The news is true, my lord; he is descried.
Caesar has taken Toryne.

ANTONY Can he be there in person? 'Tis impossible;
Strange that his power should be. Canidius,
Our nineteen legions thou shalt hold by land,
And our twelve thousand horse. We'll to our ship.
Away, my Thetis!

Enter a SOLDIER

How now, worthy soldier?

51 Actium] F2; Action F 56 impossible;] *Pope subst.*; impossible F

42 **absolute soldiership** consummate generalship. The argument is given to Canidius in North's Plutarch (1000B).

43 **Distract** divide, disrupt. In North's Plutarch, Canidius argues that Antony 'would weaken his army by dividing them into ships' (1000B–C).

44 **footmen** foot-soldiers (as opposed to marines).

44 **leave unexecuted** 'give no scope for the use of' (Arden).

47 **merely** utterly; as at 8.

50 **overplus...burn** i.e. so that Antony can fully man the rest, as in North's Plutarch, 1000C–D; see 36 n. on Antony's shortage of rowers.

51 **head** headland. The term is from North; see 3.7 headnote on location.

57 **his power** i.e. his army, let alone himself.

58–9 **nineteen legions...twelve thousand horse** The figures are from North's Plutarch (1002D), where they are offered as evidence of Antony's cowardice in deserting the leadership of such a large force. Shakespeare instead emphasises Antony's bravado in taking the riskier action first.

60 **Thetis** One of the Nereids or nymphs of the sea (compare 2.2.216), and the mother of Achilles. Wilson suggests that Shakespeare confuses her with her grandmother Tethys, wife of Oceanus and mother of the Nile among other rivers, hence equated with the goddess Isis. The confusion was common. Both goddesses are appropriate here.

60 SD **SOLDIER** J. Leeds Barroll argues that this character is to be identified with Scarus in 3.10 and 4.7–8 ('Scarrus and the scarred soldier', *HLQ* 22 (1958), 31–9).

SOLDIER O noble emperor, do not fight by sea;
Trust not to rotten planks. Do you misdoubt
This sword and these my wounds? Let th'Egyptians
And the Phoenicians go a-ducking; we
Have used to conquer standing on the earth
And fighting foot to foot.
ANTONY Well, well, away!
Exeunt Antony, Cleopatra, and Enobarbus
SOLDIER By Hercules, I think I am i'th'right.
CANIDIUS Soldier, thou art; but his whole action grows
Not in the power on't. So our leader's led,
And we are women's men.
SOLDIER You keep by land
The legions and the horse whole, do you not?
CANIDIUS Marcus Octavius, Marcus Justeius,
Publicola, and Caelius are for sea,
But we keep whole by land. This speed of Caesar's
Carries beyond belief.
SOLDIER While he was yet in Rome,
His power went out in such distractions as
Beguiled all spies.

66 SD *Exeunt*] F *(exit)* 69 leader's led] F (Leaders leade) 72 SH CANIDIUS] *Pope; Ven.* F 72 Justeius] *Theobald (following North's Plutarch); Iusteus* F; *Iustius* F2 73 Caelius] *Theobald (following North's Plutarch); Celius* F

61–6 O noble...away Shakespeare closely follows North's Plutarch (1000D–E) for the wording of this incident. The Morality-play-like ominousness of this passage reinforces a pervasive concern with superstition, with Antony's bad luck in his dealings with Caesar, etc., as at 2.3.10–38 (see n.).

62 rotten planks Compare North's Plutarch (1000D): 'vile brittle ships'.

64 go a-ducking (1) fall into the sea, (2) cringe, in contrast with the Romans (Wilson).

65 Have used Are accustomed.

65 standing on the earth (1) fighting on land, (2) standing tall, in contrast with 'ducking'.

66 foot to foot with one's foot right against the enemy's. Compare 'hand to hand'.

66 Well, well, away North's Plutarch (1000D–E): 'Antonius passed by him and said never a word, but only beckoned to him with his hand and head, as though he willed him to be of good courage, although indeed he had no great courage himself.' Shakespeare's interpretation of this incident may have been coloured by North's marginal comment: 'Antonius regardeth not the good counsel of his soldier.'

67 Hercules An ominous oath, since Hercules was Antony's supposed ancestor. Compare 4.3.21 and 4.12.44.

68–9 his whole...on't his whole course of action does not grow from a real source of strength. 'On't' = 'in it'.

70 men servingmen.

71 horse whole cavalry undivided and held in reserve (in order to 'do't at land' if the sea action fails, 53). Compare 3.8.3, where Caesar adopts the same strategy. North's Plutarch (1002D) reports that after the battle Antony's men loyally 'kept themselves whole together seven days'.

72–3 Marcus Octavius...Caelius The names are from North (1000E).

75 Carries Sweeps forward, carries a long distance. (A term from archery.)

77 power army.

77 distractions detachments, separate groups.

CANIDIUS Who's his lieutenant, hear you?
SOLDIER They say, one Taurus.
CANIDIUS Well I know the man.

Enter a MESSENGER

MESSENGER The emperor calls Canidius.
CANIDIUS With news the time's in labour, and throws forth
Each minute some.

Exeunt

[3.8] *Enter* CAESAR [*and* TAURUS] *with his army, marching*

CAESAR Taurus!
TAURUS My lord?
CAESAR Strike not by land; keep whole. Provoke not battle
Till we have done at sea. Do not exceed
The prescript of this scroll.
[*He gives a scroll*]
Our fortune lies
Upon this jump.

Exeunt

[3.9] *Enter* ANTONY *and* ENOBARBUS

ANTONY Set we our squadrons on yond side o'th'hill,
In eye of Caesar's battle, from which place
We may the number of the ships behold
And so proceed accordingly.

Exeunt

79 Taurus] *Theobald (following North's Plutarch); Towrus* F *(so throughout)* 79 Well I] *Rowe*[3]*;* Well, I F 81 in labour] *Rowe;* with Labour F 81 throws] F (throwes)*;* throes *Theobald* **Act 3, Scene 8** 3.8] *Capell; no scene division in* F 0 SD *and* TAURUS] *Capell subst.; not in* F 5 SD *He gives a scroll*] *Bevington subst., not in* F 6 SD *Exeunt*] F *(exit)* **Act 3, Scene 9** 3.9] *Dyce; no scene division in* F 4 SD *Exeunt*] F *(exit)*

81–2 ***With news...some** More news is born each minute. 'Throws forth' = 'gives birth'. Rowe's emendation of 'with Labour', the F reading, to 'in labour' clarifies the metaphor and corrects what is probably the simple error of repeating 'With' at the start of the line.

Act 3, Scene 8

Location Actium, with virtually no interruption in the action, as commonly in Shakespeare's battle scenes. In highly stylised and visually exciting display, the opposing sides appear by turns, probably at stage doors to left and right, as later at Act 4, Scene 5 and following.

3 **whole** undivided; as at 3.7.71.

5 **prescript** instructions, orders.

6 **jump** hazard.

Act 3, Scene 9

Location Actium, as before.

2 **In eye of** In sight of.

2 **battle** A line of fighting forces in battle array (*OED* sv *sb* 8), here applied to a battle line of ships.

[3.10] CANIDIUS *marcheth with his land army one way over the stage, and* TAURUS *the lieutenant of Caesar the other way. After their going in is heard the noise of a sea fight*

Alarum. Enter ENOBARBUS

ENOBARBUS Naught, naught, all naught! I can behold no longer.
Th'Antoniad, the Egyptian admiral,
With all their sixty, fly and turn the rudder.
To see't mine eyes are blasted.

Enter SCARUS

SCARUS Gods and goddesses,
All the whole synod of them!
ENOBARBUS What's thy passion?
SCARUS The greater cantle of the world is lost
With very ignorance. We have kissed away
Kingdoms and provinces.
ENOBARBUS How appears the fight?
SCARUS On our side like the tokened pestilence,
Where death is sure. Yon ribaudred nag of Egypt –

Act 3, Scene 10 3.10] *Dyce; no scene division in* F 0 SD.4 ENOBARBUS] *Rowe*[3]; *Enobarbus and Scarus* F 10 ribaudred] F; ribauldred F4; ribauld *Rowe*

Act 3, Scene 10

Location Actium, as before.

0 SD *noise of a sea fight* At 4.12.3, another sea fight is conveyed theatrically by an *Alarum afar off*. Auditory signals using drums, trumpets, etc., were crucial to the rendition of battle on the Elizabethan stage, and used a recognisable vocabulary of sound effects.

1 Naught Ruined. Compare 3.5.20.

2 admiral flagship. 'The admiral-galley of Cleopatra was called *Antoniad*', North's Plutarch reports (999A).

3 sixty 'the threescore ships of Cleopatra' (North's Plutarch, 1001D). Shakespeare borrowed other details for this scene from what follows in North.

4 SD SCARUS Not mentioned in Plutarch. Perhaps he is to be identified with the Soldier in 3.7; see 3.7.60 SD n. See 4.7.3 SD and n. on Scarus's role as a soldier who takes on something of Enobarbus's function with Antony when Enobarbus deserts. The F spelling, *Scarrus*, may be a rendition of *Scaurus*, the name of Sextus Pompeius's half-brother (see Furness, p. 4, n. 10), or a phonetic spelling of the Latin word *scarus*, scar, a kind of sea-fish; it may also play on the scars jested about in 4.7.6–10.

5 synod assembly.

6 cantle A section or segment cut out.

7 With very ignorance With out-and-out stupidity.

7 kissed away lost, said goodbye to (*OED* Kiss *v* 4); but with resonances of literal meaning too: kingdoms have been lost by kissing.

9 the tokened pestilence i.e. the final stages of the plague, when 'the Lord's tokens' (*LLL* 5.2.423) or reddish spots ominously appear.

10 ribaudred Perhaps a way of spelling 'ribald-rid', i.e. one who is common to every ribald or scurrilous, licentious knave (Steevens). 'Ribaud' is an old form (borrowed from the French) of 'ribald'. Both were often applied to loose women as well as men, and other coinages like 'ridaudrous' (i.e. 'foul' or 'filthy') and 'ribaudry', cited by Steevens and Singer, make clear that Enobarbus means something like 'obscene, abominable'. Henn (p. 123) pictures an old 'over-ridden' horse that has carried many

Whom leprosy o'ertake! – i'th'midst o'th'fight,
When vantage like a pair of twins appeared
Both as the same, or rather ours the elder,
The breeze upon her, like a cow in June,
Hoists sail and flies.

ENOBARBUS That I beheld.
Mine eyes did sicken at the sight, and could not
Endure a further view.

SCARUS She once being loofed,
The noble ruin of her magic, Antony,
Claps on his sea wing, and, like a doting mallard,
Leaving the fight in height, flies after her.
I never saw an action of such shame.

14 June] F2; Inne F

men and now gauntly shows its rib-cage through its skin. Robert Miola, *Shakespeare's Rome*, 1983, pp. 138–41, points to parallels in Virgil's *Georgics*, III, 209–74, stressing the sexual desires of mares as well as those of stallions and the gentle breezes (see 14 n. below) that blow on mares in heat, conveying their scent to the eager males.

10 **nag** i.e. whore, as when Pistol refers to Doll Tearsheet in *2H4* 2.4.190–1: 'Know we not Galloway nags?'

13 **elder** 'and so the heir of victory' (Wilson). North's Plutarch (1001D): 'the battle was yet of even hand, and the victory doubtful, being indifferent to both'.

14 **breeze** gadfly (with perhaps a pun on the ordinary kind of breeze, such as is needed to fill Cleopatra's sails). Scarus compares Cleopatra to a filthy nag which, bitten by a gadfly, turns tail like a fly-plagued cow in the hot month of June and flees from the battle. The image of a stung heifer, running tail erect across a meadow, suggests a sailing vessel in cowardly flight (Wilson). The image may ultimately be derived from the story of Io, one of Jove's conquests, whom he disguised as a heifer to conceal her from the jealous Juno, but to no effect; Juno had her vengeance by sending a gadfly to plague Io. Io is by some accounts an ancestor of Hercules. She is also equated with the goddess Isis, with whom Cleopatra is repeatedly associated in this play. See Robert G. Hunter, 'Cleopatra and the "oestre junonicque"', *S.St.* 5 (1969), 236–8, and 10 n. above on 'ribaudred' and Virgil's *Georgics*.

15 **Hoists sail and flies** North's Plutarch (1001D): 'hoising sail to fly'.

17 **loofed** luffed, steered close to the wind, headed into the wind (*OED* Luff *v* 2); perhaps with a pun on 'aloofed' = became distant. The tactical situation is unclear. Possibly Cleopatra's vessels luff in order to hoist sail; sail-handling is possible only when the wind is spilled out of the sails by heading upwind. Henn (p. 121) argues instead that Cleopatra's sails are luffed in the sense that the Roman vessels have got to windward of them – an attractive reading in context but one requiring a definition of 'luff' not sanctioned by the *OED* until 1894. North's Plutarch (1001D) says only that Cleopatra's ships hoisted sail and 'fled through the midst of them that were in fight', i.e. right through the battle formation. As for Antony, 'when he saw Cleopatra's ship under sail, he forgot, forsook, and betrayed them that fought for him'. It seems unlikely in any event that Shakespeare means to have Cleopatra's ships come upwind as their adopted course of flight; instead, they would turn and flee 'with full sail' (Plutarch) before the wind.

19 **sea wing** i.e. means of flight by sea (*OED*); more concretely, the square-sails (Henn, p. 122). A nonce use.

19 **mallard** wild drake. Falstaff twice equates the wild duck with cowardice (*1H4* 2.2.101 and 4.2.20), though the image here is more one of following after the female (Arden).

20 **in height** at its height.

21–3 **I never saw...itself** Scarus vigorously expresses the 'Roman' view of North's Plutarch: 'There Antonius showed plainly that he had not only lost the courage and heart of an emperor but also of a valiant man' (1001D–E).

Experience, manhood, honour, ne'er before
Did violate so itself.

ENOBARBUS Alack, alack!

Enter CANIDIUS

CANIDIUS Our fortune on the sea is out of breath,
And sinks most lamentably. Had our general
Been what he knew himself, it had gone well.
O, he has given example for our flight
Most grossly by his own!

ENOBARBUS Ay, are you thereabouts? Why then good night indeed.

CANIDIUS Toward Peloponnesus are they fled.

SCARUS 'Tis easy to't, and there I will attend
What further comes.

CANIDIUS To Caesar will I render
My legions and my horse. Six kings already
Show me the way of yielding.

ENOBARBUS I'll yet follow
The wounded chance of Antony, though my reason
Sits in the wind against me.

[*Exeunt separately*]

27 he] F2; his F 36 SD] *Theobald subst.; not in* F *(see Commentary for other possible arrangements)*

26 Been...himself Compare 1.1.44–5 and n., and North's Plutarch ('he was not his own man', 1001E), on the Roman ideal of being oneself.

29 thereabouts i.e. of that mind, thinking of desertion.

29 good night indeed i.e. it's all over.

30 Peloponnesus i.e. in southern Greece.

31 to't to get to it.

31 attend await.

32–4 To Caesar...yielding North's Plutarch (1002D) reports Canidius's desertion after the battle, though not his joining with Caesar. Domitius (Shakespeare's Enobarbus) deserts before the battle. Shakespeare manipulates his sources to dramatise the crisis in Antony's camp and the nature of Enobarbus's loyalty.

32 render surrender.

33 legions and my horse infantry and my cavalry.

33 Six kings The details are from North's Plutarch, 1000A and 1004A.

35 wounded chance 'broken fortunes' (Malone).

36 Sits...against me i.e. is on my trail. To 'sit in the wind' is to be on the downwind side, having the scent coming towards you. Thus Enobarbus's reason is scenting and tracking him down as a victim. See *OED* Wind *sb*[1] 20.

36 SD *Exeunt separately* Capell plausibly arranges for Canidius to leave at 34. If so, Scarus probably leaves before him, at 32. Enobarbus's last speech would be effective if delivered when he is alone onstage. F gives no indication either way.

[3.11] *Enter* ANTONY *with* ATTENDANTS

ANTONY Hark! The land bids me tread no more upon't;
It is ashamed to bear me. Friends, come hither.
I am so lated in the world that I
Have lost my way for ever. I have a ship
Laden with gold. Take that, divide it; fly,
And make your peace with Caesar.
ALL Fly? Not we.
ANTONY I have fled myself, and have instructed cowards
To run and show their shoulders. Friends, begone.
I have myself resolved upon a course
Which has no need of you. Begone.
My treasure's in the harbour. Take it. O,
I followed that I blush to look upon!
My very hairs do mutiny, for the white
Reprove the brown for rashness, and they them
For fear and doting. Friends, begone. You shall
Have letters from me to some friends that will

Act 3, Scene 11 3.11] *Dyce; no scene division in* F 6 SH ALL] F *(Omnes)*

Act 3, Scene 11

Location From this point onwards, the scene remains in the vicinity of Alexandria until the end of the play, as details like the presence of Charmian and Iras, the mention of the schoolmaster, and the immediate transition to Caesar's besieging of Alexandria (3.13.172) confirm. Shakespeare begins, however, with matters located elsewhere in his source, especially Antony's self-loathing in defeat and his first meeting with Cleopatra after Actium (located on board ship *en route* to the Peloponnesus in southern Greece, according to Plutarch; compare 3.10.30 above), and does so with such freedom of stage location that we cannot be sure until well into this present scene that we are in Egypt. To achieve dramatic concentration, Shakespeare also omits a considerable amount of history from Plutarch before Antony finally reaches Egypt and is confronted by Caesar.

2 ashamed i.e. because he has refused to fight on land and has been ignominiously defeated at sea. Shakespeare maintains continuity with 3.7.

3 lated belated; like a traveller still journeying when night falls, as in *Mac.* 3.3.6.

4–6 I have a ship...Not we North's Plutarch gives these details (1002B), but locates the action at Taenarus in the Peloponnesus (as 3.10.30 above leads us to expect at the start of this present scene).

7 instructed taught by example.

8 shoulders i.e. backs.

9 a course Shakespeare adapts an incident from North's Plutarch in which Antony, hearing of the treachery of the Governor of Libya, 'was so mad withal that he would have slain himself for anger, had not his friends about him withstood him and kept him from it' (1003A). By eliminating Antony's voyage into Libya *en route* from Greece to Egypt, Shakespeare not only compresses his narrative but uses this suicidal threat as a direct anticipation of his decision to kill himself in 4.14. To follow the source would have been to lose this dramatic effect.

12 that that which.

13 mutiny contend with each other, quarrel.

14 they them i.e. the brown hairs reprove the white.

Sweep your way for you. Pray you, look not sad,
Nor make replies of loathness. Take the hint
Which my despair proclaims. Let that be left
Which leaves itself. To the seaside straightway!
I will possess you of that ship and treasure.
Leave me, I pray, a little. Pray you now,
Nay, do so, for indeed I have lost command.
Therefore I pray you. I'll see you by and by.
[*Exeunt Attendants. Antony*] *sits down*

Enter CLEOPATRA *led by* CHARMIAN, [IRAS], *and* EROS

EROS Nay, gentle madam, to him, comfort him.
IRAS Do, most dear queen.
CHARMIAN Do. Why, what else?
CLEOPATRA Let me sit down. O Juno!
ANTONY No, no, no, no, no.
EROS See you here, sir?
ANTONY O fie, fie, fie!
CHARMIAN Madam!
IRAS Madam, O good empress!
EROS Sir, sir!
ANTONY Yes, my lord, yes. He at Philippi kept
His sword e'en like a dancer, while I struck

19 that] *Capell;* them F 24 SD.1 *Exeunt... Antony*] *Capell subst.; not in* F 24 SD.2 IRAS] *Pope subst.; not in* F

17 Sweep your way Clear your path – to Caesar, as North's Plutarch makes clear, though again Shakespeare sets the incident in a different place; historically, Antony wrote to the Governor of Corinth with a request to see his followers safe and hide them 'until they had made their way and peace with Caesar' (1002C).

18 loathness unwillingness.

18 hint opportunity.

19–20 Let...itself Leave the man (Antony) who is no longer himself (Jones).

23 lost command i.e. of self and of authority. Antony must now entreat, not order them. His ability to use pathos reveals an eloquent side of him we haven't seen before.

24 SD.2 EROS Not mentioned in North's Plutarch (see 4.4.2 SD and n.); according to Shakespeare's source, it was Cleopatra's women who, at Taenarus in southern Greece, 'first brought Antonius and Cleopatra to speak together' (1002B). It is worth noting Enobarbus's absence; Shakespeare perhaps reserves him for 3.13 where his caustic assessment replaces the sense of temporary recovery at the end of the present scene.

35 Yes, my lord, yes Antony, absorbed in bitter thoughts, seems at first not to recognise Eros or what is being said to him. His reproaches in 29 and 31 are similarly directed at himself and give no certain evidence of his being aware of the women's presence.

35 He i.e. Octavius Caesar.

35 kept kept in its sheath. North's Plutarch reports that in their wars against the republican leaders 'Caesar did no great matter, but Antonius had alway the upper hand', adding however that when Antony overthrew Cassius and Brutus in battle, 'Caesar was sick at that time' (979D–E).

36 e'en like a dancer i.e. as though for ornament only. A 'dancing rapier' was literally 'one to dance with', i.e. wear with formal attire while dancing (*AWW* 2.1.33, *Tit.* 2.1.39), and it could not be heavy.

The lean and wrinkled Cassius, and 'twas I
That the mad Brutus ended. He alone
Dealt on lieutenantry, and no practice had
In the brave squares of war. Yet now – no matter.

CLEOPATRA Ah, stand by.

EROS The queen, my lord, the queen.

IRAS Go to him, madam, speak to him.
He's unqualitied with very shame.

CLEOPATRA Well then, sustain me. O!

EROS Most noble sir, arise. The queen approaches.
Her head's declined, and death will seize her but
Your comfort makes the rescue.

ANTONY I have offended reputation,
A most unnoble swerving.

EROS Sir, the queen.

ANTONY O, whither hast thou led me, Egypt? See
How I convey my shame out of thine eyes
By looking back what I have left behind
'Stroyed in dishonour.

46 seize] F (cease) 50 led] F (lead)

37 **The lean and wrinkled Cassius** Compare *JC* 1.2.194: 'Yond Cassius has a lean and hungry look.'

38 **the mad Brutus** At 3.2.56 Antony is recalled as having wept for the slain Brutus, and in *JC* 5.5.68–75 he accords Brutus generous praise for nobility and gentleness, but Brutus was still in Antony's eyes one who assassinated out of misguided ideals. Perhaps too Antony suggests that Brutus inherited the tendency towards madness of his famous ancestor, Junius Brutus, who overthrew Tarquin (Wilson).

38 **ended** i.e. defeated. Brutus and Cassius committed suicide after defeat.

38 **alone** only, merely.

39 **Dealt on lieutenantry** Let his subordinates do the fighting. Shakespeare makes Antony recreate the past in a partial way to emphasise his sense of difference from Caesar. The charge was actually levelled against both. (See North's Plutarch, 986A, and 3.1.16–17.)

40 **brave squares** splendid squadrons, troops drawn up in square formation.

41 **stand by** i.e. I'm going to faint. Compare 'sustain me', hold me up, at 44.

43 **unqualitied** beside himself, not himself. 'Quality' means nature, character. The word provides a remarkably compressed way of suggesting his complete loss of distinctive virtue.

43 **with** by.

46 **but** unless.

47 **Your comfort** Your comforting of her; perhaps also with a suggestion of 'Your comforting of yourself'.

48 **reputation** honour. The concept is of paramount importance in the play, as also in *Oth.* 2.3.262 ff. and elsewhere.

49 **swerving** error, transgression (*OED* sv *vbl sb*).

50–3 **See...dishonour** See how I transfer the emblems of shame from your eyes to mine in calling back to sight that which I have left behind dishonourably destroyed. 'Looking back' = 'calling back to sight' (by analogy with 'calling back'), not 'looking back at', as Wilson glosses it. Wilson argues that Antony is trying to cover up his shame from her sight by brooding over the ruins of his past, but the idea is more probably that Antony explains his unmanly weeping by saying that he only apprehends the loss in terms of her, borrowing or transferring to himself her tears as the register of loss.

CLEOPATRA O my lord, my lord,
Forgive my fearful sails! I little thought
You would have followed.
ANTONY Egypt, thou knew'st too well
My heart was to thy rudder tied by th'strings,
And thou shouldst tow me after. O'er my spirit
Thy full supremacy thou knew'st, and that
Thy beck might from the bidding of the gods
Command me.
CLEOPATRA O, my pardon!
ANTONY Now I must
To the young man send humble treaties, dodge
And palter in the shifts of lowness, who
With half the bulk o'th'world played as I pleased,
Making and marring fortunes. You did know
How much you were my conqueror, and that
My sword, made weak by my affection, would
Obey it on all cause.
CLEOPATRA Pardon, pardon!
ANTONY Fall not a tear, I say; one of them rates
All that is won and lost. Give me a kiss.
[*They kiss*]

57 shouldst tow] *Rowe* (towe)*;* should'st stowe F 58 Thy] *Theobald*[2]*;* The F 69 SD] *Bevington subst.; not in* F

56 th'strings the heart strings (Johnson); also a cable or rope forming part of the rigging of a ship (*OED* String *sb* 1a). The image, not found in North's Plutarch (where Antony chases after Cleopatra in the battle 'as if he had been glued unto her', 1001E), is closer to the admittedly conventional image in the Countess of Pembroke's *Antonie* (1592): 'forgetful of his charge, as if his soul / Unto his lady's soul had been enchained...' (2.2; 439–40).

57 *tow To be towed at sea is usually a sign of being disabled and a mark of great ignominy. (F's 'stowe' erroneously picks up *st* from the previous word.)

59–60 Thy beck...Command me Your mere beckoning could command my services away even from the bidding of the gods. Perhaps another echo of the Dido episode in the *Aeneid*, as at 1.3.20 ff. and 4.14.53.

61 young man Compare 1.1.22: 'the scarce-bearded Caesar', and 3.13.17: 'the boy Caesar'. The age theme seems to intensify as defeat has made Antony review his past.

61 treaties entreaties, proposals for negotiation.

61–2 dodge...lowness shuffle and equivocate in the pitiful evasions used by those who lack power.

64 Making and marring A favourite Shakespearean antithesis (Dent M48); see 5.2.271 below.

66 affection passion.

67 on all cause whatever was at stake.

68 Fall Let fall (Abbott 291).

68 rates equals, is worth. The recalling of Antony's opulent gifts to Cleopatra in 1.5.41 ff. signals an extraordinary shift in the basis of evaluation from that earlier scene. Antony's speech here is marked by rapid vacillations from simple intimate language (68–9) to that used in addressing matters of business, and from brooding uncertainty to a regained composure (perhaps bravado) that is reinforced by energetic speech rhythms and the rhyming of the last couplet.

69 won and lost A conventional antithesis about war; compare Dent W43.1, W408.1.

Even this repays me. – We sent our schoolmaster;
Is a come back? – Love, I am full of lead. –
Some wine within there, and our viands! Fortune knows
We scorn her most when most she offers blows.
Exeunt

[3.12] *Enter* CAESAR, AGRIPPA, [THIDIAS], *and* DOLABELLA, *with others*

CAESAR Let him appear that's come from Antony.
Know you him?
DOLABELLA Caesar, 'tis his schoolmaster –
An argument that he is plucked, when hither
He sends so poor a pinion of his wing,
Which had superfluous kings for messengers
Not many moons gone by.

Enter AMBASSADOR *from Antony*

CAESAR Approach and speak.
AMBASSADOR Such as I am, I come from Antony.
I was of late as petty to his ends
As is the morn-dew on the myrtle leaf
To his grand sea.

Act 3, Scene 12 3.12] *Dyce; no scene division in* F 0 SD THIDIAS] *Rowe; not in* F 0 SD DOLABELLA] F2; *Dollabello* F

70 Even this This by itself.

70 schoolmaster North's Plutarch: 'And because they had no other men of estimation about them, for that some were fled, and those that remained they did not greatly trust them, they were enforced to send Euphronius, the schoolmaster of their children' (1004D–E). Shakespeare defers the explanation of why the schoolmaster was sent until the next scene, where it gives a sharp edge to Dolabella's appraisal of Antony's situation.

71 a he.

71 full of lead 'As heavy as lead' is a conventional comparison (Dent L134).

Act 3, Scene 12

Location Egypt. Caesar's camp. Caesar 'sits down in Alexandria', i.e. lays siege to it (3.13.172).

0 SD AGRIPPA Sometimes omitted by editors because he does not speak, but see 1.2.0 SD n. on Lamprius, Rannius, and Lucillius, supplementary note (p. 259 below) on Menecrates, and 2.6.0 SD n. on Agrippa, all of whom are silent in the scenes in question. Agrippa is silent in 4.1 as well, and Mardian in 5.2. Editors who omit such characters are perhaps not being sensitive to the theatrical possibilities of having these characters onstage.

0 SD THIDIAS This rendition in F (which also has *Thidius*) of *Thyreus* in North's Plutarch is phonetic, unlike some other proper names such as *Camidius* (*Canidius*) or *Decretas* (*Dercetus*), and is therefore less likely to be compositorial.

3 An argument An indication.

3 plucked Compare 'plume-pluck'd Richard' in *R2* 4.1.108, and Dent P441.1.

4 pinion feather (*OED* sv *sb*[1] 3).

5 Which Who.

6 SD AMBASSADOR i.e. the schoolmaster.

8 as petty to his ends as insignificant in terms of his plans.

10 To his grand sea As compared with its, the dew's, great source, the sea. The dewdrop,

CAESAR Be't so. Declare thine office.
AMBASSADOR Lord of his fortunes he salutes thee, and
Requires to live in Egypt; which not granted,
He lessens his requests, and to thee sues
To let him breathe between the heavens and earth
A private man in Athens. This for him.
Next, Cleopatra does confess thy greatness,
Submits her to thy might, and of thee craves
The circle of the Ptolemies for her heirs,
Now hazarded to thy grace.
CAESAR For Antony,
I have no ears to his request. The queen
Of audience nor desire shall fail, so she
From Egypt drive her all-disgracèd friend
Or take his life there. This if she perform
She shall not sue unheard. So to them both.
AMBASSADOR Fortune pursue thee!
CAESAR Bring him through the bands.
[*Exit Ambassador, attended*]
[*To Thidias*] To try thy eloquence now 'tis time. Dispatch.
From Antony win Cleopatra. Promise,

13 lessens] F2; Lessons F 25 SD *Exit Ambassador, attended*] *Rowe subst.; not in* F 26 SD *To Thidias*] *Rowe; not in* F

drawn up by the sun, is 'exhaled' from the sea and will return to it. 'His' can also refer to Antony, to whom the schoolmaster has been but as a dewdrop compared with the ocean. Antony has been his source and master. (This pompous display of schoolmasterly rhetoric perhaps deserves the laconic response it gets from Caesar. At any rate, the schoolmaster thereupon gets down to business.)

10 thine office the business you have been charged with.

11 Lord...thee He acknowledges you to be lord over his fortunes; or, possibly, 'As lord of such fortune as he now possesses, he salutes you.'

12 Requires Asks. The requests, rattled off like a schoolboy's lesson (Wilson), are closely based on North's Plutarch, 1004D, including that Antony be allowed to live 'at Athens, like a private man' (compare 15).

12 which not granted and if that request is not granted.

13 *lessens Some editors defend the F reading, 'Lessons', in the sense of 'disciplines', but the *e:o* error is common; compare 'now'/'new' at 1.1.49, and Wilson, p. 126.

13 sues petitions.

14 breathe i.e. live. Another faint flicker of surviving 'rhetoric'. The schoolmaster's part, sometimes played with a kind of half-triumphant, half-apologetic grimace, is a good cameo role, and functional too: we are shown embodied the withered fortunes of Antony, instead of hearing a mere critique from Caesar.

18 circle crown.

19 hazarded to thy grace staked on your favour, dependent for its fate on your mercy.

19 For As for. Caesar's reply is as in North's Plutarch, 1004F–1005A.

21 Of audience...so Will not fail to win a hearing and a granting of her wish, provided that.

22 friend lover. Shades of meaning are possible, though Caesar's intent may be belittling.

25 Bring him Escort him in safety.

25 bands troops, soldiers on guard.

And in our name, what she requires; add more,
From thine invention, offers. Women are not
In their best fortunes strong, but want will perjure
The ne'er-touched vestal. Try thy cunning, Thidias.
Make thine own edict for thy pains, which we
Will answer as a law.

THIDIAS Caesar, I go.

CAESAR Observe how Antony becomes his flaw,
And what thou think'st his very action speaks
In every power that moves.

THIDIAS Caesar, I shall.

Exeunt

[3.13] *Enter* CLEOPATRA, ENOBARBUS, CHARMIAN, *and* IRAS

CLEOPATRA What shall we do, Enobarbus?

ENOBARBUS Think, and die.

CLEOPATRA Is Antony or we in fault for this?

ENOBARBUS Antony only, that would make his will
Lord of his reason. What though you fled
From that great face of war, whose several ranges
Frighted each other? Why should he follow?

31 Thidias] F *throughout, except / Thidius / at 3.13.106* SD*;* Thyreus *Theobald and some subsequent eds., following North's Plutarch* Act 3, Scene 13 3.13] *Dyce; no scene division in* F

28 requires asks; as at 12.

28–9 add...offers offer more things that you have thought to mention. Caesar's tactic, and his more general view of women as corruptible, is invented from the bare hint of Thyreus's eloquence in North's Plutarch (1005A). Caesar's ruthlessly pragmatic plan of separating Antony from Cleopatra and thus isolating him sets in motion the suspicions and jealousies of the next scene.

30 In their best fortunes Even in their most happy circumstances.

30 want need, lack.

30 perjure cause to break her vows (of chastity).

31 ne'er-touched vestal immaculate Vestal virgin.

31 cunning skill.

32–3 Make...a law Decree your own reward for your efforts (if you succeed), which I will confirm as if it were a law. To 'answer' is to be accountable or undertake responsibility for, fulfil.

34 becomes his flaw bears his misfortune and disgrace. A 'flaw' is a crack or fault. This interpretative observation of every gesture seems to be typical of Caesar's thoroughness and efficiency.

35 speaks signifies.

36 In...moves In every motion he makes (Kittredge). 'Power' means bodily faculty.

Act 3, Scene 13

Location Egypt. Cleopatra's palace.

1 Think, and die Think despondently and die of it, or commit suicide. At 4.6.36–7 Enobarbus resolves to die by one means or the other. On Enobarbus's function in this scene – sardonically aborting the spirit of bravado in which Antony takes refuge at the end of 3.11, during Enobarbus's absence – see 3.11.24 SD.2 n.

2 we I.

3 will desire, especially sexual desire.

5 ranges Battle units (of ships) drawn up in rows or lines (*OED* Range *sb*[1] 2).

The itch of his affection should not then
Have nicked his captainship, at such a point,
When half to half the world opposed, he being
The merèd question. 'Twas a shame no less
Than was his loss, to course your flying flags
And leave his navy gazing.

CLEOPATRA Prithee, peace.

Enter the AMBASSADOR, *with* ANTONY

ANTONY Is that his answer?

AMBASSADOR Ay, my lord.

ANTONY The queen shall then have courtesy, so she
Will yield us up.

AMBASSADOR He says so.

ANTONY Let her know't. –
To the boy Caesar send this grizzled head,
And he will fill thy wishes to the brim
With principalities.

CLEOPATRA That head, my lord?

ANTONY To him again. Tell him he wears the rose
Of youth upon him, from which the world should note
Something particular. His coin, ships, legions,
May be a coward's, whose ministers would prevail

10 merèd] F (meered)

7 **affection** sexual passion; as at 2.6.126 and 3.11.66.

8 **nicked** cut short or maimed (*OED* Nick v^2 2), or got the better of, cheated (see *OED* Nick v^2 10, 'to make (a winning cast) at hazard', and 11, 'to trick, cheat'), or made a fool of (from the custom of notching the hair of fools, as in *Err.* 5.1.175: 'His man with scissors nicks him like a fool').

8 **captainship** generalship.

8 **point** crisis.

10 **The merèd question** The sole ground of quarrel, only point at issue (from *OED* Mere adj^2 2, 4, sole, entire + *-ed*), or the limited, exclusive ground of quarrel (from *OED* Mere sb^2 1, boundary, especially of a piece of land). Enobarbus will have nothing to do with Cleopatra's earlier argument that the war was declared against her too (3.7.5–6). Enobarbus has a clear sense of what is really at issue, and he intuits here Caesar's position as declared in the previous scene.

11 **course** pursue (as in hunting).

12 **gazing** i.e. staring in astonishment at Antony's ignominious flight. North's Plutarch stresses the wonderment of the seamen of both sides in beholding this spectacle (1001D).

15 **so** provided that.

16–19 Antony's gesture is often represented as an act of admirable honesty, but of course he doesn't allow Cleopatra a choice even if she wanted it, and he may simply be testing her loyalty, of which he is already suspicious.

21–2 **note Something particular** i.e. expect something exceptional.

22–3 **His coin...coward's** i.e. the paraphernalia of authority might belong to one who is merely a coward unless he proves otherwise by some act of exceptional courage befitting his romantic show of youthful vigour.

23 **ministers** agents, subordinates.

Under the service of a child as soon
As i'th'command of Caesar. I dare him therefore
To lay his gay caparisons apart
And answer me declined, sword against sword,
Ourselves alone. I'll write it. Follow me.
[*Exeunt Antony and Ambassador*]

ENOBARBUS [*Aside*] Yes, like enough, high-battled Caesar will
Unstate his happiness and be staged to th'show
Against a sworder! I see men's judgements are
A parcel of their fortunes, and things outward
Do draw the inward quality after them
To suffer all alike. That he should dream,
Knowing all measures, the full Caesar will
Answer his emptiness! Caesar, thou hast subdued
His judgement too.

26 caparisons] *Pope;* Comparisons F **28** SD *Exeunt Antony and Ambassador*] *Rowe subst.; not in* F **29** SD *Aside*] *Capell; not in* F **34** alike. That] *Rowe;* alike, that F

26 *caparisons F's 'comparisons' has been defended by Warburton and Heath (p. 460), who read the whole line as meaning: 'To lay aside the attributes of youthful vigour and showy wealth of coin, ships, and legions which Caesar would flatteringly compare with those of Antony'. Pope's emendation adopted here, 'caparisons', i.e. trappings, refers more specifically to Caesar's material advantage. It is attractive as a reading because 'gay' is idiomatically used in Shakespeare to modify clothes and the like; see *Venus and Adonis*, 286 (George W. Williams, *Explicator* 20.9 (May 1962), no. 79).

27 answer me declined meet me in combat as I am, fallen in power and reputation and older in years. Compare *Oth.* 3.3.265–6: 'or for I am declin'd / Into the vale of years'. Antony compares himself 'declined' with the 'rose / Of youth' at 20–1. This is the second such challenge to personal combat (see 3.7.30), as in North's Plutarch: 'Antonius sent again to challenge Caesar to fight with him hand to hand' (1005D). In Plutarch, however, this second challenge is sent after Antony's victory dramatised by Shakespeare in 4.7. Here therefore the gesture is born of a desperate bravado rather than in the hubris of success.

29 high-battled possessing a mighty army. 'Battle' often means a line of troops in battle array, as at 3.9.2.

30 Unstate his happiness Depose his good fortune, i.e. strip it of its state and dignity, take away the advantages bestowed by fortune. Compare *Lear* 1.2.99: 'I would unstate myself', i.e. I would forfeit my noble rank and fortune.

30 be staged to th'show be exhibited publicly, as in a gladiatorial contest, make a spectacle of himself.

31 sworder one who habitually fights with a sword, a gladiator (*OED* sv *sb* 1). Kittredge notes, with examples, that 'prize fights with swords were common London shows in Elizabethan times and later'.

32 parcel part and parcel. When fortune turns, judgement turns also.

32–4 things...alike outward circumstances affect the inner nature so that both decline together.

35 Knowing all measures Having been acquainted with every measure of fortune, from 'full' to 'emptiness'. Shakespeare compresses into a phrase the comment in North's Plutarch: 'as if he had not oftentimes proved both the one and the other fortune, and that he had not been thoroughly acquainted with the divers changes and fortunes of battles' (1002D).

35 full at full measure; with suggestion of completeness and being a source of abundance.

36 Answer (1) Meet when challenged (as at 27), (2) Agree with, correspond to (Kittredge).

Enter a SERVANT

SERVANT A messenger from Caesar.
CLEOPATRA What, no more ceremony? See, my women,
Against the blown rose may they stop their nose
That kneeled unto the buds. – Admit him, sir.
[*Exit Servant*]
ENOBARBUS [*Aside*] Mine honesty and I begin to square.
The loyalty well held to fools does make
Our faith mere folly; yet he that can endure
To follow with allegiance a fall'n lord
Does conquer him that did his master conquer
And earns a place i'th'story.

Enter THIDIAS

CLEOPATRA Caesar's will?
THIDIAS Hear it apart.
CLEOPATRA None but friends. Say boldly.
THIDIAS So haply are they friends to Antony.
ENOBARBUS He needs as many, sir, as Caesar has,
Or needs not us. If Caesar please, our master
Will leap to be his friend. For us, you know
Whose he is we are, and that is Caesar's.
THIDIAS So.
Thus then, thou most renowned: Caesar entreats
Not to consider in what case thou stand'st
Further than he is Caesar.

40 SD *Exit Servant*] *Capell subst.; not in* F **41** SD *Aside*] *Capell; not in* F **51** us, you know] *Steevens subst.;* vs you know, F **56** Caesar] F2*; Cæsars* F

39 blown overblown, starting to decay.

41 honesty personal integrity, sense of honour.

41 square quarrel.

42–6 The loyalty...i'th'story When we hold fast in loyalty to fools, our faithfulness becomes utter folly; on the other hand, anyone who has the stoic fortitude to remain loyal to a lord who has suffered misfortune achieves a moral victory over fortune itself, the very fortune that has overthrown his master, and deserves recognition for it. (As Enobarbus deliberates what to do, the central question for him becomes whether Antony is more fool or unfortunate hero.)

47 apart in private.

47 None but friends A conventional saying (Dent F743.1).

48 haply perhaps, probably.

50 Or needs not us Or else he might as well have no friends at all, his case being hopeless.

51 For As for.

52 i.e. we are Antony's friends, and he is Caesar's, and so we too are Caesar's.

55–6 Not to consider...Caesar i.e. not to worry about your situation other than to consider that you are dealing with Caesar, the embodiment of magnanimity. (But, as Kittredge observes, Thidias 'speaks with such equivocation that he actually promises nothing whatever'.)

CLEOPATRA Go on: right royal.
THIDIAS He knows that you embrace not Antony
As you did love, but as you feared him.
CLEOPATRA O!
THIDIAS The scars upon your honour therefore he
Does pity as constrainèd blemishes,
Not as deserved.
CLEOPATRA He is a god and knows
What is most right. Mine honour was not yielded,
But conquered merely.
ENOBARBUS [*Aside*] To be sure of that,
I will ask Antony. Sir, sir, thou art so leaky
That we must leave thee to thy sinking, for
Thy dearest quit thee. *Exit Enobarbus*
THIDIAS Shall I say to Caesar
What you require of him? For he partly begs
To be desired to give. It much would please him
That of his fortunes you should make a staff
To lean upon. But it would warm his spirits
To hear from me you had left Antony
And put yourself under his shroud,
The universal landlord.

57 embrace] F; embrac'd *Hudson, conj. Capell* 63 SD] *Hanmer; not in* F

57 **embrace** Capell's conjectural emendation to 'embrac'd' (*Notes*, I, 42) is perfectly possible in view of the past tenses in 58, and could represent an easy *e:d* error (as at 1.4.8, 1.5.52, and 2.5.12), but 'embrace' is not manifestly wrong.

58 **as you feared him** Shakespeare credits Thidias with improvising this excuse for Cleopatra as part of his seductive rhetoric; in North's Plutarch (1008E), Cleopatra herself offers this justification after she has been captured in her monument.

62 **right** true.

62–3 **Mine...merely** Cleopatra wants Thidias to hear her say things that he can report back to Caesar in her favour, but a good actress (like Peggy Ashcroft) can suggest to those who know Cleopatra better that she is merely playing up to Thidias, restating Caesar's position with a kind of deflating mockery aimed at a man who fancies himself a 'god' and claims to know 'What is most right'. But one cannot be certain; Enobarbus is not.

63 **merely** utterly; as at 3.7.8 and 47.

64–6 **so leaky...quit thee** Enobarbus has in mind the proverbial image of rats leaving a sinking ship (Dent M1243). The 'dearest' who are quitting Antony are the great (as opposed to the lowly) and also those whose love is most dear to him – implicitly Enobarbus as well as Cleopatra. The ambivalence betrays a sense of humiliation at the course to which Enobarbus's judgement, if not his instinct, is drawing him.

67 **require** ask.

67 **partly** i.e. as commensurate with his dignity.

72 **shroud** shelter, protection. Harold C. Goddard (*The Meaning of Shakespeare*, 1951, II, 191) sees a pun on the winding-sheet wrapped round a corpse, grimly suggesting that 'domination of the earth is death'.

73 **landlord** 'The language of feudalism' (Wilson). Goddard (see previous note) proposes that Thidias's meaning, 'an offer of protection', is undercut by a more denigrating suggested sense of 'innkeeper'. Things have changed radically since 2.6.10, where the triumvirate were the gods' stewards or land-agents.

CLEOPATRA What's your name?
THIDIAS My name is Thidias.
CLEOPATRA Most kind messenger,
Say to great Caesar this in deputation:
I kiss his conqu'ring hand. Tell him I am prompt
To lay my crown at's feet, and there to kneel.
Tell him, from his all-obeying breath I hear
The doom of Egypt.
THIDIAS 'Tis your noblest course.
Wisdom and fortune combating together,
If that the former dare but what it can,
No chance may shake it. Give me grace to lay
My duty on your hand.
[*He kisses her hand*]
CLEOPATRA Your Caesar's father oft,
When he hath mused of taking kingdoms in,
Bestowed his lips on that unworthy place,
As it rained kisses.

Enter ANTONY *and* ENOBARBUS

ANTONY Favours? By Jove that thunders!
What art thou, fellow?
THIDIAS One that but performs
The bidding of the fullest man, and worthiest
To have command obeyed.
ENOBARBUS [*Aside*] You will be whipped.
ANTONY [*Calling for Servants*]
Approach, there! – Ah, you kite! – Now, gods and devils,

75 this in deputation:] *Arden;* this in disputation, F; this; in Deputation *Theobald, conj. Warburton* **77–8** kneel. / Tell him,] F; kneel, / Till *Jones, conj. Muir* **83** SD] *Rowe subst.; not in* F **90, 96** SD *Aside*] *Capell; not in* F **91** SD *Calling for Servants*] *Wilson subst.; not in* F

75 **in deputation** i.e. as my deputy, on my behalf.

78 **all-obeying** obeyed by all.

79 **The doom of Egypt** My fate.

80–2 **Wisdom**...**shake it** i.e. when fortune assails the wise, if they remain but wise (in not daring the impossible, in accepting the limits of necessity dictated by fortune), no fortune can harm them. (Wilson notes that this is a Stoic truism – to which, however, one must add that Thidias gives the saying a pragmatic turn entirely characteristic of Caesar the politician: Play along with fortune – i.e. Caesar – and you won't get hurt.)

83 **duty** reverence, homage.

84 **father** i.e. by adoption (actually, his great-uncle).

85 **taking kingdoms in** conquering; as at 1.1.24 and 3.7.23.

87 **As** As if.

89 **fullest** most prosperous. Compare 'the full Caesar' at 35 and n.

91 **kite** bird of prey that feeds on ignoble objects; i.e. whore. The proverbial 'kite of Cressid's kind' (Dent K116) is mentioned in *H5* 2.1.76.

Authority melts from me. Of late, when I cried 'Ho!',
Like boys unto a muss kings would start forth
And cry 'Your will?' – Have you no ears? – I am
Antony yet.

Enter Servants

Take hence this jack and whip him.

ENOBARBUS [*Aside*] 'Tis better playing with a lion's whelp
Than with an old one dying.

ANTONY Moon and stars!
Whip him. Were't twenty of the greatest tributaries
That do acknowledge Caesar, should I find them
So saucy with the hand of she here – what's her name
Since she was Cleopatra? Whip him, fellows,
Till like a boy you see him cringe his face
And whine aloud for mercy. Take him hence.

THIDIAS Mark Antony –

ANTONY Tug him away! Being whipped,
Bring him again; this jack of Caesar's shall
Bear us an errand to him.

Exeunt [Servants] with Thidias

[*To Cleopatra*] You were half blasted ere I knew you. Ha?
Have I my pillow left unpressed in Rome,
Forborne the getting of a lawful race,
And by a gem of women, to be abused
By one that looks on feeders?

CLEOPATRA Good my lord –

92 me. Of late, when] *Johnson subst.;* me of late. When F **95** SD] *Placed as in Dyce; after 95 in* F **95** SD *Servants*] *Capell subst.; a Seruant* F **105** this] *Pope;* the F **106** errand] F (arrant) **106** SD *Servants*] *Capell subst.; not in* F **106** SD *Thidias*] F (*Thidius*) **107** SD *To Cleopatra*] *This edn; not in* F

93 muss A game in which small objects are thrown down to be scrambled for (*OED* sv *sb*[1]).

95 jack fellow (said contemptuously) or low-bred servant; perhaps also (especially at 105) something which 'in some way' takes 'the place of a lad or man' (*OED sb*[1] 1, 2, 7 ff.), i.e. a lowly substitute.

95 whip him The detail is from North's Plutarch, 1005A.

96 lion's whelp Enobarbus drily improves upon the sententious warning against playing with lions (Gen. 49.9 and Dent L321.1).

100 she Used contemptuously as a noun for a woman too bad to name. Compare Othello's unnaming of Desdemona, *Oth.* 4.2.88–90.

102 cringe contract or distort in shrinking from pain (*OED* sv *v* 1).

107 blasted withered, blighted.

109 Shakespeare intensifies the cost to Antony (and to Octavia) of his sojourn in Egypt by suppressing the fact that Antony had children by Octavia as well as by Fulvia (North's Plutarch, 985B, 986D). Antony's calling Octavia 'a gem of women' (110) sounds hypocritical and may chiefly reflect his fury with Cleopatra here, but see 3.2.43–4 and n. on the possibility that Antony combines genuine tenderness towards Octavia with his brusque pragmatism.

110 abused deceived.

111 feeders servants, dependants who eat at one's expense.

ANTONY You have been a boggler ever.
But when we in our viciousness grow hard –
O, misery on't! – the wise gods seel our eyes,
In our own filth drop our clear judgements, make us
Adore our errors, laugh at's while we strut
To our confusion.
CLEOPATRA O, is't come to this?
ANTONY I found you as a morsel cold upon
Dead Caesar's trencher; nay, you were a fragment
Of Cneius Pompey's, besides what hotter hours,
Unregistered in vulgar fame, you have
Luxuriously picked out. For I am sure,
Though you can guess what temperance should be,
You know not what it is.
CLEOPATRA Wherefore is this?
ANTONY To let a fellow that will take rewards
And say 'God quit you!' be familiar with
My playfellow, your hand, this kingly seal
And plighter of high hearts! O, that I were

115–16 eyes, / In our own filth drop] *Warburton subst.*; eyes / In our owne filth, drop F **121** Cneius] F2 *(following North's Plutarch / Cneus)*; *Gneius* F

113 boggler 'fickle jade' (Wilson), one who shies like a horse, plays fast and loose, equivocates (*OED* Boggle *v* 1 and 3). Henn (p. 120) sees the word as describing a hawk that will not keep to one quarry, and hence anticipating 'seel' of 115 (see next note), but *OED* provides no authority for this.

115 seel close up, hoodwink; literally, sew the eyelids shut as was done with falcons temporarily to prepare them for the hood. Antony expresses the Greek doctrine of *Ate*, according to which the gods allow anyone who hubristically believes in his own self-sufficiency to persevere in his delusion until he brings about his own fall (Kittredge, citing the character of Julius Caesar in *JC* 2.2 and 3.1 as an example). As Wilson and others (including Kittredge) point out, the ideas are also found in Jewish and Christian writing: in Ps. 2.4, 'He that dwelleth in the heaven shall laugh; the Lord shall have them in derision', and John 12.40 (citing Isa. 6.10), 'He hath blinded their eyes and hardened their heart...' Compare the proverb 'When God will punish he will first take away the understanding' (Dent G257).

118 confusion ruin.

119 morsel cold At 2.6.123, Cleopatra is referred to as Antony's 'Egyptian dish', and at 1.5.32 she describes herself as 'A morsel for a monarch'. Food and sex are constantly related in the play.

120 trencher wooden plate.

120 fragment leftover. On Shakespeare's fascination with 'broken meats', 'orts', and the like, see *Tro.* 5.2.158, *Tim.* 4.3.399, *JC* 4.1.37, *Lear* 2.2.15, and Whiter, pp. 121–2.

121 Cneius Pompey's See 1.5.32 and n. for Shakespeare's conflating of Pompey the Great and his son Cneius or Gnaeus.

122 vulgar fame common gossip.

123 Luxuriously picked out Chosen for lascivious indulgence.

127 God quit you Said by a lowly person who receives a tip or alms. To 'quit' is to reward, requite.

128–9 seal And plighter The hand attests to the lover's oath and pledges the heart's affection, as in *MND* 3.2.143–4: 'thy hand...this seal of bliss'.

Upon the hill of Basan, to outroar
The hornèd herd! For I have savage cause,
And to proclaim it civilly were like
A haltered neck which does the hangman thank
For being yare about him.

Enter a SERVANT *with* THIDIAS

Is he whipped?

SERVANT Soundly, my lord.
ANTONY Cried he? And begged a pardon?
SERVANT He did ask favour.
ANTONY [*To Thidias*] If that thy father live, let him repent
Thou wast not made his daughter; and be thou sorry
To follow Caesar in his triumph, since
Thou hast been whipped for following him. Henceforth
The white hand of a lady fever thee;
Shake thou to look on't. Get thee back to Caesar.
Tell him thy entertainment. Look thou say
He makes me angry with him; for he seems
Proud and disdainful, harping on what I am,
Not what he knew I was. He makes me angry,
And at this time most easy 'tis to do it,
When my good stars that were my former guides
Have empty left their orbs and shot their fires

134 SD] *Placed as in Collier; after 134 in* F 136 a] F*;* he *Capell* 138 SD] *Oxford; not in* F 141 whipped for following him. Henceforth] *Rowe subst.;* whipt. For following him, henceforth F

130 hill of Basan The version of Ps. 68.15 and 22.12 in the Book of Common Prayer reads: 'As the hill of Basan, so is God's hill: even an high hill, as the hill of Basan'; 'Many oxen are come about me: fat bulls of Basan close me in on every side' (quoted by Steevens[4]). 'Basan' is the spelling of the Elizabethan and Jacobean Book of Common Prayer (though generally spelt 'Bashan' today); it appears as both 'Basan' and 'Bashan' in the Bishops' Bible and as 'Bashan' in the Genevan (Noble, p. 263). Antony imagines himself a cuckolded beast of that herd, ready to outroar the rivals who press him from every side. On cuckold's horns, see 1.2.3–4 and n.

131 savage cause 'cause enough to run wild' (Kittredge).

134 yare ready, quick; as at 2.2.221, 3.7.38, and 5.2.277.

136 a he.

140 follow...triumph (1) serve Caesar in his time of triumph, (2) follow in Caesar's triumphal procession. Compare 3.1.0 SD and 3.1.10 n., and 5.2.108.

142 fever thee (may it) 'give you the shivers' (Wilson), as from a malarial attack.

144 entertainment reception. (No irony is intended.)

144 Look See to it that, be sure that.

145–6 angry...Proud and disdainful North's Plutarch: 'and bade him tell him that he made him angry with him, because he showed himself proud and disdainful towards him' (1005A). The close borrowing continues to 151.

146 harping A conventional metaphor of harping on one string (Dent S936).

149 stars i.e. including the planets, sun, and moon.

150 orbs orbits; the fixed concentric spheres of the celestial bodies. Compare 2.7.13–15 and n. The imagery may recall Rev. 9.1–2: 'And the

Into th'abysm of hell. If he mislike
My speech and what is done, tell him he has
Hipparchus, my enfranchèd bondman, whom
He may at pleasure whip, or hang, or torture,
As he shall like to quit me. Urge it thou.
Hence with thy stripes, begone!

Exeunt [Servant and] Thidias

CLEOPATRA Have you done yet?

ANTONY Alack, our terrene moon is now eclipsed,
And it portends alone the fall of Antony.

CLEOPATRA I must stay his time.

ANTONY To flatter Caesar would you mingle eyes
With one that ties his points?

CLEOPATRA Not know me yet?

ANTONY Cold-hearted toward me?

CLEOPATRA Ah, dear, if I be so,
From my cold heart let heaven engender hail,
And poison it in the source, and the first stone
Drop in my neck; as it determines, so

156 SD *Exeunt [Servant and] Oxford subst.; Exit* F

fifth angel blew the trumpet, and I saw a star fall from heaven unto the earth, and to him was given the key of the bottomless pit. And he opened the bottomless pit' (Seaton, p. 222). See also Rev. 6.13. Morris (pp. 252–62) notes an iconographical tradition embodied in Albrecht Dürer's *Die Verteilung der weissen Gewander und der Sternenfall*, the Dividing of the White Garments and the Fall of the Stars.

153–5 This passage follows North's Plutarch closely (1005A–B). But Shakespeare suppresses the information found earlier in Plutarch that Hipparchus was 'the first of all his [Antony's] enfranchised bondmen that revolted from him and yielded unto Caesar' (1002C) – a man whom Antony might willingly see treated thus.

153 enfranchèd enfranchised, freed.

155 As he...quit me According as he pleases to repay me. Compare 'quit' in 127. What will need repaying is not the harm done to Thidias but the insult to the noble sender, as in the stocking of Kent, *Lear* 2.2. Editors often add a comma after 'like', but the phrase makes sense as punctuated in F.

157 our terrene...eclipsed (1) the earth's satellite, the moon, is now eclipsed, portending disaster, (2) the love of Cleopatra, who is a veritable Isis or moon goddess alive here on earth (see 3.6.16–18) and the light of Antony's world, is 'now withdrawn from him; an eclipse more "disastrous" than any defeat in battle' (Wilson). Antony continues the metaphor of astrology. Compare 5.2.239–40, where Cleopatra resolves that 'the fleeting moon' is no longer her planet, and p. 11 above.

159 stay his time i.e. be patient until his fury subsides.

161 one that ties his points i.e. Caesar's valet. 'Points' were laces with metal tags used to fasten together articles of clothing, especially the trunk hose or breeches to the doublet or upper garment.

165 in my neck i.e. in my throat or on my head (*OED* Neck *sb*[1] 1d). Cleopatra's speech is full of apocalyptic imagery, anticipating that of Acts 4 and 5; compare Exod. 8.24, 9.23–5 and Rev. 16.21: 'And there fell a great hail, like talents, out of heaven upon the men, and men blasphemed God because of the plague of the hail, for the plague thereof was exceeding great' (Seaton, p. 221, Shaheen). The imagery is a part of the play's fascination with hyperbole – here the hyperbole of self-invective – and with motifs of dissolution, poisoning, the death of all lineage and loyal subjects, the decaying of rituals of civilised burial, etc.

165 determines comes to an end, melts.

Dissolve my life! The next Caesarion smite,
Till by degrees the memory of my womb,
Together with my brave Egyptians all,
By the discandying of this pelleted storm
Lie graveless till the flies and gnats of Nile
Have buried them for prey!

ANTONY I am satisfied.
Caesar sits down in Alexandria, where
I will oppose his fate. Our force by land
Hath nobly held; our severed navy too
Have knit again, and fleet, threat'ning most sea-like.
Where hast thou been, my heart? Dost thou hear, lady?
If from the field I shall return once more
To kiss these lips, I will appear in blood;
I and my sword will earn our chronicle.
There's hope in't yet.

CLEOPATRA That's my brave lord!

ANTONY I will be treble-sinewed, hearted, breathed,

166 Caesarion] *Hanmer subst. (following North's Plutarch);* Cæsarian F **166** smite] *Rowe;* smile F **169** discandying] *Theobald, conj. Thirlby;* discandering F **172** sits] F (sets)

166 Caesarion See 2.2.238, 3.6.6 and nn.

166 *smite Rowe's emendation of F 'smile' is supported by Exod. 9.25: 'And the hail smote throughout all the land of Egypt...'

167 memory memorials; i.e. my offspring. Traditionally, the most powerful curse a woman can utter.

168 brave splendid.

169 discandying melting. As the poisoned hail melts or *determines* (165), it does its work. A culinary image; here, and at 4.12.22, '*discandying* is the dissolving of what is *candied*'. 'Pelleted', in the same line, is also used in a culinary sense, as a compressed meat ball; compare *A Lover's Complaint*, 15–21 (Whiter, pp. 122–3, citing Steevens).

169 pelleted falling in pellets (of hail). See previous note.

171 for prey i.e. by eating them, as in *Mac.* 3.4.71–2: 'our monuments / Shall be the maws of kites'.

172 sits down in lays siege to.

173 oppose his fate i.e. resist by force the fate that seems inevitable, as Antony partly believes already at 2.3.15–38; see also 80–2 and n. in this scene, where fortune itself is equated with Caesar. Macbeth similarly resolves: 'Rather than so, come fate into the list, / And champion me to th'utterance!' (*Mac.* 3.1.70–1, cited by Kittredge).

174 Hath nobly held Antony's armed supporters 'kept themselves whole together seven days' after Actium, according to North's Plutarch (1002D), but much happened afterwards that Shakespeare has omitted in order to give the impression that Antony and Caesar fight again in Egypt soon after Actium.

175 fleet are afloat.

175 sea-like trimmed for sea duty; or tempestuous, swelling, strong, like the sea.

176 my heart my courage or spirit (Delius). Probably not addressed to Cleopatra.

178 in blood (1) bloody from battle, (2) full-spirited, full of vigour (*OED* Blood *sb* 7). A hunting phrase used of a stag, as in *LLL* 4.2.3–4 and *1H6* 4.2.48, and of hounds, as in *Cor.* 4.5.211. When applied to hounds, the phrase may refer to the tasting of blood.

179 our chronicle i.e. a place in history. Compare 46, 'a place i'th'story'.

180 There's hope in't yet Compare 196 below, 'There's sap in't yet', and Dent L265.

182 treble-sinewed, hearted, breathed thrice myself in strength, courage, and endurance. 'Breathed' more often means 'exercised' or 'out of breath', but here in combination with 'treble' it means 'having breath' (*OED* Breathed *ppl adj* 6).

And fight maliciously. For when mine hours
Were nice and lucky, men did ransom lives
Of me for jests; but now I'll set my teeth
And send to darkness all that stop me. Come,
Let's have one other gaudy night. Call to me
All my sad captains. Fill our bowls once more;
Let's mock the midnight bell.

CLEOPATRA It is my birthday.
I had thought t'have held it poor; but since my lord
Is Antony again, I will be Cleopatra.

ANTONY We will yet do well.

CLEOPATRA [*To Attendants*] Call all his noble captains to my lord.

ANTONY Do so; we'll speak to them, and tonight I'll force
The wine peep through their scars. Come on, my queen,
There's sap in't yet. The next time I do fight
I'll make Death love me, for I will contend
Even with his pestilent scythe.

Exeunt [*all but Enobarbus*]

ENOBARBUS Now he'll outstare the lightning. To be furious
Is to be frighted out of fear, and in that mood
The dove will peck the estridge; and I see still

193 SD] *This edn; not in* F 198 SD *all but Enobarbus*] *Capell subst.; not in* F

183 maliciously fiercely, savagely (*OED* Malicious *adj* 2b).

183–5 when mine...jests in my heyday I was magnanimous with my enemies, allowing men to be ransomed for trifles.

184 nice delicate, refined.

187 gaudy festive, luxurious.

189–91 It is...Cleopatra The factual details are from North's Plutarch: 'Cleopatra, to clear herself of the suspicion he had of her, she made more of him than ever she did. For, first of all, where she did solemnize the day of her birth very meanly and sparingly, fit for her present misfortune, she now in contrary manner did keep it with such solemnity that she exceeded all measure of sumptuousness and magnificence' (1005B). In Shakespeare, however, the motivation is notably altered. Here Cleopatra has been responding rhythmically to the access of energy and spirits in Antony, and not, as in Plutarch, tactically excusing herself. The need for excuses seems to die at 171.

197–8 I will contend...scythe I will kill as many as Death himself with his scythe of pestilence (i.e. plague).

199 outstare the lightning i.e. stare it down, eyeball to eyeball.

199 furious raging, frenzied.

201 estridge ostrich, or goshawk. Examples of the word from inside and outside Shakespeare (such as *1H4* 4.1.98, and others cited by Arden) are more equivocal in meaning than *OED* allows for in treating 'estridge' as simply a variant of 'ostrich'. Elsewhere in Shakespeare doves do battle with falcons (*3H6* 1.4.41) and griffins (*MND* 2.1.232), a mousing owl hawks at a falcon (*Mac.* 2.4.12–13), and a wren defends its family against an owl (*Mac.* 4.2.9–11). Enobarbus's return to the hunting metaphor he used at 3.10.35–6 suggests his sense of threat in the moment of crisis.

201 still constantly. The deterioration Enobarbus lamented in 29–37 above seems to be increasing, with access of spirits now linked to loss of judgement.

A diminution in our captain's brain
Restores his heart. When valour preys on reason,
It eats the sword it fights with. I will seek
Some way to leave him. *Exit*

[4.1] *Enter* CAESAR, AGRIPPA, *and* MAECENAS, *with his army, Caesar reading a letter*

CAESAR He calls me boy, and chides as he had power
To beat me out of Egypt. My messenger
He hath whipped with rods, dares me to personal combat,
Caesar to Antony. Let the old ruffian know
I have many other ways to die, meantime
Laugh at his challenge.

MAECENAS Caesar must think,
When one so great begins to rage, he's hunted
Even to falling. Give him no breath, but now
Make boot of his distraction. Never anger
Made good guard for itself.

CAESAR Let our best heads
Know that tomorrow the last of many battles
We mean to fight. Within our files there are,

203 on] *Rowe;* in F **205** SD] *Rowe; Exeunt* F **Act 4, Scene 1** 4.1] *Rowe; no act or scene division in* F 3 combat,] *Rowe;* Combat. F

202–3 A diminution...heart An understood word must be supplied, either (1) *that* a diminution...restores his heart, or (2) a diminution in our captain's brain *which* restores his heart.

Act 4, Scene 1

Location Before Alexandria. Caesar's camp.

1 **as** as if.

4 **to** against. Compare *1H6* 1.3.47: 'Blue coats to tawny coats'.

5 **I have...to die** North's Plutarch: 'Antonius sent again to challenge Caesar, to fight with him hand to hand. Caesar answered him that he had many other ways to die than so' (1005D). These exchanges occur in Plutarch after the events of 4.7–9. Kittredge notes that the pronoun 'he' is ambiguous in North, as in his immediate source, Amyot's French translation, and that in the Greek original Plutarch clearly means that many ways are open for Antony to die rather than Caesar.

6 **Laugh** i.e. tell him I laugh.

8 **to rage** to rave. Compare Enobarbus's word 'furious' at 3.13.199 and n., and 3.13.115 and n. Such a furious rage manifests itself as incautious anger, as Maecenas makes clear in 10–11.

9 **breath** breathing space; as in *R3* 4.2.24: 'Give me some little breath, some pause.' Antony is compared here to a pursued and exhausted animal, foaming at the mouth. The hunting metaphor is proliferating and accumulating, being transferred from one character to another until it serves as an index to the condition of Antony (and his followers).

10 **Make boot** Take advantage.

10 **distraction** violent perturbation of mood, approaching temporary madness (*OED* sv 4), suggesting that Antony already resembles his great ancestor in being Hercules Furens. See references to Hercules at 1.3.84–5, 4.3.21, and 4.12.44. The idea is planted early and grows to a climax in 4.12.

11 **best heads** commanding officers.

13 **files** As in 'rank and file'.

Of those that served Mark Antony but late,
Enough to fetch him in. See it done,
And feast the army; we have store to do't,
And they have earned the waste. Poor Antony!

Exeunt

[4.2] *Enter* ANTONY, CLEOPATRA, ENOBARBUS, CHARMIAN, IRAS, ALEXAS, *with others*

ANTONY He will not fight with me, Domitius?
ENOBARBUS No.
ANTONY Why should he not?
ENOBARBUS He thinks, being twenty times of better fortune,
He is twenty men to one.
ANTONY Tomorrow, soldier,
By sea and land I'll fight. Or I will live
Or bathe my dying honour in the blood
Shall make it live again. Woo't thou fight well?
ENOBARBUS I'll strike, and cry 'Take all.'
ANTONY Well said. Come on!
Call forth my household servants. Let's tonight

Enter three or four SERVITORS

Act 4, Scene 2 4.2] *Rowe; no scene division in* F 1 Domitius] *Rowe (following North's Plutarch and 3.5.18); Domitian* F 10 SD] F*; after* meal *at 11 by Dyce and many subsequent eds.*

14 late lately.

15 fetch him in close in upon him, surround him (*OED* Fetch *v* 15b).

16 store abundant supply (*OED* sv *sb* 4).

17 waste consumption of material (*OED* sv *sb* 8), but for the prudent Caesar there is probably a suggestion of 'squandering' as well.

Act 4, Scene 2

Location Alexandria. Cleopatra's palace.

4–5 He thinks...to one i.e. he considers himself to be in such a superior position that his army is sure to win (and that he need not risk anything in personal combat).

5–46 Shakespeare follows North's Plutarch, 1005E ff., for many details in this scene.

6 Or Either.

7–8 Or bathe...again *OED* Blood *sb* 19 defines 'blood-bath' as 'a bath in warm blood...supposed to be a very powerful tonic in great debility from long-continued diseases, etc.', and Arden cites contemporary examples. The idea of thus invigorating a diseased body gets caught up with the notion of earning eternal fame by heroic deeds of blood.

8 Shall Which shall.

8 Woo't Wilt.

9 I'll...'Take all' (1) I'll fight to the finish, crying 'Winner take all', (2) I'll strike sail and surrender (Wilson). Enobarbus, already resolved to leave Antony, says what Antony wants to hear but words it ambiguously.

10 SD The placing of the stage direction follows F and Arden, unlike most editions, which place it after 'meal' in 11. The F placing, as Ridley argues, does least to interrupt the action and allows time for the servants to enter on the deep Elizabethan stage before Antony addresses one of them. Oxford observes that the dialogue in 11–13 seems to call for at least six servants; the stage direction *three or four* is not to be taken too literally.

Be bounteous at our meal. – Give me thy hand,
Thou hast been rightly honest – so hast thou –
Thou – and thou – and thou. You have served me well,
And kings have been your fellows.

CLEOPATRA [*Aside to Enobarbus*] What means this?

ENOBARBUS [*Aside to Cleopatra*]
'Tis one of those odd tricks which sorrow shoots
Out of the mind.

ANTONY And thou art honest too.
I wish I could be made so many men,
And all of you clapped up together in
An Antony, that I might do you service
So good as you have done.

ALL The gods forbid!

ANTONY Well, my good fellows, wait on me tonight:
Scant not my cups, and make as much of me
As when mine empire was your fellow too,
And suffered my command.

CLEOPATRA [*Aside to Enobarbus*] What does he mean?

ENOBARBUS [*Aside to Cleopatra*]
To make his followers weep.

ANTONY Tend me tonight;
May be it is the period of your duty.
Haply you shall not see me more, or if,
A mangled shadow. Perchance tomorrow
You'll serve another master. I look on you
As one that takes his leave. Mine honest friends,
I turn you not away, but, like a master
Married to your good service, stay till death.

14, 15, 24, 25 SD] *Johnson and Capell subst.; not in* F 20 SH ALL] F *(Omnes)*

12 honest honourable, true.

14 fellows i.e. fellow servants in my service. Compare 3.12.5 and 3.13.92–4.

17 made so many men divided into as many men as are here.

18 clapped up together hastily combined.

20 as as that.

23 fellow i.e. fellow servant.

24 suffered acknowledged, submitted to, allowed.

26 period end.

27 if if you do.

28 shadow ghost.

31–2 like... death i.e. like a devoted master keep faith with you until my death (which will be soon). Antony echoes (unconsciously) the marriage service, 'Till death us do part'. J. Middleton Murry (*Shakespeare*, 1936, p. 303) finds echoes in this scene of Christ's Last Supper.

Tend me tonight two hours, I ask no more,
And the gods yield you for't!

ENOBARBUS What mean you, sir,
To give them this discomfort? Look, they weep,
And I, an ass, am onion-eyed. For shame,
Transform us not to women.

ANTONY Ho, ho, ho!
Now the witch take me if I meant it thus!
Grace grow where those drops fall! My hearty friends,
You take me in too dolorous a sense,
For I spake to you for your comfort, did desire you
To burn this night with torches. Know, my hearts,
I hope well of tomorrow, and will lead you
Where rather I'll expect victorious life
Than death and honour. Let's to supper, come,
And drown consideration.

Exeunt

[4.3] *Enter a Company of* SOLDIERS

1 SOLDIER Brother, good night. Tomorrow is the day.

39 fall! My hearty friends,] *Theobald;* fall (my hearty Friends) F **Act 4, Scene 3** 4.3] *Hanmer; no scene division in* F

34 yield reward.

35 discomfort distress, grief (*OED* sv *sb* 2).

36 onion-eyed A proverbial idea (Dent O67) used before by Enobarbus at 1.2.162–3, though with an ironic sense that is missing here. Despite his secret resolve to leave Antony (9 and n.) and his sceptical asides about a pathos induced by a Herculean frenzy (15–16, 25), Enobarbus is no doubt sincere in confessing that he is moved and distressed. Compare Antony's command of pathos at 3.11.8 ff.

38 the witch take me may I be bewitched. 'Take' means 'blast, enchant', as in *Ham.* 1.1.163: 'No fairy takes', and *Wiv.* 4.4.32.

39 Grace grow (1) May virtue and goodness flourish, (2) May 'herb of grace' grow. Antony means that their honest tears ought to betoken growing loyalty and faith among men; but rue or 'herb of grace' is symbolic of repentance or sorrow for another's misery, as in *R2* 3.4.106–7: 'Rue, even for ruth, here shortly shall be seen, / In the remembrance of a weeping queen.' Rue was mingled with holy water to make herb of grace; compare *Ham.* 4.5.182.

39 hearty kind-hearted (*OED* sv *adj* 3).

41 comfort encouragement, strengthening (*OED* sv *sb* 1).

42 To burn...torches i.e. to revel through the night. Compare Caesar's complaint at 1.4.4–5 that Antony 'wastes / The lamps of night in revel'.

46 drown consideration drown brooding reflection in our cups.

Act 4, Scene 3

Location Alexandria. Soldiers of Antony's army are on guard duty at the time of the posting or relieving of the watch. North's Plutarch provides several details for this scene and indicates that the episode of hearing strange music takes place on 'the self same night, within little of midnight' (1005E–1006A), though Plutarch does not mention soldiers on guard.

1–30 The company consists of two groups of two soldiers each. The first two enter and bid one another good night as they prepare to separate to their respective posts. When they meet two other soldiers coming on watch at 6, 2 Soldier wishes

2 SOLDIER It will determine one way. Fare you well.
Heard you of nothing strange about the streets?
1 SOLDIER Nothing. What news?
2 SOLDIER Belike 'tis but a rumour. Good night to you.
1 SOLDIER Well, sir, good night.

They meet other SOLDIERS

2 SOLDIER Soldiers, have careful watch.
3 SOLDIER And you. Good night, good night.
They place themselves in every corner of the stage
2 SOLDIER Here we; and if tomorrow
Our navy thrive, I have an absolute hope
Our landmen will stand up.
1 SOLDIER 'Tis a brave army, and full of purpose.
Music of the hautboys is under the stage
2 SOLDIER Peace, what noise?
1 SOLDIER List, list!
2 SOLDIER Hark!
1 SOLDIER Music i'th'air.
3 SOLDIER Under the earth.
4 SOLDIER It signs well, does it not?
3 SOLDIER No.
1 SOLDIER Peace, I say! What should this mean?
2 SOLDIER 'Tis the god Hercules, whom Antony loved,
Now leaves him.

8 SH 3 SOLDIER] *Capell;* 1 F

them 'careful watch' and is answered in 8 seemingly by one of the new arrivals; the designation of this speaker as '1' in F is accordingly emended to '3 Soldier' in this edition as in most modern editions. The four soldiers then disperse themselves to their posts, schematically represented by the four corners of the stage, two upstage and two downstage. These posts are understood to be separated by distance and the dark, although in the flexible conventions of the Elizabethan theatre the soldiers are then allowed to interchange comments on what they have heard. At 23 they advance towards one another to compare their experiences of what they have heard.

2 **determine one way** determine the outcome one way or the other.

5 **Belike** Very probably.

9 **Here we** i.e. here we are, on station where we are to watch.

9 **and** Perhaps this should be modernised as 'an', in the phrase 'an if', meaning 'if', but it can be read colloquially as 'and' in the modern sense.

12 **brave** splendid, gallant.

12 SD ***hautboys*** oboe-like instruments; F reads 'hoboys'. They are played *under the stage*, in the 'cellarage', to suggest other-worldly music.

18 **signs well** is a good omen.

21 **Hercules** See 1.3.84–5 n. on Antony's claim of descent from Hercules. In North's Plutarch, it is Bacchus whose music is heard as a sign of his forsaking his favourite (1005F–1006A).

1 SOLDIER Walk. Let's see if other watchmen
Do hear what we do.
2 SOLDIER How now, masters?
[*They*] *speak together*
ALL How now? How now? Do you hear this?
1 SOLDIER Ay, is't not strange?
3 SOLDIER Do you hear, masters? Do you hear?
1 SOLDIER Follow the noise so far as we have quarter.
Let's see how it will give off.
ALL Content. 'Tis strange.
Exeunt

[4.4] *Enter* ANTONY *and* CLEOPATRA *with* [CHARMIAN *and*] *others* [*attending*]

ANTONY Eros! Mine armour, Eros!
CLEOPATRA Sleep a little.
ANTONY No, my chuck. Eros, come, mine armour, Eros!

Enter EROS [*with armour*]

Come, good fellow, put thine iron on.
If fortune be not ours today, it is
Because we brave her. Come.
CLEOPATRA Nay, I'll help too.
What's this for?

24 SD *They*] *This edn; not in* F **25,30** SH ALL] F (*Omnes*) **Act 4, Scene 4** 4.4] *Hanmer; no scene division in* F **0** SD] *Capell subst.; Enter Anthony and Cleopatra, with others* F **2** SD *with armour*] *Capell; not in* F **3** thine] F; mine *Hanmer* **5–8** Nay...be] *Malone, conj. Capell; assigned to Cleopatra* F *(reading* Nay, Ile helpe too, *Anthony / at 5)*

24 **masters** i.e. sirs.

28 **as we have quarter** as our watch post extends.

29 **give off** cease.

Act 4, Scene 4

Location Alexandria. Antony and Cleopatra appear to have just risen (1, 35).

2 **chuck** i.e. chick. A term of endearment.

2 SD ***Enter Eros*** North's Plutarch reports that Antony 'had a man of his called Eros, whom he loved and trusted much, and whom he had long before caused to swear unto him that he should kill him when he did command him' (1006C). The business of arming Antony is Shakespeare's invention, as are Eros's earlier appearances in 3.5 and 3.11.

3 **thine iron** i.e. the armour you have there for me. (At 10 Antony tells Eros to arm himself also.) Some editors prefer Hanmer's emendation of 'thine' to 'mine'.

5 **brave** defy.

5–8 ***Nay...must be*** F cannot be right in assigning this whole speech to Cleopatra (see collation). Wilson suggests that '*Anthony*. Ah, let be...This, this' was added in the margin of Shakespeare's text and misinterpreted by the compositor. Ridley speculates that 'Sooth-law Ile helpe', with the appropriate speech heading for Cleopatra, may also have been a marginal addition – perhaps a Shakespearean afterthought.

[*She tries to help arm him*]

ANTONY Ah, let be, let be! Thou art
The armourer of my heart. False, false; this, this.

CLEOPATRA Sooth, la, I'll help. Thus it must be.

ANTONY Well, well,
We shall thrive now. Seest thou, my good fellow?
Go, put on thy defences.

EROS Briefly, sir.

CLEOPATRA Is not this buckled well?

ANTONY Rarely, rarely.
He that unbuckles this, till we do please
To doff't for our repose, shall hear a storm.
Thou fumblest, Eros, and my queen's a squire
More tight at this than thou. Dispatch. O love,
That thou couldst see my wars today, and knew'st
The royal occupation, thou shouldst see
A workman in't.

Enter an armed SOLDIER

Good morrow to thee; welcome.
Thou look'st like him that knows a warlike charge.
To business that we love we rise betime
And go to't with delight.

6 SD] *Oxford subst., after* must be *in 8; not in* F 13 doff't] F (daft)

7 **heart** Emphatic. You are the armourer of my heart, not my body. (Cleopatra inspires bravery in Antony and steels his heart with courage.)

7 **False** i.e. the wrong piece. Antony laughs at Cleopatra for not knowing how the pieces of armour are supposed to fit. Ironically, and charmingly too, the queen who would be warrior proves to be clumsily inexperienced.

8 **Sooth** In truth.

8–9 **Well, well...now** 'i.e. Cleo[patra] is doing better' (Wilson).

10 **defences** armour.

10 **Briefly** Soon, in a minute.

11 **Rarely** Excellently.

12–13 **He that...storm** i.e. anyone who grapples with me and attempts to break apart my armour until I choose to doff it for my own ease will hear a rain of blows on his armour. The image of binding and unbinding is essential to the pattern of the play; compare the symbolic sense of 'buckling' here with the buckles on Antony's breast at 1.1.8, the 'unslipping knot' at 2.2.135, and the 'knot intrinsicate' at 5.2.298.

14 **squire** The chivalric connotations of the word suggest that for Antony the reality is becoming nostalgic play.

15 **tight** deft, skilful.

15 **Dispatch** Get on with it.

16–17 **knew'st...occupation** i.e. if you were a judge of warfare, 'which is the trade of kings' (Kittredge).

18 **workman** skilled or expert craftsman (*OED* sv *sb* 2).

18–23 This brief exchange looks a bit like a first attempt by Shakespeare at something he goes on to develop more pointedly at 4.5.1 ff. If so, the Soldier here is perhaps to be identified with the Soldier of 3.7.60 ff. and with Scarus in 3.10 and 4.7–8; see 3.7.60 SD n.

19 **charge** duty, responsibility, commission.

20 **betime** betimes (as at 27), early.

SOLDIER A thousand, sir,
Early though't be, have on their riveted trim
And at the port expect you.
Shout. Trumpets flourish

Enter CAPTAINS *and* SOLDIERS

CAPTAIN The morn is fair. Good morrow, general.
ALL Good morrow, general.
ANTONY 'Tis well blown, lads.
This morning, like the spirit of a youth
That means to be of note, begins betimes.
So, so. Come, give me that. This way. Well said.
Fare thee well, dame. Whate'er becomes of me,
This is a soldier's kiss.
[*He kisses her*]
Rebukable,
And worthy shameful check it were, to stand
On more mechanic compliment. I'll leave thee
Now like a man of steel. – You that will fight,
Follow me close. I'll bring you to't. Adieu.
Exeunt [*Antony, Eros, Captains, and Soldiers*]
CHARMIAN Please you retire to your chamber?
CLEOPATRA Lead me.
He goes forth gallantly. That he and Caesar might
Determine this great war in single fight!
Then Antony – but now – Well, on.
Exeunt

24 SH CAPTAIN] *Rowe; Alex.* F 30 SD] *Johnson subst.; not in* F 32 compliment. I'll leave thee] F2 *subst.;* Complement, Ile leaue thee. F 34 SD *Antony...Soldiers*] *Capell subst.; not in* F

22 riveted trim array, trappings, armour, riveted in part as it was being put on; compare *H5* 4 Prologue 12–13: 'The armourers, accomplishing the knights, / With busy hammers closing rivets up'.

23 port gate.

24 *The morn...general F assigns this speech to *Alex.*, who, we learn at 4.6.12–13, has deserted Antony. Capell suggests that the actor of Alexas doubled the part of the Captain (*Notes*, I, 44).

25 'Tis well blown (1) That was well blown on the trumpets, or (2) The morning begins well, blossoms into day – a metaphor that responds to 'The morn is fair' (24) and continues into Antony's next two lines. The image of 'the spirit of a youth' suggests chivalric romance, as in 'squire' in 14 above and in Antony's earlier reference to Caesar's 'gay caparisons' at 3.13.26. Perhaps 'dame' in 29 below uses this kind of language as well (*OED* Dame 5). The whole is completed with Cleopatra's wistful fantasy at 36–8 that the war could be played out as a heroic romance, though knowing it can't be. This nostalgic undercurrent affects our critical sense of the occasion and of impending disaster.

28 Antony gives orders for the completion of his arming. 'That' refers to a piece of his equipment; 'Well said' means 'Well done'.

31 check reproof.

31–2 to stand...compliment to insist on further ceremonies of parting, such as would vulgarly befit common people. A 'man of steel' (33) leaves his mistress with a soldier's kiss only.

[4.5] *Trumpets sound. Enter* ANTONY *and* EROS[, *a* SOLDIER *meeting them*]

SOLDIER The gods make this a happy day to Antony!
ANTONY Would thou and those thy scars had once prevailed
To make me fight at land!
SOLDIER Hadst thou done so,
The kings that have revolted, and the soldier
That has this morning left thee, would have still
Followed thy heels.
ANTONY Who's gone this morning?
SOLDIER Who?
One ever near thee. Call for Enobarbus,
He shall not hear thee, or from Caesar's camp
Say 'I am none of thine.'
ANTONY What sayest thou?
SOLDIER Sir,
He is with Caesar.
EROS Sir, his chests and treasure
He has not with him.
ANTONY Is he gone?
SOLDIER Most certain.
ANTONY Go, Eros, send his treasure after. Do it.
Detain no jot, I charge thee. Write to him –
I will subscribe – gentle adieus and greetings;

Act 4, Scene 5 4.5] *Hanmer; no scene division in* F **0** SD *a* SOLDIER *meeting them*] *Theobald; not in* F **1** SH SOLDIER] *Theobald, conj. Thirlby; Eros* F **3, 6** SH SOLDIER] *Capell; Eros* F **6** Who's] F (Whose)

Act 4, Scene 5

Location Before Alexandria. This and succeeding scenes switch rapidly from Antony's camp to Caesar's (see 8) and then to the field of battle, without scenery and probably by the alternating use of stage doors to left and right, as in 3.8 ff.

1 happy lucky.

2 *once formerly (at 3.7.60–6). Antony's response makes clear that he addresses the soldier who spoke to him at Actium, not Eros as erroneously assigned in F at 1, 3, and 6. Perhaps Compositor B was misled by the naming of Eros and the casual omission of the unnamed soldier in the opening stage direction; F gets the text right once Eros and the soldier both speak at 9–11. The soldier at Actium (and here) is perhaps to be identified with the Scarus of 3.10 and 4.7–8; see 3.7.60 SD n.

4–5 the soldier...left thee North's Plutarch (1000A) provides Shakespeare with several details here: Antony's regret, his sending after Domitius 'all his carriage, train, and men' (see 12–16), and Domitius's penitent death. As part of his dramatic design and development of the role of Enobarbus, however, Shakespeare transposes the desertion from before the battle of Actium to its present location.

14 subscribe sign.

Say that I wish he never find more cause
To change a master. O, my fortunes have
Corrupted honest men. Dispatch. – Enobarbus!
Exeunt

[4.6] *Flourish. Enter* AGRIPPA, CAESAR, *with* ENOBARBUS, *and* DOLABELLA

CAESAR Go forth, Agrippa, and begin the fight.
Our will is Antony be took alive;
Make it so known.
AGRIPPA Caesar, I shall. [*Exit*]
CAESAR The time of universal peace is near.
Prove this a prosp'rous day, the three-nooked world
Shall bear the olive freely.

Enter a MESSENGER

MESSENGER Antony
Is come into the field.
CAESAR Go charge Agrippa
Plant those that have revolted in the van,

17 Dispatch. – Enobarbus!] *Steevens subst.;* Dispatch *Enobarbus.* F 17 SD *Exeunt*] F *(Exit)* **Act 4, Scene 6** 4.6] *Hanmer; no scene division in* F 4 SD] *Capell subst.; not in* F 9 van] F (Vant)

17 **Dispatch** See to it, quickly. (Said to Eros.)

Act 4, Scene 6

Location Before Alexandria. Caesar's camp. (See 4.5.8.)

5 To Renaissance audiences, the name of the Emperor Augustus (as Octavius was subsequently titled) was equated with his *Pax Romana*, peace under the Roman empire. Caesar is here made prophetic of his own great achievement. Conceivably, an audience would also recall the historical irony that the birth of Christ and its 'time of universal peace' occurred under the reign of Caesar Augustus (Luke 2.1). Caesar recognises his own historical myth, as Antony and Cleopatra will later create their ahistorical myths.

6 **Prove this** If this prove to be.

6 **three-nooked** three-sectored: Europe, Asia, Africa, henceforward to be governed not by the three triumvirs (compare 'triple pillar of the world', 1.1.12 and n., and 2.7.84) but by Caesar Augustus. According to Donald K. Anderson, Jr, *ELN* 17 (1979), 103–6, 'nook' here means 'sector of a circle'; the image is from the so-called T-in-O maps in which a T, inscribed within a circle, divides that circle into three sectors, one (representing Asia) twice the size of the other two.

7 **bear** (1) bring forth as in childbearing, (2) wear as a triumphal garland.

7 **the olive** Roman symbol of peace and prosperity, used to crown the emperors and vanquishers in war; also a Jewish and Christian symbol of divine promise of peace, as in the olive leaf brought to Noah by the dove (Gen. 8.11).

7 **freely** (1) readily, unreservedly, (2) with freedom of choice.

8–9 **charge Agrippa Plant** order Agrippa to place.

9 **van** front line. F's 'vant' is 'the old form of the word, short for *vantwarde*, whence *vangard* and so *van*' (Arden). This cold calculation of Caesar towards those who have defected to him is not reported in North's Plutarch. Even more

That Antony may seem to spend his fury
Upon himself.

Exeunt [all but Enobarbus]

ENOBARBUS Alexas did revolt and went to Jewry on
Affairs of Antony, there did dissuade
Great Herod to incline himself to Caesar
And leave his master Antony. For this pains,
Caesar hath hanged him. Canidius and the rest
That fell away have entertainment but
No honourable trust. I have done ill,
Of which I do accuse myself so sorely
That I will joy no more.

Enter a SOLDIER *of Caesar's*

SOLDIER Enobarbus, Antony
Hath after thee sent all thy treasure, with
His bounty overplus. The messenger
Came on my guard, and at thy tent is now
Unloading of his mules.

ENOBARBUS I give it you.

SOLDIER Mock not, Enobarbus,
I tell you true. Best you safed the bringer
Out of the host; I must attend mine office,
Or would have done't myself. Your emperor
Continues still a Jove. *Exit*

11 SD *all but Enobarbus*] *Capell subst.; not in* F 13 dissuade] F (disswade); perswade *Rowe* 16 Canidius] *Rowe; Camindius* F 20 more] F2; mote F

striking theatrically, and original to Shakespeare, is Caesar's indifference to Enobarbus's hearing this admission of realpolitik. Enobarbus is allowed to know at once that he has fallen into Caesar's trap.

12–16 Alexas...him Shakespeare alters his source to emphasise the cold-bloodedness and ingratitude of Caesar's calculation. In North's Plutarch, it is Herod who rewards Alexas for his treason to Antony by having him sent in chains to his own country and put to death. Although this execution is carried out 'by Caesar's commandment' (1004E–F), Herod is chiefly responsible for the ironic turn of events.

13 dissuade Some editors emend to 'persuade', since the word in North's Plutarch is 'persuaded' (1004E; see previous note), but 'dissuade' probably means 'persuade away from his allegiance to Antony'.

16 Canidius On Canidius's desertion of Antony after Actium, and his subsequent rejoining of Antony, see 3.10.32–4 and n. The report of Caesar's grudging reception of Canidius is Shakespeare's invention.

17 entertainment employment in Caesar's service.

20 SD *a* SOLDIER *of Caesar's* 'Soldiers of either side were probably distinguished by costume' (Wilson).

23 on my guard while I was standing guard.

27 Best you safed You'd better provide safe conduct for.

28 host army.

28 office duty.

ENOBARBUS I am alone the villain of the earth,
And feel I am so most. O Antony,
Thou mine of bounty, how wouldst thou have paid
My better service when my turpitude
Thou dost so crown with gold! This blows my heart.
If swift thought break it not, a swifter mean
Shall outstrike thought; but thought will do't, I feel.
I fight against thee? No, I will go seek
Some ditch wherein to die. The foul'st best fits
My latter part of life. *Exit*

[4.7] *Alarum. Drums and Trumpets. Enter* AGRIPPA [*and others*]

AGRIPPA Retire! We have engaged ourselves too far.
Caesar himself has work, and our oppression
Exceeds what we expected.
Exeunt

Alarums. Enter ANTONY, *and* SCARUS *wounded*

SCARUS O my brave emperor, this is fought indeed!

35–8 heart. / If...not, a...thought; but...do't, I feel. / I...thee?] *Rowe subst.;* hart, / If...not: a...thought, but...doo't. I feele / I...thee: F **Act 4, Scene 7** 4.7] *Hanmer; no scene division in* F **0** SD *and others*] *Capell subst.; not in* F 3 SD.1 *Exeunt*] F *(Exit)*

31 alone the villain beyond all others the greatest villain (Abbott 18).

32 And feel... most And am the one who realises it the most.

33 mine of bounty Compare *1H4* 3.1.166–7: 'as bountiful / As mines of India'.

35 blows causes to swell to the bursting point. Compare Antony's 'Heart...Crack thy frail case!' (4.14.40–1). A sudden, violent rush of melancholy blood (cold and dry) to the heart was thought to strangle it and make it heavy (Bamborough, pp. 121–2).

36 thought grief, melancholy, despair. Compare 'Think, and die' at 3.13.1.

36–37 a swifter...thought i.e. suicide will be a means to strike more swiftly than thought itself, which is proverbially swift (Dent T240). Even in his grief, Enobarbus plays with the word 'thought'.

37 thought will do't grief alone will break it (as indeed happens at 4.9.23).

Act 4, Scene 7

Location The field of battle.

0 SD *Alarum* A call to battle by drums and trumpets (Naylor, pp. 165–6). Auditory signals were an essential means in the Elizabethan theatre of conveying an impression of battle, as at 3.10.0 SD and 4.12.3 SD. *Alarums* were often accompanied by *excursions* or issuings forth onstage of groups of soldiers.

2 has work has his work cut out for him. 'Work' can mean 'trouble', 'affliction' (*OED* Work *sb* 6).

2 our oppression the oppressive weight of the attacks on us.

3 SD.1 *Exeunt* Technically a new scene begins here if the stage is bare, but the *Alarums* provide a sense of continuous action.

3 SD.2 SCARUS As Capell observes, Scarus takes the place of the deserter Enobarbus (*Notes*, I, 45). In North's Plutarch, Antony commends to Cleopatra for valour in the skirmish an unnamed soldier who subsequently deserts (1005D). Here Shakespeare maintains dramatic unity by making him the Scarus of 3.10, and alters his source to provide a contrast in loyalty with Enobarbus. See also 3.7.60 SD n. for another unnamed soldier who is perhaps to be identified with Scarus.

Had we done so at first, we had droven them home
With clouts about their heads.

ANTONY Thou bleed'st apace.

SCARUS I had a wound here that was like a T,
But now 'tis made an H.

[*Sound retreat*] *far off*

ANTONY They do retire.

SCARUS We'll beat 'em into bench-holes. I have yet
Room for six scotches more.

Enter EROS

EROS They are beaten, sir, and our advantage serves
For a fair victory.

SCARUS Let us score their backs
And snatch 'em up as we take hares, behind!
'Tis sport to maul a runner.

ANTONY I will reward thee
Once for thy sprightly comfort and tenfold
For thy good valour. Come thee on.

SCARUS I'll halt after.

Exeunt

8 SD *Sound retreat*] *Capell subst.; not in* F 8 SD *far off*] *Placed as in Wilson subst.; opposite* With...heads *in* 6 F

5 **droven** driven.

6 **clouts** (1) clothes, bandages, tattered rags (often a contemptuous term), (2) heavy blows, cuffs (*OED* Clout *sb*[1] 7). The wordplay is denied by some editors, but it is entirely in character in the exhilaration of victory, and continues in Scarus's next speech.

8 **'tis made an H** Scarus makes light of his wounds by jesting about them: one cut across the bottom of a previously T-shaped wound has made it into an H lying on its side, or perhaps has added to a *t*-shaped wound (as written in Secretary hand) another wound in the shape of a large hanging loop, thus completing the appearance of an *h* as written in Secretary hand (Maunde Thompson, cited by Wilson). In either case, Scarus quibbles on the similar pronunciation of the noun 'ache' ('aitch') and the letter H (Cercignani, p. 324): 'It has begun to ache', he jests.

9 **bench-holes** the holes of privies; i.e. any desperate hiding-place.

10 **scotches** gashes.

11 **beaten** i.e. probably 'struck with repeated blows' or 'beaten down' rather than 'defeated'; see next note.

11–12 **our advantage...victory** the advantage we have already gained may well pass for a brilliant victory (Kittredge); or our present advantage gives us the favourable opportunity of obtaining a complete victory (Capell, *Notes*, I, 45). Scarus's eagerness to continue the pursuit tends to favour the latter meaning.

12 **fair** 'A fair day' means 'success in battle' (*OED* Fair *adj* 14b).

12–14 **Let us...runner** The earlier idea of Antony and his men being hunted is now reversed: they are the hunters. Compare 3.13.200 ff., 4.1.8–9, etc.

14 **a runner** one who runs away.

15 **sprightly** high-spirited, cheerful.

17 **halt** limp.

[4.8] *Alarum. Enter* ANTONY *again in a march;* SCARUS, *with others*

ANTONY We have beat him to his camp. Run one before,
And let the queen know of our gests.
[*Exit a Soldier*]
Tomorrow,
Before the sun shall see's, we'll spill the blood
That has today escaped. I thank you all,
For doughty-handed are you, and have fought
Not as you served the cause, but as't had been
Each man's like mine; you have shown all Hectors.
Enter the city, clip your wives, your friends,
Tell them your feats, whilst they with joyful tears
Wash the congealment from your wounds and kiss
The honoured gashes whole.

Enter CLEOPATRA, [*with Attendants*]

[*To Scarus*] Give me thy hand;
To this great fairy I'll commend thy acts,
Make her thanks bless thee. [*To Cleopatra*] O thou day o'th'world,
Chain mine armed neck; leap thou, attire and all,
Through proof of harness to my heart, and there
Ride on the pants triumphing!

Act 4, Scene 8 4.8] *Capell; no scene division in* F 2 gests] *Theobald, conj. Warburton;* guests F 2 SD] *Oxford; not in* F 11 SD.1 *with Attendants*] *Capell subst.; not in* F 11 SD.2 *To Scarus*] *Rowe; not in* F 13 SD] *Cam.; not in* F

Act 4, Scene 8

Location See next note.

0 SD Antony's successful pursuit of Caesar's retreating forces is here represented by drum and trumpet signals and probably by excursions onstage of groups of soldiers; see 4.7.3 SD.1 n. The action is virtually continuous from scene to scene. When Antony re-enters in a victory march, we are to envisage him returning to Alexandria; at 35–9, he and Cleopatra are about to enter the city. Foreshortening of distance and time is evident when a follower is sent 'before' (1) to tell Cleopatra the news of the victory, whereupon she approaches at 11. North's Plutarch (1005D) gives a detailed account of this occasion, describing it as taking place when Antony 'came again to the palace'.

2 *gests deeds, exploits (Latin *res gestae*). The F reading, 'guests', is not listed in *OED* as a spelling variant of 'gests', but 'gest' is a variant of 'guest' and the words were easily confused.

3 see's see us.

6–7 Not...mine Not as if you were in service merely, but as if the cause had been each man's own as much as mine.

7 shown shown yourselves.

8 clip embrace.

11 SD.2 *To Scarus* In North's Plutarch the man 'of arms' thus favoured is unnamed (1005D). See 4.7.3 SD.2 n.

12 fairy i.e. one endowed with magical power and beauty, a dispenser of good fortune, like the Fairy Queen (Delius). The notion of Cleopatra's supernatural or magical authority is restored.

13 day light.

15 proof of harness armour of proof, armour that is proved invulnerable (*OED* Proof *sb* 10).

16 triumphing Accented on the second syllable.

[*They embrace*]

CLEOPATRA Lord of lords,
O infinite virtue, com'st thou smiling from
The world's great snare uncaught?

ANTONY My nightingale,
We have beat them to their beds. What, girl, though grey
Do something mingle with our younger brown, yet ha' we
A brain that nourishes our nerves and can
Get goal for goal of youth. Behold this man;
Commend unto his lips thy favouring hand. –
Kiss it, my warrior.

[*Scarus kisses Cleopatra's hand*]

He hath fought today
As if a god in hate of mankind had
Destroyed in such a shape.

CLEOPATRA I'll give thee, friend,
An armour all of gold; it was a king's.

ANTONY He has deserved it, were it carbuncled
Like holy Phoebus' car. Give me thy hand.
Through Alexandria make a jolly march;

16 SD] *Oxford subst., at 13; not in* F **18** My] F2; Mine F **23** favouring] *Theobald;* savouring F **24** SD] *Oxford; not in* F

16 Lord of lords Compare Rev. 17.14, 19.16 (Shaheen).

17 virtue valour (Latin *virtus*).

18 world's great snare This hyperbolic expression continues the hunting metaphor of 3.13.200–1, 4.1.8–9, 4.7.12–14, etc.

18 *My F's 'Mine' is an anticipation of the *n* sound in the next word, 'nightingale' – an easy error in copying. Compare F's 'mine Nailes' at 5.2.222.

18 nightingale 'A compliment to the fascination of her voice' (Deighton). 'Sweetest at night' (Wilson).

20 something somewhat.

21 nerves sinews, tendons.

22 Get...of youth Win as many goals as young men, prove their equal in this sport. Johnson speculates that the goals are in the play of barriers, or tilting, but *OED* supports the image of playing with a ball, 'the which soever can catch and carry through his adversary's goal, hath won the game' (*OED* Goal *sb* 3, citing Richard Carew's *Survey of Cornwall* (1602), 73b), or simply a race with a winning-post as its terminal (*OED* Goal *sb* 2). Shakespeare elsewhere refers to football as a violent and lower-class sport (*Err.* 2.1.83, *Lear* 1.4.86). The earlier art of romantic chivalry has given way to violent conflict.

23 Commend Entrust.

25 mankind Accented on the first syllable, as often in Shakespeare.

28 carbuncled studded with bright gems. Compare *Cym.* 5.5.189–90: 'a carbuncle / Of Phoebus' wheel'. The image may come from Ovid, *Metamorphoses*, II, 143–8 (in Golding's translation), where Phoebus's chariot is set with chrysolites and gems. Pliny (*Natural History*, Book XXXVII, chap. 7, trans. Philemon Holland (1601), pp. 616–18) describes twelve varieties, all of a red or fiery colour, including probably sapphires, garnets, and rubies. In the Middle Ages and later, 'the term was especially applied to a mythological gem said to emit a light in the dark' (*OED* Carbuncle 1).

29 holy Phoebus' car the chariot of the sun god.

30 jolly march This celebratory entry into Alexandria seems to include distinctively Egyptian elements, both contrasted and paralleled with a Roman 'triumph'.

Bear our hacked targets, like the men that owe them.
Had our great palace the capacity
To camp this host, we all would sup together
And drink carouses to the next day's fate,
Which promises royal peril. Trumpeters,
With brazen din blast you the city's ear;
Make mingle with our rattling taborins,
That heaven and earth may strike their sounds together,
Applauding our approach.

[Trumpets sound.] Exeunt

[4.9] *Enter a* SENTRY *and his Company* [*of* WATCH]. ENOBARBUS *follows*

SENTRY If we be not relieved within this hour,
We must return to th'court of guard. The night
Is shiny, and they say we shall embattle
By th'second hour i'th'morn.

1 WATCH This last day was
A shrewd one to's.

39 SD *Trumpets sound*] *Jones; not in* F **Act 4, Scene 9** 4.9] *Capell; no scene division in* F 0 SD SENTRY] F (*Centerie*) 0 SD *of* WATCH] *This edn; not in* F

31 **targets** light round shields.

31 **like...owe them** 'with spirit and exultation, such as become the brave warriors that own them' (Johnson); or 'hacked as much as the men are to whom they belong' (Warburton).

33 **camp this host** lodge this army.

34 **carouses** full bumpers drained in a toast; as in *Ham.* 1.4.8–10 (from German *gar aus*, all out).

35 **royal peril** i.e. war, the sport of kings; as at 4.4.16–17.

36 **brazen** (1) of brass, referring to the sound of the metallic instrument, (2) bold, unabashed.

37 **taborins** drums.

38 The music is to be so loud that it will appear to re-echo from heaven. The close resemblance of this line to Claudius's vaunts in *Ham.* 1.2.126–8 and 5.2.275–8 is suggestive of the *Ate* or self-destructive infatuation to which Antony is prone. Compare 3.13.115 n. Antony's hyperbole rashly claims divine as well as human sanction for his victory.

Act 4, Scene 9

Location Caesar's camp.

0 SD SENTRY i.e. leader of those who are standing watch.

0 SD ENOBARBUS ***follows*** The details of Enobarbus's death are Shakespeare's own invention. North's Plutarch reports simply of Domitius that he 'repented his open treason' in deserting Antony (before the battle of Actium) and 'died immediately after' (1000A).

2 **court of guard** guard-room or other place where the guard musters; as in *1H6* 2.1.4. *OED* explains it as a perversion of *corps de garde*, meaning the guard-room as well as the guard itself (Arden).

3 **shiny** full of light.

3 **embattle** arm, prepare for battle; as in Spenser, *Faerie Queene*, II, v, 2, 3: 'One in bright armes embatteiled full strong' (*OED* Embattle v^1 1). 'Embattle' may also mean 'to form in order of battle, take up positions in the field', though the 'second hour i'th'morn', i.e. after midnight, seems early for this.

5 **shrewd** cursed, unlucky. 'Often used as we use "plaguy", "confounded", and the like' (Kittredge).

ENOBARBUS O, bear me witness, night –
2 WATCH What man is this?
1 WATCH Stand close and list him.
[*They stand aside*]
ENOBARBUS Be witness to me, O thou blessèd moon,
When men revolted shall upon record
Bear hateful memory: poor Enobarbus did
Before thy face repent.
SENTRY Enobarbus?
2 WATCH Peace! Hark further.
ENOBARBUS O sovereign mistress of true melancholy,
The poisonous damp of night disponge upon me,
That life, a very rebel to my will,
May hang no longer on me. Throw my heart
Against the flint and hardness of my fault,
Which, being dried with grief, will break to powder
And finish all foul thoughts. O Antony,
Nobler than my revolt is infamous,
Forgive me in thine own particular,
But let the world rank me in register
A master-leaver and a fugitive.

6 SD] *Wilson subst.; not in* F

6 **close** concealed.

6 **list** listen to.

8 **revolted** who have broken their allegiance.

8 **upon record** in the record of history. ('Record' is accented on the second syllable.) The place they will have in history is a constant preoccupation of the play's chief characters.

12 **sovereign mistress** i.e. the moon, goddess of the melancholy to which Enobarbus has been subject (3.13.1, 4.6.35–7). The association of the moon with mental disorders is evident in such phrases as 'lunatic', 'moonstruck', and 'to moon'. The moon in Shakespeare is often cold and fruitless (*MND* 1.1.73), pale-faced (*1H4* 1.3.202), inconstant, watery, envious (*Rom.* 2.2.4). Since the moon is associated throughout this play with Isis and Cleopatra, it might be that Enobarbus, in his specific attachment to Antony, here conflates queen and moon as the 'blessèd' agent of dissolution, fluctuation, and destruction.

13 **disponge** drop as from a squeezed sponge. Damp night air was considered noxious, as when Portia chides Brutus in *JC* for exposing himself to 'the humors / Of the dank morning' and 'the vile contagion of the night' with its 'rheumy and unpurged air' (2.1.261–7).

16 **flint** Enobarbus adapts to his use the proverbial metaphor, 'A heart of flint' (Dent H311).

17 **Which** i.e. the heart.

17 **being dried with grief** Nicholas Coeffeteau, *The Table of Humane Passions*, trans. Edward Grimeston (1621), p. 333, asserts that when they come to open those that have been 'smothered with melancholy', 'instead of a heart, they find nothing but a dry skin like to the leaves in autumn' (quoted in Bamborough, p. 121). Such was thought to be the effect of cold and dry melancholic blood rushing to the heart in grief and strangling it; see 4.6.35 and n. In any event, the collision here of the ideas of moisture and dryness is arresting.

20 **in thine own particular** as far as you personally are concerned. (The world will not be so forgiving.)

21 **in register** in the catalogue or record of men's deeds. Compare 'upon record' at 8, and Enobarbus's earlier concern about his 'place i'th'story' (3.13.46).

22 **master-leaver** (1) one who leaves a master, a runaway servant (*OED* Master *sb*[1] 27), (2) the greatest of deserters.

22 **fugitive** 'one who flees or tries to escape

O Antony! O Antony! [*He dies*]
1 WATCH Let's speak to him.
SENTRY Let's hear him, for the things he speaks
May concern Caesar.
2 WATCH Let's do so. But he sleeps.
SENTRY Swoons rather, for so bad a prayer as his
Was never yet for sleep.
1 WATCH Go we to him.
[*They approach Enobarbus*]
2 WATCH Awake, sir, awake. Speak to us.
1 WATCH Hear you, sir?
SENTRY The hand of death hath raught him.
Drums afar off
Hark, the drums demurely wake the sleepers.
Let us bear him to th'court of guard;
He is of note. Our hour is fully out.
2 WATCH Come on, then. He may recover yet.
Exeunt [*with the body*]

[4.10] *Enter* ANTONY *and* SCARUS, *with their army*

ANTONY Their preparation is today by sea;
We please them not by land.
SCARUS For both, my lord.
ANTONY I would they'd fight i'th'fire or i'th'air;

23 SD] *Rowe subst.; not in* F 26 Swoons] F (Swoonds) 27 SD] *This edn; not in* F 33 SD *with the body*] *Capell; not in* F Act 4, Scene 10 4.10] *Capell; no scene division in* F

from...an owner', a deserter (*OED* Fugitive *sb* 1). 'An apprentice who broke his indenture and ran away was a reprobate' (Wilson) and hence a fugitive from the law.

23 SD ***He dies*** Enobarbus dies of a broken heart, as he has repeatedly anticipated. The idea is not the trite and hyperbolic metaphor it has become for us but a physiological process in which grief or melancholy 'blows' the heart by swelling it until it 'breaks' (3.13.1, 4.6.35–7; see Bamborough, pp. 121–2). Paul Jorgensen ('Enobarbus' broken heart and *The Estate of English Fugitives*', *PQ* 30 (1951), 387–92) proposes that Shakespeare may have known Sir Lewis Lewkenor's *The Estate of English Fugitives under the King of Spain* (1595), a popular work that portrayed many a traitor as suffering scorn and dying of passionate melancholic heartbreak.

27 **for** a prelude to. 'Such an unquiet conscience can hardly sleep' (Wilson). Enobarbus's 'bad' prayer is contrasted with the night-charm or the 'Third Collect, For Aid against All Perils', in the service for Evening Prayer.

29 **raught** reached.

30 **demurely** 'with solemn sound' (Onions).

32 **of note** a person of rank and importance.

Act 4, Scene 10

Location The field of battle.

1 **by sea** A very ominous note in a play full of omens.

3 **i'th'fire or i'th'air** i.e. as well as in the other two elements, water and earth, the 'sea' and 'land' of 1–2 (Wilson). Compare Cleopatra's 'I am fire and air' (5.2.283).

We'd fight there too. But this it is: our foot
Upon the hills adjoining to the city
Shall stay with us – order for sea is given;
They have put forth the haven –
Where their appointment we may best discover
And look on their endeavour.

Exeunt

[4.11] *Enter* CAESAR *and his army*

CAESAR But being charged, we will be still by land –
Which, as I take't, we shall, for his best force
Is forth to man his galleys. To the vales,
And hold our best advantage.

Exeunt

[4.12] *Enter* ANTONY *and* SCARUS

ANTONY Yet they are not joined. Where yond pine does stand
I shall discover all. I'll bring thee word
Straight how 'tis like to go. *Exit*

6–7 us – order...haven –] *Knight subst.;* vs. Order...Hauen: F **Act 4, Scene 11** 4.11] *Dyce; no scene division in* F **Act 4, Scene 12** 4.12] *Dyce; no scene division in* F **0** SD] *Capell subst.; Alarum afarre off, as at a Sea-fight. Enter Anthony, and Scarrus* F

4–9 our foot...endeavour North's Plutarch describes how Antony, at break of day, 'went to set those few footmen he had in order upon the hills adjoining unto the city; and there he stood to behold his galleys which departed from the haven' (1006A). 'Foot' (4) means foot-soldiers.

7 They i.e. Antony's galleys.

7 forth forth from.

8 From which hills we may best descry the disposition and equipment of the naval forces.

Act 4, Scene 11

Location Continues at the field of battle.

1 But being charged Unless we are attacked. The implication is that Antony has been manoeuvred into committing himself first to the sea action.

1 still quiet, inactive.

2 we shall i.e. we will be left undisturbed.

4 hold our best advantage take the strongest position possible.

Act 4, Scene 12

Location The scene continues at the battle. Antony has taken up position on the 'hills adjoining to the city' mentioned in 4.10.5, but the imagined location shifts to Alexandria by the time of Cleopatra's entry at 30 (see n.).

1 *Yet...joined The contending forces have not yet joined in battle. Unless Antony is simply wrong in saying this, the stage direction *Alarum afar off, as at a sea fight*, placed in the Folio at the head of this scene, must belong later, at 3 as in this and other editions, or when Antony re-enters at 9, as in still other editions. The stage direction may have been written somewhat imprecisely in the margin, as Wilson speculates.

3 Straight Straightway.

3 like likely.

Alarum afar off, as at a sea fight

SCARUS Swallows have built
In Cleopatra's sails their nests. The augurers
Say they know not, they cannot tell, look grimly,
And dare not speak their knowledge. Antony
Is valiant, and dejected, and by starts
His fretted fortunes give him hope and fear
Of what he has and has not.

Enter ANTONY

ANTONY All is lost!
This foul Egyptian hath betrayèd me.
My fleet hath yielded to the foe, and yonder
They cast their caps up and carouse together
Like friends long lost. Triple-turned whore! 'Tis thou
Hast sold me to this novice, and my heart
Makes only wars on thee. Bid them all fly;
For when I am revenged upon my charm,
I have done all. Bid them all fly. Begone!

[*Exit Scarus*]

3 SD.2 *Alarum...sea fight*] *Placed as in Wilson; at 0* SD *in* F 4 augurers] *Capell;* Auguries F 17 SD] *Capell; not in* F

3–6 Swallows...knowledge In North's Plutarch, swallows not only breed 'under the poop of her [Cleopatra's] ship', but are driven away by others and their nests 'plucked down' (999A) – a distinctly ominous sign. The warning occurs before Actium, not the fighting at Alexandria; Shakespeare has reserved this touch until the play has entered a later, more fatalistic stage.

4 sails Shakespeare's use of North's Plutarch (see previous note) makes it clear that he means 'ships' here (as earlier at 2.6.24 and 3.7.49). The sails themselves are not good places to build nests.

4 *augurers augurs, soothsayers; as in *JC* 2.1.200 and 2.2.37 ('What say the augurers?'), *Cor.* 2.1.1, and *Ant.* 5.2.328. Shakespeare's preference for this now-obsolete form suggests that F's 'auguries' is an error. Pope's 'augurs' is less demonstrably Shakespearean.

8 fretted (1) worn, eaten away, (2) vexed, chafed, (3) chequered; as in *JC* 2.1.103–4: 'yon grey lines / That fret the clouds'.

13 Triple-turned Three times faithless (to Julius Caesar, Gneius Pompey, and now Antony). Compare 3.13.119–21. Neither in North's Plutarch nor in Shakespeare is Cleopatra in fact responsible for this naval defeat, as she was in part at Actium. As in his source, Shakespeare records the event and Antony's accusation without telling us whether the accusation is true; we are left with one more indication of Cleopatra's enigmatic quality (Fredson Bowers, 'Shakespeare's dramatic vagueness', *VQR* 39 (1963), 475–84). Still, Antony's sense of her malign influence provides another occasion for a *tour de force* in invective.

14 sold i.e. by black magic; see 16 n.

15 all even those who have not already deserted; emphatic.

16 my charm this witch who practises charms or spells on me. Antony repeatedly accuses Cleopatra of being a 'false soul' or 'grave charm' (25), a 'gipsy' (28), a 'spell' whom he must bid 'Avaunt' (30), and a 'witch' (47). This is no mere figure of speech; Antony has lost the battle, he thinks, because of her black magic. Contrast his more positive sense of her magical powers at 4.8.12, for example.

O sun, thy uprise shall I see no more.
Fortune and Antony part here; even here
Do we shake hands. All come to this? The hearts
That spanieled me at heels, to whom I gave
Their wishes, do discandy, melt their sweets
On blossoming Caesar; and this pine is barked
That overtopped them all. Betrayed I am.
O, this false soul of Egypt! This grave charm,
Whose eye becked forth my wars and called them home,
Whose bosom was my crownet, my chief end,
Like a right gipsy hath at fast and loose
Beguiled me to the very heart of loss.
What, Eros, Eros!

Enter CLEOPATRA

Ah, thou spell! Avaunt!

20 hands.] *Capell;* hands? F **21** spanieled] *Hanmer;* pannelled F

20 shake hands i.e. in parting, as in *Mac.* 1.2.21.

20 hearts good fellows, boon companions. Compare *Temp.* 1.1.5: 'Heigh, my hearts!' and *Wiv.* 3.2.87; frequent in Shakespeare. *OED* Heart *sb* 14b misleadingly gives the earliest citation as 1663, though it provides earlier uses of 'heart' as a term of endearment (sv *sb* 14).

21 *spanieled Hanmer's emendation of F's 'pannelled' is strengthened by the various possible spellings of 'spaniel', including the dialectal 'span(n)ell' (*OED* sv *sb*[1]), and by the proverbial association of spaniels with fawning and sweetmeats (Dent S704, and M. M. Mahood, *Shakespeare's Wordplay*, 1957, p. 22).

22 Their wishes Their hearts' desire.

22 discandy melt, dissolve; with a culinary sense, as at 3.13.169. Caroline Spurgeon, *Shakespeare's Imagery and What It Tells Us*, 1935, pp. 195–9, shows that the previously noticed association in Shakespeare of fawning dogs and flattery with 'candy' or 'candied' (compare *1H4* 1.3.251–2 and *Ham.* 3.2.60–2, also *Tim.* 4.3.225–7 and *JC* 3.1.42–3) is derived from the practice of feeding dogs at meals under the table.

22–3 melt...Caesar Antony's former followers lavish their sweet flatteries now on Caesar, whose fortunes are blossoming.

23 barked stripped of its bark and thus killed. The 'pine', recalling 1 above, is tall and straight, like Antony in his prime. Compare *MV* 4.1.75–7, *2H6* 2.3.45, etc.

25 false soul evil, disembodied spirit.

25 grave charm deadly witch. 'Grave' can mean heavy, deadening, potent, commanding (Latin *gravis*).

26 becked beckoned.

27 i.e. whose love was the crown of my achievements, the object and reward of my labours. Johnson cites the proverb *finis coronat opus* ('the end crowns the work'), rendered by Shakespeare as 'The fine's the crown' (*AWW* 4.4.35).

28 right true.

28 gipsy See 1.1.10 n.

28 at fast and loose A proverbial image; compare Dent P401 and *John* 3.1.242. Fast and loose is a cheating game played by gipsies in which the victim bets he can make fast a knot in a string or belt, whereupon the ingeniously woven knot is pulled loose. (*OED* Fast and loose cites Whetstone's *Promos and Cassandra* (1578), 1.2.5: 'at fast or loose, with my Giptian I mean to have a cast', and Jonson's *The Gipsies' Metamorphosis* (1621), Song 1.)

29 loss ruin.

30 SD This meeting is Shakespeare's own conception. North's Plutarch merely reports that after his defeat Antony 'fled into the city, crying out that Cleopatra had betrayed him unto them' (1006B). Shakespeare's fluid stage allows us to imagine that the scene is now in Alexandria, at court, rather than on the field of battle where the scene began (see note on location above).

30 spell enchantment.

30 Avaunt Begone. (Usually said to ward off the power of a witch or devil.)

CLEOPATRA Why is my lord enraged against his love?
ANTONY Vanish, or I shall give thee thy deserving
And blemish Caesar's triumph. Let him take thee
And hoist thee up to the shouting plebeians!
Follow his chariot, like the greatest spot
Of all thy sex; most monster-like be shown
For poor'st diminutives, for dolts, and let
Patient Octavia plough thy visage up
With her preparèd nails!

Exit Cleopatra

'Tis well thou'rt gone,
If it be well to live. But better 'twere
Thou fell'st into my fury, for one death
Might have prevented many. Eros, ho!
The shirt of Nessus is upon me. Teach me,
Alcides, thou mine ancestor, thy rage.
Let me lodge Lichas on the horns o'th'moon,

37 dolts] F; doits *Warburton, conj. Thirlby* 45 Lichas] *Theobald; Licas* F

33 **triumph** triumphal procession (in Rome); as at 3.13.140 and 5.2.108. Cleopatra's death would deprive such a triumphal procession of its chief attraction, as Caesar himself notes at 5.1.65–6.

34 **plebeians** Accented on the first syllable, as in *Cor.* 1.9.7 and 5.4.36. Cleopatra thinks again of this ignoble prospect at 5.2.54–6 and 207–20.

35 **spot** blemish.

36 **monster-like be shown** be exhibited like a freak in a travelling show; as in *Temp.* 2.2.27–33 and *Mac.* 5.8.25–6: 'We'll have thee, as our rarer monsters are, / Painted upon a pole.'

37 **For...dolts** For the entertainment of puny commoners and idiots. Thirlby's emendation of 'dolts' to 'doits', small coins, depends on a reading of 'diminutives' in the same sense, for which no other instances have been found, whereas the application to living creatures is common (as in *Tro.* 5.1.34).

39 **preparèd** 'sharpened for the purpose' (Wilson).

41 **Thou fell'st into** You had fallen a victim to.

42 **Might have prevented many** i.e. might have forestalled the shame and mental anguish that are as terrible as many deaths. Compare *JC* 2.2.32: 'Cowards die many times before their deaths.' Or Antony could mean, in his fury, that many others will die as a result of this.

43 **The shirt of Nessus** When Hercules, or 'Alcides' (44), had fatally shot the centaur Nessus with a poisoned arrow for trying to rape Hercules' wife Deianira, Nessus vengefully gave the shirt soaked with his poisoned blood to Deianira as a supposed love-charm for her husband. She later sent it to Hercules by the innocent hand of the page, Lichas (45). The poison so maddened Hercules with agony that he cast Lichas from Mount Oeta into the sea and then mounted a funeral pyre. The story is told in Ovid's *Metamorphoses*, IX, 117 ff. (in Golding's translation) and *Heroides*, IX, and in Seneca's *Hercules Oetaeus*. Antony blames his downfall and death on the treachery of a woman, thus missing the irony of Deianira's innocence.

44 Antony claims descent from Anton, son of Hercules, and has long emulated the fury for which Hercules was famous, not only in Hercules' death but when, maddened by Hera, he killed his wife and children. (See Seneca, *Hercules Furens*, and 1.3.84–5 above and n.)

45 The hyperbole may derive from Seneca's *Hercules Oetaeus* 3. 817 (trans. John Studley, in Thomas Newton (ed.), *Seneca His Ten Tragedies* (1581), p. 201): 'With Lycas thus his labours end, thrown up to heaven they say, / That with his dropping blood the clouds he stainèd all the way' ('In astra missus fertur, et nubes vago / spargit cruore'; cited by Warburton). Compare *Cor.* 1.1.213, when the plebeians throw their caps 'As they would hang them on the horns a'th'moon'.

And with those hands that grasped the heaviest club
Subdue my worthiest self. The witch shall die.
To the young Roman boy she hath sold me, and I fall
Under this plot. She dies for't. Eros, ho! *Exit*

[4.13] *Enter* CLEOPATRA, CHARMIAN, IRAS, [*and*] MARDIAN

CLEOPATRA Help me, my women! O, he's more mad
Than Telamon for his shield; the boar of Thessaly
Was never so embossed.
CHARMIAN To th'monument!
There lock yourself and send him word you are dead.
The soul and body rive not more in parting
Than greatness going off.
CLEOPATRA To th'monument!
Mardian, go tell him I have slain myself.
Say that the last I spoke was 'Antony',
And word it, prithee, piteously. Hence, Mardian,
And bring me how he takes my death. To th'monument!
Exeunt

Act 4, Scene 13 4.13] *Dyce; no scene division in* F 1 he's] F (hee's); he is F2 10 death. To th'monument!] *Pope subst.;* death to'th'Monument. F

46 **club** Hercules' weapon.

47 **worthiest** most heroic and noble. Like Hercules, Antony will end his own life and thereby subdue that part of his noble nature that has striven for glory.

Act 4, Scene 13

Location Alexandria, following immediately after the previous scene. The sense of location in these scenes is very fluid. There is no reason to suppose a change of scene between 4.12 and 4.13, as Wilson and others insist, if we accept that by the end of 4.12 the imagined place of action is the palace.

2 **Telamon** Ajax, son of Telamon (properly called Telamonius), one of the Greek heroes of Troy, who after the capture of Troy went mad and slew himself when the shield and armour of Achilles were awarded to Odysseus or Ulysses rather than to himself. In his madness he slaughtered sheep, thinking they were Greeks. In Chapman's *Iliad*, *Telamonios* is translated 'Telamon' (Wilson).

2 **the boar of Thessaly** The boar sent by Diana or Artemis to ravage the fields of the King of Calydon, in eastern Greece, and slain by his son Meleager, the brother of Deianira. In Golding's translation of the *Metamorphoses*, the boar's eyes 'did glister blood and fire' (VIII, 376).

3 **embossed** frenzied and foaming at the mouth from exhaustion. Said of a hunted animal.

5 **rive not more** do not create a more terrible cleavage.

6 **going off** i.e. bidding farewell to its glory.

10 ***death. To th'monument** F's punctuation, 'death to th'Monument', is possible, and it is preserved by Arden with the meaning that Mardian is to bring the news to the monument, but the repetition of 'To th'monument!' in 3 and 6 suggests that this final utterance of the scene is another refrain.

[4.14] *Enter* ANTONY *and* EROS

ANTONY Eros, thou yet behold'st me?
EROS Ay, noble lord.
ANTONY Sometime we see a cloud that's dragonish,
A vapour sometime like a bear or lion,
A towered citadel, a pendent rock,
A forkèd mountain, or blue promontory
With trees upon't that nod unto the world
And mock our eyes with air. Thou hast seen these signs;
They are black vesper's pageants.
EROS Ay, my lord.
ANTONY That which is now a horse, even with a thought
The rack dislimns and makes it indistinct
As water is in water.
EROS It does, my lord.
ANTONY My good knave Eros, now thy captain is
Even such a body. Here I am Antony,
Yet cannot hold this visible shape, my knave.
I made these wars for Egypt, and the queen,

Act 4, Scene 14 4.14] *Dyce; no scene division in* F 4 towered] *Rowe;* toward F 10 dislimns] *Rowe* (dislimn's); dislimes F 14–15 shape, my knave. / I] *Rowe*[2] *subst.;* shape (my Knaue) / I F

Act 4, Scene 14

Location Continues at the palace. At the end of 4.12, Antony was looking for Eros.

1 thou yet behold'st me? 'This question, which, of course, Eros cannot understand, is explained by what follows (in ll. 2–14). Antony seems to himself such a faded, shadowlike figure of what he had been, that he wonders if he is still visible and recognizable' (Kittredge).

2–14 Sometime...knave The use of clouds and vapours to suggest the insubstantial and evanescent nature of human life is universal, found for example in Aristophanes' *The Clouds*, Pliny's *Natural History*, Book II, chap. 3, *Ham.* 3.2.376–82, and *Temp.* 4.1.148–58. Arden gives other citations. At the same time Shakespeare's treatment of the topic is highly distinctive, providing a vision of the solid and substantial as melting and undergoing metamorphosis until Cleopatra imaginatively recreates her reality into quasi-myth in the final stages of the play.

8 black vesper's pageants the illusory and fading spectacle of sunset, heralding the approach of night. Prospero calls his masque in *Temp.* 4.1.155–6 an 'insubstantial pageant' that has 'faded', just as the world itself will dissolve and 'Leave not a rack behind'. 'Pageant' is often synonymous with 'theatrical representation', 'spectacle', or 'masque' in Shakespeare, as in *R2* 4.1.321 and in *MND* 3.2.114: 'Shall we their fond pageant see?'

9 even with a thought as quick as thought.

10 The rack dislimns The mass of cloud or vapour effaces, blots out the picture. To 'limn' is to paint, as in *Venus and Adonis* 290. The metaphor of the pageant and theatrical illusion probably continues; compare Jonson's masque, *Hymenaei*, 192 SD: 'Here the upper part of the scene, which was all of clouds and made artificially to swell and ride like the rack, began to open' (Orgel, p. 82).

12 knave boy, fellow.

15 Egypt The Queen of Egypt.

15 the queen Grammatically this phrase can be construed as in apposition with 'she' in 18 and hence the subject of 'has / Packed cards', or as governed by 'for' in a prepositional phrase ('for Egypt and for the queen'). In the latter case a

Whose heart I thought I had, for she had mine –
Which whilst it was mine had annexed unto't
A million more, now lost – she, Eros, has
Packed cards with Caesar and false-played my glory
Unto an enemy's triumph.
Nay, weep not, gentle Eros; there is left us
Ourselves to end ourselves.

Enter MARDIAN

O, thy vile lady!
She has robbed me of my sword.

MARDIAN No, Antony,
My mistress loved thee, and her fortunes mingled
With thine entirely.

ANTONY Hence, saucy eunuch, peace!
She hath betrayed me and shall die the death.

MARDIAN Death of one person can be paid but once,
And that she has discharged. What thou wouldst do
Is done unto thy hand. The last she spake
Was 'Antony, most noble Antony!'
Then in the midst a tearing groan did break

16 mine –] *Hanmer subst.;* mine: F 18 more] F (moe) 18 lost –] *Capell subst.;* lost:) F 19 Caesar] *Rowe; Cæsars* F 22 vile] F (vilde)

comma would be required after 'mine' in 16 and a full stop after 'lost' in 18. The former reading better connects the logic in Antony's mind of his devoted service and of Cleopatra's betraying him nonetheless.

18 more more in number. F's 'moe', a variant of 'mo', is sometimes used in Elizabethan texts to mean 'more in number' as distinguished from 'greater in size', 'additional to', etc., but the spelling 'more' is also used so often in Shakespeare to mean 'more in number' that the distinction tends to become arbitrary and archaic; compare 'enow' and 'enough' at 1.4.11.

19–20 Packed...triumph Shuffled or stacked the cards in Caesar's favour and falsely played away my glory, thus allowing my enemy to triumph – literally, to trump. Cleopatra, supposedly Antony's partner in the game, is suspected of having arranged and played her cards in such a way as to leave Antony's high card vulnerable to Caesar's trump card. 'Trump' is a corruption of 'triumph', and both words were applied in Shakespeare's time to cards and a card game (*OED* Triumph *sb* 8a and b, Trump *sb*[2]). 'Knave', 'queen', and 'heart' (12–16) are card terms that probably suggested the metaphor (Whiter, pp. 106–7). Perhaps Antony's mind is supposed to be returning to the talk about games of chance at 2.3.33 ff.

23 robbed me of my sword (1) 'degraded me; literally, made me surrender my sword' (Wilson), (2) taken away my prowess as a soldier, my very masculinity.

25 saucy insolent.

26 die the death 'A solemn phrase for death inflicted by law' (Johnson, note to *MM* 2.4.165; *OED* Die *v*[1] 2c); as also in *MND* 1.1.65 and *Cym.* 4.2.96. Shaheen cites numerous uses in the Bible.

27 of by.

27 can...once Compare the proverb 'A man can die but once' (Dent M219).

28 that she has discharged she has paid that debt in full.

29 unto thy hand without effort on your part (*OED* Hand *sb* 34c).

The name of Antony; it was divided
Between her heart and lips. She rendered life
Thy name so buried in her.

ANTONY Dead, then?

MARDIAN Dead.

ANTONY Unarm, Eros. The long day's task is done,
And we must sleep. [*To Mardian*] That thou depart'st hence safe
Does pay thy labour richly; go.

Exit Mardian

Off, pluck off!

[*Eros unarms him*]

The sevenfold shield of Ajax cannot keep
The battery from my heart. O, cleave, my sides!
Heart, once be stronger than thy continent;
Crack thy frail case! Apace, Eros, apace!
No more a soldier. Bruisèd pieces, go;
You have been nobly borne. – From me awhile.

Exit Eros

I will o'ertake thee, Cleopatra, and
Weep for my pardon. So it must be, for now
All length is torture; since the torch is out,

36 SD *To Mardian*] *Globe; not in* F 37 SD.2 *Eros unarms him*] *Wilson subst.; not in* F

32–3 **it was...lips** i.e. she pronounced only half of Antony's name and then her heart groaned as she died as though keeping the rest to herself.

33–4 **She rendered...in her** She gave up to the living world that part of your name which was buried in her. Some editors provide a comma after 'life', taking the phrase to mean 'she gave up life, with your name thus buried in her', but F makes sense as punctuated.

35 **Unarm** North's Plutarch (1006B–C) reports Antony's unarming himself, his vowing to overtake Cleopatra (compare 44), and his condemnation of himself for being 'of less courage and noble mind than a woman' (compare 59–60). Only at that point in Plutarch is Eros called to Antony to remember his oath to assist in Antony's suicide (compare 62–7). Antony's using Eros as a naïve audience for his meditations on dissolution, and the hauntingly simple eloquence of Antony's response to the seeming news of Cleopatra's death in 35–6, are Shakespeare's invention.

37 **thy labour** i.e. as messenger. Such a message might deserve death. Another variation on the messenger-and-his reward in the play; see pp. 42–3 above.

38–9 **The sevenfold...heart** Even the great shield of Ajax, with its seven thicknesses of oxhide, could not protect my heart from this deadly assault of grief. A 'battery' is an artillery bombardment or other succession of heavy blows.

40–1 **Heart...case** Unhindered by his breastplate, Antony feels the violent agitation of his heart as though it wished to free itself from his body – not to crack yet, as in death, but to swell towards bursting. Compare Enobarbus at 4.6.35 above, 'This blows my heart', and *Lear* 2.4.121, 197–8: 'O me, my heart! my rising heart!...O sides, you are too tough! / Will you yet hold?'

40 **thy continent** that which contains you, the heart; the 'frail case' of 41.

41 **Apace** Quickly.

46 **length** prolongation of life, duration.

46 **the torch** i.e. the life of Cleopatra.

Lie down and stray no farther. Now all labour
Mars what it does; yea, very force entangles
Itself with strength. Seal then, and all is done.
Eros! – I come, my queen. – Eros! – Stay for me.
Where souls do couch on flowers, we'll hand in hand,
And with our sprightly port make the ghosts gaze.
Dido and her Aeneas shall want troops,
And all the haunt be ours. – Come, Eros, Eros!

Enter EROS

EROS What would my lord?
ANTONY Since Cleopatra died
I have lived in such dishonour that the gods
Detest my baseness. I, that with my sword
Quartered the world, and o'er green Neptune's back
With ships made cities, condemn myself to lack
The courage of a woman – less noble mind

60 mind] F; minded *Rowe*

47–9 Now...strength Any act now would be self-defeating; indeed, all strenuous efforts merely entangle themselves in their own exertions. Walker (III, 309) compares Sonnet 23, especially 3–4 and 7–8.

49 Seal Finish the business, complete the agreement, as in sealing a document. The action is like that of York in *H5* 4.6.26–7, dying as he bids farewell to the slain Suffolk: 'And so espous'd to death, with blood he seal'd / A testament of noble-ending love.' The imagery of seals and torches (46) is reminiscent of the Book of Revelation, e.g. 5.1, as Seaton, p. 223, observes. See Morris, pp. 252–62, for the iconographical tradition based on Revelation that includes the work of Albrecht Dürer.

51 couch recline (in the Elysian fields).

52 sprightly port high-spirited bearing, demeanour. 'Sprightly' may also suggest 'spirit-like', 'ghostly'; 'sprite' = 'spirit' (Wilson).

53 i.e. Antony and Cleopatra will be the most famous lovers in the Elysian fields, outshining even the Queen of Carthage and her lover. In the *Aeneid*, Book VI, Aeneas does sport with Dido for a time but then dutifully leaves her to fulfil the destiny of Rome, unlike Antony, and is repulsed by a scornful Dido when he encounters her in Hades. Shakespeare consciously fashions a myth that transcends the recorded 'history' of his sources, while at the same time inviting us to see an ironic discrepancy between the myth that Antony imagines and the often dismaying failures of his actual life. On the pervasiveness of the Dido and Aeneas story throughout the play, see 1.3.20 ff., 3.11.59–60 and nn., and p. 7 above.

53 shall want troops will have no entourage of admiring 'ghosts' (i.e. souls, spirits) to gaze at them.

54 all the haunt be ours i.e. all will flock to gaze on us. 'Haunt' can mean the act of resorting, companionship, company, or a place of frequent resort, especially of ghosts.

56 in such dishonour i.e. the dishonour of outliving Cleopatra and of lacking 'The courage of a woman' (60).

58 Quartered i.e. divided and conquered. The business of hanging and quartering a criminal is often generalised into an image of slaughter and dismemberment in Shakespeare, as in *1H6* 4.2.11: 'Lean famine, quartering steel, and climbing fire'.

59 With ships made cities Assembled as it were whole cities of ships, as in *H5* 3 Prologue 15–16: 'A city on th'inconstant billows dancing; / For so appears this fleet majestical'.

59 to lack for lacking.

60 less noble mind This phrase is either in apposition with 'I' (57) (Arden), or else it means 'I...condemn myself to have, i.e., for having, a less noble mind' (Kittredge). The corresponding sentence in North's Plutarch (1006C) tends to support the latter.

Than she which by her death our Caesar tells
'I am conqueror of myself.' Thou art sworn, Eros,
That when the exigent should come – which now
Is come indeed – when I should see behind me
Th'inevitable prosecution of
Disgrace and horror, that on my command
Thou then wouldst kill me. Do't. The time is come.
Thou strik'st not me, 'tis Caesar thou defeat'st.
Put colour in thy cheek.

EROS The gods withhold me!
Shall I do that which all the Parthian darts,
Though enemy, lost aim and could not?

ANTONY Eros,
Wouldst thou be windowed in great Rome and see
Thy master thus with pleached arms, bending down
His corrigible neck, his face subdued
To penetrative shame, whilst the wheeled seat
Of fortunate Caesar, drawn before him, branded
His baseness that ensued?

EROS I would not see't.

ANTONY Come, then, for with a wound I must be cured.
Draw that thy honest sword, which thou hast worn
Most useful for thy country.

EROS O, sir, pardon me!

ANTONY When I did make thee free, swor'st thou not then

63 **exigent** extremity, time of extreme and compelling necessity.

65 **inevitable prosecution** inexorable pursuit.

68 **'tis Caesar thou defeat'st** i.e. you frustrate Caesar's plan, undo his triumph. Compare 5.1.64–5.

69 **The gods withhold me** i.e. the gods forbid.

70 **Parthian darts** See 3.1.1 n.

71 **enemy** Here an adjective.

72 **windowed** placed in a window; either to look on or to be looked at, probably the former. (The only *OED* citation in this sense – Window *v* 2.)

73 **pleached** folded. The actor gestures 'thus', suggesting either a captive whose arms are bound together or one in deep melancholy. Folded arms betoken melancholy in *Tit.* 3.2.6–7 ('passionate our tenfold grief / With folded arms'), *JC* 2.1.240, *LLL* 3.1.181, etc., and in the frontispiece of Robert Burton's *The Anatomy of Melancholy* (1621).

74 **corrigible** submissive to correction.

74–5 **subdued...shame** overpowered by deep shame, so wholly submissive as to express nothing but shame.

75 **wheeled seat** chariot.

76–7 **branded...ensued** stigmatised as by a brand the abjectness of the poor wretch who followed his chariot. As Wilson points out, the vanquished preceded the victor in the Roman triumph, and Romans were themselves never subjected to this indignity, but Shakespeare makes the same assumptions in *JC* 5.1.108–9, that Brutus will be 'led in triumph / Thorough the streets of Rome'.

79 **honest** honourable.

80 **pardon me** i.e. excuse me from performing the act.

To do this when I bade thee? Do it at once,
Or thy precedent services are all
But accidents unpurposed. Draw, and come.

EROS Turn from me then that noble countenance
Wherein the worship of the whole world lies.

ANTONY Lo thee! [*He turns from him*]

EROS My sword is drawn.

ANTONY Then let it do at once
The thing why thou hast drawn it.

EROS My dear master,
My captain, and my emperor, let me say
Before I strike this bloody stroke, farewell.

ANTONY 'Tis said, man, and farewell.

EROS Farewell, great chief. Shall I strike now?

ANTONY Now, Eros.

EROS (*Kills himself*)
Why, there then! Thus I do escape the sorrow
Of Antony's death.

ANTONY Thrice nobler than myself!
Thou teachest me, O valiant Eros, what
I should, and thou couldst not. My queen and Eros
Have by their brave instruction got upon me
A nobleness in record. But I will be
A bridegroom in my death and run into't
As to a lover's bed. Come then, and Eros,
Thy master dies thy scholar. To do thus
I learned of thee.
[*He falls on his sword*]
How, not dead? Not dead?
The guard, ho! O, dispatch me!

87 SD] *Rowe subst.; not in* F 94 SD] *Placed as in Rowe subst.; after 93 in* F 103 SD *He falls on his sword*] *Rowe subst.; not in* F 104 ho!] F (how?)

83 **precedent** former; accented on the second syllable.

84 **accidents unpurposed** events leading to no purpose.

86 **the worship...world** everything that the world holds in esteem and veneration.

94 SD This stage direction, sometimes moved by editors to the end of Eros's speech, may simply mean that he stabs himself mortally. Stage action is necessary at this point. See collation for placing in F.

96–7 **Thou teachest...couldst not** The meaning is more explicit in North's Plutarch: 'O noble Eros, I thank thee for this, and it is valiantly done of thee to show me what I should do to myself which thou couldst not do for me' (1006C).

98–9 **got upon...record** gained over me a noble place in history. Enobarbus too thought about his place in the 'record' of history, at 4.9.8 and 21–2.

101 **As to a lover's bed** Compare the proverbial phrase 'To go to one's grave (death) like a bed' (Dent B192.1).

Enter a [*Company of the*] GUARD, [*one of them* DERCETUS]

1 GUARD What's the noise?
ANTONY I have done my work ill, friends.
O, make an end of what I have begun!
2 GUARD The star is fall'n.
1 GUARD And time is at his period.
ALL Alas, and woe!
ANTONY Let him that loves me strike me dead.
1 GUARD Not I.
2 GUARD Nor I.
3 GUARD Nor anyone.

Exeunt [*all the Guard but Dercetus*]

DERCETUS Thy death and fortunes bid thy followers fly.
This sword but shown to Caesar with this tidings
Shall enter me with him.

[*He takes up Antony's sword*]

Enter DIOMEDES

104 SD *Enter...*DERCETUS] *Pope subst.* (*Enter* Dercetas *and guard*); *Enter a Guard* F; *Enter* Decretas *and Guard / Rowe* **108, 113** SH 2 GUARD] *Rowe;* 2 F **109, 111, 138** SH 1 GUARD] 1 F **114** SH 3 GUARD] *Rowe;* 3 F **114** SD *all...Dercetus*] *Capell subst.; not in* F **115** SH DERCETUS] F; *Dercetas / Pope* **117** SD.1 *He takes up Antony's sword*] *Wilson subst.; not in* F

104 SD ***DERCETUS** This character is not named in this scene, and to the theatre audience is simply an anonymous soldier, one of the guard who stays behind briefly when the rest flee at 114. North's Plutarch (1007A) makes clear that 'Dercetaeus' is one of the guard. The name is a problem for editors. F calls him *Dercetus* in the first speech heading, at 115 below, but *Decre.* at 119. Later, in 5.1, he is *Decretas* in the entering stage direction (3) and *Dec.* in the speech headings. Many editors choose the form *Decretas* because it enjoys a numerical advantage in the samples. Nevertheless, Compositor B could not have happened on the historically correct *Dercetus* (a spelling variant of *Dercetaeus*) unless it was in his copy. Shakespeare evidently followed North's Plutarch when he first set the word down, and went to the unusual length of writing out the full name in the speech heading. Whether he or someone else then got it wrong (an easy error of metathesis), there is good authority for following the correct first impression. The Countess of Pembroke's *Antonie* refers to him as *Dircetus*. Pope's *Dercetas* is something of a hybrid. On Compositor B's difficulty with unfamiliar proper names, and his tendency to persist in what may well be his own idiosyncratic spelling, see 3.7.19 SD *Canidius*, and n.

108 The star is fall'n This and the following four lines echo a number of apocalyptic phrases from the Book of Revelation, e.g. 8.10–13 ('and there fell a great star from heaven...And I beheld and heard one angel...saying with a loud voice, "Woe, woe, woe, to the inhabitants of the earth..."'), 9.6, and 10.6 (Seaton, pp. 219–24), and may also reflect an iconographical tradition exemplified by Albrecht Dürer (Morris, pp. 252–62).

109 his period its end.

117 enter me with him admit me to his service, put me in his good graces.

117 SD.2 *Enter* DIOMEDES North's Plutarch identifies Diomedes only as a 'secretary unto him...who was commanded to bring him [Antony] into the tomb or monument where Cleopatra was' (1006D). Shakespeare correctly infers that it was by such a messenger, sent from Cleopatra, that Antony 'heard that she was alive' (1006D), and from this brief circumstance Shakespeare provides Diomedes with his report of Cleopatra's 'prophesying fear' (125 ff.).

DIOMEDES Where's Antony?
DERCETUS There, Diomed, there.
DIOMEDES Lives he? Wilt thou not answer, man?
[*Exit Dercetus*]
ANTONY Art thou there, Diomed? Draw thy sword and give me
Sufficing strokes for death.
DIOMEDES Most absolute lord,
My mistress Cleopatra sent me to thee.
ANTONY When did she send thee?
DIOMEDES Now, my lord.
ANTONY Where is she?
DIOMEDES Locked in her monument. She had a prophesying fear
Of what hath come to pass. For when she saw –
Which never shall be found – you did suspect
She had disposed with Caesar, and that your rage
Would not be purged, she sent you word she was dead;
But fearing since how it might work, hath sent
Me to proclaim the truth, and I am come,
I dread, too late.
ANTONY Too late, good Diomed. Call my guard, I prithee.
DIOMEDES What ho, the emperor's guard! The guard, what ho!
Come, your lord calls.

Enter four or five of the GUARD *of Antony*

ANTONY Bear me, good friends, where Cleopatra bides.
'Tis the last service that I shall command you.
1 GUARD Woe, woe are we, sir, you may not live to wear
All your true followers out.
ALL Most heavy day!
ANTONY Nay, good my fellows, do not please sharp fate
To grace it with your sorrows. Bid that welcome
Which comes to punish us, and we punish it,
Seeming to bear it lightly. Take me up.

119 SH DERCETUS] *Wilson; Decre.* F; *Der. / Pope* **120** SD] *Capell subst.; not in* F **129** you word] F; word *Pope*

127 found found true.

128 disposed with come to terms with. (The only instance of this meaning, *OED* Dispose *v* 7b.)

129 purged i.e. as though by a purging medicine. 'Rage' or choler is a bodily humour, dangerous in excess.

136 bides abides, is to be found.

138–9 live. . . out i.e. outlive those who serve you.

141 To grace By gracing or honouring (Abbott 356).

I have led you oft; carry me now, good friends,
And have my thanks for all.

Exeunt, bearing Antony [*and Eros*]

[4.15] *Enter* CLEOPATRA *and her Maids aloft, with* CHARMIAN *and* IRAS

CLEOPATRA O Charmian, I will never go from hence.
CHARMIAN Be comforted, dear madam.
CLEOPATRA No, I will not.
All strange and terrible events are welcome,
But comforts we despise. Our size of sorrow,
Proportioned to our cause, must be as great
As that which makes it.

Enter [*below*] DIOMEDES

How now? Is he dead?
DIOMEDES His death's upon him, but not dead.
Look out o'th'other side your monument;
His guard have brought him thither.

Enter [*below*] ANTONY, *and the* GUARD [*bearing him*]

CLEOPATRA O sun,
Burn the great sphere thou mov'st in; darkling stand

145 SD *Exeunt*] F (*Exit*) 145 SD *and Eros*] *Oxford; not in* F Act 4, Scene 15 4.15] *Dyce; no scene division in* F 0 SD *and her Maids*] F; *omitted by Rowe* 6 SD *below*] *Collier; not in* F 9 SD] *Collier subst.; Enter Anthony, and the Guard* F

145 SD *and Eros* As Oxford notes, editors have generally failed to provide for the removal of Eros's body. Conceivably the matter could be taken care of earlier, at 114 possibly; at all events, the stage must be cleared before Scene 15.

Act 4, Scene 15

Location Cleopatra's monument. North's Plutarch reports that she built many such tombs or monuments 'joining hard to the temple of Isis' (1005C).

0 SD *and her Maids* As Oxford notes, in support of Rowe's omission of this phrase, the stage direction may simply duplicate itself when it adds '*with* CHARMIAN *and* IRAS'. In no other scene do additional 'maids' accompany Cleopatra, though she is at times attended by eunuchs and other followers, and in Enobarbus's description (2.2.216) she is accompanied in her barge by 'gentlewomen, like the Nereides'.

0 SD *aloft* in the gallery above the main stage; as in *Rom.* 3.5.0, *Tit.* 1.1.0, and *R3* 3.7.94, etc. Similar to *above*, as in *Oth.* 1.1.81, etc.

8 o'th'other side your monument In the Elizabethan theatre, Diomedes may perhaps refer to Antony's being carried through the stage door opposite to that by which Diomedes has entered. See pp. 43–4 above and illustration 4 for various options in staging this scene.

9 SD *below* See 14, 'Help friends below!'

11 the great sphere The hollow sphere in which the sun (according to Ptolemaic astronomy) was thought to be fixed; the motion of the sphere whirled the sun around the earth like a planet. If the sun were to consume its sphere, the earth would be left 'darkling', in darkness. For

The varying shore o'th'world! O Antony,
Antony, Antony! Help, Charmian, help, Iras, help!
Help friends below! Let's draw him hither.

ANTONY Peace!
Not Caesar's valour hath o'erthrown Antony,
But Antony's hath triumphed on itself.

CLEOPATRA So it should be, that none but Antony
Should conquer Antony, but woe 'tis so!

ANTONY I am dying, Egypt, dying; only
I here importune death awhile, until
Of many thousand kisses the poor last
I lay upon thy lips.

CLEOPATRA I dare not, dear –
Dear my lord, pardon – I dare not,
Lest I be taken. Not th'imperious show
Of the full-fortuned Caesar ever shall
Be brooched with me. If knife, drugs, serpents, have
Edge, sting, or operation, I am safe.
Your wife Octavia, with her modest eyes
And still conclusion, shall acquire no honour
Demuring upon me. But come, come, Antony –

26 me. If] *Rowe subst.;* me, if F **27** operation, I] F2*;* operation. I F

biblical parallels, see Rev. 8, esp. 8.12: 'And the fourth angel blew the trumpet, and the third part of the sun was smitten, and the third part of the moon, and the third part of the stars, so that the third part of them was darkened...' (Seaton, p. 220).

12 The varying shore o'th'world The ever-changing world, alternating between day and night and as the tide ebbs and flows on the shore. Compare *Mac.* 1.7.6: 'this bank and shoal of time', and *H5* 4.1.265: 'the high shore of this world'.

15–18 Not Caesar's...conquer Antony The idea was probably suggested by Ovid's *Metamorphoses*, XIII, 472 (Golding's translation): 'That none may Ajax overcome save Ajax' ('ne quisquam Aiacem possit superare nisi Aiax'); see J. A. K. Thomson, *Shakespeare and the Classics*, 1952, p. 150).

20 importune i.e. beg a delay of.

22 I dare not i.e. I dare not come down to you, Antony. Wilson is possibly right in arguing that Cleopatra's plea for help in hoisting Antony aloft at 13–14 is an interpolation, since Antony's request to kiss her once more and her timorous refusal would seem unnecessary in view of the plan to lift him up to her, but the passage may make sense as it stands if Antony ignores her first suggestion or simply fails to hear it in his weakened condition. North's Plutarch emphasises her desire for security in describing how she 'locked the doors unto her and shut all the springs of the locks with great bolts' (1006B). See David Galloway, *N&Q* 203, ns 5.8 (August 1958), 330–5.

24 th'imperious show the imperial triumphal procession.

26 brooched adorned as with a brooch.

26–7 knife...operation A parallel construction would end in 'Edge, operation, or sting', since drugs have operation and serpents sting, but Shakespeare similarly avoids a precise parallel in *Ham.* 3.1.151: 'The courtier's, soldier's, scholar's, eye, tongue, sword' (Arden).

28 modest 'governed by the proprieties of the sex' (*OED* sv *adj* 3).

29 still conclusion silent judgement (of me), 'quiet summing of me up' (Wilson).

30 Demuring upon Looking demurely at, or looking doubtfully askance upon. Cleopatra supposes that Octavia will be smug and moralistic – intolerably virtuous.

Help me, my women – we must draw thee up.
Assist, good friends.

ANTONY O, quick, or I am gone.

[*They begin lifting*]

CLEOPATRA Here's sport indeed! How heavy weighs my lord!
Our strength is all gone into heaviness,
That makes the weight. Had I great Juno's power,
The strong-winged Mercury should fetch thee up
And set thee by Jove's side. Yet come a little;
Wishers were ever fools. O, come, come, come!

They heave Antony aloft to Cleopatra

And welcome, welcome! Die when thou hast lived;
Quicken with kissing. Had my lips that power,
Thus would I wear them out.

[*She kisses him*]

ALL A heavy sight!

ANTONY I am dying, Egypt, dying.
Give me some wine, and let me speak a little.

CLEOPATRA No, let me speak, and let me rail so high
That the false huswife Fortune break her wheel,
Provoked by my offence.

32 SD] *Wilson subst.; not in* F 39 when] F; where *Pope* 41 SD] *Wilson subst.; not in* F

32 SD The staging method of Antony's raising is not made clear. In North's Plutarch, 'Cleopatra would not open the gates, but came to the high windows, and cast out certain chains and ropes in the which Antonius was trussed; and Cleopatra her own self, with two women only, which she had suffered to come with her into these monuments, trised Antonius up' (1006D). See pp. 43–4 above, and illustration 4.

33 **sport indeed** Cleopatra bitterly contrasts her present occupation with 'the diversions of happier times', especially perhaps when she would draw up fish on her hook and 'think them every one an Antony' (Staunton, Malone, Wilson; see 2.5.14 above). In the same vein, 'How heavy weighs my lord!' dolefully recalls 'O happy horse, to bear the weight of Antony!' (1.5.22).

34 **heaviness** (1) sorrow, (2) weight (Malone). The double meaning has biblical precedent, as in Ecclus. 38.18: 'the heaviness of the heart breaketh the strength' (Noble, p. 239).

38 **Wishers were ever fools** Proverbial-sounding.

39 **Die . . . lived** i.e. live a little longer before you die. Pope's emendation of 'when' to 'where' is unnecessary, as the next line shows. The sexual possibilities of 'die' may be continued in 'Quicken' (40), 'I am dying' (43), and indeed throughout the dialogue about 'sport', 'heaviness', 'weight', and so on (J. A. Bryant, Jr, *Hippolyta's View*, 1961, pp. 184–5).

40 **Quicken** Revive.

42 **heavy** doleful.

46 **false huswife Fortune** Compare the proverb 'Fortune is a strumpet' (Dent F603.1). Fortune is a 'huswife' also in *AYLI* 1.2.31 and *H5* 5.1.80, and a 'strumpet' in *Ham.* 2.2.493. 'Huswife' more frequently means simply 'housewife', of which it is a spelling variant, and could be modernised here, but 'huswife' catches some of the meaning of 'hussy' (a phonetic reduction of 'housewife'). The blend of meanings here suggests that the wheel of Fortune is like the spinning-wheel of a busy housewife, as in *AYLI*.

47 **offence** i.e. insulting language. The language of invective in the play is felt to have an almost magical potency.

ANTONY One word, sweet queen:
Of Caesar seek your honour, with your safety. O!
CLEOPATRA They do not go together.
ANTONY Gentle, hear me.
None about Caesar trust but Proculeius.
CLEOPATRA My resolution and my hands I'll trust,
None about Caesar.
ANTONY The miserable change now at my end
Lament nor sorrow at, but please your thoughts
In feeding them with those my former fortunes,
Wherein I lived the greatest prince o'th'world,
The noblest; and do now not basely die,
Not cowardly put off my helmet to
My countryman – a Roman by a Roman
Valiantly vanquished. Now my spirit is going;
I can no more.
CLEOPATRA Noblest of men, woo't die?
Hast thou no care of me? Shall I abide
In this dull world, which in thy absence is
No better than a sty? O see, my women:
[*Antony dies*]
The crown o'th'earth doth melt. My lord!
O, withered is the garland of the war;
The soldier's pole is fall'n! Young boys and girls

56 lived the] *Theobald;* liued. The F 64 SD] *Placed as in Capell; not in* F; *after* more *in 61, Rowe; after* melt *in 65, Arden*

49 They...together Cleopatra may have in mind the proverb 'The more danger the more honour' (Dent D35).

51 Compare Daniel's *Cleopatra*: 'I have both hands and will, and I can die' (1; 54).

53–60 The miserable...vanquished This speech is closely paraphrased from North's Plutarch, beginning where Antony bids Cleopatra 'that she should not lament nor sorrow for the miserable change of his fortune at the end of his days' (1007A). Other borrowed particulars include his calling for wine (compare 44) and his advice 'that chiefly she should trust Proculeius above any man else about Caesar' (1006F; compare 50). Even when the borrowing is most detailed, however, Shakespeare's reworking is fitted to character and situation; in particular, the remarkable syntactical structure in 53–60, comprising a single, agrammatical period or unit that defies all attempts at punctuation, is expressive of the dying Antony.

59 a Roman by a Roman As Reuben Brower (*Hero and Saint*, 1971, pp. 336–7) observes, this could mean simply 'that Antony had fought bravely until beaten by Octavius', but almost surely means instead that, as Cleopatra put it earlier in this scene, 'none but Antony / Should conquer Antony' (4.15.17–18).

61 woo't wilt (thou).

66–7 garland...soldier's pole 'Shakespeare was thinking of the village festivities in which a pole, the central point of the sports, is decked with garlands of flowers' (Deighton). The village pole further suggests the 'Young boys and girls' of 67 (Furness). A 'garland' is also a wreath or crown of victory, and a 'soldier's pole' may be a standard around which soldiers rally, or the pole star. John Wallace has pointed out to me the implication of sexual insufficiency and male impotency in these lines; it is also suggested by Philip Traci, *The Love Play of Antony and Cleopatra*, 1970, p. 90, and by Fitz, p. 302.

Are level now with men; the odds is gone,
And there is nothing left remarkable
Beneath the visiting moon. [*She starts to faint*]
CHARMIAN O, quietness, lady!
IRAS She's dead too, our sovereign.
CHARMIAN Lady!
IRAS Madam!
CHARMIAN O madam, madam, madam!
IRAS Royal Egypt! Empress!
[*Cleopatra stirs*]
CHARMIAN Peace, peace, Iras.
CLEOPATRA No more but e'en a woman, and commanded
By such poor passion as the maid that milks
And does the meanest chares. It were for me
To throw my sceptre at the injurious gods,
To tell them that this world did equal theirs
Till they had stol'n our jewel. All's but naught;
Patience is sottish, and impatience does
Become a dog that's mad. Then is it sin
To rush into the secret house of death

70 SD] *Rowe subst.; not in* F; *after 71 in Wilson* **76** SD] *Wilson subst.; not in* F **78** e'en] F (in)

68 the odds is gone the difference between great and small has vanished (*OED* Odds *sb* 2b). Without Antony, distinctions in worth are meaningless.

69 remarkable A new and rare word in Shakespeare's day (*OED*'s earliest example is from 1604) and hence more 'remarkable' in its full etymological sense than is the devalued modern expression. Shakespeare uses it once more, in *Cym.* 4.1.13.

70 visiting here today and gone tomorrow; perhaps too with a sense of baleful influence, as in *Oth.* 5.2.109–11: 'It is the very error of the moon, / She comes more nearer earth than she was wont, / And makes men mad.' The 'visiting' of a deity (*OED* sv *vbl sb* 1) is in order to comfort, try, or punish.

71 O, quietness Possibly Charmian is urging Cleopatra not to be too passionate, in which case the fainting should occur after this speech (as in Wilson's edition); but Charmian's cry of alarm may mean that she sees her mistress going into a faint and needing assistance. 'Please calm yourself!' she urges, as she helps Cleopatra down.

78 No more...woman Prompted by Iras's addressing her as 'Royal Egypt' and 'Empress', Cleopatra says that she is only a woman like them, one who can be overwhelmed by grief. Again she stresses the collapsing of distinctions between great and small, as at 67–8.

80 chares household tasks; compare 'charwomen'. According to *OED* 'chores' is a dialect variant of 'chare' or 'char', used especially in the U.S. Shakespeare uses 'chare' and 'chares' only in this play (see also 5.2.230), though the form was common in the period (Arden).

80 were would be fitting.

81 i.e. 'to let them know how little she now esteems it, and how much she despises them' (Furness). The gesture is like that in *Tit.* 4.3.50 ff., where Titus and his kinsmen shoot arrows to heaven with petitions complaining of the lack of justice 'in earth nor hell'.

81 injurious wilfully inflicting injury or wrong (*OED* sv *adj* 1).

83 our jewel i.e. Antony.

84–5 Patience...mad Patience is for fools, and impatience is for the mad; both are useless here. This is Shakespeare's only use of 'sottish', but it is common enough elsewhere in the period (Arden).

Ere death dare come to us? How do you, women?
What, what, good cheer! Why, how now, Charmian?
My noble girls! Ah, women, women! Look,
Our lamp is spent, it's out. Good sirs, take heart.
We'll bury him; and then, what's brave, what's noble,
Let's do't after the high Roman fashion
And make death proud to take us. Come, away.
This case of that huge spirit now is cold.
Ah, women, women! Come, we have no friend
But resolution and the briefest end.
Exeunt, [those above] bearing off Antony's body

[5.1] *Enter* CAESAR, AGRIPPA, DOLABELLA, MAECENAS, [GALLUS, PROCULEIUS,] *with his council of war*

CAESAR Go to him, Dolabella, bid him yield;
Being so frustrate, tell him, he mocks
The pauses that he makes.
DOLABELLA Caesar, I shall. [*Exit*]

Enter DERCETUS, *with the sword of Antony*

CAESAR Wherefore is that? And what art thou that dar'st
Appear thus to us?

88 what, good] *Theobald;* what good F **92** do't] F (doo't)*;* do it *Pope* **96** SD *those above*] *Capell; not in* F **Act 5, Scene 1 5.1**] *Pope; no scene division in* F **0** SD MAECENAS, GALLUS, PROCULEIUS] *Hanmer; Menas* F **2** he mocks] F*;* he but mocks *Hanmer* **3** SD.1 *Exit*] *Theobald subst.; not in* F **3** SD.2 DERCETUS] *Wilson; Decretas* F*;* Dercetas *Pope*

90 Our lamp is spent Compare 'the torch is out' (4.14.46), and the parable of the foolish and wise virgins, Matt. 25.8: 'Our lamps are out' (Shaheen).

90 Good sirs Addressed to the women. Compare 'Sirrah Iras' at 5.2.228. Furness cites examples from contemporary dramatists.

91 brave fine. Cleopatra seems to mean suicide. She is already glamorising Antony's far from glamorous and dignified suicide.

96 briefest swiftest.

96 SD ***Exeunt*** The members of Antony's guard who bore him in at 9 may remain silently and respectfully below until this *Exeunt* at the end of the scene, but perhaps they leave instead after heaving Antony aloft at 38. The scene of Antony's death and Cleopatra's grieving among her women is hardly one in which they can take part, and because they are on the main stage they cannot help in bearing off Antony's body from the acting space above.

Act 5, Scene 1

Location Alexandria. Caesar's camp.

0 SD GALLUS, PROCULEIUS Shakespeare's manuscript evidently did not specify these members of Caesar's *council of war*, who figure briefly at 61–9.

2–3 Being. . .he makes Tell him that, being so helpless and baffled as he is, he makes himself ridiculous by his delays in yielding.

4–48 Shakespeare makes Caesar's grief more public than in his source, allowing Caesar to use the occasion for a display of his greatness that contrasts strikingly with Cleopatra's more intimate and personal grief in the previous scene.

DERCETUS I am called Dercetus.
Mark Antony I served, who best was worthy
Best to be served. Whilst he stood up and spoke
He was my master, and I wore my life
To spend upon his haters. If thou please
To take me to thee, as I was to him
I'll be to Caesar; if thou pleasest not,
I yield thee up my life.
CAESAR What is't thou say'st?
DERCETUS I say, O Caesar, Antony is dead.
CAESAR The breaking of so great a thing should make
A greater crack. The round world
Should have shook lions into civil streets
And citizens to their dens. The death of Antony
Is not a single doom; in the name lay
A moiety of the world.
DERCETUS He is dead, Caesar,
Not by a public minister of justice,
Nor by a hirèd knife; but that self hand
Which writ his honour in the acts it did

5, 13, 19 SH DERCETUS] *Wilson; Dec.* F 5 Dercetus] *Wilson; Decretas* F 18 the] F; that *Pope*

North's Plutarch (1007A–B) describes how, when Dercetaeus had brought the news to Caesar of Antony's death, Caesar withdrew into the privacy of his tent, 'and there burst out with tears [compare 26–33], lamenting his hard and miserable fortune, that had been his friend and brother-in-law, his equal in the empire, and companion with him in sundry great exploits and battles' (compare 40–8).

4–5 that dar'st...to us It was a treasonable offence in medieval and Tudor England to enter the king's presence with weapons drawn, as when Suffolk and Warwick do so in *2H6*, prompting King Henry to exclaim, 'Why, how now, lords? your wrathful weapons drawn / Here in our presence? Dare you be so bold?' (3.2.237–8). Compare also *Temp.* 2.1.294 ff. For the most important Tudor statute on this, see John Bellamy, *The Tudor Law of Treason*, 1979.

9 spend expend.

14 breaking (1) breaking apart, (2) disclosing (Wilson).

15 crack (1) cracking apart, (2) loud report; suggesting 'the crack of doom', i.e. the thunderclap of the Day of Judgement, or the blast of the archangel's trumpet (*OED* sv *sb* 1).

15 round world Donne's Holy Sonnet 7 uses this image in an apocalyptic vision: 'At the round earth's imagined corners, blow / Your trumpets, angels, and arise, arise / From death.' Donne is perhaps indebted in turn to Rev. 8, and to Ps. 93.1: 'He hath made the round world so sure that it cannot be moved' (in the Book of Common Prayer; both the Genevan and the Bishops' Bible, worded somewhat differently, omit 'round', as Noble observes, p. 79). Some editors find the image unsatisfactory and emend it, especially in view of the metrical irregularity, but the biblical usage lends support to its credibility.

16 shook lions Compare *JC* 1.3.20 ff.: 'Against the Capitol I met a lion...'

16 civil city; with suggestion of 'civilised' and 'well-regulated' (Kittredge).

17 to their dens i.e. to the lions' dens, or else scurrying to safety indoors, to the citizens' dens, as though they were animals. In either case, the apocalyptic inversions of wildness and civilisation cause humans and animals to exchange roles.

18 Is not...doom Is more than the downfall and death of this one individual. 'Doom' also contains the metaphor of the crack of doom, the Day of Judgement.

19 moiety half.

21 self same.

Hath, with the courage which the heart did lend it,
Splitted the heart. This is his sword;
[*He offers the sword*]
I robbed his wound of it. Behold it stained
With his most noble blood.

CAESAR Look you sad, friends?
The gods rebuke me, but it is tidings
To wash the eyes of kings.

AGRIPPA And strange it is
That nature must compel us to lament
Our most persisted deeds.

MAECENAS His taints and honours
Waged equal with him.

AGRIPPA A rarer spirit never
Did steer humanity; but you gods will give us
Some faults to make us men. Caesar is touched.

MAECENAS When such a spacious mirror's set before him,
He needs must see himself.

CAESAR O Antony,
I have followed thee to this; but we do launch
Diseases in our bodies. I must perforce
Have shown to thee such a declining day,

24 SD] *This edn; not in* F **26** you sad, friends?] *Capell;* you sad Friends, F*;* you, sad friends, F3*;* you sad, friends: – *Theobald* **27** tidings] F (Tydings)*;* a Tydings F2 **28** SH AGRIPPA] *Theobald; Dol.* F **31** Waged] F*;* way F2*;* weigh'd *Rowe* **31** SH AGRIPPA] Theobald; Dola. F **36** launch] F*;* launce *Pope;* lance *Theobald*

26–7 *Look...gods F punctuation would also allow 'Look you, sad friends, / The gods...'

27 but it is if it is not. Caesar's weeping appears genuine, as in North's Plutarch (1007B), but here Caesar is not averse to having an audience who can then testify to his humanity and largeness of spirit; as Agrippa observes, 'Caesar is touched' (33).

28,31 SH ***AGRIPPA** As Oxford notes, the F readings *Dol.* and *Dola.* presumably represent Shakespeare's error.

30 persisted persistently desired or pursued.

31 Waged equal with him Were equally matched in him.

32 steer humanity guide any person.

32 will give insist on giving.

35 He...himself Maecenas is moved by Caesar's public display of grief to praise Caesar as one who can draw self-knowledge from this momentous event: he will be aware of his mortality, as all mortals must, and realise that he too will decline some day. Presumably this achieving of self-knowledge will be more wisely attained than in Antony's case, and will thereby give Caesar the advantage in seeking to make the most of his gifts. The idea of a 'mirror' as pattern or exemplar to be emulated or avoided (*OED* Mirror *sb* 5b and c) reinforces a more literal meaning in which Caesar sees Antony as a mirror image of himself – a 'brother', 'competitor', 'mate', and 'friend', as he proceeds to explain in 42–6. Compare 1.1.59–61, 2.2.4, etc., on being and knowing oneself.

36–7 I have...bodies I regret having pursued you to this extremity, but I had to, just as we lance boils or infections to cure ourselves by means of a painful operation. 'Launch' and 'lance' are both derived from Latin *lancere*, to handle a lance, but developed along slightly divergent paths. The metaphor is perhaps anticipated in Lepidus's urging that the wound of discord be probed lightly (2.2.24–7).

38 shown i.e. in my own downfall.

Or look on thine; we could not stall together
In the whole world. But yet let me lament
With tears as sovereign as the blood of hearts
That thou, my brother, my competitor
In top of all design, my mate in empire,
Friend and companion in the front of war,
The arm of mine own body, and the heart
Where mine his thoughts did kindle – that our stars,
Unreconciliable, should divide
Our equalness to this. Hear me, good friends –

Enter an EGYPTIAN

But I will tell you at some meeter season.
The business of this man looks out of him;
We'll hear him what he says. – Whence are you?
EGYPTIAN A poor Egyptian yet, the queen my mistress,

39 look] F (looke); look'd *Hanmer* 48 SD] *Placed as in Capell; after* says *at 51 in* F 52 Egyptian yet, the] F; *Ægyptian* yet; the *Rowe*[3]; Egyptian, yet the *Wilson, conj. William Watkiss Lloyd, cited in Cam.*

39 look F's 'looke' could be an error for 'lookd' in Shakespeare's manuscript; Hanmer and others have emended.

39 stall dwell. Several connotations are possible: to tolerate the presence of (see *OED* Stall v^1 1), to be enthroned or installed in high office (see *OED* sv v^1 7), and perhaps also, with intended or unintended irony, to be kept like animals in a stall for fattening (see *OED* sv v^1 8, 8b).

41 as sovereign...hearts as precious and as efficacious as heart's blood. Caesar, continuing the medical metaphor of 'launching' or lancing diseases (36–7), prefers healing by tears to bleeding; bleeding connotes both a medical remedy for disease and bleeding in battle. Compare 4.2.7–8 and n. Moved as he no doubt is, Caesar takes care to enhance the image of healer and peacemaker he appealed to earlier in speaking of a 'Time of universal peace' near at hand (4.6.5).

42 competitor partner; as at 1.4.3 and 2.7.66; but the added sense of 'rival' would seem to follow from 39–40, and is common in Shakespeare. Compare *Tit.* 2.1.77: 'cannot brook competitors in love'.

43 In top of all design In loftiest enterprise.

44 front forehead, face. The brow of war is menacing, as in *R3* 1.1.9: 'Grim-visag'd War hath smooth'd his wrinkled front', and *H5* 3.1.11–14.

46 Where...kindle Where my heart kindled its ('his') thoughts of courage. Antony's virtues as a soldier inspired emulation in me. Compare 1.4.56–72.

46 stars Compare Prince Henry to Hotspur in *1H4* 5.4.65: 'Two stars keep not their motion in one sphere', where 'stars' means planets.

47 Unreconciliable This spelling from F is metrically preferable. *OED* cites examples from the later sixteenth and earlier seventeenth centuries along with this one.

47–8 should...to this should tear apart our equal partnership, leading to this end.

49 meeter season more suitable time. This comment is often taken as evidence that Caesar has been merely rehearsing a set piece in obituary, but it needn't be so at all. The pattern of heightened set pieces falling back into the imperatives of continuing action is common in the play. Compare, for example, the interplay of tender sentiment and political expediency in the scene of Caesar's farewell to his sister and Antony, 3.2.36 ff.

50 The urgency of this man's business reveals itself in his eyes and expression.

52 yet still (though soon to become a subject of Rome). The F punctuation, retained here, suggests that 'A poor Egyptian yet' is in apposition to 'the queen, my mistress'; though a queen, Cleopatra is poor in being confined to 'all she has, her monument' (53). With a semicolon or period after 'yet', the phrase 'A poor Egyptian

Confined in all she has, her monument,
Of thy intents desires instruction,
That she preparedly may frame herself
To th'way she's forced to.

CAESAR Bid her have good heart.
She soon shall know of us, by some of ours,
How honourable and how kindly we
Determine for her; for Caesar cannot live
To be ungentle.

EGYPTIAN So the gods preserve thee! *Exit*

CAESAR Come hither, Proculeius. Go and say
We purpose her no shame. Give her what comforts
The quality of her passion shall require,
Lest, in her greatness, by some mortal stroke
She do defeat us; for her life in Rome
Would be eternal in our triumph. Go,
And with your speediest bring us what she says
And how you find of her.

PROCULEIUS Caesar, I shall. *Exit Proculeius*

CAESAR Gallus, go you along.
[*Exit Gallus*]

53 all she has,] *Rowe;* all, she has F 54 intents desires] *Pope;* intents, desires, F; intents, desires *Rowe*[2] 59 live] *Rowe*[2], *conj. Southern MS., cited in Cam.;* leaue F; learn *Dyce, conj. Tyrwhitt* 64 Lest, in] F (Least in) 69 SD *Exit Gallus*] *Theobald; not in* F

yet' might refer to Cleopatra (i.e. 'from a poor Egyptian yet') in answer to Caesar's question 'Whence are you?'; or it might refer to the speaker, who acknowledges that he will soon owe allegiance to Rome, or perhaps proudly declares himself to be an Egyptian still. With a comma after 'Egyptian', the 'yet' would imply that Cleopatra is still very much a queen, though poor.

55 **preparedly may frame herself** may prepare to shape her course of action.

57 **ours** my people.

58 **honourable** honourably. The *-ly* termination in 'kindly' answers for both adverbs; compare *JC* 2.1.224: 'Good gentlemen, look fresh and merrily' (Kittredge).

59 ***live** Wilson speculates that F's 'leaue' resulted from MS. 'leue'; compare 'leave' at 1.2.172.

61–8 **Come hither...I shall** North's Plutarch reports that Caesar 'sent Proculeius and commanded him to do what he could possible to get Cleopatra alive', thinking that 'she would marvellously beautify and set out his triumph'. Before doing so, according to Plutarch, Caesar 'called for all his friends and showed them the letters Antonius had written to him and his answers also sent him again during their quarrel and strife, and how fiercely and proudly the other answered him to all just and reasonable matters he wrote unto him' (1007B). Shakespeare places this episode afterwards at 73–7, slightly altering the emphasis of his source to bring out not the fierceness of Antony's letters but Caesar's parading of his own temperateness, as well as his characteristic circumspection in keeping copies of his own share of the correspondence 'for the record'. The messenger from Cleopatra at 52–6 is not in Plutarch.

63 **The quality of her passion** The nature of her passionate grief.

65–6 **for her life...triumph** for her presence in Rome alive, in my triumphal procession, would make it eternally memorable.

67 **with your speediest** as speedily as you can.

68 **of** concerning.

Where's Dolabella,
To second Proculeius?
ALL Dolabella!
CAESAR Let him alone, for I remember now
How he's employed. He shall in time be ready.
Go with me to my tent, where you shall see
How hardly I was drawn into this war,
How calm and gentle I proceeded still
In all my writings. Go with me and see
What I can show in this.

Exeunt

[5.2] *Enter* CLEOPATRA, CHARMIAN, IRAS, *and* MARDIAN

CLEOPATRA My desolation does begin to make
A better life. 'Tis paltry to be Caesar;
Not being Fortune, he's but Fortune's knave,
A minister of her will. And it is great
To do that thing that ends all other deeds,
Which shackles accidents and bolts up change,

Act 5, Scene 2 5.2] *Pope; no scene division in* F

71 Let him alone Don't bother about him now.
74 hardly reluctantly.
76 my writings i.e. to Antony.

Act 5, Scene 2

Location Alexandria. Cleopatra's monument.

0 SD *Enter* The stage direction says nothing about entering *aloft* as at 4.15.0. With no need in the present scene for a visual separation between those *aloft* and those below, as at 4.15.9 ff., the whole action of 5.2 was probably presented on the main Elizabethan stage. See pp. 43–4 above and 8 SD n. below.

0 SD MARDIAN Mardian is given nothing to say in this scene, and we cannot be certain if he is to remain as a mute witness of these great events or exit at some unspecified point; possibly Shakespeare forgot that he had brought him onstage. North's Plutarch does not mention Mardian here, and stresses that Cleopatra retired to her monument 'with two women only' (1006D). Mardian is not addressed in Cleopatra's farewell to her women, nor is he questioned about the suicides. On the other hand, mute characters are common enough in this play, including Rannius, Lucillius, and perhaps Lamprius in 1.2, perhaps Menecrates in 2.1, and Agrippa at 2.6, 3.12, and 4.1.0. At 4.13.7–10 Cleopatra bids Mardian come to her in the monument and tell her how Antony takes her death (Ridley, Kittredge).

2 A better life i.e. 'a life in which Fortune's gifts are rightly estimated and despised' (Arden).

3 Fortune's knave Compare the proverbial phrase 'He is Fortune's fool' (Dent F617.1). 'Knave' here means 'servant', and perhaps also a card in Fortune's deck. The possibility of a pun on 'nave', with Antony and Cleopatra at the periphery of Fortune's wheel, is discussed by J. P. Brockbank, 'Shakespeare and the fashion of these times', *S.Sur.* 16 (1963), 30–41, p. 31.

5 that thing i.e. suicide.

6 Which locks up the chances and changes of this mortal life. (Death puts an end to all such tribulations.)

Which sleeps, and never palates more the dung,
The beggar's nurse and Caesar's.

Enter [to the gates of the monument] PROCULEIUS

PROCULEIUS Caesar sends greeting to the Queen of Egypt,
And bids thee study on what fair demands
Thou mean'st to have him grant thee.
CLEOPATRA What's thy name?
PROCULEIUS My name is Proculeius.
CLEOPATRA Antony
Did tell me of you, bade me trust you, but
I do not greatly care to be deceived
That have no use for trusting. If your master
Would have a queen his beggar, you must tell him
That majesty, to keep decorum, must
No less beg than a kingdom. If he please
To give me conquered Egypt for my son,
He gives me so much of mine own as I
Will kneel to him with thanks.
PROCULEIUS Be of good cheer;
You're fall'n into a princely hand. Fear nothing.

7 dung] F; dug *Theobald, conj. Warburton* 8 SD] *This edn; Enter Proculeius* F; *Enter* PROCULEIUS *and* GALLUS, *with Soldiers, to the Door of the Monument, without / Capell*

7–8 Which sleeps...Caesar's Which is a sleep that relishes no more this dungy earth, nurse of beggar and Caesar alike. The F reading, 'dung', which some editors have questioned (see collation), gains plausibility from the proverbial phrase 'to foresee (despise) as dung' (Dent D645.1), and from 1.1.37–8: 'our dungy earth alike / Feeds beast as man'. Compare also 4.15.62–4: 'Shall I abide / In this dull world, which in thy absence is / No better than a sty?' For 'palates', meaning 'tastes' or 'enjoys the taste of', compare *Tro.* 4.1.60: 'Not palating the taste of her dishonor'.

8 SD ***to the gates of the monument*** Proculeius's entrance must be staged in such a way as to make it appear that he cannot reach Cleopatra, but there is no evidence to suggest that Shakespeare tried to reproduce the description in North's Plutarch (1007C) by having Proculeius set up a ladder 'against that high window by the which Antonius was triced up' and then come down into some special stage structure representing the monument, as Wilson and other editors have speculated. For fuller discussion, see pp. 43–4 above.

10 study...demands consider what requests for favourable terms.

14–15 I do not...trusting Perhaps, as Hudson and other editors suggest, Cleopatra shrewdly wants Proculeius to think that she doesn't much care whether he is to be trusted or not, as a way of throwing Caesar off his guard. Caesar will then be sure of her and less secret as to his purpose. A larger wary meaning is apparent as well: I have no great fondness for the idea of being deceived, I who know how dangerous trusting can be.

16 a queen his beggar Seemingly one of Shakespeare's several allusions (as in *Rom.* 2.1.14 and *LLL* 1.2.109–10 and 4.1.65–6) to the old ballad of 'King Cophetua and the Beggar Maid' in which a king falls in love with a beggar maid and makes her his queen. The allusion is grotesquely apt here.

17 to keep decorum to behave as majesty ought.

Make your full reference freely to my lord,
Who is so full of grace that it flows over
On all that need. Let me report to him
Your sweet dependency, and you shall find
A conqueror that will pray in aid for kindness
Where he for grace is kneeled to.

CLEOPATRA Pray you tell him
I am his fortune's vassal, and I send him
The greatness he has got. I hourly learn
A doctrine of obedience, and would gladly
Look him i'th'face.

PROCULEIUS This I'll report, dear lady.
Have comfort, for I know your plight is pitied
Of him that caused it.

[*Some of the Guard come behind Cleopatra and seize her*]

You see how easily she may be surprised.
Guard her till Caesar come.

IRAS Royal queen!

CHARMIAN O Cleopatra! Thou art taken, queen.

26 dependency] F2; dependacie F 34 SD *Some...her*] *Jones subst.; not in* F; *Here* Gallus, *and Guard, ascend the Monument by a Ladder, and enter at a back-Window / Theobald* 35–6 You see...come] F *(repeating the* SH *Pro.); assigned by Malone to Gallus*

23 **Make your full reference freely** Refer your case without reserve.

24 **flows over** Proculeius speaks of Caesar as though he were the fertile Nile. The image is now ironically co-opted from 'Egypt' to Caesar.

27 **pray in aid for kindness** beg your assistance in order that he may omit no kindness. 'Pray in aid' is a legal term meaning 'to pray or crave the assistance of someone' (*OED* Pray *v* 6). Alternatively the phrase may mean that Caesar will 'sue for your kindness as an ally, and as having an interest in common with him' (Hudson).

29 **his fortune's vassal** A touch of veiled irony here, since her speech is addressed to one whom she has just called 'Fortune's knave' (3) (Wilson).

29–30 **I send...got** 'I allow him to be my conqueror; I own his superiority with complete submission' (Johnson), but said with the same telling irony as in her equivocal reference to 'fortune's vassal' (see previous note); Cleopatra has already recognised the greatness he has got as worthless.

31 **doctrine** lesson; such as could be found in the Elizabethan homily 'Of Order and Obedience' (Milward, pp. 137–8).

34 **Of** By.

35–6 **You see...come** These lines are often assigned by editors to Gallus, who was ordered by Caesar to go along with Proculeius at 5.1.69 and who is described in North's Plutarch as holding Cleopatra in conversation at the barred gate while Proculeius climbs to the high window and enters the monument (1007C). But Shakespeare seemingly chooses not to follow Plutarch in this critical regard, perhaps because a fully staged re-enactment of Plutarch was not feasible or necessary. If Gallus is present at all, he may be nothing more than the mute he was in 5.1. F makes sense as it stands, but see p. 43 n. 4 above for fuller discussion and for evidence of a possible omission in the text.

35 **surprised** captured.

CLEOPATRA Quick, quick, good hands. [*Drawing a dagger*]
PROCULEIUS Hold, worthy lady, hold!
[*He seizes and disarms her*]
Do not yourself such wrong, who are in this
Relieved, but not betrayed.
CLEOPATRA What, of death too,
That rids our dogs of languish?
PROCULEIUS Cleopatra,
Do not abuse my master's bounty by
Th'undoing of yourself. Let the world see
His nobleness well acted, which your death
Will never let come forth.
CLEOPATRA Where art thou, Death?
Come hither, come! Come, come, and take a queen
Worth many babes and beggars.
PROCULEIUS O, temperance, lady!
CLEOPATRA Sir, I will eat no meat, I'll not drink, sir;
If idle talk will once be necessary
I'll not sleep, neither. This mortal house I'll ruin,
Do Caesar what he can. Know, sir, that I
Will not wait pinioned at your master's court,
Nor once be chastised with the sober eye
Of dull Octavia. Shall they hoist me up

38 SD.1 *Drawing a dagger*] *Theobald; not in* F 38 SD.2 *He seizes and disarms her*] *Malone subst.; not in* F

38 SD.1, 38 SD.2 The staging here seems to follow North's Plutarch, which describes how Cleopatra 'thought to have stabbed herself in with a short dagger she ware of purpose by her side', and how Proculeius, coming suddenly upon her and 'taking her by both the hands, said unto her: "Cleopatra, first thou shalt do thyself great wrong..."' (1007D).

40 **Relieved...of death too** By 'Relieved', Proculeius means 'rescued' (*OED* Relieve *v* 1). In her answer, however, Cleopatra implies that 'relieved' can instead mean 'eased of', 'set free from' (*OED* sv *v* 3–5). 'What, am I deprived of death, too?' Her answer may also depend on 'betrayed', as Kittredge suggests: 'I am too betrayed, even of the ability to die.' Cleopatra's speeches to Proculeius are not in North's Plutarch.

41 **our dogs of languish** even our dogs of their lingering diseases.

44 **acted** accomplished.

45 **come forth** be revealed.

47 **babes and beggars** i.e. those whom death takes easily and in large numbers.

48 **meat** food.

49–50 **If...neither** Compare Daniel's *Cleopatra*, in which the queen says, 'Words are for them that can complain and live' (4; 1154). Shakespeare's Cleopatra may mean here that she will deny herself life-sustaining sleep, using idle talk if necessary to keep herself awake.

52 **wait pinioned** attend in servile manner like a bird with clipped wings, unable to fly.

53 **chastised** Accented on the first syllable.

53 **the sober eye** Compare 4.15.28–30: 'Octavia, with her modest eyes...Demuring upon me', and n. Shakespeare's language is close here to that of Daniel's *Cleopatra*: 'Think, Caesar, I that liv'd and reign'd a queen / Do scorn to buy my life at such a rate...That I should pass whereas Octavia stands / To view my misery, that purchas'd hers' (1; 63–70).

And show me to the shouting varletry
Of censuring Rome? Rather a ditch in Egypt
Be gentle grave unto me! Rather on Nilus' mud
Lay me stark nak'd and let the water-flies
Blow me into abhorring! Rather make
My country's high pyramides my gibbet
And hang me up in chains!

PROCULEIUS You do extend
These thoughts of horror further than you shall
Find cause in Caesar.

Enter DOLABELLA

DOLABELLA Proculeius,
What thou hast done thy master Caesar knows,
And he hath sent for thee. For the queen,
I'll take her to my guard.

PROCULEIUS So, Dolabella,
It shall content me best. Be gentle to her.
[*To Cleopatra*] To Caesar I will speak what you shall please,
If you'll employ me to him.

55 varletry] F2 (Varlotry); Varlotarie F 68 SD *To Cleopatra*] *Hanmer; not in* F

55 varletry rabble. Compare 4.12.34 ff.: 'And hoist thee up to the shouting plebeians...'

56 censuring passing judgement.

56–9 Rather...abhorring Cleopatra's speech recalls her oath at 3.13.170–1: 'Lie graveless till the flies and gnats of Nile / Have buried them for prey'. The splendid hyperbole turns here to images of corruption and festering.

58 water-flies This is *OED*'s earliest citation. Compare *Ham.* 5.2.82 and *Tro.* 5.1.34, where the word is used of annoying, vain, diminutive creatures like Osric and Patroclus.

59 Blow me into abhorring (1) deposit eggs on or in me, fill me with eggs, and thus make me abhorrent (*OED* Blow v^{1} 28), or (2) cause me to swell abhorrently with maggots (see *OED* sv v^{1} 22). Following 'Lay me stark nak'd', the image takes on an erotic suggestion, one that couples sexuality and death.

60 pyramides Four syllables, accented on the second. Compare 2.7.17 and n. on Elizabethan conceptions of pyramids as shaped like obelisks, from which a hanging would be possible as it would not from a true pyramid.

61 extend magnify.

63 SD North's Plutarch mentions Cornelius Dolabella, 'a young gentleman' and 'one of Caesar's very great familiars', only after Caesar's visit to Cleopatra, and then reports simply that Dolabella 'sent her word secretly, as she had requested him, that Caesar determined to take his journey through Syria, and that within three days he would send her away before with her children' (1009A–B; compare 199–201 below). Shakespeare alters the sequence of events and expands this mere hint into two encounters with Cleopatra, making Dolabella so sympathetic towards the queen that she at last responds with her moving tribute to Antony as a mythic hero. Shakespeare's design presumably requires such a figure to offset the untrustworthiness of Proculeius and thus enforce a double sense of political and personal values. At 5.1.69–70 Caesar wished to send Dolabella to 'second Proculeius' but then remembered he had sent Dolabella to bid Antony yield (5.1.1); since that time, Caesar has heard of Antony's death.

65 For As for.

68 what whatever.

CLEOPATRA Say I would die.
Exit Proculeius [*with Soldiers*]
DOLABELLA Most noble empress, you have heard of me?
CLEOPATRA I cannot tell.
DOLABELLA Assuredly you know me.
CLEOPATRA No matter, sir, what I have heard or known.
You laugh when boys or women tell their dreams;
Is't not your trick?
DOLABELLA I understand not, madam.
CLEOPATRA I dreamt there was an emperor Antony.
O, such another sleep, that I might see
But such another man!
DOLABELLA If it might please ye –
CLEOPATRA His face was as the heav'ns, and therein stuck
A sun and moon, which kept their course and lighted
The little O, the earth.
DOLABELLA Most sovereign creature –
CLEOPATRA His legs bestrid the ocean; his reared arm

69 SD *Exit Proculeius*] *Placed as in Pope; after* to him *at 69 in* F **69** SD *with Soldiers*] *Capell subst.; not in* F **80** O, the] *Steevens subst.;* o'th' F*;* O o'th' *Theobald*

70 empress The title flatteringly acknowledges Cleopatra to be Antony's widow and ignores Octavia (H. Granville-Barker, *Prefaces to Shakespeare*, 2nd ser., 1930, p. 157), or simply equates 'empress' with 'queen'.

74 trick way, manner.

78 stuck were set.

79 A sun and moon In the familiar image of the human being as a microcosm or 'little world' resembling the macrocosm of the universe, the eyes are often likened to heavenly spheres. Compare the speech of Cleopatra to Antony (as reported by Dircetus) in the Countess of Pembroke's *Antonie* 4; 1596: 'your eyes, my sun', and also Tamburlaine's 'piercing instruments of sight, / Whose fiery circles bear encompassèd / A heaven of heavenly bodies in their spheres' (*1 Tamburlaine* 2.1.14–16). The entire description of Tamburlaine in 2.1 is like Cleopatra's of Antony in its Herculean portraiture. Compare also Lady Percy on the dead Hotspur, *2H4* 2.3.17–38. Such descriptions were a feature, as Whiter (pp. 160–7) observes, of pageants, masques, and processions; see Ruth Nevo, 'The masque of greatness', *S.St.* 3 (1967), 111–28, for further evidence of allusions to Jacobean court masques. Seaton (pp. 219–24) observes that Cleopatra's whole speech here resembles the description in Rev. 10.1–6 of the mighty angel who 'came down from heaven, clothed with a cloud...and his face was as the sun...' For Albrecht Dürer's contribution to the iconographical interpretation of this image, see Morris, p. 259. Janet Adelman, *The Common Liar*, p. 98, points out that Antony's attributes in this speech are not unlike those ascribed by Orpheus to Jupiter himself in Richard Linche's translation of Cartari's *Imagines deorum*: the feet reaching down from heaven to earth, the eyes that 'are the sun and the moon' (*The Fountain of Wisdom* (1599), sig. 12^{v}).

80 O A tiny circle; as in *H5* 1 Chorus 12–14: 'may we cram / Within this wooden O the very casques / That did affright the air at Agincourt'. In *MND* 3.2.188, the figure of O is associated with heavenly bodies: 'yon fiery oes and eyes of light'. Some editors, including Oxford, prefer Theobald's emendation: 'The little O o'th'earth'.

81 His legs...ocean i.e. he stood like the Colossus astride the entrance to the harbour of Rhodes (one of the Seven Wonders of the ancient world), cited in *JC* 1.2.135–6. On grand image-making here and elsewhere in the play, see pp. 29–30 above.

Crested the world; his voice was propertied
As all the tunèd spheres, and that to friends;
But when he meant to quail and shake the orb,
He was as rattling thunder. For his bounty,
There was no winter in't; an autumn 'twas
That grew the more by reaping. His delights
Were dolphin-like; they showed his back above
The element they lived in. In his livery
Walked crowns and crownets; realms and islands were
As plates dropped from his pocket.

DOLABELLA Cleopatra –

CLEOPATRA Think you there was or might be such a man
As this I dreamt of?

86 autumn 'twas] *Theobald, conj. Thirlby; Anthony* it was F

82 Crested Formed a crest for, surmounted; like a warrior's upreared arm often seen in heraldry cresting a coat-of-arms or mounted on a helmet.

82–3 was propertied...spheres was as musical in quality as that of the concentric spheres in Ptolemaic astronomy, revolving harmoniously about the earth. Shakespeare invokes the mysterious, supremely beautiful, and almost divine 'music of the spheres', inaudible to human hearing, in *MV* 5.1.60 ff. Spheres figure prominently in courtly masques, replete with sun, moon, stars, music, armorial bearings, and the like; see Whiter, pp. 161–2.

83 tunèd tuneful.

83 and that to friends when he spoke to friends.

84 quail make quail, overawe.

84 the orb the world, 'The little O'.

85 For As for.

86 *autumn 'twas Wilson observes that the Folio's *'Antony'* is an easy minim error if Compositor B misread Shakespeare's 'autome' as 'antonie' and then adjusted the following word to his misreading. (On the other hand, R. C. Hood observes that the unusual idiom at 1.3.91, 'my oblivion is a very Antony', gives some support to the F reading here.) Possibly Shakespeare knew the passage in Plutarch's 'The Life of Alcibiades' in which that person's physical beauty in his later years is compared to 'the fair time of the year, the autumn or latter season' (Howard Erskine-Hill, 'Antony and Octavius: the theme of temperance in Shakespeare's "Antony and Cleopatra"', *RMS* 14 (1970), 42).

87–9 His delights...lived in i.e. just as the dolphin shows his back above the water, so Antony rose above the pleasures that were his element; his sporting in a sea of pleasure displayed his greatness, not his submission or drowning. The erotic possibilities of the image, reminiscent of Cleopatra's 'O happy horse, to bear the weight of Antony!' (1.5.22), are pointed out by Kenneth Burke, *Language as Symbolic Action*, 1966, p. 113. The passage may also evoke the idea of the Aldine dolphin, well known in Renaissance iconography as an image of ripeness and wholeness combining growth of strength and steady quickness; see Edgar Wind, *Pagan Mysteries in the Renaissance*, 1968, pp. 98–9 and fig. 52. For a description of huge sea-creatures bearing men on their backs in Jonson's *Masque of Blackness*, presented at court on Twelfth Night, 1605, see Orgel, pp. 47–60, esp. p. 49, and Whiter, p. 160.

89–90 In his livery...crownets i.e. among his retainers, those who wore his livery, were kings and princes. (Some are mentioned at 3.6.71–7 and 3.13.93.)

91 plates silver coins. Antony's bounty spills from him as he walks the earth, giantlike.

92–3 Think...dreamt of 'She demands to know, not whether there has ever been a historical Antony, but whether the physical universe has contained, or could contain, *her* Antony, the god-like figure of her imagination' (John Armstrong, *The Paradise Myth*, 1969, p. 52).

92 might could.

DOLABELLA Gentle madam, no.
CLEOPATRA You lie up to the hearing of the gods.
But if there be nor ever were one such,
It's past the size of dreaming. Nature wants stuff
To vie strange forms with fancy; yet t'imagine
An Antony were Nature's piece 'gainst fancy,
Condemning shadows quite.
DOLABELLA Hear me, good madam:
Your loss is as yourself, great; and you bear it
As answering to the weight. Would I might never
O'ertake pursued success but I do feel,
By the rebound of yours, a grief that smites
My very heart at root.
CLEOPATRA I thank you, sir.
Know you what Caesar means to do with me?
DOLABELLA I am loath to tell you what I would you knew.
CLEOPATRA Nay, pray you, sir.
DOLABELLA Though he be honourable –
CLEOPATRA He'll lead me then in triumph.
DOLABELLA Madam, he will, I know't.

Flourish. Enter PROCULEIUS, CAESAR, GALLUS, MAECENAS, *and others of his train*

ALL Make way there! Caesar!

95 nor] F; or F3 **103** smites] *Capell;* suites F **106** what] *Rowe*[3]*;* what, F

95 if...one such i.e. whether or not such a man ever existed.

96 It's past...dreaming i.e. no dream could come up to my image of him, the transcendent reality I invoke.

96 size capacity.

96–9 Nature...quite Mere Nature lacks material to contend with the fancy or imagination in creating fantastic forms; yet an Antony such as I have pictured forth would be in himself Nature's masterpiece in competition with imagination, a masterpiece utterly surpassing any of the illusory images created by the imagination. Cleopatra insists on the superiority of the *idea* of Antony, whether or not such a man ever existed; the idea perfects Nature and yet is no idle imagining either, for it is invested in the reality of Antony.

101 As answering to the weight In proportion to its heavy weight of grief.

101–2 Would...but I do feel May I never succeed in what I desire if I do not feel.

103 rebound reflection or recoil. The image is perhaps that of a blow with an axe rebounding from the root of one tree to another or recoiling onto the woodsman.

103 *smites As Wilson notes, the F reading 'suites' is a single minim error.

109 SD *Enter* PROCULEIUS...*train* North's Plutarch (1008D–1009A) provides many details for Caesar's visit to Cleopatra: her presenting him with 'a brief and memorial of all the ready money and treasure she had', Seleucus's contradicting her, Cleopatra's rage at Seleucus, and Caesar's indulgent response. But see 139 SD n. for important changes by Shakespeare.

110 Make way there Presumably this cry begins, perhaps from offstage, as Caesar and his train enter.

CAESAR Which is the Queen of Egypt?
DOLABELLA It is the emperor, madam.
Cleopatra kneels
CAESAR Arise, you shall not kneel.
I pray you, rise. Rise, Egypt.
CLEOPATRA [*Rising*] Sir, the gods
Will have it thus. My master and my lord
I must obey.
CAESAR Take to you no hard thoughts.
The record of what injuries you did us,
Though written in our flesh, we shall remember
As things but done by chance.
CLEOPATRA Sole sir o'th'world,
I cannot project mine own cause so well
To make it clear, but do confess I have
Been laden with like frailties which before
Have often shamed our sex.
CAESAR Cleopatra, know
We will extenuate rather than enforce.
If you apply yourself to our intents,
Which towards you are most gentle, you shall find
A benefit in this change; but if you seek
To lay on me a cruelty by taking
Antony's course, you shall bereave yourself
Of my good purposes and put your children
To that destruction which I'll guard them from
If thereon you rely. I'll take my leave.

114 SD] *Oxford; not in* F

111 Which...Egypt This is often taken – perhaps wrongly – as an insult or as evidence of a coldness in Caesar that makes him unable to recognise the inimitable Cleopatra. The line may instead indicate Caesar's desire, as he is in the process of entering, to be conducted forward and be introduced to the Queen of Egypt. Dolabella's response seems to comply with this wish.

116 Take...thoughts Do not torment yourself with reproaches.

119 sir master.

120 project set forth.

121 clear free from blame, innocent.

122 like frailties Compare the proverb 'Women are frail' (Dent W700.1).

124 enforce press home.

125 If you fall in with my plans for you.

128 lay...cruelty make me look cruel. Caesar intimates that her children will suffer if Cleopatra commits suicide. Caesar probably has in mind the laying of a formal charge against him, a public accusation; he is being cautiously legalistic and concerned with the public record of history, as in 118–19 and earlier at 5.1.73–6. Cleopatra correspondingly defends herself in terms with legal application, such as 'cause' and 'confess' (120–1). This legalistic manoeuvring leads up to the inventory of her wealth at 135 ff. and the issue of whether she is guilty of perjury and fraud.

CLEOPATRA And may through all the world! 'Tis yours, and we,
Your scutcheons and your signs of conquest, shall
Hang in what place you please. Here, my good lord.
[*She offers him a scroll*]
CAESAR You shall advise me in all for Cleopatra.
CLEOPATRA This is the brief of money, plate, and jewels
I am possessed of. 'Tis exactly valued,
Not petty things admitted. Where's Seleucus?

[*Enter* SELEUCUS]

SELEUCUS Here, madam.
CLEOPATRA This is my treasurer. Let him speak, my lord,
Upon his peril, that I have reserved
To myself nothing. Speak the truth, Seleucus.
SELEUCUS Madam, I had rather seal my lips
Than to my peril speak that which is not.

135 SD] *Craig subst. after Collier MS.; not in* F 137–8 brief of. . .of. 'Tis] *Pope subst.;* breefe: of. . .of, 'tis F 139 SD] *Oxford; not in* F 144 seal] F3 (seale)*;* seele F (*perhaps a spelling variant*)

133 **And may** Cleopatra plays on Caesar's 'I'll take my leave', conventionally said on the point of intended departure, in a punning sense: 'You may *take your leave*, have your will, anywhere in the world.'

134 **scutcheons** Shields showing armorial bearings, here the captured shields of those whom Caesar has conquered.

135 **Hang** Be hung up like captured trophies; but with a mocking hidden sense, 'be hanged as foes', that is understood by those who know what Cleopatra thinks of Caesar's seemingly fair words. Cleopatra's hidden sense continues the legalistic play noted above at 128.

136 Your advice will be consulted in all matters pertaining to yourself. Caesar repeats the offer at 185–6.

137 **brief** inventory, summary.

139 **Not petty things admitted** Petty things omitted.

139 SD Whether Seleucus enters at this point or comes onstage at 109 as part of Caesar's train, as Capell proposed and several editors have followed, is hard to determine. An entry at 109 would imply that he has already gone over to Caesar, but, if so, why does Cleopatra need to introduce him to Caesar? More likely, the little scene that follows is 'a put-up job between Cleo[patra] and Sel[eucus]' (Wilson), one calculated to give Caesar the impression that Cleopatra desires to live and thus reduce his wariness about the possibility of her suicide. Seleucus may then belong to the monument and its treasures, and now enters (or comes forward) when summoned. North's Plutarch speaks of Seleucus as standing apart, happening to be there at the interview: 'by chance there stood Selecucus by, one of her treasurers, who, to seem a good servant, came straight to Caesar to disprove Cleopatra, that she had not set in all but kept many things back of purpose' (1008E). Plutarch makes it plain that Cleopatra is hoping to trick Caesar into thinking she wants to live; Shakespeare leaves room for doubt as to her intentions and success. Similarly, Shakespeare leaves room to suppose Cleopatra and Seleucus are playing a prearranged scene of deception, whereas Plutarch's Seleucus is motivated simply by a desire to put himself in favour with Caesar. In Daniel's *Cleopatra*, on the other hand, it is plain that Seleucus has betrayed Cleopatra (4; 844 ff.).

144 ***seal** F 'seele' is often retained by editors as 'seel', to sew up, literally to shut the eyes of wild hawks in order to tame them, as at 3.13.115. Although normally said of eyes, 'seel' might here be applied in a vivid metaphorical sense to lips; the F spelling 'seele' is not used elsewhere in Shakespeare for 'seal' (Ridley). However, in the theatre the normal phrase, 'seal my lips', would inevitably be the understood meaning, since 'seal' and 'seel' are indistinguishable to the ear.

CLEOPATRA What have I kept back?
SELEUCUS Enough to purchase what you have made known.
CAESAR Nay, blush not, Cleopatra. I approve
Your wisdom in the deed.
CLEOPATRA See, Caesar! O, behold
How pomp is followed! Mine will now be yours,
And should we shift estates yours would be mine.
The ingratitude of this Seleucus does
Even make me wild. – O slave, of no more trust
Than love that's hired! What, goest thou back? Thou shalt
Go back, I warrant thee! But I'll catch thine eyes
Though they had wings. Slave, soulless villain, dog!
O rarely base!
CAESAR Good queen, let us entreat you.
CLEOPATRA O Caesar, what a wounding shame is this,
That thou vouchsafing here to visit me,
Doing the honour of thy lordliness
To one so meek, that mine own servant should
Parcel the sum of my disgraces by
Addition of his envy! Say, good Caesar,
That I some lady trifles have reserved,
Immoment toys, things of such dignity
As we greet modern friends withal, and say
Some nobler token I have kept apart
For Livia and Octavia, to induce
Their mediation, must I be unfolded
With one that I have bred? The gods! It smites me

156 soulless] *Pope;* Soule-lesse, F

150 How pomp is followed How greatness is served.

151 shift estates exchange places and conditions.

154 love that's hired i.e. a prostitute's love.

157 rarely exceptionally.

161 meek Irony plays about Cleopatra's use of such a word, especially in view of her flying out at Seleucus, and calls attention to the comic contradictions in her play-acting at submissiveness. She may also mean 'subdued by adversity'.

162 Parcel (1) particularise, enumerate by item, (2) add one more item to.

163 envy malice.

164 lady suitable for a lady.

165 Immoment toys Trifles of no moment or importance. (The only recorded use of 'immoment'.) In Daniel's *Cleopatra*, the queen speaks of 'some certain women's toys' (3; 687), and there are other parallels as well; compare, for example, 'Ah, Caesar, what a great indignity / Is this' in Daniel (684–5) with 158 above. See Arthur M. Z. Norman, 'Daniel's *The Tragedie of Cleopatra* and *Antony and Cleopatra*', *SQ* 9 (1958), 11–18, for further details.

166 modern ordinary.

166 withal with.

168 Livia Octavius Caesar's wife (though one would never know till now that he is married).

169–70 unfolded With exposed by.

170 one that I have bred a member of my household.

Beneath the fall I have. [*To Seleucus*] Prithee, go hence,
Or I shall show the cinders of my spirits
Through th'ashes of my chance. Wert thou a man,
Thou wouldst have mercy on me.

CAESAR Forbear, Seleucus.
[*Seleucus withdraws*]

CLEOPATRA Be it known that we, the greatest, are misthought
For things that others do; and when we fall,
We answer others' merits in our name,
Are therefore to be pitied.

CAESAR Cleopatra,
Not what you have reserved nor what acknowledged
Put we i'th'roll of conquest. Still be't yours;
Bestow it at your pleasure, and believe
Caesar's no merchant, to make prize with you
Of things that merchants sold. Therefore be cheered.
Make not your thoughts your prisons. No, dear queen,
For we intend so to dispose you as
Yourself shall give us counsel. Feed and sleep.
Our care and pity is so much upon you
That we remain your friend; and so adieu.

CLEOPATRA My master, and my lord!

CAESAR Not so. Adieu.
Flourish. Exeunt Caesar and his train

CLEOPATRA He words me, girls, he words me, that I should not
Be noble to myself. But hark thee, Charmian.

171 SD] *Johnson; not in* F 174 SD] *Capell subst.; not in* F 177 merits in our name,] *Johnson subst.;* merits, in our name F

172 **cinders** smouldering hot coals.

173 **chance** (fallen) fortune.

173 **Wert thou a man** i.e. instead of a eunuch.

174 **Forbear** Withdraw. Compare 'Forbear me' at 1.2.118.

175 **misthought** misjudged.

177 We have to answer for the misdeeds done by others in our name. ('Merits' means that which is desired or has been earned, whether good or evil (*OED* Merit *sb* 1).) Cleopatra speaks as though the attempted concealment of valuables were Seleucus's misdeed, even though she has just admitted to having done it herself. Also, given the game she is playing with Caesar, her words permit the interpretation that she has similarly had to answer for the misdeeds of Antony, who made war in her name.

180 **i'th'roll of conquest** Caesar is still being very formal and legalistic, as at 118–19 and 128.

181 **Bestow** Use (*OED* sv *v* 5).

182 **make prize** haggle.

184 **Make not...prisons** 'Be not a prisoner in imagination, when in reality you are free' (Johnson).

185 **dispose you** arrange your affairs.

186 **Feed and sleep** An ironic recall of Cleopatra's resolve, spoken to Proculeius, to eat and sleep no more (48–50). Either Proculeius has reported back to Caesar, who doesn't miss a detail, or Cleopatra has shrewdly anticipated the way Caesar thinks.

190–1 **He words me...to myself** He attempts to deceive me with mere words to keep me from suicide.

[*She whispers to Charmian*]

IRAS Finish, good lady. The bright day is done,
And we are for the dark.
CLEOPATRA Hie thee again.
I have spoke already, and it is provided;
Go put it to the haste.
CHARMIAN Madam, I will.

Enter DOLABELLA

DOLABELLA Where's the queen?
CHARMIAN Behold, sir. [*Exit*]
CLEOPATRA Dolabella!
DOLABELLA Madam, as thereto sworn by your command,
Which my love makes religion to obey,
I tell you this: Caesar through Syria
Intends his journey, and within three days
You with your children will he send before.
Make your best use of this. I have performed
Your pleasure and my promise.
CLEOPATRA Dolabella,
I shall remain your debtor.
DOLABELLA I your servant.
Adieu, good queen. I must attend on Caesar.
CLEOPATRA Farewell, and thanks.

Exit [*Dolabella*]

Now, Iras, what think'st thou?
Thou an Egyptian puppet shall be shown
In Rome as well as I. Mechanic slaves
With greasy aprons, rules, and hammers shall

191 SD *She whispers to Charmian*] *Theobald subst.; not in* F **196** SD *Exit*] *Capell subst.; not in* F; *at 195, Theobald* **206** SD] *Capell; Exit* F *(placed after* Caesar *in 205)* **207** shall] F; shalt F2

193 Hie thee again Come back quickly.

194 spoke given orders (for the means of suicide).

199–202 Caesar...of this For North's Plutarch on this speech, see 1009B and 63 SD n. above. The dialogue here from 199 to 205 is close to Daniel's *Cleopatra* (4; 1090–7), though there Cleopatra, in soliloquy, is speaking of the contents of a letter sent her by Dolabella. See Arthur M. Z. Norman, 'Daniel's *The Tragedie of Cleopatra* and *Antony and Cleopatra*', *SQ* 9 (1958), 11–18, esp. p. 16.

207 puppet Cleopatra has in mind a tableau or pageant drawn through the streets in Caesar's triumph.

208 Mechanic slaves Artisans, labourers; like the 'rude mechanicals' of *MND* 3.2.9, or the 'poor mechanic porters' of *H5* 1.2.200.

209 aprons Workmen's aprons, the visually recognisable badges of tradesmen, tapsters, etc., as in *2H6* 2.3.75 and 4.2.13, *2H4* 2.2.171 ff., etc.

209 rules Straight-edged measuring-sticks.

Uplift us to the view. In their thick breaths,
Rank of gross diet, shall we be enclouded
And forced to drink their vapour.

IRAS The gods forbid!

CLEOPATRA Nay, 'tis most certain, Iras. Saucy lictors
Will catch at us like strumpets, and scald rhymers
Ballad us out o'tune. The quick comedians
Extemporally will stage us and present
Our Alexandrian revels; Antony
Shall be brought drunken forth, and I shall see
Some squeaking Cleopatra boy my greatness
I'th'posture of a whore.

IRAS O the good gods!

CLEOPATRA Nay, that's certain.

IRAS I'll never see't! For I am sure my nails
Are stronger than mine eyes.

CLEOPATRA Why, that's the way
To fool their preparation and to conquer
Their most absurd intents.

215 Ballad] F2; Ballads F **215** o'] *Theobald;* a F **222** my] F2; mine F

210 Uplift us Cleopatra again recalls, as she did at 5.2.54–6, Antony's taunt that Caesar will 'hoist thee up to the shouting plebeians' (4.12.34). The image is more offensive here; the common labourers will themselves lift up Cleopatra and her women, taking rude familiarities, instead of merely seeing the women elevated for all to behold. Cleopatra is strengthening her resolution to do what must be done (Wilson, Kittredge).

211 Rank of gross diet Stinking with bad food. The attributing of strong breath to labourers is a commonplace in Shakespeare, as in *Cor.* 1.1.60 and 2.1.236, *2H6* 4.7.12, and *JC* 1.2.246–7. Onions, cheese, and musty bread contributed to the problem.

212 drink drink in, inhale (as in the 'drinking' of tobacco).

213 Saucy Insolent and lascivious (*OED* sv *adj* 2 and 2b); as in *Cym.* 1.6.151 and *MM* 2.4.45.

213 lictors Minor officials attending a magistrate and carrying out his sentences on offenders, hence comparable in England to beadles. Wilson observes that beadles dealt officially with 'strumpets' (214), as in *Lear* 4.6.160 and *2H4* 5.4.5.

214 scald scurvy, contemptible.

215 Ballad us Sing our story in ballads. Compare *1H4* 2.2.45–6, where Falstaff proposes to have 'ballads made on you all and sung to filthy tunes', and *AWW* 2.1.171–2: 'a divulged shame, / Traduc'd by odious ballads'. On Cleopatra's concern (as with the other major characters of the play) for her place in history, see pp. 25–30 above. She is aware here that her name will become a powerful historical and literary stereotype, like Cressida's, and that her role will be 'played' in Rome and elsewhere. Even in an intimate moment such as this, Cleopatra is self-conscious in her artistry and aware of some kind of audience.

215 quick quick-witted, sprightly (*OED* sv *adj* 12).

219 boy The boy who played Cleopatra in Shakespeare's company is daringly invited to break theatrical illusion and call attention to the way in which the actors, centuries after the fact and on a bare stage, are bringing Antony drunken forth and 'boying' the greatness of Cleopatra.

220 posture demeanour, attitude. (The earliest citation in the *OED*.)

222 *my nails The F reading, 'mine Nailes', may have been affected by 'mine eyes' in the next line, or 'mine' may have anticipated the *n* sound in 'Nailes'. Compare F's 'mine nightingale' at 4.8.18.

Enter CHARMIAN

Now, Charmian!
Show me, my women, like a queen. Go fetch
My best attires. I am again for Cydnus,
To meet Mark Antony. Sirrah Iras, go –
Now, noble Charmian, we'll dispatch indeed –
And when thou hast done this chare I'll give thee leave
To play till Doomsday. Bring our crown and all.
[Exit Iras.] A noise within
Wherefore's this noise?

Enter a GUARDSMAN

GUARDSMAN Here is a rural fellow
That will not be denied your highness' presence.
He brings you figs.
CLEOPATRA Let him come in.
Exit Guardsman
What poor an instrument
May do a noble deed! He brings me liberty.
My resolution's placed, and I have nothing
Of woman in me. Now from head to foot

227 Cydnus] *Rowe* (Cidnus); *Cidrus* F 231 SD *Exit Iras*] *Capell; not in* F; *Exeunt Charmian and Iras / Arden*

227 Cydnus See 2.2.201 ff. for Enobarbus's description of the meeting of Antony and Cleopatra on the river of Cydnus. Shakespeare may be recalling Daniel's *Cleopatra* (5; 1473–84), in which Cleopatra's 'pompeous rich array' in her death scene is compared with her appearance on the river of Cydnus.

228 Sirrah A common form of address to inferiors and servants, whether male or female; compare 2.3.10 and 'sirs' at 4.15.90.

229 dispatch (1) make haste (*OED* sv *v* 9), (2) finish off (*OED* sv *v* 5).

230 chare household task; as at 4.15.80.

231 SD *Exit Iras* Some editors (the Arden editors among them) provide for Charmian to exit here too, noting that Cleopatra addresses both her women at 226–7: 'Show me, my women, like a queen. Go fetch / My best attires.' Yet her further remarking, 'Sirrah Iras, go – / Now, noble Charmian, we'll dispatch indeed –' seems to differentiate the tasks of the two women, and her 'thou' and 'thee' in 230 seem addressed to Iras (though depending on how the sentence is punctuated). At 273, in the absence of a Folio stage direction, one or two women could re-enter, but the particular addressing of Iras ('Yare, yare, good Iras') in 277 points to her arrival with the royal garments. Surely Cleopatra would not object to Charmian's presence during the interim, including the interview with the Clown; she likes an audience, and is not given to soliloquising.

234–5 figs...What poor an instrument Suggesting the proverbial comparison 'Not worth a fig' (Dent F211), and probably with erotic overtones (Fitz, p. 302). 'Poor an instrument' may also, or instead, refer to the Clown, the 'He' of 236.

235 What How.

237 placed fixed.

237–8 I have...in me This resolve contrasts sharply with Cleopatra's tactical admission to Caesar of womanly frailty at 121–3 above and with her 'No more but e'en a woman' on the occasion of Antony's death at 4.15.78.

I am marble-constant; now the fleeting moon
No planet is of mine.

Enter GUARDSMAN, *and* CLOWN [*bringing in a basket*]

GUARDSMAN This is the man.
CLEOPATRA Avoid, and leave him.

Exit Guardsman

Hast thou the pretty worm of Nilus there,
That kills and pains not?

CLOWN Truly I have him, but I would not be the party that should desire you to touch him, for his biting is immortal. Those that do die of it do seldom or never recover.

CLEOPATRA Remember'st thou any that have died on't?

CLOWN Very many, men and women too. I heard of one of them no longer than yesterday – a very honest woman, but something given to lie, as a woman should not do but in the way of honesty – how she died of the biting of it, what pain she felt. Truly, she makes a very good report o'th'worm. But he that will believe all that they say shall never be saved by half that they do. But this is

239 marble-constant] *Capell;* Marble constant F **240** SD *bringing in a basket*] *Rowe subst.; not in* F

239 fleeting changeful. ('Fleeting moon' is a proverbial idea; Dent M1111.)

240 No planet is of mine Compare 3.6.16–18, where Cleopatra is described as appearing 'In th'habiliments of the goddess Isis', and also 3.13.157, where Antony laments that 'our terrene moon', i.e. Cleopatra, is now 'eclipsed'. Cleopatra now resolves to have no more to do with mortality and human vicissitude.

240 SD CLOWN Countryman (the word used in North's Plutarch); rustic. Cleopatra's interview with him is factually based on North's Plutarch, 1009D, where Shakespeare could even find a suggestion of laughter in the countryman's banter with the guards about the goodly figs he is taking to the queen: but the conversation between Cleopatra and the Clown, with its rich ironies about death and sexuality, is entirely Shakespeare's. Ruth Nevo ('The masque of greatness', *S.St.* 3 (1967), 111–28, p. 124) compares this countryman to the antimasque figures of Jacobean masques, given the prominent masque element in all of 5.2; see 79, 82–3, and 87–9 nn. above.

241 Avoid Depart.

242 worm serpent.

243 That kills and pains not North's Plutarch reports earlier, during the time of the battle of Actium, that Cleopatra conducted tests to see what poisons 'made men die with least pain', concluding that the 'aspic' was best of all, since its fatal bite induced only a 'heaviness of the head' and 'a great desire also to sleep' (1004C–D).

245 immortal The Clown's blunder for 'mortal', but anticipating Cleopatra's 'Immortal longings' at 275.

248 of one from one.

249 honest (1) truthful, (2) chaste, respectable. The wordplay continues in 'honesty' (250).

249–50 something given to lie (1) rather addicted to telling lies, (2) sexually wanton, ready to 'lie' with men. The bawdy wordplay continues in 'died', came to orgasm (251), the 'pain she felt' in the sharp pleasure of sex (251), and the 'very good report' she makes of the 'worm' or phallus (252). Compare Enobarbus on Cleopatra's 'dying' at 1.2.137–40.

252–3 But he . . . they do The Clown comically transposes the expected order of 'all' and 'half', and misapplies religious teachings on salvation by faith rather than works (Arden, Wilson). Harold Fisch ('*Antony and Cleopatra*: the limits of mythology', *S.Sur.* 23 (1970), 59–67, p. 64) proposes that 'the man who believed what the woman said of the serpent (worm) but could not be saved by what she had done is of course Adam'.

most falliable, the worm's an odd worm.

CLEOPATRA Get thee hence, farewell.

CLOWN I wish you all joy of the worm. [*Setting down his basket*]

CLEOPATRA Farewell.

CLOWN You must think this, look you, that the worm will do his kind.

CLEOPATRA Ay, ay, farewell.

CLOWN Look you, the worm is not to be trusted but in the keeping of wise people, for indeed there is no goodness in the worm.

CLEOPATRA Take thou no care; it shall be heeded.

CLOWN Very good. Give it nothing, I pray you, for it is not worth the feeding.

CLEOPATRA Will it eat me?

CLOWN You must not think I am so simple but I know the devil himself will not eat a woman. I know that a woman is a dish for the gods, if the devil dress her not. But truly, these same whoreson devils do the gods great harm in their women, for in every ten that they make, the devils mar five.

CLEOPATRA Well, get thee gone. Farewell.

CLOWN Yes, forsooth. I wish you joy o'th'worm. *Exit*

[*Enter* IRAS *with royal attire*]

CLEOPATRA Give me my robe. Put on my crown. I have
Immortal longings in me. Now no more
The juice of Egypt's grape shall moist this lip.
[*The women dress her*]
Yare, yare, good Iras; quick. Methinks I hear
Antony call. I see him rouse himself
To praise my noble act. I hear him mock

256 SD] *Capell; not in* F **273** SD.2 *Enter...attire*] *Capell subst.; not in* F*; Re-enter Charmian and Iras with a robe, crown, and other jewels / Arden* **276** SD] *Bevington; not in* F

254 falliable A blunder for 'infallible'.

258–9 do his kind act according to its nature. The risible suggestion of a sexual instinct not easily controlled may linger in the Clown's jesting as far as 273.

263 Take thou no care Don't you worry.

266 Will it eat me (1) Will it bite me as a serpent bites, (2) Will it consume my flesh once I am dead, as worms do.

269 dress (1) prepare for use as food, (2) attire in alluring clothes.

269–70 whoreson i.e. rascally, abominable. (A slang expression.)

271 make...mar A favourite Shakespearean antithesis, as at 3.11.64 (Dent M48).

274 robe...crown According to North's Plutarch, Cleopatra was found 'stark dead, laid upon a bed of gold, attired and arrayed in her royal robes' (1009E).

275 Immortal longings Longings for immortality.

277 Yare Quickly, deftly.

The luck of Caesar, which the gods give men
To excuse their after wrath. Husband, I come!
Now to that name my courage prove my title!
I am fire and air; my other elements
I give to baser life. So, have you done?
Come, then, and take the last warmth of my lips.
Farewell, kind Charmian. Iras, long farewell.
[*She kisses them. Iras falls and dies*]
Have I the aspic in my lips? Dost fall?
If thou and nature can so gently part,
The stroke of death is as a lover's pinch,
Which hurts, and is desired. Dost thou lie still?
If thus thou vanishest, thou tell'st the world
It is not worth leave-taking.

CHARMIAN Dissolve, thick cloud, and rain, that I may say
The gods themselves do weep!

CLEOPATRA This proves me base.
If she first meet the curlèd Antony,
He'll make demand of her, and spend that kiss

286 SD] *Hanmer subst.; not in* F **293** Dissolve, thick] *Theobald;* Dissolue thicke F

280–1 The luck...wrath Octavius Caesar's notorious good luck in defeating Antony even at games of chance (see 2.3.26–9, 4.14.76, and North's Plutarch, 985A–B) is mocked by Cleopatra as the kind of undeserved good fortune given to some men by the gods, a fortune that induces arrogance (hubris) and thereby justifies the gods' subsequent retribution (nemesis).

281 Husband, I come The word 'come' often includes an erotic suggestion, especially in this play, as Fitz (p. 302) observes.

282 May my courage prove my right to call Antony husband, to call myself his wife.

283 I am fire and air i.e. the lighter two of the four elements from which all life is composed (Dent A94.1). The 'other elements', earth and water, belong to the lower region of mortality, to the 'clay' and 'dungy earth' of 1.1.37.

286 SD *Iras falls and dies* North's Plutarch reports simply that Cleopatra is found dead with 'one of her two women, which was called Iras, dead at her feet' (1009E). The cause of death is not specified in Plutarch or in Shakespeare. Some editors (e.g. Wilson, Jones) conjecture that Iras has allowed an asp to bite her, but it is not like Iras to upstage her mistress, and death by grief is no more improbable than Enobarbus's demise (4.9). On the other hand, Cleopatra's 'This' in 294 implies a recognition that Iras has chosen to precede Cleopatra in death.

287 aspic asp; as in North's Plutarch, 1004D and 1010A.

289–90 The stroke...desired As before at 1.2.137–40 and 5.2.251, death is likened to an amorous embrace, to a physical climax both painful and delicious. This motif of erotic violence is not in North's Plutarch.

292 leave-taking 'any ceremony when one departs' (Kittredge); or 'taking leave of' (Riverside).

294 This i.e. Iras's dying first.

295 curlèd with curled hair; recalling her first meeting with Antony, he 'Being barbered ten times o'er' (2.2.234). The image suggests handsomeness in men, as in 'The wealthy curlèd darlings of our nation' (*Oth.* 1.2.68) and in many Renaissance portrait representations.

296–7 He'll...to have Johnson's explanation, that Antony 'will enquire of her concerning me, and kiss her for giving him intelligence', though endorsed by more recent editors, is surely too demure and circumspect to represent Cleopatra's whole meaning. Cleopatra jestingly imagines herself cheated of her sexual desire for Antony by a younger woman who gets there first.

296 spend expend (with sexual suggestion).

Which is my heaven to have. Come, thou mortal wretch,
[*She applies an asp*]
With thy sharp teeth this knot intrinsicate
Of life at once untie. Poor venomous fool,
Be angry, and dispatch. O, couldst thou speak,
That I might hear thee call great Caesar ass
Unpolicied!

CHARMIAN O eastern star!

CLEOPATRA Peace, peace!
Dost thou not see my baby at my breast,
That sucks the nurse asleep?

CHARMIAN O, break! O, break!

CLEOPATRA As sweet as balm, as soft as air, as gentle –
O Antony! – Nay, I will take thee too.
[*She applies another asp*]
What should I stay – *Dies*

CHARMIAN In this wild world? So, fare thee well.
Now boast thee, Death, in thy possession lies
A lass unparalleled. Downy windows, close;
And golden Phoebus never be beheld

297 SD] *Hanmer subst.; not in* F **306** SD] *Theobald subst.; not in* F **308** wild] F (wilde); vile *Capell*

297 mortal deadly.

297 wretch creature. (Often a term of affectionate abuse.)

298 intrinsicate intricate, hidden, occult. The idea of intricate mystery applies to the delicate link between our vital spirit and our bodily frame, a link that death must somehow untie, and also to the vast complexity of life (see Kittredge).

299 fool A term of endearment, like 'wretch' at 297. Often used of children, like the 'baby at my breast' (303).

302 Unpolicied Outmanoeuvred in the contest of 'policy' or craft, including statecraft, for Cleopatra has foiled Caesar's ambitions.

302 eastern star Venus, the morning star. Cleopatra is compared with Venus at 2.2.210, and the paradox of holy amorousness is invoked by Enobarbus at 2.2.248–50.

303 baby at my breast In North's Plutarch (1010B), the asp bites are found in Cleopatra's arm (according to some authorities), but Shakespeare could have read the following in Thomas Nashe's *Christ's Tears over Jerusalem* (1593): 'At thy breasts (as at Cleopatra's), asps shall be put out to nurse' (*Works*, ed. R. B. McKerrow, II, 140). See also George Peele's *Edward I* (1593), Scene 15, 2095–6, in *Works*, ed. Prouty, II, 69–212, p. 148, where Queen Eleanor cruelly applies a serpent to the Mayoress's breast: 'Why so; / Now she is a nurse. Suck on, sweet babe'; also Sir Thomas Browne, *Pseudodoxia Epidemica, or Enquiries into Vulgar and Common Errors*, Book V, chap. 12 (noted by Arden and Wilson). G. Watson, 'The death of Cleopatra', *N&Q* 223, ns 25 (1978), 409–14, summarises the uncertainties of classical authors regarding Cleopatra's means of death and concludes that Shakespeare's referring to breast and arm may be his own innovation, though Shakespeare may have drawn on Galen (who describes Cleopatra's queenly greatness in her death) and probably on Paul of Aegina. See also Mary Olive Thomas, 'Cleopatra and the "mortal wretch"', *SJ* 99 (1963), 174–83, concerning Shakespeare's possible artistic intentions.

305 As sweet...as gentle A series of proverbial comparisons (Dent B63.1, A91.1, A88.1), here imbued with an erotic, even orgasmic sense that fuses sexuality and dying.

307 What Why.

308 wild savage. The emendation adopted by some editors to 'vile' or 'vilde' is possible.

310 windows eyelids.

311 Phoebus The sun god.

Of eyes again so royal! Your crown's awry;
I'll mend it, and then play –

Enter the GUARD *rustling in*

1 GUARD Where's the queen?
CHARMIAN Speak softly. Wake her not.
1 GUARD Caesar hath sent –
CHARMIAN Too slow a messenger.
[*She applies an asp*]
O, come apace, dispatch! I partly feel thee.
1 GUARD Approach, ho! All's not well. Caesar's beguiled.
2 GUARD There's Dolabella sent from Caesar. Call him.
[*Exit a Guardsman*]
1 GUARD What work is here, Charmian? Is this well done?
CHARMIAN It is well done, and fitting for a princess
Descended of so many royal kings.
Ah, soldier! *Charmian dies*

Enter DOLABELLA

DOLABELLA How goes it here?
2 GUARD All dead.
DOLABELLA Caesar, thy thoughts
Touch their effects in this. Thyself art coming
To see performed the dreaded act which thou
So sought'st to hinder.

312 awry] *Rowe*[3]; away F 313 SD *in*] *Rowe; in, and Dolabella* F 315,317,319 SH 1 GUARD] 1 F 315 SD *She applies an asp*] *Pope subst.; not in* F 318,323 SH 2 GUARD] 2 F 318 SD *Exit a Guardsman*] *Oxford; not in* F 319 here, Charmian? Is] *Rowe;* heere *Charmian?* / Is F; here? – *Charmian,* is *Capell*

312 **Of** By.

312 ***awry** Rowe's correction of F's 'away' is graphically easy (the *a:r* confusion). It is further confirmed by the description in North's Plutarch ('her other woman called Charmian, half dead and trembling, trimming the diadem which Cleopatra ware upon her head', 1009F), and in Samuel Daniel's *Cleopatra* (5; 1651–2): 'in her sinking down she wries / The diadem' (cited in Wilson).

313 **mend** adjust.

313 **and then play** Charmian recalls Cleopatra's words at 231, 'To play till Doomsday'.

313 SD ***rustling*** i.e. moving swiftly, their armour clattering.

317 **beguiled** tricked, cheated.

319–22 **What work...Ah, soldier** Shakespeare follows in remarkable detail the language of North's Plutarch: 'One of the soldiers, seeing her, angrily said unto her, "Is that well done, Charmian?" "Very well," said she again, "and meet for a princess descended from the race of so many noble kings." She said no more, but fell down dead hard by the bed' (1009F–1010A).

322 SD.2 ***Enter*** DOLABELLA The repetitiveness of this entry in F, where Dolabella first enters with the Guard at 313 (see collation), is further evidence that the text is based on Shakespeare's foul papers. The dramatist evidently changed his plans and neglected to delete the first entry. The book-keeper would not allow such a discrepancy to stand.

324 **Touch their effects** Meet their realisation.

Enter CAESAR *and all his train, marching*

ALL A way there, a way for Caesar!
DOLABELLA O sir, you are too sure an augurer:
That you did fear is done.
CAESAR Bravest at the last,
She levelled at our purposes and, being royal,
Took her own way. The manner of their deaths?
I do not see them bleed.
DOLABELLA Who was last with them?
1 GUARD A simple countryman, that brought her figs.
This was his basket.
CAESAR Poisoned, then.
1 GUARD O Caesar,
This Charmian lived but now; she stood and spake.
I found her trimming up the diadem
On her dead mistress; tremblingly she stood,
And on the sudden dropped.
CAESAR O, noble weakness!
If they had swallowed poison, 'twould appear
By external swelling; but she looks like sleep,
As she would catch another Antony
In her strong toil of grace.
DOLABELLA Here on her breast
There is a vent of blood, and something blown;
The like is on her arm.
1 GUARD This is an aspic's trail, and these fig-leaves

336–7 diadem / On her dead mistress;] *Pope subst.;* Diadem; / On her dead Mistris F

327 **A way there** The repetition of this formula heralding the arrival of the emperor, previously heard when Caesar made his visit to the live Cleopatra (110), underscores the irony of his defeated plans in this moment of otherwise complete triumph.

329 **That** That which.

330 **levelled at** aimed at, guessed. The image is of a weapon levelled in aiming at a target (*OED* Level v^{1} 6, 7).

333 **simple** poor or humble in condition.

336 **trimming up** straightening.

340 **like sleep** as if asleep.

341 **As** As if. Caesar momentarily transcends himself in the perfectly cadenced image of 340–2.

342 **toil** net, snare.

342 **grace** attractive quality, beauty, but with a suggestion also of a heavenly and transcendent virtue (Harold Fisch, '*Antony and Cleopatra*: the limits of mythology', *S. Sur.* 23 (1970), 59–67, p. 67).

343 **vent** discharge.

343 **blown** swollen, or, more probably, 'deposited'. Compare 59 above, 'Blow me into abhorring.' North's Plutarch says nothing of swelling from the asp's bite, and insists that there was 'no mark seen of her body, or any sign discerned that she was poisoned' (1004C–D, 1010B). 'This' in 345, the asp's trail, seems to refer to 'something blown' on her breast and arm.

Have slime upon them, such as th'aspic leaves
Upon the caves of Nile.

CAESAR Most probable
That so she died; for her physician tells me
She hath pursued conclusions infinite
Of easy ways to die. Take up her bed,
And bear her women from the monument.
She shall be buried by her Antony.
No grave upon the earth shall clip in it
A pair so famous. High events as these
Strike those that make them; and their story is
No less in pity than his glory which
Brought them to be lamented. Our army shall
In solemn show attend this funeral,
And then to Rome. Come, Dolabella, see
High order in this great solemnity.

Exeunt omnes, [*bearing the dead bodies*]

360 SD *bearing the dead bodies*] *Wilson subst.; not in* F; *bearing Cleopatra* [*on her bed*], *Charmian, and Iras / Oxford*

349 **conclusions infinite** innumerable experiments.

353 **clip** embrace; as at 4.8.8: 'clip your wives'.

355 **Strike...make them** Touch with sorrow those who brought about these deeds.

355–7 **their story...lamented** the history of these high events is no less deserving of pity than the glory of him who performed these lamentable deeds is deserving of renown. Although Caesar's words here are often quoted as evidence that he is merely self-regarding, there may well be more poignancy than contempt in Caesar's recognition of the nature of his own role. Reuben Brower proposes in fact that 'their' and 'them' might refer to Antony and Cleopatra; if so, the passage may mean that 'their story is no less pitiable than Caesar's glory is, and his glory is as "miserable" as the changed fortunes of Antony and Cleopatra. Shakespeare leaves the audience with the feeling that greatness in victory and greatness in defeat are equally glorious, equally pitiable' (*Hero and Saint*, 1971, p. 346). The fortunes of Antony, Cleopatra, and Caesar are all intimately bound together in the story.

360 **solemnity** occasion of ceremony, or special formality on an important occasion (*OED*).

SUPPLEMENTARY NOTE

2.1.2, 5 SH MENAS Whether the speaker in 2–3 and 5–8 is Menas or Menecrates is open to debate. Shakespeare must have intended to have both men on stage, since they are mentioned in North's Plutarch (984C–E) and earlier in this play (1.4.49) as Pompey's piratical associates, and are both named in the opening stage direction to the present scene. Still, Pompey addresses only Menas in this scene. His doing so explicitly at 33 and 43 requires the assignment of the intervening speech, 39–43, to Menas. The difficulty is that the speech heading at 39 in F, and indeed throughout the scene, reads *Mene.* Editors since Malone have assigned the speech at 39 to Menas and have added those at 16 and 18 to his assignment for good measure, but have left those at 2 and 5 to Menecrates, presumably because the spelling of *Mene.* suggests Menecrates rather than Menas.

Does Menecrates speak at all? Pompey exits at the end of this scene saying, 'Come, Menas', with no acknowledgement of Menecrates' presence. Menecrates does not appear in 2.7 with Menas, and is not mentioned in the comparable incident in North's Plutarch (984E). When Menas enters at 2.7.15 SD, his name is spelled *Menes* in F. The speech headings in 2.7 all read *Men.* except for one *Menas* at 34. Clearly the speech heading *Mene.* is not a reliable abbreviation for Menecrates. Although Shakespeare's intentions may have been unclear at first, the surest way out of arbitrary editorial choice is to assign all speeches to Menas. The speeches at 2 and 5 are not inappropriate to him. As Johnson observes, 'I know not why Menecrates appears; Menas can do all without him.' Shakespeare's manuscript had already introduced non-speaking named characters (Rannius, Lucillius, probably Lamprius) in 1.2, so that Menecrates' undoubted presence in 2.1 is no guarantee that he is to speak. If Shakespeare was not being particularly careful about his speech headings while he worked out the roles of his two pirates, and then did not go back to straighten out the speech headings after he had settled on Menas as the only speaker, editors might be attempting to preserve an intention prior to Shakespeare's final decision.

TEXTUAL ANALYSIS

This edition is based on the First Folio of 1623 (F), the only authority for the text of *Antony and Cleopatra*. Editors generally agree that the Folio text was based on Shakespeare's own manuscript, or perhaps, in view of the unusual stage direction *Omnes*, of a punctuation system uncharacteristic of Shakespeare, and of the predominance of the longer 'oh' spelling that is at variance with Shakespeare's apparent practice, from some kind of transcript.[1] To a significant extent, the Folio text retains what appear to be characteristically Shakespearean spellings, such as *One* for *on* (1.1.41), *Scicion* for *Sicyon* (1.2.109 ff.), *how* for *ho* (1.2.109 and 4.14.134), *reciding* for *residing* (1.3.104), *hard* for *heard* (2.2.233), *arrant* for *errand* (3.13.106), *triumpherate* (compare *triumphery* in *LLL* 4.3.51) for *triumvirate* (3.6.29), *cease* for *seize* (3.11.46), and *in* for *e'en* (4.15.78).[2] *Ventigius* may also be authorial, since it is spelt thus and in other unusual forms in *Timon of Athens*; it appears in *Antony* twice, at 2.3.31 and 40 SD, on a page set by Compositor E, though more often correctly as *Ventidius*, twice in 2.2 on a page set by Compositor B and thrice in 3.1 on pages set by Compositor E. Some Shakespearean spellings, in other words, seem to have survived a possible transcription and the spelling practices of two compositors.

Whether in Shakespeare's hand or that of some transcriber, the papers used as printer's copy were not yet prepared to serve as the prompt-book. Stage directions are at times expressive of matters that Shakespeare, as a theatrical professional, evidently cared about: *She hales him up and down* (2.5.65), *Whispers in's ear* (2.7.34), *Enter Ventidius as it were in triumph, the dead body of Pacorus borne before him* (3.1.0), *Enter the Guard rustling in* (5.2.313). W. W. Greg, noting that such stage directions are not always convenient in actual performance, wonders if Shakespeare, contemplating retirement and thus less directly in touch with his acting company than before, prepared these directions with a view to providing a 'producer's copy' rather than a prompter's.[3]

At other times, stage directions are apt to be laconic or simply missing. Much crucial information is missing as to the staging of the scene when Cleopatra is

[1] Wilson, p. 127; W. W. Greg, *The Editorial Problem in Shakespeare: A Survey of the Foundations of the Text*, 1942, p. 148; Ridley, p. vii; Stanley Wells and Gary Taylor, *A Textual Companion*, 1987, p. 549. I am indebted also to the 'Appendix on Text' in Marvin Spevack's forthcoming Variorum edition of *Antony and Cleopatra*, which the editor has generously allowed me to see.

[2] Some of these are listed by Wilson, pp. 124–5. Spevack's 'Appendix on Text' takes some of these spellings to be common variants, but agrees that *triumpherate* and *in*, for example, are very likely to be Shakespeare's. On the assignment of Folio pages to Compositors B and E, see T. H. Howard-Hill, 'New light on Compositor E of the Shakespeare First Folio', *The Library* 6th ser., 2 (June 1980), 156–78, and an unpublished essay, 'A Reassessment of Compositors B and E in the First Folio Tragedies', privately distributed.

[3] Greg, *The Editorial Problem*, p. 148; discussed in Wilson, p. 127.

captured in her monument (5.2.8 ff.). Gallus, dispatched by Caesar at the end of 5.1 to assist Proculeius in the capture, fails to appear in 5.2, though here the omission is probably the result of faulty casting-off of copy (see Commentary at 5.2.35–6).[1] The number of messengers appearing to Antony at 1.2.81 ff., and the assignment of speeches to them, are left unclear (see Commentary at 1.2.108 SD.2). The number of soldiers and the assignment of speeches to them in 4.3 are similarly left vague, as in other texts based on authorial papers; see for instance the numbering of the citizens in *Coriolanus* 2.3 and the French captains in *All's Well That Ends Well.* Throughout, the entrances and exits of messengers and ambassadors are apt to be unrecorded, as at 1.4.47–56, 2.5.108, 3.3.37, 3.12.25, 3.13.40, and 3.13.156. Soldiers and guardsmen are similarly taken for granted at 4.5.0, 4.7.0, 4.8.2, 4.14.120, 5.2.69, and 5.2.318; the same is true of attendants at 3.13.156 and 4.8.11.

Seemingly necessary exits of named characters, like those of Alexas at 1.3.5 and 2.5.116, Antony and the Ambassador at 3.13.28, Agrippa at 4.6.4, Scarus at 4.12.17, Dolabella at 5.1.3, and Gallus at 5.1.69, are omitted. An *Exeunt* at the end of a scene may stand imprecisely for a series of exits in sequence, as at the end of 2.7, 3.13, 4.4, and perhaps 3.10. *Exit* stands not infrequently for *Exeunt*, as at 4.14.145. No provision is made for the removal of dead bodies at 4.9.33 (of Enobarbus), 4.14.145 (of Eros), and 5.2.360 (of Cleopatra and her maids), though the bearing of the wounded and then dead Antony is indicated at 4.14.145 and 4.15.96.

Nor is provision made at 2.7.15 for the entry of the boy who is to sing the drinking song at 107. Iras is not explicitly brought on at 3.11.24, or Thidias at 3.12.0, or Charmian at 4.4.0, or Gallus and Proculeius at 5.1.0, though they are (except Gallus) assigned speeches in the scenes that follow. The text does not make clear whether Seleucus should enter with Octavius's train in the final scene (5.2.109), or, more probably, when his presence is required (at 139); nor is it clear whether Seleucus exits at 174 or simply stands back. On the intriguing question as to whether Charmian is present at Cleopatra's interview with the Clown in 5.2, or whether she has gone with Iras at 231 to fetch Cleopatra's regal attire, the text is silent. Such matters of detail Shakespeare presumably left to the prompter and to his fellow actors.

Ghost characters are sometimes named in opening stage directions without any subsequent mention or assignment of speeches, as with Rannius, Lucillius, and perhaps Lamprius (unless he is the Soothsayer) in 1.2. In 2.1 the text brings on Menas and Menecrates, both named in Plutarch, as associates of Pompey, and then assigns the speeches throughout the scene to *Mene.*, a spelling that suggests Menecrates; but some speeches must be assigned to Menas, to whom alone Pompey speaks, and since in 2.7 Menecrates does not appear with Menas and is never mentioned again, and since Menas's name is now confusingly spelled

[1] Charlton Hinman, *The Printing and Proof-Reading of the First Folio of Shakespeare*, 2 vols., 1963, II, 508–9.

'Menes' (as in North's Plutarch), the possibility emerges that 'Menecrates' is a non-speaking character who disappears once Shakespeare has focused on Menas as Pompey's chief ally (see Supplementary Note, p. 259 above). No prompter has straightened out this confusion, at any rate. Mardian is brought on at the beginning of 5.2 and is never instructed to exit, though he has no lines (as also in 1.2), and whether he is to remain onstage throughout 5.2 is unclear. The reference in the opening stage direction of 4.15 to Cleopatra *and her maids* is ambiguous as to whether unspecified extras are meant, since the stage direction goes on to specify *with Charmian and Iras*.

For the most part, however, the copy submitted to the printer seems to represent a late stage in Shakespeare's composition; some editors posit an authorial fair copy. The author's work seems pretty well completed. J. Dover Wilson's suggestion that certain apparent repetitions in Cleopatra's speech at 4.15.30 ff. can be regarded as 'notes for a proposed cut of some seventeen lines' (p. 129) has been convincingly refuted by David Galloway.[1] Speech headings present a few ambiguities, especially *Mene.* in 2.1 as noted above, and generic speech headings are sometimes supplied in place of proper names, such as *Romaine* or *Rom.* for Silius in 3.1, but for the most part are reasonably consistent for author's papers. Some other occasional inconsistencies appear to be Shakespeare's own. Scarus and the wounded soldier of 3.7 may be the same character, as J. Leeds Barroll has argued;[2] if so, Shakespeare's manuscript has not clarified the identification. Alexas enters *from Caesar* (1.5.35) when in fact he has come from Antony. The speech headings *Alex.* instead of *Captain* at 4.4.24 and *Dol.* instead of *Agrippa* at 5.1.28 and 31 are unlikely to be compositorial. The speech heading *Eros* instead of *Soldier* at 4.5.1, 3, and 6 may also be authorial, though the absence of an entry stage direction for the Soldier at the start of the scene might have misled the compositor (B) into supposing that Eros was the Soldier until the assignment of speeches at 9 to the Soldier and then to Eros convinced him of his error. At any rate the inconsistencies of this sort are few.

In the spelling of proper names, to be sure, both Shakespeare and the compositors (B and E, especially B) appear to have taken considerable liberties, so much so that it is often difficult to know where the responsibility lies. *Thidias*, sounding like a phonetic rendering of Plutarch's *Thyreus* and thereby adapted to conditions of performance, is more likely to be Shakespeare's choice than the compositor's. *Licoania* for *Lycaonia* and *Brandusium* for *Brundusium* (3.6.77 and 3.7.21), on the other hand, which are both corrected in F2 to conform with North's Plutarch, are easy errors for the compositor to have made in following manuscript copy. *Camidias*, *Camidius*, and *Camindius* for Plutarch's *Canidius* suggest Compositor B's uncertainty with letters easily confused in reading manuscript (*m*:*n*, *a*:*u*); although the consistency in substituting *m* for *n* could be authorial, it is an easy minim error and may also represent a tendency on the part of Compositor B

[1] Wilson, p. 129; David Galloway, *N&Q* 203 (1958), 330–5.
[2] 'Scarrus and the scarred soldier', *HLQ* 22 (1958), 31–9.

to hit on his version of a word and stick to it, as with *Decretas* for *Dercetus* (see below). *Pausa* for *Pansa* at 1.4.59 is an easy compositorial error, as are *Mauchus* for *Manchus* (3.6.74), *Troine* for *Toryne* (3.7.23), *Iusteus* for *Justeius* (probably a spelling variant) at 3.7.72, *Thidius* for *Thidias* (Plutarch: *Thyreus*) at 3.13.106 SD, *Dollabello* for *Dolabella* (3.12.0; elsewhere correct), *Domitian* for *Domitius* (4.2.1), and *Sidnis* and *Cidrus* for *Cydnus* (2.2.197, 5.2.227). The spelling *Cleopater*, occurring thrice in Act 2 and always on pages set by Compositor E (2.2.129 and 227, 2.5.0 SD), is unlikely to be authorial.

Some spellings could certainly be Shakespeare's, such as *Hirsius* for *Hirtius* (a simple spelling variant; Plutarch reads *Hircius*) at 1.4.59. *Menacrates* for *Menecrates* (1.4.49) may give further testimony to the difficulty Shakespeare seems to have encountered in distinguishing Menas and Menecrates, as noted above. *Anthonio's* instead of *Antonius* at 2.2.7 and 2.5.26 may be Shakespeare's way of indicating familiar address; the spelling is found elsewhere in Elizabethan usage.[1] *Scicion* for *Sicyon* (1.2.109, etc.), *Towrus* for *Taurus* (3.7.79, etc.), *Cicelie* for *Sicily* (2.6.7, etc.), *Scarrus* for *Scarus* (4.12.0 SD, etc.), and *Licas* for *Lichas* (4.12.45), some of them perhaps normal spelling variants, may be authorial, though by no means necessarily. *Orades* for *Orodes* (3.1.4), *Adullas* for *Adallas* (3.6.73), *Polemen* for *Polemon* (3.6.76), *Celius* for *Caelius* (a normal spelling variant) at 3.7.73, and *Caesarian* for *Caesarion* (perhaps a spelling variant) at 3.13.166 could be authorial or compositorial. Because many of these variations in proper names, including *Ventigius*, sound 'auditory', Ridley (p. x) speculates about an auditory link somewhere in the chain of transmission.

This edition preserves spellings like *Thidias* and *Antonio's* that appear to be authorial choices, but emends in accord with North's Plutarch where the F reading may be compositorial or where a purportedly Shakespearean reading can be regarded as a spelling variant or minor inconsistency. There seems no point in preserving *Ventigius*, even if Shakespeare sometimes wrote it that way, and few if any editors do so; yet some editors (such as Oxford) retain *Camidius*, despite the obvious potential for a minim error. (It is true that *Ventigius* appears less often in F than *Ventidius*, but the evidence from *Timon* suggests that *Ventigius* was a Shakespearean spelling; *Camidius* or *Camidias* in F invariably preserves the *m*, but the inconsistency of spelling nonetheless suggests uncertainty and the potential for error.) *Scarrus* is probably best regarded as a spelling variant of *Scaurus*, the name of Sextus Pompeius's half-brother, M. Æmilius Scaurus (see Furness, p. 4, n. 10), or *scarus*, a good Latin word even if it doesn't appear in North's Plutarch. *Decretas* is popular with editors, but surely it is perverse to ignore the fact that the first use of the name in F gives it as *Dercetus*, a predictable Elizabethan spelling of Plutarch's *Dercetaeus*.

Emendation of words other than proper names is often assisted by an awareness of the authorial copy underlying F and the difficulties encountered by the

[1] Kittredge cites Greene, *Ciceronis Amor* (1589; ed. Grosart, VII, 142): 'Is not Anthonio enamoured of the black Egyptian Cleopatra?' See Wilson, p. 141, note 1.1.10.

compositors in deciphering the handwriting of Shakespeare or a possible transcriber. Minim errors are common. Those involving *m*, *n*, *u*, *v*, *i*, and *w* include *windes/minds* (1.2.106), *Saue/Saw* (1.2.73), *me/we* (1.4.77), *gloue/glow* (2.2.214), *Vassailes/wassails* (1.4.57), *high Conlord/high-coloured* (2.7.3), *Inne/June* (3.10.14), and *suites/smites* (5.2.103); those involving *a*, *r*, *u*, and *n* include *Mandragoru/mandragora* (1.5.3), *away/awry* (5.2.312), *change/charge* (1.2.4), *would/world* (3.5.11), and *wan'd/warr'd* (*warred*) (2.1.42); those involving *e:o* include *Lessons/lessens* (3.12.13); those involving *e:d* include *dumbe/dumb'd* (*dumbed*) (1.5.52), *ioyne/join'd* (*joined*) (2.1.22), *vouchsafe/Vouchsaf'd* (*Vouchsafed*) (1.4.8), *a feare/afeard* (2.3.23), and *Tawny fine/Tawny-finn'd* (*Tawny-finned*) (2.5.12); those involving *l:t* include *smile/smite* (3.13.166) and *look'd/took't* (3.4.9).[1] No less easy for the compositor are errors like *Gentlewoman* for *gentlewomen* (2.2.216) and *savouring* for *favouring* (4.8.23).

These simple compositorial errors are not uncommonly found in proper names as well, as we saw above. Recognising the ease and frequency of errors of this sort does not of course always settle the question of whether to emend; editors divide, for example, on *ioyne/join'd* (2.1.22), among others, and some editors carry emendation further than this edition in such cases as *now/new* (1.1.49), *knew/know* (1.4.86), *graceful/grateful* (2.2.66), *greet/gree* (2.1.40), *noble/nobly* (2.2.105), *art/act* (2.5.105), *there/then* (2.7.69), and *embrace/embrac'd* (3.13.57). In bibliographical terms they are all plausible enough.

Some other errors are easily recognisable as errors in transmission, whether by Shakespeare himself or a scribe or the compositors. *My nightingale* is transcribed as *Mine nightingale* (4.8.18), anticipating in *Mine* the *n* sound of the next word, and at 5.2.222 *mine nails* is probably an anticipation of *mine eyes* in the next line. Other words or parts of words repeated in error include *a compelling an/a compelling* (1.2.134), *Say not, say/Say not so* (2.2.128), and *should'st stowe/should'st tow* (3.11.57). According to Oxford, *Seruicles* at 1.3.43 is probably a misprint for *seruicies*, an archaic spelling of *services*. *Fore-tell* at 1.2.37, Wilson argues, is a misprint for *fertill*, i.e. *fertile*; *One* at 1.4.3 is a misinterpretation of *o*ʳ, a contraction of *our*; *leaue* for *live* at 5.1.59 and *loue* for *leave* at 1.2.177 may both be a misreading of *leue* (though *leue* as a spelling for *liue* or *live* occurs nowhere else in Shakespeare); and *Anthony* for *autumn* at 5.2.86 may be a misreading of the manuscript *autome*.[2] Eyeskip accounts for *by* in place of *by my* at 1.3.82. Confusion of singular and plural is common, as *man/mans* (1.5.64), *grow/growes* (2.7.93), *yours/your* (3.4.24), *knows/know* (3.6.23), and so on, and perhaps in *smell/smels* (1.4.21), although the editor must not take this frequency as a licence to regularise matters of number and agreement to suit modern practice; Shakespearean usage must be the guide. Confusions are not uncommon in *Thy/The* (3.11.58), *this/the* (3.13.105), *is/'tis* (2.5.44), *is/his* (2.6.19), *he/his* (3.10.27), and so on, though again caution is necessary in each case.

[1] Some of these are listed by Wilson, p. 126.

[2] Wilson, pp. 126–7. Spevack's 'Appendix on Text' points out that the Shakespearean spelling elsewhere is 'Autumne' and 'Autume', not 'autome'.

Errors in punctuation are common, suggesting that the compositors not only did what they could with Shakespeare's sparsely-pointed manuscript but regarded punctuation as their responsibility. The F punctuation is notwithstanding often very helpful and must be carefully considered throughout, even though the need for emendation is also ever-present. By the same token, an editor should exercise judgement but not be overly reticent about adding stage directions in square brackets (including indications of persons addressed) in a manuscript text that left so much up to the prompter and the acting company.

Mislining or ambiguous lineation is common in this play, owing perhaps in part, as Greg suggests (though Ridley, p. ix, disagrees), to Shakespeare's having run on half-lines to economise space, in part to the compositors' practice of starting each new speech without indentation even if in the middle of a line of verse, and more generally to the increasing freedom of late Shakespearean versification. This edition takes a more sceptical view of editorial tradition in the arranging of half-lines into purported full lines of verse than do most editors (excepting my Scott, Foresman and Bantam editions). The problems are of two kinds.

The first occurs when three half-lines in a row can be arranged with either the first two or the last two linked into an iambic pentameter, that is, when the middle half-line can be linked either way.

MESSENGER News, my good lord, from Rome.
ANTONY Grates me! The sum.
CLEOPATRA Nay, hear them, Antony. (1.1.18–20)

or, a few lines later,

CLEOPATRA . . .
Perform't, or else we damn thee.'
ANTONY How, my love?
CLEOPATRA Perchance? Nay, and most like. (1.1.25–7)

Fredson Bowers and Paul Werstine, among others, have wrestled with the problem, and Bowers has done statistical analyses to determine whether half-lines are more apt to occur generally at the beginnings or ends of speeches, a factor which could, he argues, sway editorial choice in the case of three half-lines in sequence,[1] but the evidence is inconclusive, and this edition, along with Oxford, chooses to print all such three-half-line sequences without indentation. The use of indentation to indicate linkage is, after all, an editorial convention not found (except in cases of crowded spacing) in the original quartos or the First Folio. And whereas it serves the useful purpose in many instances of indicating Shakespeare's presumed intention of regarding two or more half-lines as making up a single

[1] Paul Werstine, 'Line division in Shakespeare's dramatic verse: an editorial problem', *Analytical and Enumerative Bibliography* 8 (1984), 73–125, and Fredson Bowers, 'Establishing Shakespeare's text: notes on short lines and the problem of verse division', *Studies in Bibliography* 33 (1980), 74–130. See also George Walton Williams, 'The year's contributions to Shakespearean studies', *S.Sur.* 34 (1981), 191–3.

pentameter verse, the frequency (especially in the late plays) of such sequences of three half-lines suggests that Shakespeare may have regarded such versification as perfectly correct in its indeterminacy. The metrical effect, in performance or in reading, is supple and continuous. The editorial impulse to choose one of two possibilities at the expense of the other may well misrepresent the author's intention. Shakespeare's verse, especially in his late plays, constantly warns us not to impose preconceived notions of metrical conventionality.

The other problem of lineation seems to me to be of a comparable sort, though here I go against a virtually unanimous editorial tradition. Many links urged on us by that tradition as a way of combining two or more half-lines into one verse line do not produce very plausible pentameter verse. Some are plausible hexameter lines, as in the following:

> CAESAR...
> To rot itself with motion.
> [*Enter a second* MESSENGER]
> MESSENGER Caesar, I bring thee word... (1.4.47–8)

or

> CLEOPATRA...
> My Antony is away.
> CHARMIAN You think of him too much. (1.5.6–7)

Shakespeare did occasionally write hexameter lines, to be sure, but to add such hypothetically constructed hexameters by the hundreds to the meagre store of undoubted hexameters occurring elsewhere is to increase the percentage out of all recognisable proportion. Moreover, the first of these examples occurs in a passage generally in verse, but the second does not. Cleopatra and Charmian have been speaking in short exchanges, evidently in prose. And even if the first passage is set in the midst of blank verse, so is the following metrically uncertain dialogue occurring in the preceding scene:

> CAESAR...
> So much as lanked not.
> LEPIDUS 'Tis pity of him.
> CAESAR Let his shames quickly... (1.4.72–4)

Either proposed link here produces lameness compared with the fine verse that surrounds this passage. In conversation onstage, on the other hand, it flows perfectly naturally, and in verse. A similar effect occurs at 2.2.123–5:

> CAESAR...
> O'th'world I would pursue it.
> AGRIPPA Give me leave, Caesar.
> CAESAR Speak, Agrippa.

Using the purely editorial convention of indenting one of these half-lines invokes a standard of regularity that may well not apply.

Sometimes editorial tradition insists on dividing a good blank verse line in the interests of further linking fore and aft, as in the following, lineated here as in most editions:

> ANTONY...
> Hark, Ventidius.
> CAESAR I do not know,
> Maecenas. Ask Agrippa.
> LEPIDUS Noble friends... (2.2.17–19)

By itself, 'I do not know, Maecenas. Ask Agrippa' has the effective integrity of a whole speech in one verse line, as it appears in the Folio, and it is metrically superior to the fabricated line, 'Hark, Ventidius. / I do not know'.

Many short phrases in succession can offer the temptation to arrange a blank verse line, and earlier Shakespeare (*King John* 3.3.65–6, for example) affords numerous instances where the results are metrically convincing. In the late plays, on the other hand, attempts of this sort not infrequently run into the difficulty that one or two phrases cannot quite be accommodated and are thus left dangling by the hypothetical lineation. An example occurs in 1.2.71–7, here printed as it is usually lineated by editors:

> ENOBARBUS Hush, here comes Antony.
> CHARMIAN Not he. The queen.
> CLEOPATRA Saw you my lord?
> ENOBARBUS No, lady.
> CLEOPATRA Was he not here?
> CHARMIAN No, madam.
> CLEOPATRA He was disposed to mirth, but on the sudden...

Sometimes the hypothesised verse is more irregular:

> CAESAR Welcome to Rome.
> ANTONY Thank you.
> CAESAR Sit.
> ANTONY Sit, sir.
> CAESAR Nay, then. (2.2.30–4)

Here the attempted line is hard to scan, notably so in relation to the surrounding verse, and forces on the reader a sense of cadence that may well be at variance with the staccato nervousness needed for this first taut encounter of Antony and Octavius Caesar.

Sometimes the linking of two half-lines seems to urge the compression into metrical regularity of speeches that require a slower and fuller rate. The following are presented here in the form adopted by editorial tradition:

> CAESAR...
> With what is spoke already.
> ANTONY What power is in Agrippa... (2.2.149–50)

or

VENTIDIUS...
Should my performance perish.
SILIUS Thou hast, Ventidius, that... (3.1.27–8)

or

1 SOLDIER...
Let's see how it will give off.
ALL Content. 'Tis strange. (4.3.29–30)

Other hypothetical linkages seem to urge a metrical expansion of what might well be spoken more succinctly:

CAESAR...
Where is he now?
OCTAVIA My lord, in Athens. (3.6.65–6)

or

ANTONY...
There's hope in't yet.
CLEOPATRA That's my brave lord! (3.13.180–1)

or

CAESAR...
Laugh at his challenge.
MAECENAS Caesar must think... (4.1.6–7)

Other purported linkages are simply questionable in their irregularity. I suppose a case could be made for the sound echoing the sense if we line as follows:

ANTONY...
For thy good valour. Come thee on.
SCARUS I'll halt after. (4.7.16–17)

but since the linking is only editorial fabrication, the hypothesis is entirely a circular one. Even harder to justify, in terms of sound and sense, is the following:

DIOMEDES His guard have brought him thither.

Enter [*below*] ANTONY, *and the* GUARD [*bearing him*]

CLEOPATRA O sun, (4.15.9–10)

Surely this does little more than tuck away into the neat appearance of blank verse a half-line better left to its own expressive sense of dislocation and change.

On occasion the desire to link a longer passage may distort the dramatic intensity of short exchanges uttered under great emotional distress. Consider the moment of Antony's bungled suicide, lined here in accordance with editorial tradition:

ANTONY...
The guard, ho! O, dispatch me!

Enter a GUARD

1 GUARD What's the noise?
ANTONY I have done my work ill, friends. O, make an end
Of what I have begun!
2 GUARD The star is fall'n.
1 GUARD And time is at his period.
ALL Alas,
And woe!
ANTONY Let him that loves me strike me dead.
1 GUARD Not I.
2 GUARD Nor I.
3 GUARD Nor anyone. (4.14.104–14)

Surely the dividing of 'Alas, and woe!' runs counter to theatrical experience, and the final supposed blank verse line falls notably short. This entire passage is better presented for the reader as it appears in the Folio, thus preserving among other things the perfectly good blank verse line as printed there, 'O, make an end of what I have begun.'

A moment of no less intensity is distorted when the editorial arrangement implies blank verse regularity in the following:

CLEOPATRA...
Beneath the visiting moon.
CHARMIAN O, quietness, lady!
IRAS She's dead too, our sovereign.
CHARMIAN Lady!
IRAS Madam!
CHARMIAN O madam, madam, madam!
IRAS Royal Egypt! Empress!
CHARMIAN Peace, peace, Iras. (4.15.70–7)

All this is not to say that arrangement into blank verse is uniformly inappropriate. Shakespeare's apparent practice of running on half-lines in his manuscript to economise space leaves the editor with a consistent problem, and too much would be lost by simply setting all half-lines to the left margin. Still, discrimination is necessary and clear enough in principle even if difficult in individual cases of judgement. The same editorial responsibility applies here as in deciding whether a passage crowded into prose in the Folio is intended to be versified, and, if so, how it is to be divided.

READING LIST

This list comprises those critical works that have been particularly important to the editor in preparing the Introduction and Commentary, and that may be useful to the reader in further studies of the play.

Adelman, Janet. *The Common Liar: An Essay on 'Antony and Cleopatra'*, 1973

Barroll, J. Leeds. 'The chronology of Shakespeare's Jacobean plays and the dating of *Antony and Cleopatra*', in Gordon Ross Smith (ed.), *Essays on Shakespeare*, 1965, pp. 115–62

'Shakespeare and Roman history', *MLR* 53 (1958), 327–43

Shakespearean Tragedy: Genre, Tradition, and Change in 'Antony and Cleopatra', 1984

Beckerman, Bernard. 'Past the size of dreaming', in Mark Rose (ed.), *Twentieth Century Interpretations of 'Antony and Cleopatra'*, 1977, pp. 99–112

Bethell, S. L. *Shakespeare and the Popular Dramatic Tradition*, 1944, pp. 116–33

Bono, Barbara J. *Literary Transvaluation: From Vergilian Epic to Shakespearean Tragicomedy*, 1984, pp. 1–6, 140–224

Bradley, A. C. 'Shakespeare's *Antony and Cleopatra*', in *Oxford Lectures on Poetry*, 1909, pp. 279–305

Brower, Reuben A. *Hero and Saint: Shakespeare and the Graeco-Roman Heroic Tradition*, 1971, pp. 317–53

Brown, John Russell (ed.). *Shakespeare: Antony and Cleopatra: A Casebook*, 1969

Burckhardt, Sigurd. 'The king's language: Shakespeare's drama as social discovery', *AR* 21 (1961), 369–87

Cantor, Paul. *Shakespeare's Rome: Republic and Empire*, 1976, pp. 125–208

Charney, Maurice. *Shakespeare's Roman Plays: The Function of Imagery in the Drama*, 1961, pp. 79–141

Coates, John. '"The choice of Hercules" in *Antony and Cleopatra*', *S.Sur.* 31 (1978), 45–52

Coleridge, S. T. *Samuel Taylor Coleridge: Shakespeare Criticism*, ed. T. M. Raysor, 2 vols., 2nd edn, 1960, I, 76–9

Colie, Rosalie. *Shakespeare's Living Art*, 1974, pp. 168–207

Conti, Natale. *Natalis Comitis Mythologiae*, 1581

Danby, John F. *Poets on Fortune's Hill: Studies in Sidney, Shakespeare, Beaumont and Fletcher*, 1952, pp. 128–51

Dickey, Franklin. *Not Wisely But Too Well: Shakespeare's Love Tragedies*, 1957

Dollimore, Jonathan. *Radical Tragedy: Religion, Ideology, and Power in the Drama of Shakespeare and His Contemporaries*, 1984, pp. 204–17

Doran, Madeleine. '"High events as these": the language of hyperbole in *Antony and Cleopatra*', *QQ* 72 (1965), 26–51

Dorius, R. J. 'Shakespeare's dramatic modes and *Antony and Cleopatra*', in Rudolf Hess *et al.* (eds.), *Literatur als Kritik des Lebens*, 1975, pp. 83–96

Eagleton, Terence. *Shakespeare and Society*, 1967, pp. 122–9

Erickson, Peter. *Patriarchal Structures in Shakespeare's Drama*, 1985, pp. 123–47

Fisch, Harold. '*Antony and Cleopatra*: the limits of mythology', *S.Sur.* 23 (1970), 59–67

Fitz, L. T. 'Egyptian queens and male reviewers: sexist attitudes in *Antony and Cleopatra* criticism', *SQ* 28 (1977), 297–316

French, A. L. *Shakespeare and the Critics*, 1972, pp. 206–35

Goddard, Harold C. *The Meaning of Shakespeare*, 2 vols., 1951, II, 184–208

Goldberg, S. L. 'The tragedy of the imagination: a reading of *Antony and Cleopatra*', *Melbourne Critical Review* 4 (1961), 41–64

Goldman, Michael. *Acting and Action in Shakespearean Tragedy*, 1985, pp. 112–39

Granville-Barker, Harley. *Prefaces to Shakespeare*, 2nd ser., 1930, pp. 116–66

Harris, Duncan S. '"Again for Cydnus": the dramaturgical resolution of *Antony and Cleopatra*', *SEL* 17 (1977), 219–31

Harrison, Thomas P. 'Shakespeare and Marlowe's *Dido, Queen of Carthage*', *UTSE* 35 (1956), 57–63

Heffner, Ray L., Jr. 'The messengers in Shakespeare's *Antony and Cleopatra*', *ELH* 43 (1976), 154–62.

Henn, T. R. *The Living Image*, 1972, pp. 117–36

Hibbard, G. R. '*Feliciter audax:* "Antony and Cleopatra", I, i, 1–24', in Philip Edwards *et al.* (eds.), *Shakespeare's Styles: Essays in Honour of Kenneth Muir*, 1980, pp. 95–109

Holloway, John. *The Story of the Night: Studies in Shakespeare's Major Tragedies*, 1961, pp. 99–120

Honigmann, E. A. J. *Shakespeare: Seven Tragedies: The Dramatist's Manipulation of Response*, 1976, pp. 150–69

Hume, Robert D. 'Individuation and development of character through language in *Antony and Cleopatra*', *SQ* 24 (1973), 280–300

Jones, Emrys (ed.). *Antony and Cleopatra*, 1977

Kaula, David. 'The time sense of *Antony and Cleopatra*', *SQ* 15 (1964), 211–23

Knight, G. Wilson. 'The transcendental humanism of Antony and Cleopatra', in *The Imperial Theme*, 1931, rev. edn, 1951, pp. 199–262

Knights, L. C. 'On the tragedy of Antony and Cleopatra', *Scrutiny* 16 (1949), 318–23; reprinted in *Some Shakespearean Themes*, 1959

Krook, Dorothea. 'Tragic and heroic in Shakespeare's *Antony and Cleopatra*', in Ariel Sachs (ed.), *Scripta Hierosolymitana*, 1967, pp. 231–61

Lee, Robin. *Shakespeare: 'Antony and Cleopatra'*, 1971

Lloyd, Michael. 'Cleopatra as Isis', *S.Sur.* 12 (1959), 88–94

McAlindon, T. *Shakespeare and Decorum*, 1973, pp. 167–213

MacCallum, M. W. *Shakespeare's Roman Plays and Their Background*, 1910, pp. 300–453

Macdonald, Ronald R. 'Playing till Doomsday: interpreting *Antony and Cleopatra*', *ELR* 15 (1985), 78–99

Mack, Maynard. 'The Jacobean Shakespeare: some observations on the construction of the tragedies', in J. R. Brown and Bernard Harris (eds.), *Jacobean Shakespeare*, 1960, pp. 11–41

'*Antony and Cleopatra*: the stillness and the dance', in Milton Crane (ed.), *Shakespeare's Art: Seven Essays*, 1973, pp. 79–113

Markels, Julian. *The Pillar of the World: 'Antony and Cleopatra' in Shakespeare's Development*, 1968

Mason, H. A. *Shakespeare's Tragedies of Love*, 1970

Merchant, W. M. 'Classical costume in Shakespearian productions', *S.Sur.* 10 (1957), 71–6

Miola, Robert. *Shakespeare's Rome*, 1983, pp. 116–63

Morris, Helen. 'Shakespeare and Dürer's Apocalypse', *S.St.* 4 (1968), 252–62

Nandy, Dipak. 'The realism of *Antony and Cleopatra*', in Arnold Kettle (ed.), *Shakespeare in a Changing World*, 1964, pp. 172–94

Norman, Arthur M. Z. 'Daniel's *The Tragedie of Cleopatra* and *Antony and Cleopatra*', *SQ* 9 (1958), 11–18

Oakeshott, Walter. 'Shakespeare and Plutarch', in John Garrett (ed.), *Talking of Shakespeare*, 1954, pp. 111–25

Odell, George C. D. *Shakespeare from Betterton to Irving*, 2 vols., 1920

Ornstein, Robert. 'The ethic of the imagination: love and art in *Antony and Cleopatra*', in J. R. Brown and Bernard Harris (eds.), *Later Shakespeare*, 1966, pp. 31–46

Phillips, James Emerson, Jr. *The State in Shakespeare's Greek and Roman Plays*, 1940, pp. 188–205

Rackin, Phyllis. 'Shakespeare's boy Cleopatra, the decorum of nature, and the golden world of poetry', *PMLA* 87 (1972), 201–11

Ridley, M. R. (ed.). *Antony and Cleopatra*, based on the edition of R. H. Case, 1954

Riemer, A. P. *A Reading of Shakespeare's 'Antony and Cleopatra'*, 1968

Schanzer, Ernest. *The Problem Plays of Shakespeare: A Study of 'Julius Caesar', 'Measure for Measure', and 'Antony and Cleopatra'*, 1963, pp. 132–83

Seaton, Ethel. '*Antony and Cleopatra* and the Book of Revelation', *RES* 22 (1946), 219–24

Shapiro, Stephen A. 'The varying shore of the world: ambivalence in *Antony and Cleopatra*', *MLQ* 27 (1966), 18–32

Simmons, J. L. *Shakespeare's Pagan World: The Roman Tragedies*, 1973, pp. 109–63

Snyder, Susan. 'Patterns of motion in *Antony and Cleopatra*', *S.Sur.* 33 (1980), 113–22

Stein, Arnold. 'The image of Antony: lyric and tragic imagination', *KR* 21 (1959), 586–606

Stone, George Winchester, Jr. 'Garrick's presentation of *Antony and Cleopatra*', *RES* 13 (1937), 20–38

Traci, Philip J. *The Love Play of Antony and Cleopatra: A Critical Study of Shakespeare's Play*, 1970

Traversi, Derek. *Shakespeare: The Roman Plays*, 1963, pp. 79–203

Waddington, Raymond B. 'Antony and Cleopatra: "What Venus did with Mars"', *S.St.* 2 (1966), 210–26

Waith, Eugene. *The Herculean Hero in Marlowe, Chapman, Shakespeare, and Dryden*, 1962, pp. 113–21

Wells, Stanley, and Gary Taylor, *William Shakespeare: A Textual Companion*, 1987

Williamson, Marilyn L. *Infinite Variety: Antony and Cleopatra in Renaissance Drama and Earlier Tradition*, 1974

Wilson, John Dover (ed.). *Antony and Cleopatra*, 1950

Wind, Edgar. *Pagan Mysteries in the Renaissance*, 1968

Worthen, W. B. '"The weight of Antony": staging "character" in *Antony and Cleopatra*', *SEL* 26 (1986), 295–308